THE BIBLICAL *ḤEREM*
A Window on Israel's Religious Experience

Program in Judaic Studies
Brown University
BROWN JUDAIC STUDIES

Edited by
Ernest S. Frerichs, Wendell S. Dietrich,
Calvin Goldscheider, David Hirsch, Alan Zuckerman

Project Editors (Projects)

David Blumenthal, Emory University (Approaches to Medieval Judaism)
Ernest S. Frerichs, Brown University (Dissertations and Monographs)
Lenn Evan Goodman, University of Hawaii (Studies in Medieval Judaism)
Norbert Samuelson, Temple University (Jewish Philosophy)
Jonathan Z. Smith, University of Chicago (Studia Philonica)

Number 211

THE BIBLICAL *ḤEREM*

A Window on Israel's Religious Experience

by

Philip D. Stern

THE BIBLICAL *ḤEREM*
A Window on Israel's Religious Experience

by

Philip D. Stern

Scholars Press
Atlanta, Georgia

THE BIBLICAL *ḤEREM*
A Window on Israel's Religious Experience

Library of Congress Cataloging-in-Publication Data

Stern, Philip D.
The Biblical *Ḥerem* : a window on Israel's religious experience / by Philip D. Stern.
p. cm. — (Brown Judaic studies ; no. 211)
Includes bibliographical references and index.
ISBN 1-55540-552-5 (alk. paper)
1. Excommunication—Biblical teaching. 2. Bible. O.T.—Criticism, interpretations, etc. I. Title. II. Title: *Ḥerem*. III. Series.
BM565.S82 1990
221.6'7--dc20 90-19170
CIP

Printed in the United States of America
on acid-free paper

To my parents, my brothers,

ולמורי נעורי

Rabbi Dov Taylor and Rabbi Manuel Gold

CONTENTS

Preface ix

Abbreviations xi

Introduction 1

Chapter 1: Introductory: Philological Observations on the Root *ḤRM*--חרם 5

Chapter 2: Implications of the Mesha Inscription 19

Chapter 3: Previously Suggested Parallels 57

Chapter 4: Further Parallels 67

I: A Mari Letter 67

II: The Utuḫegal Inscription 70

III: Hittite 72

IV: The [d]Idi-Sin Inscription 78

V: Ugarit 79

VI: Egypt: Osorkon, High Priest of Thebes 81

Chapter 5: The Book of Deuteronomy 89

I: The Deuteronomic Ḥerem and the Lists of Nations 89

II: Deut 13:13-19 104

III: Deut 7:25-6 110

IV: The Last Battles of Moses; Sihon and Og 116

Chapter 6: The Tetrateuch 123

I: Exodus 20:19 123

II: Priestly Writings 125

III: Num 21:1-3 135

Chapter 7: Joshua-Judges 139

I: Joshua 6 139

II: Joshua 7-8 145

III: Joshua 9 156

IV: Joshua 10-11 157

V: The Book of Judges 161

Chapter 8: Samuel-Kings 165

I: I Samuel 15 165

II: I Kings 20:42 178

III: I Kings 9:20-22 183

IV: 2 Kings 19:11=Isa 37:11 185

Chapter 9: Literary Prophets 189

I: Isaiah 34 189

II: Isaiah 11:15 192

III: Isaiah 43:28 193

IV: Jeremiah 25:9 197

V: Jeremiah 50-1 199

VI: Micah 4:13 201

VII: Malachi 3:24 and Zechariah 14:11 204

Chapter 10: The Writings 209

I: Ezra 10:8 209

II: The Book of Chronicles and Daniel 212

Chapter 11: Conclusion 217

Select Bibliography 227

Index 235

PREFACE

The term חרם or *ḥerem* which is the focus of this study, is still commonly recognized and even used by traditional Jews, although no longer with the biblical meaning. The same root also occurs in modern Hebrew with connotations that are well removed from the kind of divine-and-human warfare that characterizes most of the root's usage in the Hebrew Bible. Due to the fact that the חרם weds large scale massacre of an enemy with the biblical concept of holiness, the subject is one which may easily cause gnashings of teeth, chills of the spine, and head-scratching bewilderment to many readers of the Bible. Such a reaction is understandable, but it unless it leads to a search for answers, it does not lead to greater understanding. The two greatest prophets of ancient Israel, Moses and Samuel, were each associated with the חרם, so it is plain that this behavior was no embarrassment to the people better known today for the Ten Commandments.

My own interest in this fairly obscure practice was quite minimal until a different project brought it indirectly into view, and my teacher, Baruch A. Levine, suggested it as a dissertation topic. My response was somewhat tentative, as I wondered whether such a subject could sustain a new, large scale treatment. Time and tide proved that it could. Moreover, research into such a area, so foreign to our modern way of thinking, proved fascinating, since the only approach that made sense was to try and understand how the ancients came to create and take pride in this particular action. The results of that attempt are here now in this revised work; additional results will undoubtedly come in the future and different approaches will be tried, as this extraordinary topic will continue to attract new ways of thinking about it. I hope that one of the consequences of this essay will be to stimulate a rethinking of the subject.

Prof. Levine not only provided me with the benefit of his wide knowledge and insight into the Bible, but he predicted early on that the result would be published, making him a better candidate than Saul for a place among the prophets.

Prof. William W. Hallo has shown me a great deal of generosity; he showed much interest in my work, which would be substantially poorer in its comparative reach as well as in its bibliography, if he had not donated so much of his time.

Prof. Jeffrey Tigay, a former teacher of mine, helped me avoid certain methodolgical pitfalls and demonstrated his helpfulness, which is well known to his students.

Prof. Jacob Milgrom read a section of my dissertation and sent me his encouraging critique. Prof. Susan Niditch has been a great source of encouragement, for which I am thankful.

I am extremely grateful to Prof. Stephen Dempster for sending me a copy of his very fine master's thesis, which was both interesting and of material assistance to me.

Closer to home, Profs. Cyrus H. Gordon, Norman K. Gottwald, and S. David Sperling read all or part of the original dissertation, offering me friendly criticism and the opportunity to test my evolving ideas on them.

Profs. Michael Carter and Larry Schiffman were most helpful in dealing with areas of my research which touched their fields. Prof. Mervin Dilts steered me away from a chimera in Sophocles.

On the ancient Egyptian side, Prof. Ogden Goelet kept me on track and away from various pitfalls. Mr. Paul O'Rourke of the Brooklyn Museum graciously supplied me with the Egyptian parallel found in chapter four. At that same museum, I met Prof. Alan R. Schulman, who gave me important references. Prof. Edward Greenstein gave me both lunch and his opinions, an excellent combination.

In all-too-brief encounters with Profs. Michel C. Astour and Erica Reiner, I had the opportunity to discuss technical philological points. I also had the good fortune to consult and benefit from the expertise of a number of other distinguished Assyriologists: Douglas Frayne, William Lambert, Ira Spar, and Christopher Walker. I also had the privilege of consulting with two scholars from Jerusalem, Profs. Jonas Greenfield and Ephraim Stern. To all of the above I am grateful for sharing their time and thought.

I am pleased to record something of my debt of gratitude to my father, Rabbi Chaim Stern; in this case for his assistance in various ways, notably in taking on the role of computer consultant and in other ways helping me prepare the manuscript.

Lastly, but scarcely leastly, I would like to thank Profs. Jacob Neusner and Ernest Frerichs for giving me the opportunity to bring my work to the Brown Judaic Series, and to thank Dr. Dennis Ford of Scholar's Press for his ready assistance.

LIST OF ABBREVIATIONS

AB	Anchor Bible series
AfO	*Archiv für Orientforschung*
AHw	von Soden, *Akkadisches Handwörterbuch*
Akk.	Akkadian
ANET	Pritchard, ed. *Ancient Near Eastern Texts*
AnOr	*Analecta orientalia*
AOAT	Alter Orient und Altes Testament
ARAB	Luckenbill, *Ancient Records of Assyria and Babylonia*
ARM	Dossin et al., eds., Archives Royales de Mari, textes transcrits et traduits
ASOR	Annual of the American Schools of Oriental Research
AThANT	Abhandlungen zur Theologie des Alten und Neuen Testaments
BA	*Biblical Archeologist*
BAR	*Biblical Archeology Review*
BASOR	*Bulletin of the American Schools for Oriental Research*
BDB	Brown, Driver, and Briggs *Hebrew and English Lexicon*
BETL	*Biblotheca ephemeridum theologicarum lovansienum*
BH	Biblical Hebrew
BHK	Kittel, ed. *Biblica hebraica*
BHS	Elliger and Rudolph, eds. *Biblica hebraica stuttgartensia*
Bib	*Biblica*
BN	*Biblische Notizen*
BWANT	Beiträge zur Wissenschaft vom Alten und Neuen Testaments
BWL	Lambert, *Babylonian Wisdom Literature*
BZAW	Beiträge zur ZAW
CAD	Gelb et al. *The Assyrian Dictionary of the University of Chicago*
CBQ	*Catholic Biblical Quarterly*
CRB (CB)	Cahiers de RB
CTA	Herdner, *Corpus des tablettes en cunéiformes alphabétiques*
DBS	Pirot et al., eds. *Dictionnaire de la Bible, Supplement*
DN	Divine name

EJ	Roth et. al., eds *Encyclopedia Judaica*
EM	Sukenik et al., eds. *Encyclopedia Miqra'it*
Gilg.	The Gilgamesh Epic
GThA	Göttinger theologische Arbeiten
HAT	Handkommentar zum AT
HSM	Harvard Semitic Monographs
HSS	Harvard Semitic Studies
HUCA	Hebrew Union College Annual
ICC	International Critical Commentary
Il.	*The Illiad*
JANES	*Journal of the Ancient Near Eastern Society of Columbia University*
JAOS	*Journal of the American Oriental Society*
JBL	*Journal of Biblical Literature*
JNES	*Journal of Near Eastern Studies*
JQR	*Jewish Quarterly Review*
JRAS	*Journal of the Royal Asiatic Society*
JSOT	*Journal for the Study of the Old Testament*
JSS	*Journal of Semitic Studies*
KAI	Donner-Röllig, *Kanaanäische und aramäische Inschriften* (3 vols.)
KAR	Keilschrifttexten aus Assur, religiösen Inhalts
KzAT	Kommentar zum Alten Testament
KBL	Kohler and Baumgartner, *Lexicon in Veteris Testamenti Libros*
KTU	Dietrich and Sanmartin, eds., *Die keilaphabetischen Texte aus Ugarit*
LAPO	Littératures anciennes du Proche-Orient
LCL	Loeb Classical Library
MDOG	Mitteilungen der deutschen Orient-Gesellschaft
MI	Mesha Inscription
MT	Massoretic Text
NCB	New Century Bible

NEB	New English Bible
NJV	New Jewish Version of the Jewish Publication Society
OA	*Oriens Antiquus*
OBO	Orbis Biblicus et Orientalia
Od.	*The Odyssey*
Or	*Orientalia*
OSA	Old South Arabic
OTL	Old Testament Library
OuTWP	De Ou Testamentiese Werkgemeenskap in Suid-Afrika
PEQ	Palestine Exploration Quarterly
POS	Pretoria Oriental Series
POTT	Wiseman, ed. *Peoples of Old Testament Times*
RA	*Revue d'assyrologie et d'archéologie orientale*
RAC	Klauser, ed. *Reallexikon für Antike und Christentum*
RB	*Revue Biblique*
RHA	Revue hittite et asiatique
SANT	Studien im Alten and Neuen Testament
SBLDS	Society of Biblical Literature, Dissertation Series
SBLMS	Society of Biblical Literature, Monograph Series
SMIM	Dearman, ed. *Studies in the Mesha Inscription and Moab*
StBoT	Studien zu den Boğazkoy-Texten
StTh	Studia Theologica
SVT	Supplement to VT
TDOT	Botterweck and Ringgren, eds. *Theological Dictionary of the Old Testament*
THAT	Jenni & Westermann, eds. *Theologische Handwörterbuch zum AT*
TM	Tell Mardikh (Ebla)
TWAT	Botterweck and Ringgren, eds. *Theologisches Wörterbuch zum Alten Testament*
UF	Ugarit-Forschungen
UI	Utuhegal Inscription
UT	Gordon, *Ugaritic Textbook*

VT	*Vetus Testamentum*
WCJS	World Congress of Jewish Studies, Proceedings of Panel Sessions, Bible Studies and Hebrew Language Jerusalem
ZA	*Zeitschrift für Assyriologie und vorderasiatische Archäologie*
ZAW	*Zeitschrift für alttestamentliche Wissenschaft*

INTRODUCTION

This study is a revised version of my 1989 doctoral dissertation. I have taken the opportunity to make many revisions, including both excisions and additions. I have added some material from the ongoing stream of scholarly work as well as further developed the ideas found in the dissertation itself. Sometimes this came in the form of new exegesis of biblical passages, frequently in the light of my central theses. I have also benefited from the additional time which was not always available when working on the original dissertation, allowing me the possibility of reevaluating particular judgements or delving more deeply into specific texts. The result is a work which attacks its subject, the biblical חרם or *ḥerem* in its ancient Near Eastern context, and in a fundamentally new way when one looks at the history of the study of the subject. The חרם. is obscure even to the biblical scholar, despite the work that has been done on it (particularly notable is the work of Christian Brekelmans, whose monograph is the most cited secondary source in this monograph). Yet it is a fasinating phenomenon in human behavior, and one far from unimportant for the understanding of the religion of biblical Israel.

This study, then, treats a feature of Israelite warfare known as the חרם, which has long been considered as a singular "consecration-to-destruction" of a designated enemy, with some or all of the spoils of victory set apart to the deity by destruction, not subject to the usual division among the army. Normally, the booty was shared by the soldiers, even those in the baggage train, according to David's ruling of 1 Sam 30:23-5. Actually, the חרם may equally well (or even better) be described as a "consecration-through-destruction." (to a deity). I will use the two formulations indifferently, and add that a third, a "destruction through consecration," also has validity. A well-known example of this behavior is found in Joshua 6. Prior to the assault on Jericho, Joshua announced the חרם, specifying what it entailed and warning Israel against the awful consequences of an infraction. After the city walls fell, Israel executed the חרם, destroying the city and its people and devoting the city and its spoil to YHWH--consecrating Jericho to YHWH through destruction. The one exception was that of an ordinary Israelite, Achan, who appropriated some small items, including a cloak from the idolatrous city of Babylon. His transgression was detected and punished by death to avert the peril that then loomed over the entire community on his account. In normal circumstances, Achan's misbehavior would have been less serious. In brief outline, such was the Israelite war-חרם.

There also is another חרם, one which appears in less bellicose surroundings. One may cite from a legal code, as in Exod 22:19, which decrees the חרם for someone who offers sacrifices to gods other than Israel's god YHWH (Deut 20:18 links the war-.חרם with Exod 22:19, by giving the war-חרם the character of a measure against idol-worship). Presumably, Exod 22:19 was differentiated from the ordinary death penalty by the proscription of the idolator's property. This is supported by comparison with the provisions of Deut 13:13-19, which prescribes the חרם. for religious defection to other gods on a massive scale, that of whole cities. Outside of the verses in Exodus and

Deuteronomy 13, the most important peacetime application of the term חרם is undoubtedly that found in in a few verses in Leviticus and Numbers. The picture emerges of a חרם still possessing much of its original (wartime) force but at the same time domesticated, reduced to the bureaucratic control of the priests. The priestly חרם is alluded to in only a few places. We are given only a tantalizing glimpse of the war-חרם adapted to the purposes of the priestly class.

The root appears in some 40-odd verses, in a wide variety of places and contexts. Yet the biblical texts do not yield us as much information as we would like (given this many occurrences). The biblical texts were written for an audience which was conversant with the assumptions underlying the חרם, its character, and what it meant. In addition, we need not doubt that there were many more traditions of the war-חרם than appear in the Bible, which was not composed for the sake of keeping a tally of such things. The one Moabite tradition we have (see ch. 2) cannot be the sole time in Moabite history that the חרם was applied; the mere existence of a special verb for the operation indicates that. We therefore work with only a part of the total material, and the Moabite Inscription itself was found and preserved by great good luck. The fortunate unearthing and preservation of the Moabite Inscription motivates the search for additional extra-biblical evidence.

The study itself of חרם is rewarding from a certain point of view. The חרם is a salutary reminder of the truly non-Western, Oriental world of thought responsible for the forging of Israelite religion--which has been made deceptively familiar to us by the appropriation of the Hebrew Bible by later Judaism, and by Christianity as the Old Testament. As so often in life, the challenge and the difficulty of the חרם also offer an opportunity; for it gives us a window though which to view ancient Israelite religion and life, unencumbered by the stratigraphic overlay of the Jewish or Christian traditions.

With this in mind, the point of departure of this study was not the חרם as it appears in standard biblical theologies or commentaries. I sought to gather as much information as possible that could bear on the חרם from ancient sources. Happily, the perfect text for this purpose has survived in the aforementioned inscription of a ninth century Moabite king named Mesha. His 34-line text has at its epicenter an actual instance of חרם, which Mesha executed against Israel. Its close relation to the biblical narratives in language and style also helped make the Mesha Inscription (=MI) the ideal launching pad for this kind of study. Largely from its contents I derived a basic proposition or hypothesis which I then tested against the evidence of the biblical texts themselves.

I further sought corroboration and amplification of that proposition from other ancient cultures, insofar as it lay in my power to do so. As it turned out, the proposition arrived at from studying the MI was in fact a basic motif of many ancient cultures. In simple form it was the struggle of a people to overcome the forces of chaos and to establish a world order (*Weltordnung*), in which the group could survive and flourish. This motif was often expressed in ancient myths and cosmogonies, and in various kinds of biblical texts as well. I cannot claim that placing the חרם in a cosmogonic or mythic context explains everything about the war-חרם, but it does illuminate its basic thrust and puts it, I believe, in a conceptual framework which the ancients themselves would have recognized as appropriate. The ancient Near Eastern parallels to the war-חרם that appear in chapter four help demonstrate the non-Israelite origin of the חרם, as do also philological evidence (chapter one) and the evidence of the Mesha Inscription (chapter two). The contact with ancient Near Eastern thought with regard to order and the perception of foreign foes as chaos is a main source of support for this approach to the subject.

I also have been encouraged that my hypothesis has proved to be a valuable exegetical tool for analyzing biblical verses and chapters which feature the root חרם. This has enabled me to reopen the subject of the חרם from a fruitful perspective; the חרם's role as a means of creating or restoring the moral order of the universe. This helps explain what to many is this anomalous entity amidst the moral laws of the Hebrew Bible.

This investigation has been structured around these general ideas and considerations. The first chapter is basically a supplement and updating to the initial chapter--entitled "Philological Investigation," of C. H. W. Brekelmans' *De ḥerem in het Oude Testament* (1959), the pioneering large-scale systematic inquiry into the חרם. This investigation involves several new items culled from comparative Semitic lexical study of the root חרם which are relevant to the topic. The second chapter is a study of the Mesha Inscription from the religious standpoint (with particular reference to the חרם, a perspective from which (surprisingly) the MI had not been studied at length. Next I evaluate previously proposed parallels to the חרם from the ancient world (ch.3), and then propose some additional ones from the Near East (ch.4). By the nature of things, these are not as close to the Israelite חרם as the Moabite example, but they all share important features with the חרם of Canaan. The second part of the study deals with the biblical material in greater or lesser detail, depending on the nature of the material, and the degree to which the individual passages offer room for exegesis.

To moderns the חרם raises the question of theodicy. Indeed, the subject merits a more central place in biblical theology. Its current place in the shadows may be due to its obscurity, or the result of a desire to shove the bloodstained practice into a corner of decent obscurity as a 'skeleton at the feast' of biblical theology. This study has not emphasized the question of theodicy, but the reader may nevertheless find that an answer emerges out of this effort to shed new light on the חרם and on the religion and life of ancient Israel.

Finally, the laws of Deuteronomy 20, which include the laws of siege and חרם, suggest as a fitting epigraph, this quatrain of Shakespeare:

> Then tell us, shall your city call us lord,
> In that behalf, which we have challeng'd it?
> Or shall we give the signal to our rage,
> And stalk in blood to our possession?
>
> King John (II i)

CHAPTER 1

INTRODUCTORY: PHILOLOGICAL OBSERVATIONS ON THE ROOT *ḤRM*

In an investigation of a particular Hebrew practice, which, like the חרם, was encapsulated in a single word, it is traditional to begin by studying its root as it is manifested in the various Semitic languages. Fortunately for the present study, C. H. W. Brekelmans, in his pioneering dissertation published under the name *De ḥerem in het Oude Testament* (1959), has surveyed in his opening chapter a wide range of Semitic languages with a good deal of acumen. Hence it is not necessary for us to duplicate his work, but merely to supplement it and to reassess the evidence as a whole strictly in terms of the relevance of the comparative Semitic material to the understanding of the Hebrew word and practice of חרם.

In Ugaritic, there has been an interesting development since Brekelmans's monograph; the emergence of an attestation of the root חרם in a sense similar to that of the Bible. This was pointed out by J. C. de Moor in his published treatment of KTU 1.13.[1] Unfortunately, the text, which de Moor dubbed "An Incantation against Infertility" and which is addressed to the goddess Anat, is somewhat problematic (partly due to lacunae), and de Moor's translation reflects the state of the text. I reproduce here the salient lines with de Moor's translation (without his arrangement of the English lines):

(1) [ ]xx (2)[ ]	
[ ]	
[r]ḥm. tld (3) [bn. lbᶜl.]	may the Dam(sel) bear (a son to Baal!)
(2) ḫrm. ṯn . ym(4)m.	Destroy under the ban during two days,
š(ql. ṯlṯ) ymm. lk.	th(row) down for yourself (during three) days,
(5) hrg .'ar[bᶜ.] ymm . bṣr.	kill in frustration during (fo)ur days![2]

However, de Moor's recent publication (with K. Spronk)[3] of an autograph edition of the text shows that it should be read differently. Most impor-

[1] J. C. de Moor, "An Incantation against Infertility (KTU 1.13)," *UF* 12 (1980), 305-10.

[2] Ibid. 305.

[3] J. C. de Moor & K. Spronk, *A Cuneiform Anthology of Religious Texts from Ugarit* (Leiden, 1987), *Semitic Study Series* 6, 58-9.

tant for the intelligibility of the text given above is the line, *š[ql. ṯlṯ] ymm. lk.* It is now clear that the “q” of *šql* could not be a correct rendering. The remaining part of the cuneiform sign has two horizontals, while the sign for “q” has but one. The space between horizontals is too narrow for “p” or “z”, while “w” takes up more space, and does not yield a reading that makes sense. Of the eligible letters of the Ugaritic alphabet there remains only “k.” *škl* would have to be construed as an example of *kly* in shaphel (imperative), meaning “annihilate” or the like, which fits the context. The word *lk* that occurs a few words later could not only mean “for yourself,” but better (as others have also seen), probably, “go!” It would then precede the next imperative, *hrg*, “kill!” Since the occurrence of *lk* varies from the syntax of the preceding clause it might as well be construed as the verb “to go,” since “for yourself,” is difficult to understand here.

The new autograph text has one other change. Where de Moor restored *bn* (immediately after (3)) the text is now restored to read *ibr*, “bull.” This is a point to which I shall return later (ch. 4). I read as follows:

(1) [ ]xx (2)[ ]	
[ ]	
[r]ḥm. tld (3) [’ibr. lbʿl.]	may the Dam(sel) bear (a bull to Baal)
(2) ḫrm. ṯn . ym(4)m.	Devote to destruction in(?) two days,
š[kl. ṯlṯ] ymm. lk.	Annihilate in(?)(three} days. Go,
(5) hrg .’ar[bʿ.] ymm . bṣr.	kill in (fo)ur days....[4]

An important point here, which de Moor seized upon, is the parallelism between *ḫrm* and *hrg*, two lines later (cp. Josh 8:24-6}.[5] The parallelism and the context of the first lines of the incantation show that the meaning is close to the Heb. חרם (החרים), although its precise force here is hard to determine on the basis of this text alone.[6] A difficulty is that חרם, which is, as de Moor deduced, an imperative, is lacking an object; but then, so is *hrg*.[7] However, in a way, the passage, in which the goddess Anat is asked to apply the חרם to the anonymous ‘enemies,’ is a forerunner of Isa 34:5,7, where a prophet pictures YHWH applying the חרם against arch-enemy Edom. In

---

4 The last.word *bṣr* seems to go with the next clause. So A. Caquot & J.-M. de Tarragon, *Textes ougaritiques II: Textes religieux, rituels, correspondance. LAPO*, 22 n.9, following H. Cazelles. This work provides an excellent bibliography.

5 J. C. de Moor, "An Incantation," 306.

6 A..Caquot & J.-M. de Tarragon, *Textes ougaritiques II*, 22,adopt the translation, “massacre,” (following G. del Olmo) which does not seem to do justice to the context and biblical parallels.

7 J. C. de Moor & K. Spronk, *A Cuneiform Anthology*, 140.

view of all this, and the biblical picture, where the religious use of the root predominates, and more than predominates in connection with YHWH (while Anat as war goddess is a highly appropriate analogue), it seems that de Moor's seemingly bold translation is much to be preferred.

In his article of 1980, de Moor did not say in which stem Ugaritic *ḫrm* was to be placed. Recently, though, in the glossary of his cuneiform reader, he adopted the D-stem, which is unlikely, since neither the Northwest Semitic languages nor Old South Arabic attest it, and since the evidence from syllabic Ugaritic does not support it. J. Huehnergard's recent lexical study of the syllabic texts sheds light on this problem. He offers these observations regarding *ḫa-ri-mu*:

> It is likely...that two of the instances of *ḫa-ri-mu* represent a single Ugar. word glossing a single Akk. word which corresponds to different Sum. signs, viz. to both no.190 ḪUL and no.191 GUL. (...) An Akk. word...that is equated with both ḪUL and GUL is *šulputu* "desecrate(d)".... I may suggest,therefore, that Ugar. ḫa-ri-mu in lines 40' and 42' (of *Ugaritica* V 137) represents an adjective /*ḥarīmu*/ (alphab. unattested) cognate to the Hebrew verb *heḥerîm*....[8]

In his glossary, Huehnergard lists this /*ḥarīmu*/ as meaning "desecrated(?)"[9] The question mark is justified. Such a meaning would not be cognate with Heb. החרים, but would be a Ugaritic aberration from the Semitic use of the root, which deals with consecration, not desecration. The two signs ḪUL and GUL are listed as follows in Borger's *Zeichenliste*: a) ḪUL (#456) = *lapātu* Š, "zerstören"; *šalputtu*, "Ruin," and b) GUL (#429) = *abātu*, zerstören.[10] Not only is "to destroy" a more primary meaning of *šulputu* (*CAD* s.v. *lapātu*), but "to destroy" seems to be the primary meaning of the two signs. Finally, an adjective--clearly of G- not D-stem derivation--with a meaning in the area of "to destroy" would be within the semantic field required of a Ugaritic cognate to Heb. החרים, the verbal form of which appears in KTU 1.13. The adjective /*ḥa-rī-mu*/ shows that the verb is most likely a G-stem. The use of the verb makes it probable that the adjective means "consecrated to destruction," (or the like) and vice versa.

This reopens the question of the primary nature of the noun in Hebrew. The Ugaritic evidence of one text can not be judged to be definitive, but if there was a regular G-stem verb equivalent to Heb. החרים in Ugaritic, that verb may well have existed once in Hebrew, and engendered the noun חרם. It might also have begotten the verb החרים and then, in Biblical Hebrew, faded away before the competition of the hiphil verb. This would pave the way for the situation found in the Bible (which, as the Ugaritic, whatever its exact

---

[8] J. Huehnergard, *Ugaritic Vocabulary in Syllabic Transcription, Harvard Semitic Studies* 32 (1987), 89. The orthography of the root, with *ḫ* instead of *ḥ* as one would expect, may be a result of cuneiform influence spilling over from the syllabic writing to the alphabetic.

[9] Ibid. 126.

[10] R. Borger, *Assyrisch-Babylonische Zeichenliste, AOAT* Bd. 33/33A (2nd ed., 1981), 174, 169.

place among the Semitic languages, makes plain, is the end-product of centuries of development), and would help explain why biblical authors occasionally used the noun חרם + helping verb (e.g. נתן) instead of החרים, drawing a subtle and elusive distinction, but that would be less likely to be drawn if the hiphil were simply a denominative from the substantive חרם--as had been plausibly argued by Brekelmans.[11] I offer this alternative as a possibility suggested by the appearance of חרם in Ugaritic text KTU 1.13, from which one may infer that the prehistory of the Hebrew root חרם is more complex than was previously imagined.

The presence of חרם in Ugaritic provides, then, a probable precursor to Heb. החרים, but we must hope for new texts to add to this small amount of data.

From Ugaritic we travel eastwards to Akkadian. Brekelmans surveyed briefly the known forms in Akkadian, such as *ḫarāmu*, *ḫarimtu*, and *ḫarmu*, without reaching any radical conclusions which would be important for the understanding of the חרם.[12] He did not consider the word *ḫamru* (usually in *bīt ḫamri*), defined by the *CAD* (H 70a) as "sacred precinct (of Adad)." This word may be derived from the root *ḥrm* by metathesis.

In a review of a book by de Vaux, K. Deller raised the possibility of the metathesis, but said that the proof was not at hand.[13] Yet he thought another alternative to metathesis equally plausible; that the *bīt ḫamri* was the sanctuary of a particular god, like the Old Babylonian *gagû*, the Israelite shrine at Shilo, and the Memphite Sarapeum.[14] However, one has to wonder if this second alternative is really an alternative, for the *bīt ḫamri* was not a temple, but a special precinct distinct from the temple of the same deity (and so hardly analogous to the temple at Shilo; biblical religion lacks a comparable institution to the *bīt ḫamri*).[15] However, it was only with the coming of Islam, that the *ḥaram* or "sacred territory" of Mecca (and Medina) was exclusively the domain of Allah.[16] Although the *bīt ḫamri* was associated most often with the storm god (Adad), or ^{d}IM, it was also a part of the cult of the god Aššur in the Old Assyrian period. Both the Kanish colony and the city of Assur had such a precinct in that time,[17] which means other gods may have had one besides Adad or ^{d}IM.[18]

---

[11] C. H. W. Brekelmans, *De ḥerem in het Oude Testament* (Nijmegen, 1959), 43f..
[12] Ibid. 34.

[13] K. Deller in review of R. de Vaux, *Les sacrifices de l'Ancien Testament, Or* N.S. 34 (1965). 385.
[14] Ibid.
[15] KAR 154, an Assyrian ritual text, distinguishes between *bīt ^{d}Adad* and *bīt ḥamri;* after a temple ritual the hierodules (NU GIG MEŠ) go out to the sacred precinct (l.13).
[16] E. W. Lane, *Arabic-English Lexicon* I (Cambridge, England, repr. 1984, 2 vols.), 554c-555a.
[17] L. Matouš, "Der Aššur-Tempel nach altassyrischen Urkunden aus Kultepe," in *Studies Presented to Professor M. A. Beek on the Occasion of his 65th Birthday* (Assen, Netherlands, 1974). See also H. Hirsch, *Untersuchungen zur altassyrischen Religion, AfO* Bhft. 13/14 (1961), 48. There was also a *ḫamrum* of Ashur in the city of Aššur

Although the idea of metathesis can not, as Deller rightly remarked, be proved with the means at hand, there are a number of grounds which serve as a basis for the conclusion that this etymology is the most probable. One, Deller himself pointed out; that it would fit in well with the word *ḫarimtu*:

> (5) ganz unvoreingenommen, so muss der Parallelismus zu der Gestellung von gottgeweihten Personen ($^{LU/MI}$MAŠ.$^{LU/MI}$SUḪUR.LAL, *ḫarimtu* genannt) auf fallen.[19]

This parallelism is important because it places the word *ḫamru* in a philological context. Otherwise, it stands isolated (cp. *ḫemēru*, *ḫamru*, to cover, cover). In addition, the Arabic *ḥaram* in its basic signification as a holy precinct is partly analogous to the *bīt ḫamri*. The metathesis of *r* and *m* here would form a perfect parallel to the situation of *qadāšu* and *qašdu*, where the metathesis is admitted by the *CAD*.[20] The verb *qadāšu* in the G-stem means "to be free of claims(?))," (only at Ras Shamra),[21] which is not what a Hebraist would expect (i.e. to be holy). Yet *qašdu* does mean "holy." I would point to an analogy here: *ḫarāmu* "to separate,"[22] could have the same relation to *ḫamru* as *qadāšu* has to *qašdu*. A last argument is derived from the element of *ḫamru* or *ḫamri* in toponyms and personal names from the Old Babylonian period onwards (although most of the material is from the Middle Assyrian and on).[23] Although the *CAD* is reluctant to assign any semantic value to the material it covers,[24] it should be noted that the term *ḫamru* would be ideal for a toponym (cp. Qedesh); Von Soden, in fact, groups together the names which the *CAD* lists apart from (*bīt*) *ḫamri*.[25] On the geographical side, one may observe that toponyms with *ḫamru* are found in Assyrian and Babylonian volumes of the *Répertoire Géographique*, (e.g. near Nippur),[26] while the volume of the *Répertoire Géographique* which is

---

then, according to M. T. Larsen in The Old Assyrian City-State and its Colonies Mesopotamia: Copenhagen Studies in Assyriology vol. 4 (1976), 59.

[18] M. I. Gruber believes that an OB Letter is best explained as speaking of such a precinct in relation to Shamash at Sippar. See his "Hebrew *Qedeshah* and her Canaanite and Akkadian Cognates," *UF* 18 (1986), 140 n. 26.

[19] See n. 11.

[20] *CAD* 146a.

[21] Ibid. 46a.

[22] Ibid. H 89b-90a.

[23] Cf. Ibid. I/J 152a *ḫamru* C; also K. Nashef, *Die Orts- und Gewässernamen der mittelbabylonischen und mittelassyrischen Zeit*, *Répertoire Géographique des Textes Cunéiformes* Bd. 5 *Beihefte zum Tübinger Atlas des vorderen Orients* Re. B. Nr. 7 (1982), 116, 300. In the same series: R. Zadok, *Geographical Names According to New- and Late-Babylonian Texts* Bd. 8 (1985), 149.

[24] *CAD* I/J 152a *ḫamru* C.

[25] *AHw* 318a.

[26] The river Ḫamri is mentioned by J. J. Finkelstein, "Mesopotamia," *JNES* XXI (1962) 81.

*Géographique*which is devoted to Hittite (and Hurrian) toponyms lacks all reference to *ḫamru*,[27] even though both languages employed the term.

The latter point may be significant since some scholars believe that Akkadian *ḫamru* was a Hurrian loanword.[28] I may cite against this, E. Laroche, who pointed out that *ḫamri* was used by the Hurrians only within the Hittite sphere of influence, and in his Hurrian glossary defined *ḫamri* after the Hittite and Akkadian, an indication in his format that he did not consider it a Hurrian word.[29] The Old Assyrian colony in Kanish had a *ḫamru* earlier than the known Hurrian use, and it most likely was modeled on the *ḫamru* at Assur (rather than the mother-city modeling itself on the trading colony). From Kanish the use of the term then passed into other languages, such as Hurrian and Luwian. The Semitic etymology of the word *ḫamru* is thus much more likely than the Hurrian one.

The *bīt ḫamri* was a sacred area outside the city, as KAR 154, a neo-Assyrian ritual text, vividly illustrates. The action (which involved chanting and elevating the statue of the god, as well as giving offerings) took place both at the temple of Adad proper, and at the *bīt ḫamri* of Adad. The *bīt ḫamri*, like the temple, was the site of varied activities, from sacral to economic.[30] The most interesting from the viewpoint of the study of the חרם is the penalty clause of a contract: *apilšu rabû ina* ^{d}*ḫa-am-ri ša* ^{d}*Adad iššarap*: "His eldest son will be burned (to death) in the sacred precinct of Adad."[31] In contrast to the *CAD*, which takes the clause literally, Deller argued that it

---

[27] G. F. del Monte & J. Tischler, *Die Orts- und Gewässernamen der hethischen Texte, Répertoire Géographique des Textes Cunéiformes* Bd. 6, *Beihefte zum Tübinger Atlas des vorderen Orients* Reihe B. Bd. 7 This includes Hurrian names. Although the lack of *ḫamri*-names is not an absolute, it is precisely in the Hittite sphere that one would expect a Hurrian name to occur. See article cited in n. 29.

[28] W. Haas & G. Wilhelm, *Hurritische und luwische Riten aus Kizzuwatna, AOAT Sonderreihe* Bd. 3 (1974). They list *ḫamri* in the Hurrian glossary. q.v.. J. Huehnergard, *Ugaritic Vocabulary,* 173 also assumes Hurrian derivation, although E. Laroche, in "Glossaire de la langue hourrite I," *RHA* 34 (1976), 91, does not. Huehnergard goes beyond Laroche in connecting *ḫamri* with *ḫamarri.* He cites *UGARITICA* V 137 iv a 14, a polyglot god register: *Sara ḫa-ma-ar-ri qi-i* (*d-šu* (?)). To the first he uses an alternate reading, Sum. BARAG=Akk. *parakku* "socle, sanctuary." The Sumerian does not mean sanctuary (see A. Sjoberg et al., *The Sumerian Dictionary of the University Museum of the University of Pennsylvania* (Phila., 1984) B s.v. $bara_7$), nor need the Akkadian The restoration is conjectural, and the meaning of *ḫamarri* is unknown even to Laroche. If *ḫamarri* is an inflection of *ḫamri*, that does not prove it Hurrian, since loanwords enter the grammar of the new language. The Old Assyrian *ḫamru* at Kanish predates the use of the term in Hurrian in relation to the storm god Teshub. Laroche does not list *ḫamri*, in his list of Akkadian loanwords in *RHA* 35 (1977), 315, probably because the *CAD* is noncommittal.

[29] E. Laroche, "Hourrite purli, purni, maison,'" *RA* 47 (1953), 192. In conversation, E. Reiner expressed the opinion that she was extremely dubious of the Hurrian origin of the term.

[30] Cf. W. G. Lambert, "An Old Babylonian Letter and Two Amulets," *Iraq* 38 (1976), 57f..

[31] *CAD* H 70b.

was merely formulaic language, citing a still-used (c.1965) Jesuit vow-formula, *holocaustem in odorum suavitatis*.[32] Following Deller's approach, M. Weinfeld collected a number of formulations that contained a verb meaning "to burn" from Assyria, the Bible, and Arabic, and insisted they were not to be taken literally.[33] The instance of taking the eldest son to the *bīt ḫamri* is unique, though, and not necessarily on a par with the other examples Weinfeld collected--even if he is correct about those.[34] The fact that people sentenced to 'burning' might be dedicated to the temple instead, which Deller and Weinfeld cite,[35] may aid our understanding of the term in the circumstance where the person was to be "burnt before Adad," i.e. at his temple. Yet in the case in which the son was to be taken not to the temple but to the *bīt ḫamri*, Deller's and Weinfeld's interpretation would seem to be lacking in application.

Whatever the case with *holocaustem in odorum suavitatis*, it is less likely the case that a legal contract would be so formulated. By nature the vow lends itself to extravagant language, as in the instance of Jephthah. Not so the contract. Surely at some time--even if not (for the sake of argument) at the time of the particular document in question--the possibility did exist of putting an *aplu rabû* to the fire in order to enforce a contract. The language reflects the crude necessity of finding a guarantee that the person who had obligated himself would indeed fulfill the terms of the contract.

The important thing to keep in mind is that the text connects the *bīt ḫamri* with the burning to death of human beings, whatever the practice was at a given date. If I am correct in connecting the word *ḫamru* with the root חרם, then this connection is noteworthy and not purely fortuitous, any more than the use of the word חרם in the Bible with the Hebrew cognate שׂרף, "to burn," was fortuitous. Unfortunately, documentation on this point is too limited to allow us to draw far-reaching conclusions from this coincidence of usage. It is enough to say that it strengthens my interpretation of *ḫamru* or *bīt ḫamri* as a metathesized form of *ḫarāmu*, an interpretation which has the merit of bringing coherence to what would otherwise be a random collection of linguistic and cultural facts. Among these are the degree of correspondence between Ar. *ḥaram* and Akk. *ḫamru* on the one hand, and the association with burning to death (if only on a small scale) on the other. These, as well as the other arguments, make it evident that the *bīt ḫamri* belongs in a philological discussion of the חרם. Finally, I may point out that even if it could be proved that the word *ḫamru* was borrowed, its assimilation into the Akkadian vocabulary would have been facilitated by the analogy of the word as a metathesized form of *ḫarāmu* in the manner of *qašdu*. Yet there is no evidence to show that *ḫamru* is other than a good Akkadian word.

---

[32] K. Deller in review of R. de Vaux, 385.

[33] M. Weinfeld, "The Worship of Molech and of the Queen of Heaven and its Background," *UF* 4 (1972), 145-6.

[34] Cf. M. Smith's vigorous rebuttal of Weinfeld in "A Note on Burning Babies," *JAOS* 95 (1975), 477-9. Their exchange of views continued.

[35] See notes 31-2.

The Ebla finds have added a new dimension to Semitic philology. Already, material relevant to our topic has emerged in the published material. It is probable that further information will come to light in the course of time, but at present no Eblaitic verbal form of חרם has been found (to my knowledge). There is a good chance that an adjective has been found. M. Krebernik, in a 1983 article dealing with lexical texts from Ebla, noted a gloss *'a-mu* to the equation NI.GIG=*ga-ti-sum* (normalized *qadišum*), equating it to the West Semitic root חרם, although his identification of the one with the other is uncertain.[36] A meaning in the semantic field of sanctity would be indicated; it is not yet possible to narrow it down further.

More solid evidence comes from an article by G. Pettinato on the Eblaite calendar, which lists three variant names of the same month: *itu ḫu-lu-mu*, *itu ḫur-mu*, and *itu izi-gar*.[37] The first two, assuming they have been correctly read--unlike some other readings, these have not been impeached, to my knowledge--are examples of the "intercambiliabilita di l/r" at Ebla.[36] The presence of the third name, *itu izi-gar*, is interesting. Pettinato translated *itu izi-gar* as "month of ascending flames."[38] As indicated (n.37) Pettinato's reading of *izi-gar* is not correct, but the motif of the flames remains, so that here again, in a totally fresh context (cf. above, *bīt ḫamri*), we see the association of the root חרם with fire, although Pettinato, too, is not absolutely certain in his identification of the Hebrew root חרם with the Eblaite, in this case *ḫu-lu-mu* and *ḫur-mu*.[36] While caution is always indicated in dealing with this new Semitic language, it seems fairly safe to affirm this particular identity; the evolution of Muharram into a month name offers a late analogy.[39] To be sure, there is no indication that the fire involves the death of human beings; Pettinato points to a setting in the ritual cult.[36] This is logical for a cultically oriented calendar like Ebla's (a majority of the month names honor the occasion of the offering to a deity),

---

[36] M. Krebernick, "Zu Syllabar und Orthographie der lexicalischen Texte aus Ebla," *ZA* 73 (1983), 4.

[37] G. Pettinato, "Il Calendrio di Ebla al Tempo del Re Ibbi-Sipiš sulla base di TM 75.G. 427," *AfO* 25 (1978), 30. Also cf. idem "Il Calendario semitico del 3. millennio ricostruito sulla base dei testi di Ebla," *OA* 16 (1977), 280f. and *Ebla: An Empire Inscribed in Clay* (Garden City, N.Y., 1981), 150f.. There he translates *itu ḫurmu* as "month of the fires." I should add that von Soden is of the opinion that the root of Akk. *ḫarāmu* is the same as our root (*AHw* 323a.), which bolsters the Eblaite identification. According to M. C, Astour, the "ḫ" in Akk. "ḫarāmu" is retained (against expectations) for phonetic reasons, because of the presence of the liquid in the word (verbal communication).

[38] Ibid. However, Prof. W. W. Hallo has informed me that this reading is incorrect. He referred me to the glossary entry izi-ne-ne(r) gar "fan the fire" in his and J. J. A. van Dijk's *The Exaltation of Inanna* (New Haven, 1968), 79f., as well as to (among other references) B. Landsberger et. al., *Materials for the Sumerian Lexicon XIII: A Reconstruction of Sumerican and Akkadian Lexical Lists* 159 ll.191-3 (where the sign appears as NE-NE-gar, with the actual value left open) cf. esp. 192 (NE-N)E-gar = ši-ki-in IZI (=išāti), trans. by W.von Soden in *AHw*. 1234b as "Legen ins Feuer."

[39] For a short summary treatment with bibliography, see *Encylopedia of Islam* vol. 5 (Leiden, 1960-), 698b-699a.

and it suggests fire's consecrating role in the sacrificial cult. The association of *ḫurmu* and fire at Ebla may be viewed as a harbinger of biblical chapters like Deuteronomy 13; although actual sacrifice is not involved there, as we shall see. Traditional associations in antiquity could last long in one form or another.

It is the turn now of Arabic and Old South Arabic. Here I have little to add to Brekelmans' treatment.[40] The occurrence of forms such as *mḥrm* for 'temple, sanctuary,'[41] (as opposed to Heb. מקדש) shows the rather positive side of the root חרם, which is reflected in its use in personal/proper names across a broad spectrum of Semitic languages, including Hebrew (see below). It also appears in a context of war, but according to Brekelmans, *hḥrm* appears in South Arabic in a war report, not for destruction but for the sparing of a conquered city. However, he also cites the case of the Sabaen king Krb'l who:

> in his wars put many cities to flames; he banned (*hḥm*) the city of Nan, destroying it by fire, so that he might let his own folk live in the wild, and he erected a temple for Almakah (in translation).[42]

Brekelmans remarks on this that one may at least say that the religious sense of *hḥrm* here is far from clear.[43] One may take note, however, of the following elements: a) the distinction of terminology which Krb'l made in introducing *hḥrm* coupled with b) the shunning of the ruined city (cf. the curse on Jericho) c) the obviously religious motive of the temple-building and d) the association of the root *ḥrm* with fire (as seen previously) as well as with the destruction of a city. All these elements add up to something not too remote from the biblical practice of the חרם although far from identical.

With regard to Arabic proper, Brekelmans pointed out the frequency of the use of the root *ḥrm* in many forms (verbal and nominal) and meanings, but that direct contact with the OT is, in spite of the broad semantic field, absent.[44]

In Arabic, the unambiguously positive connotation of the root occurs in connection with the simple stem, which can mean "*he* (a person) *was* or *became, sacred*, or *inviolable*, or *entitled to reverence, respect*, or *honour*," which meanings are reflected in the VIIIth stem meaning "to reverence, re-

---

[40] Treated in C. H. W. Brekelmans, *De ḥerem,* 17-23.

[41] Recently reaffirmed by J. C. Biella in her *Dictionary of Old South Arabic: Sabaen Dialect Harvard Semitic Studies* 25 (1982), 190. Although Biella also gives *mḥrm,* "fortified camp" (cp. A. F. L. Beeston, "Warfare in Ancient South Arabia (2nd-3rd centuries A.D.)," *QAHTAN: Studies in Old South Arabian Epigraphy* Fasc. 3 (1976). 17f.. "ordinance depot," 65, "strongpoint"), this is corrected to "temple" with the aid of additional evidence in W.W. Müller, "Sabäische Felsinschriften von der jementischen Grenze zur Rub' al-K̄alī' in R. Degen, et. al., eds., *Neue Ephemeris für Semitische Epigraphik,* Bd. 3 (Wiesbaden, 1978). The temple had a military function as a gathering place from which to launch campaigns and so on.

[42] C. H. W. Brekelmans, *De ḥerem,* 23.

[43] Ibid. 17.

[44] Ibid. 22.

spect, honour"[45] In Biblical Hebrew such a purely positive aspect of the root (i.e., lacking the component of destruction, which in itself is negative) is preserved only in its use in names. The best example is the name Ḥarim, which was used by priests, heads of families, and a prince.[46] A DN pronounced much the same is found in the Akk. name Išar-Ḫarim.[47]

The root חרם appears (or possibly appears) in oaths or vows in more than one language. In Arabic, Lane cites the example of a man who swears that his wife is forbidden to him (form II).[48] In Palmyran and Phoenician, votive formulae involving חרם depend on restorations of damaged inscriptions.[49] As the Arabic example shows, the mere use of the root in a vow is no proof of an ultimate connection to the חרם-vow of the Bible. In the other cases, one can not make much of connections that rest entirely on restorations.

A curious case from Elephantine (also connected with oaths) is that of Ḥerem-Bethel, accepted as the name of a deity until a recent article by K. van der Toorn.[50] The sole text in which this alleged DN occurs is an enigmatic courtroom text. The text in question reads as follows:

'n' mlkyh 'qr' lk 'l ḥrmbyt'l
'lh' byn (nq)mn iv l'(mr) ...[51]

Most of the second line is enigmatic, after *'lh'*, but that is fortunately of no consequence. *ḥrmbyt'l 'lh'* had been translated as "Herem-Bethel the god."[52] This is in keeping with the use of *ḥrm* as a theophoric element in a name such as *ḥrmntn*, which van der Toorn does not dispute.[53] Of course, we have at the settlement at Elephantine (see ch.2) names combining two DNs, e.g. Anatyahu, which is a strong argument in favor of the opinion of the majority of scholars; the debate has been over the precise meaning of *ḥrm* within the framework of the larger DN Ḥerem-Bethel. Van der Toorn argues that *ḥrm* is not part of the DN, but is to be construed as an "object under taboo, sacred and inviolable," citing Nabatean and Palmyran *ḥrmyn*, "inviolable objects."[54] On one such object, according to van der Toorn, an

---

[45] E. W. Lane, *Arabic-English Lexicon,* I 553c, 554b.

[46] *BDB* 356b.

[47] W. C. Gwaltney, jr., "Indices of Proper Names from the *EL* Old Assyrian Texts," *HUCA* 48 (1977), 20.

[48] E. W. Lane, *Arabic-English Lexicon* , I 554a.

[49] C. H. W. Brekelmans, *De ḥerem*, 25,34-5. R. S. Tomback, *A Comparative Semitic Lexicon to the Phoenician and Punic Languages, SBLDS* 32 (Chico, Ca., 1978), does not mention the root which is found in PN Mlkḥrm).

[50] K. van der Toorn, "Ḥerem-Bethel and Elephantine Oath Procedure," *ZAW* 98 (1986), 282-285.

[51] Ibid. 283.

[52] P. Grelot, Documents araméens d'Egypte, *LAPO* 5 (1972), 93, M. H. Silverman, Religious Values in the Jewish Proper Names at Elephantine, *AOAT* bd. 217 (1985), 223.

[53] K. van der Toorn, "Ḥerem-Bethel," 285.

[54] Ibid. 283.

oath was sworn, as oaths were sworn by the Akk. *asakku* in Mari (also he points to Mt 23,16-22).[55]

Passing over van der Toorn's other arguments, it is possible just to compare the different interpretations of the two lines quoted above, especially l.1. "I call to you, to/on Ḥrmbyt'l, the god," is good Semitic parallelism. "I call to you, on/by the sacred object of Bethel the god," does not read as well, and the only other example of this *ḥrm*, "sacred object," at Elephantine depends, like the votive texts mentioned above, on a reconstruction.[56] The case never amounts to more than ingenious speculation.

This brings us to the question of the meaning of *ḥrm* in Ḥrmbyt'l. One cannot be certain as to the correct answer, but Brekelmans clearly chose an attractive possibility in preferring "sacred precinct,"[57] which would evoke in this context not only Ar. *ḥaram* but also, in my view, the Akk. *bīt ḫamri*. However, the presence in Egypt of names like Ḥrmntn, parallel to other theophoric names such as Jonathon, or perhaps Theodore, does not favor this view. M. H. Silverman has categorically denied the possibility of Ḥrm's representing a divine name (as Ḥrmntn seems to indicate), seeing it as a "theophorous element."[58] The existence of two divine names in Akkadian (see chart below) is a counter–argument. Another is Phoenician Mlkḥrm, which follows the pattern of מלכעשתרת, which also argues for a god. The name Ḥrmntn follows an ancient and widepread pattern, known throughout the ancient Near East. Given all this, it is hard to avoid understanding the element 'ḥrm' as the name of a god.

C. H. W. Brekelmans, in his "filologisch onderzoek," did not seek out the late Aramaic dialects, of which the most familiar dialect to the biblicist is Syriac. I may note in passing, utilizing the Syriac-English Dictionary edited by J. Payne Smith, the many late developments which this root is subject to in Syriac. The causative stem (aphel) was used as the equivalent to the hiphil stem of *ḥrm* in Biblical Hebrew.[59] In New Testament Syriac and later, the aphel meant "to excommunicate, to curse, ban." The ethpeel stem was used to express the passive, "to be excommunicated, anathematized." The ettaphal was used similarly to the ethpeel, with the added meaning of "to be threatened with excommunication." Its derivatives (half a dozen) include such meanings not familiar from the Bible as "accursed, execrable, savage, fierce, cruel, harsh." The multiplying of forms and meanings, although not with the fecundity of classical Arabic, witnesses to a possibility which I raised in regard to Ugaritic, viz. that more forms of the root were in use in the biblical period than are found in the Bible. Surely there were other nonreligious uses of the root (as in Late Hebrew) which were unutilized by

---

[55] Ibid. 283-4.

[56] Ibid. 284-5.

[57] C. H. W. Brekelmans, *De ḥerem*, 28.

[58] M. H. Silverman, *Religious Values,* 224. He defines it simply as a "theophorous element," the "subject in a verbal-sentence name." 148, with references.

[59] J. Payne Smith, *A Compendious Syriac Dictionary* (Oxford, 1903), 158.

biblical writers. The vocabulary of the Bible is only a fraction of what was in use at a given time.

The study of the Semitic root חרם in relation to the Bible suggests, that the biblical usage having to do with "consecration to destruction" was not widely shared by other Semitic speakers (excepting Moabite, see ch. 2, and possibly Ugaritic). Yet it should be easily comprehended from the foregoing why this root, with meanings of sanctity and the forbidden attached to it, and possibly still-living traditional associations with fire, should have received the kind of specialization it did in Biblical Hebrew. One may add as an important thread that חרם in Semitic denotes separation; more than one kind of separation takes place in the חרם; a separation between that which is God's and that which is human is matched by a corresponding physical action or course of action making and marking the separation.[60] Although the vast majority of instances when the hiphil of the root is used, the meaning is "consecrate through destruction," there are some anomalous usages which are secular, mainly in Chronicles and Daniel but as early as 2 Kgs 19:11 =Isa 37:11, where it was presumably not used in this way for the first time. The standard derivation of this usage has been as a weakened or secularized use of חרם I = Ar. *ḥarama*, the root I am dealing with in this study. חרם II, "to perforate," = Ar. *ḫarama* has not been considered because the secular usage follows the hiphil pattern of the חרם I usage., and is largely late. However, the existence of an eighth form of Ar. *ḫarama* meaning "to kill, extirpate, destroy," (Lane I, 730b) raises the possibility that what in the Arabic appears in the nondescript eighth form would logically appear in Hebrew as a hiphil, producing an isomorph to the hiphil of חרם I, just as two identical written (we need not enter into pronunciation) nominal forms (one meaning "net") coexisted without causing much confusion. This possibility better explains the coexistence in the Book of Kings of the hiphil of חרם in its sacral meaning along with the secular meaning of "destroy." The Arabic VIIIth form may well be of more recent vintage than the pre-exilic period of ancient Israel, but this is not a derivation, only an analogy; what could develop in Arabic at one, possibly post-biblical time, could develop in Hebrew at an earlier time through a similar process of word formation..

This concludes the chapter, but as a final illustration of the comparative breadth of this root, I offer a look at the omnastics of this root. The chart on the next page, while necessarily incomplete, gives an idea of the breadth and depth of the "Ḥerem Omnasticon." The fact that Semites from many places named their children using this root (as well as deities), shows the positivity which it could assume, as I noted above with Heb. Harim. This is also a good indication of the positive light in which biblical writers saw the practice of חרם, a point which I will have occasion to amplify in the course of this study.

---

[60] For a modern linguistic analysis of חרם along with five other verbs of separation see A. Vivian, *I campi lessicali della "separazione" nell'ebraico biblico, di Qumran e della Mishna: ovvero, applicabilita della teoria dei campi lessicali all'ebraico* (Florence, 1978).

THE חרם OMNASTICON

LANGUAGE/ DIALECT	PERSONAL NAMES	DEITY NAMES	TOPONYMS/ MISCEL-LANEOUS
SOUTH ARABIC	Ḥrm, Ḥrmm, 'ḥrm, Ḥrmt, Mḥrmt, Ḥrmlh, Yḥrm, Yḥrm'l Tḥrmn, T̲'dḥrm, Ḥrm'l, Ḥrmtm, Mḥrmh, Mḥrmm, Ḥrmšms*	Ḥrmn, Mḥrm	'ḥrm (GN) bnw ḥr'm (tribe)
CLASSICAL ARABIC	Ḥaram		Banu Ḥaram (tribe) Ḥaram, Maḥram Muḥarram (month)
NABATEAN	Ḥrim, Ḥrmw		
EGYPTIAN ARAMAIC	Ḥrmutu, Ḥrmšzb, Ḥrmntn, Ḥrmn	Ḥrmbt'l	
LATE ARAMAIC/ SYRIAC			ḥurmana' (basilisk)
UGARITIC	Ḥrm		
PHOENICIAN	Mlkḥrm		
AKKADIAN	Ḫurruma Išar-Ḫarim	Ḫurum,Ḫarim	Til-ḫamri, ḫamri (cities), ḫamri (branch) of river, canal
HEBREW	Ḥarim		Ḥarem, Ḥormah, (towns), (Mt.) Ḥermon
EBLAITE			Ḫulumu, Ḫurmu (months)

* See G. L. Harding, *An Index and Concordance of Pre-Islamic Arabian Names and Inscriptions* (Toronto, 1971), 185.

CHAPTER 2

IMPLICATIONS OF THE MESHA INSCRIPTION

The origins of the Moabites are mysterious, but the Bible clearly linked Moab's earliest beginnings to those of Israel, as Moab was derived incestuously from Lot. The Mesha stele dramatizes this connection in its language, for with some editing it would fit well into the MT (a translation of the inscription is found at the end of the chapter). The theology of warfare reflected in it is akin to that of Deuteronomy. In short, the Moabite and Israelite cultures seem to have shared similar world views.

The immediate reason for devoting a chapter to the Mesha Inscription (=MI) is that it is the one text found on Canaanite soil which explicitly mentions the חרם. The 34 line inscription gives an account in miniature of the conflict between Moab and Israel in the ninth century B.C, using many key terms which are also found in the biblical Exodus-and-conquest narratives (see below). In this chapter I will examine the MI linearly and in comparison to the Bible and explore various topics it raises. The inscription's usefulness for understanding the *Weltanschauung* which underlay the practice of the חרם will be shown in detail. The geographical and linguistic proximity of Moab and Moabite, respectively, to Israel and Hebrew, laid the ground for similarity of culture and practice. The MI provides us with an extra-biblical historical source; yet like the Bible, it requires critical handling.

King Mesha's narrative reveals that the Moabites practiced the חרם against Israel and raises the question as to why no one in the biblical narratives ever called for the use of the חרם in Israel's handling of the conflicts with Moab from Moses to Jereboam II. The Bible supplies us with more than one answer. Deut 20:16-17 preach the חרם against the autochthonous peoples of the Promised Land--the land to the west of the Jordan alone.[1] The Moabites, Ammonites, and Edomites would fall under the rules defined for those whom it was necessary to embark on a journey to fight; where the חרם need not apply (see ch. 4). Deut 2:9 records a tradition that Israel was not to disturb Moab because the Lord had given it land as a legacy from Lot. Both explanations dovetail: the חרם as a form of consecration was reserved by Israel for the land to be settled; and the feeling of kinship with Moab may have also been a restraint. Another consideration is the specific nature of the חרם, which was not a discretionary act in its pristine form. It was an extreme act done only by divine command (e.g. I Samuel 15), or by virtue of a vow, if accepted by the deity (Num 21:1-3). Such a vow was the product of dire circumstances. Mesha's חרם was not likely to have resulted from a vow, since he does not mention it, unlike Numbers 21. The fact that the Moabites seem never to have tried to settle the western side of the Jordan was probably a major factor as well. It was in the context of Edomite encroachment on the land of Judah that the prophet of Isaiah 34 raged.

---

[1] M. Weinfeld, "The Extent of the Promised Land--the Status of Transjordan," in *Das Land Israel in biblischer Zeit: Jerusalem-Symposium 1981, GThA* 25 (1983), 59.

The Moabites, the MI informs us, worshipped Kemosh as their national god.[2] This is evident both from the role Kemosh plays in the inscription, which is analogous to the role of YHWH in the Bible (which calls Moab "the people of Kemosh"), and from the personal names recovered from other sources (as well as Kemosh's role in the Bible). L.12, רית.לכמש.ולמאב might imply a second national deity named Moab (cf. ᵈAššur), but no source outside the MI uses Moab as a DN, so the line is best understood as referring to the people (cf. Num 21:29; מאב//עם כמוש). This has important implications for the meaning of רית (see below).

It is obvious that Mesha's account does not square well with 2 Kings 3, the historicity of which has recently been denied from several perspectives.[3] The question as to whether Mesha rebelled against Israel sometime during the reign of Ahab (as a literal understanding of MI would imply), or closely following his death as 2 Kgs 1:1 suggests, is an important one. It must take into account the element of legend in Kings. The aftermath of the Naboth episode brought about Ahab's sincere repentance. As a result, an oracle deferred Ahab's punishment to his 'house' (1 Kgs 21:28-9), i.e. his heirs (cp. the judgement on Solomon in 1 Kgs 11:11-13, where for David's sake it was said that the rebellion was delayed). This supplied a redactor with a motive to date the rebellion after Ahab, validating Elijah's prediction. Note that the next chapter, 1 Kings 22, raises the question of true vs. false prophets. This consideration of prophetic 'legend' as a chronological factor has been overlooked by historians in their attempts to reconstruct the chronology of Mesha's revolt.[4] On the other hand, it could work the other way; the sudden twist to the Naboth story which saves retribution for his heirs may be a way of adjusting the Naboth story and Elijah's role in it with the well-known fact that Mesha rebelled against Israel upon the death of Ahab (2 Kgs 1:1, 3:5). The question will be dealt with again below.

It is important to view Mesha's charting of his accomplishments with a skeptical eye. To read his inscription one could think that his campaign(s) had more of the nature of a royal processional than a serious military undertaking. He, too, had obvious motives of self-glorification as well as a strong religious impulse to boost Kemosh over the enemy god, YHWH.

---

[2] For the latest treatment of Moabite religion see G. L, Mattingly, "Moabite Religion and the Mesha' Inscription," *SMIM*, 211-38. Moabite's closeness to Hebrew is attributed to Israel's dominion over Moab during the United Monarchy by R. Garr, *Dialect Geography of Syria-Palestine* (Phila., 1985), 234-5.

[3] See J. R. Bartlett, "The 'United' Campaign against Moab in 2 Kings 3:4-27," in J. F. A. Sawyer & D. J. A. Clines, *Midian, Edom and Moab, JSO T* Sup 24 (1983), 135-146, R. Klein, *Textual Criticism of the Old Testament* (Philadelphia, 1974), 36-40, H. Schweizer, *Elischa in den Kriegen: Literaturwissenschaftliche Untersuchung von 2 Kön 3; 6,8--23; 6,24-7,20, SANT* XXXVII (1974) 100ff., S. Timm, *Die Dynastie Omri: Quellen und Untersuchung zum Geschichte Israels* (Göttingen, 1982), Part 3, Ch. 2 "Die Bieziehung der Meshainschrift zum Feldzug der drei Könige 2. Kön. 3," 171-80. and the appendix to this chapter.

[4] E.g., the most recent, very sold work of J. A. Dearman, "Historical Reconstruction and the Mesha' Inscription," *SMIM*, 155-210.

Hayim Tadmor has demonstrated, in his treatment of mainly neo-Assyrian royal inscriptions, how far these kings could go in straying from the exact order of events for apologetic, pietistic, or other purposes.[5] Some Assyrian documents are in several versions, allowing the scholar to practice textual criticism. Obviously, in the case of the MI there is far less evidence. Moab was a society of a different geopolitical background with a lower level of material culture, about which there is consequently far less information available than is the case with Assyria. However, Mesha does participate in the general tradition of first millennium Near Eastern royalty (e.g. the Zakur Inscription, KAI 202), and though royal Israelite inscriptions are lacking, the MI reflects a cultural similarity to the Hebrew Bible that partly compensates for that lack.

In terms of genre, the MI seems to compress all genres into one omnibus; it is a victory stele glorifying the king's prowess, a sanctuary dedication, and finally, a memorial inscription.[6] It seeks to list all of Mesha's accomplishments, among which are civic projects like the construction of a highway by the Arnon and the building of temples at major sites. The inscription refers specifically to the building of the במת of Kemosh, but in the latter part of the MI several sites whose names begin with בת are in Mesha's construction program. It is almost certain that some of these had Moabite sanctuaries which needed to be reconstructed or (at the least) restored and rededicated. Jezebel built a temple to Baal outside Samaria, at a place which the Bible calls עִיר בֵּית־הַבָּעַל (2 Kgs 10:25), a similar type of name to those in Moab, such as בת.בעלמען (MI 30). It was, of course, the task of the Near Eastern king to rebuild and restore the temples of the local gods from time immemorial (KAI 202 again). Aside from Kemosh, there were other Moabite gods, such as Baal. The biblical evidence matches Baal's frequency in Moabite toponyms.[7]

---

[5] H. Tadmor, "History and Ideology in the Assyrian Royal Inscriptions," F. M. Fales, ed., *Assyrian Royal Inscriptions: New Horizons in Literary, Ideological, and Historical Analysis* (Rome,1981), 13-33, idem "Autobiographical Apology in the Royal Assyrian Literature," H. Tadmor & M. Weinfeld, eds., *History, Historiography, and Interpretation: Studies in Biblical and Cuneiform Literature* (Jerusalem, 1982), 36-57.

[6] M. Miller, "The Mesha Stone as a Memorial Stela," *PEQ* 106 (1974), 9-18. Miller also compares the MI with Aramaic inscriptions profitably. See now also ch.5 of *SMIM*.

[7] A. H. van Zyl, *The Moabites, POS* III (1960), Baal; 193f., goddess; 195f.. L. G.Herr, "Formal Scripts of Iron Age Transjordan," *BASOR* 249 (1980), 26, lists 8 Moabite seals from 700-550 B.C, in which 6 Kemosh-names are listed, and one Baal-name. Kemosh was the national (or dynastic) deity of Moab at least from Mesha's day onward (his grandfather gave his father a Kemosh-name--we have a variety of royal Kemosh-names); Baal had the same role in Tyre.The Bible's distinction between the two seems to be accurate; Kemosh is a major deity at Ebla, Baal is not, and at Ugarit the name Kemosh (Kmṯ) occurs separately from Baal. Kemosh had a long history distinct from Baal, and the Bible keeps them distinct--Ahab worships Baal with no suggestion that he worshipped thereby Kemosh, "the abomination of Moab" in 1 Kgs 11:7. There is no evidence which suggests that it is mistaken. It may be that at this period of resurgent Moabite nationalixm, Baal was identified with Phoenician nationalism and took a back seat to Kemosh, but aside from the king we know little about exactly who in Moab

It is clear that the building activities celebrated here were on a large, even vast scale for the region, comparable perhaps to Solomon's large building operations. It is thus hard to understand how these peacetime operations could have been completed shortly after the fighting. Undoubtedly, those, like Albright, who date the stele to c.830, are correct.[8] In our view, it is also certain from other, none too subtle indications. In l.4 Mesha praises Kemosh for saving him from his enemies, but significantly he mentions only Israel, not Judah or Edom (cf. n. 2, appendix). He saw (l.7) the demise of the Omrides (841), which alone puts the earlier dating some have suggested for the MI (c.850) out of court.

Incidentally, one may infer that among the enemies that Mesha triumphed over in his career were most likely internal opponents. Mesha personally was an ardent Dibonite (ll.1,21), and his policies, e.g. his building policy, must have favored Dibon and some localities at the expense of others. Moab was also exposed to bedouin marauders from its eastern flank.

The reason the late dating is important is that, for those who believe, as J. Liver did,[9] that the stele was erected early in Mesha's tenure, before the mythical events of 2 Kings 3 (see appendix), the stele assumes a character close to a press dispatch. This position seemingly enables one to harmonize the Bible with the MI; but as noted above, the MI was written from a perspective of decades. Mesha's scribes had leisure to write and redact their *Heilsgeschichte* in a way analogous to the Assyrian manner documented by Tadmor.[10]

In Assyria, the first regnal year was considered the time for the monarch to begin his military conquests. There are examples of monarchs who in their annals appropriated achievements of their more militant immediate predecessor for their regnal year. There are also examples of kings who were in fact the model of a *šarru dannu* ("mighty king,") but whose timetable did not agree with the dictates of convention, so that a campaign involving years and great distances could be represented as having been completed in the course of the regnal year. The annalistic account of the campaign would be replete with vague indicators of time like *ina ūmēšuma* (an equivalent to "then") or round numbers such as were used in the Bible. Although the MI employs the cognate word, ים, "day, period of time,"(cf..בימי, ll.6,9,33, and

---

worshipped whom. For the complexities of evaluating onomastic evidence, see J. Tigay, *You Shall Have No Other Gods: Israelite Religion in the Light of Hebrew Inscriptions HSS* 31 (Atlanta, 1986), ch. 1. Baal was Hadad at Ugarit, another reason not to identify Baal with Kemosh, a different kind of god, especially since the MI would have used the title if it applied, instead of the epithet *ʿaštar.

8 W. F. Albright, *ANET*, 320.

9 So J. Liver, "The Wars of Mesha, King of Moab," *PEQ* 99 (1967) 21-2, followed by D. Rosner, *The Moabites and their Relationships with the Kingdoms of Israel and Judah in the Military, Political, and Cultural Spheres* (Heb.) (Jerusalem, 1976) 148f..

10 See articles cited in note 4. In addition see W. von Soden, "Die Assyrer und der Krieg," *Iraq* 25 (1963), 131-43, which gives a more general overview as well as some observations in the same vein as Tadmor's.

see ll.5,8 as well)[11] as a vague indicator of time, there is no reason to think that Moab shared directly in Assyrian imperialistic conventions. This inscription follows such a mode probably because of a similar local tradition and also because it made sense from what today is known as the public relations or propaganda point of view. Falling into one of these categories was Mesha's boast of l.29, that he had added hundreds of towns to Moab, a boast with an ancient pedigree. It was a staple of Assyrians inscriptions to boast of extending the imperium's territory, but other kings bragged of extending their domains as well. An example is found in a text of the Old Babylonian period, the "short inscription" of Yaḫdun-Lim, King of Mari, which has many features which can be profitably compared with the MI.[12] In addition to more local traditions there were broader traditions that preceded the Assyrian empire and in which it and other, smaller entities later participated.

The indications of time in the Mesha stele are mostly vague or stereotyped with the possible exception of the thirty year rule attributed to Mesha's father. On the other hand, E. Lipinski has proposed another view.[13] Proceeding from the thirty year figure, he assumes the forty years were from Omri's day (c.881) to the end of the Omrides (c.841). This is logical, and may be correct, if Mesha was indirectly or directly responsible for the end of the Omrides, as he seems to claim (l.7). In that case he also helped undermine the anti-Assyrian coalition. On the other hand, the thirty year figure may be a calculated one on the basis of the round number forty, (i.e. 3/4) and be some years off. As F. Cross has seen, the 7000 figure for Israelite casualties in l.16 is a round number, and the likelihood of the antecedently suspect '40' being round is thus greatly enhanced.[14] The number 7000 appears in the Bible a number of times, often in military contexts (cf. 1 Kgs 19:18, 20:15, and 2 Kgs 24:16, warriors deported to Babylon,1 Chr 18:4, David's captured Aramean horse, 1 Chr 19:18, David's slain Aramean charioteers. This (round) number lends itself to statements of triumph or defeat, Together with the list of kinds of people slaughtered at Nebo, the addition of the number 7000 (which is lacking in the Ataroth and other accounts) in the light of these biblical citations, comes to express Mesha's triumph over YHWH and his shrine. Given the roundness of the numbers of the MI, they do not very much help us fathom the murky chronology of the MI.[15]

---

[11] S. Segert, "Die Sprache der moabitischen Königsinschrift," *ArOr* 29 (1961), 241.
[12] Published by Thureau-Dangin,"Iaḫdun-Lim, roi de Ḫana," *RA* 33 (1936) 49ff.. The present writer hopes to write such a study at a future date.
[13] E. Lipinski, "Notes on the Meša' Inscription," *Or* N.S. 40 (1971), 330-31.
[14] F. M. Cross, "The Ammonite Oppression of the Tribes of Gad and Reuben: Missing Verses from 1 Samuel 11 Found in 4QSamuel," H. Tadmor & M. Weinfeld, eds., *History, Historiography, and Interpretation: Studies in Biblical and Cuneiform Literature* (Jerusalem, 1982), 154-55.
[15] Further explorations of this difficult subject of MI chronology may be found, *int. al*, in B. Bonder, "The Date of Mesha's Rebellion," *JANES* 3 (1971), 83-88, J. A. Dearman, "Historical Reconstruction and the Mesha Inscription," *SMIM*, 164-5. and G. Garbini, *History and Ideology in Ancient Israel* (London, 1988), 33-8. Also, S. Timm,

That murkiness is in part due to the fact that we have not learned the lesson of the Assyrian annals and *ina ūmēšuma*. The crucial lines, ll.7-8, have been dealt with from the point of view of the numbers, while the operative word, ים, has not been scrutinized to the same degree. The biblical chronology and the MI's schedule of events have generally been believed to be in conflict, or capable of being reconciled only by ingenious manipulation of figures. It may be that a study of the Moabite word 'day' resolves the problem.

Here are the lines where the word appears:

5. י.מלך.ישראל.ויענו.את.מאב.ימן.רבן.
6. צה|וילחפה.בנה.ויאמר.גם.הא.אענו.את.מאב|בימי
8. ץ.מהדבה|וישב.בה.ימה.וחצי.ימי.בנה.ארבען.שת.ויש
9. בה.כמש.בימי|
33. תחם.בקר.ואחזה.וישב.).בה.כמש.בימי

Omri was king of Israel for twelve years according to the account of his reign in 1 Kgs 16:23-28. According to that account, it was a reign evenly divided between the old capital of Tirzah and Omri's new capital of Samaria. As Tadmor points out, common sense dictates that if Omri moved to Samaria in the middle of the reign, he must have begun the construction of the new city near the beginning of his reign.[16] Yet the corvée was part of the downfall of Jereboam I, who had in the succession from his father a more solid base on which to build than Omri. It is hard to see how Omri could have consolidated his rule, built Samaria, and only then invaded Moab after he had completed the new capital, because according to ll.4-5, Omri oppressed Israel for ימן.רבן, "a long time." This seems to indicate a longer period than five or six years that would have remained to Omri at the most. A more plausible scenario is that the general-king was able to consolidate early in his reign by his uniting Israel with an attack on the ancient enemy, Moab. He then built Samaria afterwards, most likely using Moabite labor as Mesha later used Israelite workers, and in something of the manner of a conquering Sargon of Assyria building his new capital of Dur-Sharrukin. This would minimize the political cost of constructing a new capital (i.e. the corvée). It was an enormous task to build a capital at such an undeveloped site, and it reflects the confidence of a conquerer who had access to an enormous labor pool. If Moab fell quickly to Omri, as, given the length of his reign, ימן.רבן implies, construction of Samaria with forced labor could have proceeded apace.

Next we turn to l..6, "He [Ahab] said also he, 'I will oppress Moab בימי.'" Here, it is clear that "in my days" is an inadequate translation. It really means, "in the days of my reign," or just "during my reign," to which Omri's

---

(Göttingen, 1982), 163-5. On 165 n.31 he sees agreement between the chronology of the MI and 2 Kgs 1:1. and 2 Kgs 3:5.

[16] H. Tadmor, "On the History of Samaria in the Biblical Period," (Heb.), in Y. Abiram, ed., *Eretz Shomron: The Thirtieth Archeological Conference, Septermber 1972*, (Jerusalem, 1973), 68.

son had just "succeeded." The very locution, "his son succeeded him" may, by the way, be an (ironic) allusion to the dynastic instability of the Northern Kingdom, since it was by no means normal for a son to succeed his father in Ephraim (a normal succession notice would also give the name of the heir). If we look at ll.9,33, "Kemosh...in my days," we see that the meaning "during my reign" obtains. For example, l.33, in speaking of the capture of Horonaim, says, "Kemosh dwelt there during my reign," perhaps meaning on one level that a statue of Kemosh was brought to the city to dwell in a sanctuary following its liberation (ancient parlance did not require the word 'statue,' cf. KAR 154, where Adad is borne by hierodules, cp. Isa 46:1-2, esp. 1a). The introduction or reintroduction of Kemosh to Horonaim was a measure of Mesha's triumph, hence its place near the MI's end.

This brings us to the difficult sentence, ll.7-8, "Omri took possession of the land of Medeba, he occupied it ימה and half the 'days' of his son--forty years"[17] The statement thus indicates that Omri held on to his conquest until he died, for a period of half of Ahab's "days." The statement has only one subject, Omri: the second part restates the first part in terms of Ahab's life, but is still grammatically governed by Omri. According to 1 Kgs 16:29, Ahab reigned for 22 years. If he took the throne at the midpoint of his life, then Ahab was about 22 years old when he took the throne, and died at the age of forty-four or so, which is rounded off to the conventional forty, meaning one generation (the forty is the "total" column), although actually it was a maximum of Omri-11 + Ahab-22 = 33 years. On the other hand, if, as seems most likely, Omri ruled Moab 11 years, then "half the 'days' of his son" refers to the length of Omri's reign in which time he dominated Moab, put in terms of the length of Ahab's reign. The use of 'ימ. for reign would be consistent with the meaning of ים in al but one of its occurrences and the 11 year figure is supported by the earlier "many years"--ימן.רבן. The unusual wording of ll.7-8 is due to the coincidence that Ahab reigned over Moab twice as long as Omri, but it also reflects the fact that Mesha felt such resentment that he did not want to mention Ahab's unspeakable name. At the end of the line, Mesha gives a rounded total of forty, for the generation of Israelite oppression. The fact that the line ends in a total of 40, means that in a backhanded way it is indicating that not only did Omri occupy Medeba for half his son's reign, but that the occupation continued for the length of Ahab's reign. Then comes the 'total' column. Therefore one must translate: " he occupied it during his reign and [it was occupied] half the reign of his son--forty years." This interpretation fits neatly together. The sentence is written on two levels to deal with both Omri and Ahab. The generation of Moabite oppression measured by the sum of the two reigns over Moab ran close enough to the round number of 40 years. The use of 40 years in cycles of oppression and liberation is, of course, familiar from the Book of Judges.

---

[17] Although the orthography permits the reading '(grand)sons,' it seems more probable in terms of literary continuity that the identical orthography in l.6 reflects the same word, and that Mesha is continuing to speak of Ahab.

From the examination of the MI's use of ים, "day," an interpretation along these lines seems warranted, and if so, the conflict between the MI and the MT version, which twice states that the Moabite revolt came upon the death of Ahab (2 Kgs 1:1, 3:5), evaporates. Given the military strength attributed to Ahab by the Assyrians, it would not be surprising if Mesha waited until the day of Ahab's death, when he might hope for a chaotic succession, and in which he seems to have seen the hand of Kemosh. Thus MI ll.7-8, which scholars have read as indicating a revolt at a time other than that of 2 Kgs 1:1, Ahab's death, actually agrees with it, should this historical reconstruction stand. The death of a monarch was a customary time for vassals to revolt, as the histories of Assyria and Babylon, Israel and Judea illustrate.

The overwhelming importance of the conquering founder of the dynasty, Omri, is emphasized repeatedly in the MI. As stated above, the writing of the MI postdated the house of Omri. The text poetically identifies the defunct dynasty with Israel (l.7). The Assyrian inscriptions which refer to Israel as *bīt ḫumri*, also identify it with the Omride dynasty, a practice which continued after its fall.[18] To Mesha, Omri clearly dwarfed his nameless successors. It seems clear that Mesha has compressed all the action into an indefinite but extremely short period of time; for his perspective obviously includes the revolt and at the same time the life of the entire Omride dynastic line! Additional tendentious symptoms appear in Mesha's boast of the rapidity with which he took Nebo (ll.14ff.), surely a fortified city--in the space of a few hours. A similar boast was common in Assyria, too. If the traditional interpretations are correct, the capture of an originally Israelite city, Jahaz, with two hundred men כל רשה (l.20),[19] is another boast. It is not clear what these last two words refer to. Assuming that Moabite רש equals Hebrew ראש, as is generally accepted, the lack of the aleph which accompanies the "o" in l.3 זאת, "this"[20] or l.31 צאן "small cattle," is probably due to an 'aramaizing' pronunciation, found also in Akkadian and Ugaritic. J. C. L. Gibson's translation of רש as "division" is good (he cites 1 Sam 11:11, 13:17), but his rendering of the line is not as felicitous (viz. "I took from Moab two hundred men, his whole division, and I led it up against Jahaz and captured it"--the "his" hangs in the air).[21] I would construe רשה as plural: "I took from Moab two hundred men, all of its divisions, and led it (Moab) against Jahaz." That is, Mesha led an army in which all of the units

---

[18] Written *bīt ḫu-um-ri-a* in the time of Tiglath-Pileser III (*ANET* 283) and simply *mātḫu-um-ri* in the annals of Adad-Nirari III (*ANET* 281).

[19] A. Demsky in his treatment, "The Military Count of Mesha, King of Moab (Mesha Stone Line 20)," (Heb.) *Shnaton: An Annual for Biblical Studies* VII-VIII (1983-84), 255-57, sees the idiom נשא ראש 'to muster, count.' The two words belong to different clauses, as the divider indicates.

[20] On the writing of aleph in *z't*, and the shift in Moabite to from "a" to long "o," see J. Blau, "Short Philological Notes on the Inscription of Mesa'," *MAARAV* 2/2 (1979-80), 146-48.

[21] J. C. L. Gibson, *Textbook of Syrian Semitic Inscriptions I: Hebrew and Moabite Inscriptions* (Oxford, 1971),76,81.

had 200 men. The Israelite king fled before the army of Mesha, which comprised all of Moab. This could overstate Moabite strength and unity.

In contrast, a historical element in both the MI and 2 Kings 3 is found in the emphasis placed on assuring or destroying the Moabite water supply: 2 Kings 3 deals with the problem of obtaining water in Moab; in 2 Kgs 3:19 YHWH orders the stopping up of Moabite wells. Ll.24-5 of the MI deal with the digging of cisterns in a Moabite town, as well as forced labor of prisoners doing something, perhaps also connected with assuring a supply of water. Thus the MI includes not only various elements of conventional Near Eastern royal and religious propaganda but also details the verisimilitude of which is hardly to be doubted.

Let us now proceed to examine further some of the specifics of the MI. There exists a linguistic consonance between Hebrew and Moabite that often extends even to prepositions. The latter particles are crucial in any language, and native speakers rarely fail to notice the use of an incorrect preposition, although the speaker sometimes has a choice of more than one. It is indicative of close kinship between languages when cognate verbs employ the identical preposition as well. Thus in l.2 of MI one finds that Mesha מלך על מאב (lit. "reigned over Moab"), just as in BH. In lls.2-3 Mesha uses another preposition with the same verb to express the idea of (legitimate) succession: ואנך מלכתי אחר אבי; this is put in the same way by Bathsheba in 2 Kgs 1:17. There she reminds David of his promise to have Solomon succeed him: שלמה...ימלך אחרי. We do not know whether Mesha was the eldest son, but if not his father had legitimated his rule--as David did Solomon. Other examples are יסף ל (hiphil),אמר ל, and so on. Yet prepositions can be highly idiosyncratic, even within one language or locality, and change over time.

Here are some more samples of the close relation between Hebrew and Moabite. In l.3 Mesha speaks of making a במת, a 'high place' or sanctuary for Kemosh. The Bible speaks in 1 Kgs 11:7f.. of how Solomon built sanctuaries to the gods of his foreign wives, including Kemosh, using the same word for sanctuary (במה,). Kings uses a different verb (than the MI), 'to build,' (בנה). a verb that is abundantly attested in the MI, starting with l.9. L.5 has the following: ויענו.את.מאב.ימן.רבן., which is similar to Num 20:5, part of which reads, "...I dwelt in Egypt ימים רבים and the Egyptians dealt harshly (וירעו) with us." There is little difference in the meaning of the verbs ויענו and וירעו (cf. Deut 26:6, which S. D. Sperling pointed out to me), and both texts reflect traditions of an oppression prior to liberation.

The phrase of l.7, וישראל.אבד.אבד.עלם. calls for comparison with Num 21:29:

אוֹי־לְךָ מוֹאָב אָבַדְתָּ עַם־כְּמוֹשׁ
נָתַן בָּנָיו פְּלֵיטִם וּבְנֹתָיו בַּשְּׁבִית לְמֶלֶךְ אֱמֹרִי סִיחוֹן׃

Woe to you Moab! You have fled, people of Kemosh!
He has made his sons refugees, his daughters (he has made) captive to the king of the Amorites, Sihon.

First, let us consider “people of Kemosh” (עַם־כְּמוֹשׁ). Its counterpart, “people of YHWH,” appears early on, in the Song of Deborah (Jud 5:11). No other people is called “people of DN” in the Bible. I mentioned above the analogous role of Kemosh to YHWH in the MI. Num 21:29 offers tangible evidence that biblical writers saw in Kemosh a god who played a uniquely comparable role to Israel’s YHWH in the life of Moab. There is a similar equating of the two gods in Jephthah's speech to the Ammonites (Judges 11).

Next, a most fortuitous and interesting comparison arises between Num 21:29 and l.7's וישראל.אבד.אבד.עלם. The verb אבד is the key to these passages. MI l.7. has been uniformly translated, “Israel has perished completely forever,” which would be bombast. The phrase has nothing structurally in common with what precedes it. We do not have a parallel stich but a new sentence with a new verb. It is increasingly clear that Heb. אבד can mean “to flee.”[22] Num 21:29 is a good example. In it, Moab did not perish; it lived to be taunted. Num 21:29 should be translated (as above) “Woe to you, Moab. You have fled, people of Kemosh. He has made his sons fugitives, and his daughters captive....” Kemosh made the sons fugitives, he did not slay them. In l.7, we have the reverse; Mesha boasts that Israel has fled his domain forever. There is no logic to following the triumphal boast, “Israel has perished,” with “Omri took possession of the land of Mhdb’.” The logic of the MI is that Mesha was seeking to expel Israel from Moabite land, so he followed the announcement of rout with the story of how the flight came about. The גם of l.30 .בא(גם.מהדד), is not required by the syntax, but preceding Mhdb‘, emphasizes Mesha's success in reversing the settlement policy of Omri (l.7). Incidently, the MI emphasizes the activity of Omri in Moab, but never mentions Ahab. The king of Israel was occupied at home with his major building projects, and abroad with the Assyrians and the Arameans, and must have ruled through a governor (see below). Mesha's use of the חרם, &c., must have panicked many Israelites into fleeing to the safe side of the Jordan (or to the north). Num 21:29 thus throws much light on the meaning of MI l.7; and the two constitute mirror images of each other. The biblical phrases עַם־כְּמוֹשׁ and עַם־יהוה are a tacit acknowledgement of the religious kinship of Moab and Israel, to which the astonishing appearance of the חרם in the MI also testifies.[23] These ties are likely to have been far deeper and broader than it is possible to document today. So, too, the idea of war that emerges from the MI is almost identical to that of the Bible. The war of

---

[22] Cf. S. D. Sperling, "Joshua 24 Re-examined," *HUCA* LVIII (1987) 133 n.23, J. Huehnergard, *Ugaritic Vocabulary in Syllabic Transcription, Harvard Semitic Studies* 32 (Atlanta, 1987), 104. Already in W. F. Albright, *From the Stone Age to Christianity: Monotheism and the Historical Process* (2nd ed., Garden City, 1957), 238. See especially B. A. Levine, "The Triumphs of the Lord," (Heb.) in *The Book of Yigael Yadin, Eretz Yisrae*l 20 (1989), 212.

[23] Some may argue that the Moabites borrowed the חרם from Israel. This is an argument belied by the way the חרם is embedded in the religious terminology and the vital role it plays in the sacred war. They would be unlikely to choose for this the language borrowerd from the oppressor, and unlikely to need to. As we shall see, the idea of חרם originated in a polytheistic milieu,

liberation sponsored by a deity I have alluded to; but there is also a similar siege mentality in the MI and in the Bible. Mesha saw himself as surrounded (1.4); intervention by a friendly power was never a possibility.

Equally, the biblical attitude towards Moab was one of alienation and this is evident even in the Book of Ruth. The biblical writers maintain a truculent attitude towards virtually every foreign people, large or small, with few exceptions. Moab and Israel must have lived in peace some of the time, living as they did cheek by jowl. The law of Deut 23:4 could not have come about unless Moabites (and Ammonites) were 'fraternizing' with their Israelite neighbors. Still, the biblical polemics--almost always couched in religious terms--do not reveal the level of naked competition for land and its associated resources in the Transjordan which the MI highlights in regard to Gad.

According to the MI, Gad had resided in the area north of the Arnon from days of yore. Many years ago, W. F. Albright proposed a solution to the crux of MI 1.12, אראל.דודה.[24] He interpreted the latter word as **dawidum*, a Mari-Akkadian term for "tribal chieftain," but this proved to be an incorrect reading of Akk. *da-WI-du-um*, now read *dabdum*, meaning "defeat."[25] Albright identified אראל with the clan of Gad mentioned in Gen 46:16 and Num 26:15 אַרְאֵלִי, Eng. Areli,[17] an identification which still has much to commend it, given the context. Seeing that the MI deals with the Gadite (Land of) Ataroth, the orthographic distinction אראל and אַרְאֵלִי is negligible. Further, it vanishes altogether in the problematic 2 Sam 23:20a-b:

וּבְנָיָהוּ בֶן־יְהוֹיָדָע בֶּן־אִישׁ־חַי [חַיִל] רַב־פְּעָלִים מִקַּבְצְאֵל הוּא הִכָּה אֵת שְׁנֵי אֲרִאֵל מוֹאָב

Benayahu son of Yehoyada, a valiant warrior and greater in deeds than Qabzael, he slew the two אֲרִאֵל of Moab.

This text is hard to translate as it stands. Yet it clearly refers to אֲרִאֵל- in a context of war with Moab. Its orthography is the same as that of the MI--the only time in the Bible that this is the case. It is not surprising that an archaic chapter like 2 Samuel 23 would preserve the ancient spelling.This אֲרִאֵל can have nothing to do with Ariel of Isaianic fame (e.g. Isa 29:1, where, as is well known, it is used as a name for Jerusalem, a meaning that could not apply to 2 Sam 23:20). The LXX has preserved a better text:

καὶ Βαναιας ὑιὸς Ιωδαε, ἀνὴρ αὐτὸς πολλαστὸς ἔργοις ἀπο Καβεσελ. καὶ αὐτὸς ἐπάταξεν τοὺς δὺο ὑιοὺς αριηλ[26] τοῦ Μοαβ

[24] W. F. Albright, "Two Little Understood Amarna Letters from the Middle Jordan Valley," *BASOR* 89 (1943), 16 n. 55.

[25] *CAD* D 15. On אֲרִאֵל, contrast K. P. Jackson, "The Language of the Mesha Inscription," *SMIM*, 112-13

[26] The LXX follows the late vocalization, like the *Qere* of Ezek 14:14, which reads 'Daniel' instead of 'Danel,' found in the Ugaritic Aqhat Epic, a version of which was

This gives us, "he slew the two sons of Arel = בני אראל of Moab." There is an extremely high probability that this is the correct reading. A better translation would be "he smote the two Arelites of Moab." The Septuagint's reading is almost certainly correct because in the Hebrew version, the scribe would have had to write the letters בנ four times to write the sentence correctly, while at the end the similarity of שני and בני made it still more difficult to get it all right. A Greek scribe would have had no particular reason to insert the word "sons" there, and had a much easier sentence to copy, with no two words of substance exactly alike. Hence it has come down to us without the omission of the word "sons of."

Putting this all together, it would seem that the biblical verse recounts how a Davidic hero, Benayahu, fought and killed two powerful warriors of the Gadite clan of Arel(i) (which from Mesha's perspective had been in the land for generations). It is understandable that some Transjordanian Israelites in that formative period would have cast their lot with Moab and fought with it, just as the list of Davidic heroes which concludes 2 Samuel 23 includes an Ammonite (David's basic constituency was in Judah, anyway). Albright's interpretation of the Moabite word אראל meshes perfectly with the LXX-corrected version of 2 Sam 23:20.

It is worth adding that 2 Samuel 23, which I have labeled an ancient chapter, has a parallel to MI 1.28: כי.כל.דיבן.משמעת, "For all Dibonites are my personal vassals." in 2 Sam 23:23, where King David puts Benayahu, the greatest of the heroes, into his personal entourage, וַיְשִׂמֵהוּ דָוִד אֶל־מִשְׁמַעְתּוֹ. In 2 Sam 23:9, the word אִישׁ, normally "man," is used as a body of fighting men, just as in the MI and in certain biblical passages as well. These are additional indications that אראל is a word for Gadites, members of the clan known from a few places in the Bible, who in the context of the MI are caught up in war. The word is not to be taken as a cult object. This brings us to the following word, דודה.[27]

I have found an explanation of דודה, which, oddly enough, produces the same meaning for the word as did Albright's translation. There is an Akkadian word for (wild) ram which is cited in the *CAD* with *atūdu*, namely *dūdu* (found as of the A2 volume, only in lexical texts). One may draw the analogy of אלופֵי אֱדוֹם אֵילֵי מוֹאָב (Exod 15:15) and other biblical examples. Considering that Moab had conditions necessitating pastoralism, such a word as Akk. *dūdu* (which with *atūdu* is probably a West Semitic loanword) might well appear in Moabite as דוד, meaning in context, "chief." The use of internal *matres lectionis* for dipthongs or possibly vowels is found in the MI (e.g., the *yod* of in Dibon, and if the scholarly vocalization is correct, the first *he* in YHWH). There is no certain example with *waw*, but האשוח seems a likely case. B. A. Levine has drawn my attention to Ben Sira 50:3 אשיח,

---

known in Israel. So 'Arel' is an older form than 'Ariel,'and lions come in though the similarity in sound, occasioning the play on the hero's name and the killing of a lion.

27 K. P. Jackson notes this as well, "Language," *SMIM*, J. C. L. Gibson, *Textbook I*, 84 suggests that *dwdh* is King David but grammar and context make this an unlikely suggestion. Even if Mesha wished to preserve the memory of Moab's old troubler, his scribes, who could spell YHWH, spelled David's name wrongly, as never in the MT.

which supports a vowel letter here. This proposal would restore Albright's apt rendering. It would also add another parallel between the MI and MT, in equating a foreign ruler with a wild ram.

To A. F. L. Beeston, the phrase "most likely means 'the Prophet of its city-god.'"[28] He does not, however, explain the basis from which he deduced 'prophet'; nor does he supply evidence for 'city-god.' However, at one point he adduces another etymology for the meaning 'leader', starting from 'friend, protector (hence uncle)' and leading to 'governor,' as "Latin *comes* has evolved from 'friend (of the ruler)' to 'governor (count) of a province." Language need not work linearly; possibly the two may have reinforced one another. However, my proposal arises out of a well-attested phenomenon in Semitic.

It thus seems best to translate אראל.דודה as "(the clan of) Areli/Arel, its chief." This leads to a deeper understanding of the historical significance of the MI. The MI credits Gad with having dwelt in the area of Ataroth for an indefinite, but lengthy amount of time. This fits in with biblical tradition. From Moab's point of view, then, Gad was long a thorn in its side. The task of dealing with deeply-rooted Israelite Transjordan was magnified by an Israelite king's building of the fortified city of Ataroth. אראל thus refers to the clan of Gad whose chief (perhaps the leader of Gad at large) was taken by the Moabites.[29] Thus, according to our interpretation, the Moabites dragged the major leader of Gad before Kemosh, just as, for example, Assyrian texts reflect the idea of dragging the enemy before the victor, the king (*CAD* M1 *mašāru* I/3 360a). Josh 8:23,28 speak of the people handing over the enemy king alive to Joshua, who then hangs the king of Ai, this following the חרם of a city (cf. Josh 10:30-42). This interpretation is more consistent with the evidence and much more probable than a hypothetical cult object, for there is no known Israelite cult object corresponding to the combination of אראל.דודה--neither from the Bible nor from elsewhere (especially the Ugaritic ritual texts, which bear such resemblance to the later biblical cultic texts in such things as sacrificial terminology nor from the large Phoenician-Punic corpus, which also includes cult terms).

The writer(s) of the passage had it in mind to emphasize the gravity of the situation that Mesha faced, thus underlining the glory of Mesha's deeds as aided by Kemosh--but the data given are unlikely to be untrue.

The Moabites felt that the Gadites had usurped the 'land that Kemosh had sworn unto their forefathers.' Therefore, Mesha says, "I slaughtered (ואהרג) all of the people of the city--רית.לכמש.ולמאב (ll.11-12)." He uses a strikingly different terminology than later (l.17.), when the חרם makes its appearance. The presumption is that Mesha's intent is to describe actions

---

[28] A. F. L. Beeston, "Mesha and Ataroth," *JRAS* 1985, 143-9.

[29] For other suggestions, cf. S. Segert, "Die Sprache," 204, "altar hearth," but as E. Lipinski, "Notes," 333, observed, "one does not drag altar hearths." Suggestions that *dwdh* is a deity or cult object make the phrase "*'r'l dwdh*" even more obscure, since Mesha would not "drag" a Moabite deity and there is no evidence that the word--or rather phrase--corresponds to any Israelite cultic usage.

which differ in kind at Ataroth and Nebo.[30] Without even investigating the term רית, the inclusion of Moab following Kemosh, unlike l.17, indicates that the Moabite people shared in the רית after the slaughter, an inclusion which could hardly be further from the intent of the חרם in l.17 (cp. Joshua 6-7, 1 Samuel 15). On the contrary, as the lack of mention of Moab indicates, the חרם is an act of separation reflecting the profound distinction between human and divine in the religions of Israel and Moah.

It is now time to look at the question of the meaning of the old crux, רית. This, too, has been given more than one explanation.[31] However, Albright's explanation is by far the most convincing.[32] He translated as "satiation," from רוה, which not only fits the context, but is strongly supported by biblical usage, as Brekelmans was the first to note.[33] The use of the verb רִוְּתָה in contexts parallel to the MI of bloodshed and divine vengeance (Jer 46:10, Isa 34:5,7) is striking. In Isaiah 34, where YHWH lusts for Edom's gore, both רִוְּתָה and חרם are in the same text, as in the MI. The רית is the satiation of Kemosh's lust for blood on a "day of vengeance to avenge himself on his foes (Jer 46:10)" (this [non-cultic] explanation also makes it the more unlikely that אראל.דודה is to be understood as coming from a cultic context. Moreover, one can assume from the use of this term and the way it is used (including the people of Moab in the "satiation"), that after the massacre the Moabites took spoil in the normal fashion which needed no further notation.

There is a certain parallel, long since noted by scholars,[34] between the lines that describe the attack on Ataroth (ll.11-13) and the חרם at Nebo (ll.14-18). In both cases, cities were taken and the population slaughtered without quarter. But such similarities need not mean identity. The MI states clearly that the reason why Ataroth was subject to such treatment was because it was a colony (perhaps similar in function to the colonies of Alexander the Great in a later period), built by an Israelite king. "For Gadites had lived in the district (lit. land) of Ataroth from time immemorial, but the king of Israel [relatively recently] built for it [the city of] Ataroth, and I attacked the city" (ll.10-12). It was this Israelite policy of building on Moabite soil which especially outraged the Moabites, and led to the wholesale slaughter of the inhabitants. The use of the word "to drag," סחב, in the case of both Ataroth and Nebo, was undoubtedly purposeful, because it

---

30 *Contra* G. L. Mattingly, "Moabite Religion," 235. He (and his colleague J. A. Dearman) seems to see a חרם at Ataroth, as well as at Nebo.

31 See *KAI II* 175 supporting an explanation based on OSA *ryt*. Against: J. C. L. Gibson, *Textbook*, I 79, C. H. W. Brekelmans, *De ḥerem*, 29-31. It would mean a sacrifice to both god and people. The old explanation that רית comes from ראה is antecedently improbable, but has also been superseded by Albright's theory.

32 G. L. Mattingly, "Moabite Religion," 235-6 states the case for Albright's hypothesis well, but it should be noted that C. H. W. Brekelmans, *De ḥerem*, 31, was the first to observe the connection between Moabite רית and Isa 34:5ff..

33 Ibid.

34 Most recently, G. L. Mattingly in "Moabite Religion, 235. In construing אראל as a cult object, he does not explain the meaning of the term with which it is in construct.

conveyed a certain contempt for the defeated foe. It cannot mean that because in the second instance, the objects of the verb (as restored) are cult objects, that one may infer that the first case, אראל.דודה, is a cult object. This amounts to the classic fallacy of *post hoc ergo propter hoc*. Look at the differences! One cannot but notice the totally different terminology associated with רית., which unlike the hiphil of חרם is a) not even a verb and does not describe an action bur rather an emotion b) is etymologically distant from consecration through destruction c) is given a special explanation for the emotion involved, unlike the חרם d) the רית was shared by deity and people, while the whole point of the חרם is that some things are set aside for the divine sphere alone, which is separated from that of mortals. in a way that often defies human understanding (Joshua 7, 1 Samuel 15).

The passage (ll.14-17) which follows up the Ataroth episode does not start with the kind of explanation provided for Ataroth. Instead, Kemosh orders Mesha to advance on Nebo. This is surely a response to an inquiry of an oracle, a standard ancient practice. Yet whereas Mesha was content formerly with the formulation, "I slaughtered all the people of the city," here he says,

אהרג.כל(ה).שבעת.אלפן(.)ג(ב)רן.ו(גר)ן.וגברת.ו(גר) רחמתו

Instead of repeating רית &c. he now says וכי.לעשתר.כמש.החרמתה. "For to עשתר.כמש I consecrated it (the city of Nebo) to destruction."

Turning to the untranslated line (ll.16-17a), which presents us with something of a lexical problem, the general meaning is clear: all men, women and children (גר=BH גור, "whelp": possibly not the word the Moabites used for their own children). It is puzzling that some translators have seen fit to translate רחמת as handmaidens or the like. Never do the biblical descriptions of חרם, which often depict the dead as men, women, and children, mention slaves. Nor is there any mention of גרים, "aliens," "clients," a frequent translation that flies in the teeth of the biblical evidence. BH has no feminine form, and there would be little reason to list clients by sex or to give them equal prominence with the Israelites with whom they were fighting. The rendering "child" is closer to passages like Deut 3:6. *ARM* IV 33, Ishme-Dagan's victory message to his brother, mentions slaves (*wardum*) and clients (*ṣābum*),[35] but does not give masculine and feminine forms, as here. רחם (Heb. for "womb"), was a metonym for young women, as Jud 5:30 indicates. There was no reason to prefer slave girls over free. No one called *rḥm ʻnt*, "girl Anat," a slave! The Ugaritic female DN *rḥmy* (*UT* 483f.), can be linked to *aṯrt* (Asherah) in combination; a likely numen of fertility, not enslavement.[36] By devoting

[35] Following A. L. Oppenheim, *Letters from Mesopotamia* (Chicago, 1967), 106. This translation, which is not found in his dictionary, flows from the context.
[36] On these Ugaritic terms, see A. S. Kapelrud, *The Violent Goddess: Anat in the Ras Shamra Texts* (Oslo, 1969), 34-7.

captured nubile women--the most desirable booty of all (cf. Deut 21:10-14, Il. I, Od IX:40)--Mesha earned maximum credit from his god. That is the point of placing רחמת at the end of the list.[37] In Jud 5:30 "a woman, two women per capita" is the first item of plunder mentioned, indicating the most desirable. In the MI, the word is singled out for mention by being put at the end of the line, indicating the same thing; a male counterpart is lacking. The line means then, "people of all ages, even nubile women." The foregoing of spoil (in contrast to ll.11-12, where material booty was taken), especially the choicest spoil of all, in the Moabite practice of the חרם, reflected the unique nature of the practice as well as Mesha's devotion to Kemosh.

It is doubtless no coincidence that the unique use of עשתר.כמש occurs in conjunction with the sole use in the MI of החרמתה. This unique form or expression coincides with the pbysical center of the inscription as well as the high point, from Mesha's perspective, of the devotional or religious aspect of the description of events (notice that the section consisting of l..8 [end] to l.10 [start] contains building notices which belong more logically with the latter part of the MI; these have been inserted at least partly in order to place l.17's החרמתה in the center).[38] The next step is to try to find the most plausible theory to explain this unique concatenation. The conventional assumption is that the first part represents the widely-attested Semitic deity, Ashtar.

Actually, this assumption is not made by everyone. For, according to some scholars, Ashtar-Kemosh is Kemosh's consort.[39] However, this idea is unacceptable as Ashtar is too strongly attested as a masculine (though by one theory androgynous)[40] god, and replacing Kemosh with a consort (with such an unlikely name!)[41] at the climax of an inscription dedicated to him is unlikely and unparalleled in the Near East. At Ugarit, there was, of course, the female counterpart of Ashtar (*ʿṯtr*), viz. *ʿṯtrt*. Ironically, it would seem from one Ugaritic text (*UT* 129), which is unfortunately damaged, and which breaks off (hence the outcome is obscure), that Ashtar wants his own palace but is denied it because he lacks a wife. In 129:20, Ashtar descends like a lion: *...lbum ard bnpšny trḥṣn kṯrm...*, and is possibly likened to a bull or bulls as well--*kṯrm* (the condition of the line has made the correct translation of

---

[37] It seems also to reflect paranomasia, since רחם and חרם share the same root letters.

[38] The premature introduction of Moabite building puts an affirmation of the Moabite *Weltordning* before an allusion to Moab's blackest hour. Cf. l. 8, וישב בה ימה. followed by ll.8-9 וישבה קמש בימי.There is a clever play on the two similarly written verbs, with Omri's occupation anticipating Kemosh's restoration of Moabite world order. The little discursus on world order both centered the line with the חרם and foreshadowed it

[39] A. van Zyl, *The Moabites,* 195f.. So D. Rosner, *The Moabites,* 43-45.

[40] W. F. Albright, *Archeology and the Religion of Israel* (Baltimore, 1968), 83-84. Further, see T. Jacobsen, *The Treasures of Darkness: A History of Mesopotamian Religion* (New Haven, 1976), 140.

[41] We have a number of names formed from Kemosh, but it is hard to imagine forming a sentence name from *Ashtar-Kemosh.

what remains impossible, esp. given the enigmatic *bnpšny*). Given his masculine status in the texts, the view of W. Kaiser that the Ugaritic names *ʿṯtr-ab* and *ʿṯtr-um* indicate androgyny, is not likely, since just such an attribute would be seized on for the myth of his rivalry with Baal (whose absence from the MI is conspicuous, and will be considered shortly).[42] However, Kaiser wrote before Jacobsen's analysis, which accounts for the Ashtar/Baal rivalry, too:

> Ishtar--her name goes back through the form **Eshtar* to *ʿAṯtar*--corresponds to the West Semitic god of the morning star, ʿAṯtar, who was also a rain deity but of semiarid regions where agriculture was possible only with the use of irrigation. ...when ʿAṯtar tried to take the place of the dead Baʿal, the rain god of the regions of rain agriculture, he did not prove big enough to fill Baʿal's throne. His female counterpart...goddess of the evening star, was a war goddess and also goddess of sexual love.[43]

A Ugaritic polyglot deity-list equates Ashtar with the Sumerian god ^{d}LUGALMARDA (if correctly restored) and the Hurrian Ashtabi, both war gods (as is Arabian ʿAṯtar).[44] A war goddess, like Ishtar, might understandably take on male characteristics (e.g. her beard). A male war god would not need feminine traits. Thus *ʿṯtr-um* may be better explained as the Akkadian name Ishtar-ummi. Ishtar was, naturally, known at Ugarit. The *um* told the reader to read not ‘Ashtar’ but ‘Ishtar.’

In the light of the above, 'Ashtar-Kemosh' is unlikely to add up to a female deity; and we must consider the other possibilities. The most obvious is that it is a combination, e.g. *UT* gloss.# 1941 *ʿṯtr w ʿṯtpr*). Another is that it is an epithet, not unlike the biblical epithet translated as “Lord of hosts.” According to this view, Ashtar is added to enhance the depiction of Kemosh as the war god who enabled Mesha to apply the חרם in part to display his power in war.

It is necessary to make an attempt, at least, at understanding something of the thought of the author(s) of the stele insofar as it may reveal itself, as part of the larger enterprise of seeking to comprehend the mode of thought which moved the ancients to the חרם out of many possible choices. The MI is a portrait in miniature of a mentality which was certainly present elsewhere in the ancient Near East.[45]

The biblical account of Moab's origin (Gen 19:29-38) is mythic, and has its psychological raison d'être. It accounts for the kinship, which was too obvious to escape notice, between Moab and Ammon on the one hand (which was so close as to be incestuous from Israel's point of view), and between

---

[42] W. Kaiser, *The Ugaritic Pantheon,* diss. (Ann Arbor, Mich., 1973), 163-4.

[43] T. Jacobsen, *Treasures,* 140.

[44] J. Huehnergard, *Ugaritic Vocabulary*, 164.

[45] Cf. R. Labat, *Le caractère religieux de la royauté assyro-babylonienne* (Paris, 1939), ch. 3 "La guerre sainte" and M. Weippert, "'Heiliger Krieg' in Israel und Assyrien," *ZAW* LXXXIV (1972), 460-493, with extensive bibliography.

those nations and Israel. Yet by assigning Moab and Ammon to Lot, the creator of the myth put them at a comfortable distance "genetically," since the place of Lot in the Abraham saga was morally and religiously inferior. At the same time Mesha's point of view was precisely reversed; cf. ll. 8-9, וישבה.כמש.בימיו, "Kemosh restored it (the land of Moab) in my time (as king)." Like Hebrew, the verb ישׁב, "dwell" takes the preposition "b" in lls. 10,13,19,31; the verb *שׁוב, (in hiphil), the direct object suffix or the marker את as in l.12. The same word on l.13 with "b" is the hiphil of ישׁב; l.13b I settled there men of Sharon(?) and Maharit(?). Thus, Albright's translation (*ANET* 320), "Kemosh dwelt there," followed by many,[46] is questionable, and is unlikely on contextual grounds as well. Mesha was upholding the claim in this inscription that it was not YHWH who exercised the power over the land of Moab, but Kemosh. In his anger (1.5), he gave it over to Israelite rule, but after his servant Mesha assumed the throne, he restored Moab. Hence in the Moabite חרם, Mesha slaughtered the people of Nebo, but the city, the place, he consecrated through destruction, and the two acts together sanctified the city defiled by an enemy people and its god, and helped restore the Moabite world order.

It is clear from the MI as a whole, and especially from ll.12-13 and the continuation of l.17 כי.לעשתר.כמש.החרמתה, wherein booty is dragged to Kemosh alone, that Kemosh was the entity to whom Mesha was devoting Nebo. Here Kemosh has that role, not Mesha, not *Ashtar-Kemosh! One does not dedicate a city to one god and give the spoils to another god, even if the two are husband and wife. It is possible to take this further in the light of Deut 13:13-19, in which the חרם is prescribed in order that YHWH's wrath will turn away and his equanimity will return (Deut 13:18).[47] In the MI we have in 1.5, Kemosh's wrath, followed by ll.17-18, the חרם, and in 1.19, Kemosh's redemptive action on behalf of Moab, followed by the speedy end of the war. It would seem that the proper execution of the חרם then acted for Mesha and Moab in a similar way as its proper execution was prescribed in Deut 13:13-19. Therefore the god to which Nebo was devoted was Kemosh, and *Ashtar is a mere epithet. The combinatory explanation therefore fails. One may further extrapolate that the temple of YHWH that seems to have existed on Moabite soil at Nebo, which possibly attracted some Moabite worshippers (collaborators) was an abomination to Kemosh, and that the חרם of Nebo was carried out in something of the same spirit as animated the writing of Deut 13:13-19.

---

[46] W. H. Shea, "The Melqart of Stela," *MAARAV* 1/2 (1978-79), 165, argues, following J. Friedrich, that the "b" is written once but is meant to be read twice. While this is ingenious, it does not take into account the two similar widespread roots with overlapping orthographies, but forces all instances into one mold. Here Mesha speaks of a whole territory vs. 1.33, where (an image of) Kemosh enters a city. Just as one never sees "YHWH dwells in the Land of the Negev," so one should not see same of Kemosh in Medeba.

[47] The text speaks of not touching the spoil so that YHWH's wrath ישׁוב (will return),meaning that God was already angry.

Anyway, the combinations found at Ugarit (and also at Ebla),[48] e.g. Kothar–wa–Ḫasis, use the *waw* to effect the juncture, as does the Deir Allah inscription. In the light of all these considerations, the combination idea should be dropped. Before dropping it, however, let us consider it in one more form, suggested long ago, out of the onomasticon of the Elephantine papyri, which included divine names composed of two deities, such as ענתיהו, or Anat–Yahu.[49] The conception that underlies this syncretism is also uncertain in this instance. The colony at Elephantine was a special case occurring much later time in a highly unusual setting and among an atypical population. If it reflects the influence of Egyptian practice in its combination of names, a practice best known in the example of Amon-Re, it would be better to start from the Egyptian practice, which is better understood. Also, the idea that *Ashtar-Kemosh reflects Egyptian influence is a possibility worth exploring.

In the time of Rameses III's expansion into Canaan, Amon-Re was featured prominently in Rameses's inscriptions as a war god. By this theory, the Moabites adapted the Egyptian form, which E. Hornung has interpreted in an excellent fashion. He terms the Amon-Re phenomenon 'syncretism' which, in speaking of the numerous deities paired with Re, he says, "may be interpreted as meaning that Egyptians recognize Re in all these very different gods...."[50] However, unsatisfied with this formulation he adds other considerations, of which I shall cite two. Firstly, he notes that syncretism "does not imply identity or fusion of the gods involved, it can combine deities who have different forms, and even...ones of the opposite sex."[51] This observation could fit such names as Anat–Yahu, on the one hand, and *Ashtar-Kemosh, on the other. Yet whatever the relation between the god Ashtar and Kemosh, it was assuredly not that of Amon and Re. The Egyptian practice of syncretism, according to Hornung was flexible, allowing many combinations. But Hornung continues, saying that, "Amon-Re is not the synthesis of Amun and Re but a new form that exists along with the two other gods."[52] This is possibly true for Elephantine names such as Anat–Yahu, but is unlikely to be the case in the MI, where the name would undoubtedly be written in the same way as in the Elephantine papyri (without a space). This caveat is not a mere technicality; NW Semitic names follow clearly defined patterns, and in this case, the separation of the two elements in *Ashtar-Kemosh is purposeful, as the first-rate scribe(s) of the MI could hardly have erred in writing divine names.

One must conclude that the combination theory of *Ashtar-Kemosh (especially as Kemosh's consort) does not stand up well under scrutiny. S.

---

[48] For example cf. Adar-wa-An, TM 75 G 2038 pub. G. Pettinato, *OA* 18 (1979), 344-5.

[49] A. Cowley, *Aramaic Papyri of the Fifth Century,* (Oxford, 1923), 147.

[50] E. Hornung, *Conceptions of God in Ancient Egypt: The One and the Many* (Ethaca, 1982), 92.

[51] Ibid. 96-97.

[52] Ibid. 96.

Segert was thus right to use the term 'epithet,' and one may understand this by reading the name Ashtar as *ʿaštar*, viz. as a generalized form of the deity, meaning, "the warrior," or the like: one may compare the Akkadian Ishtar-derived noun *ištaru*, "goddess," and, closer to Moab, the use in Deut 7:13 and elsewhere of עשתרות with the meaning of "fertility, increase."[53] Thus the god Ashtar disappears.

The distinction between people and place existed also in the minds of some biblical writers. Joshua 6:17 introduces the חרם using the nominal form (quite unlike the usage prominent in other passages, which use the hiphil). "The city shall be חרם and everyone in it to YHWH." The passage goes on to sharpen the distinction by declaring the city's spoil off limits. The question of spoil raises the question of what we may call the economics of חרם. The MI informs that after the wholesale slaughter at Ataroth and Nebo, Mesha moved on to use Israelites as slaves. Similarly, in the time of Solomon it was also found expedient to use the ideology of חרם to justify the impressment of non-Israelites into the king's corvée (1 Kgs 9:20-1), though a later editor felt this as a failure to apply the full rigor of the חרם. In this, if Mesha's behavior is a guide, the zealous editor was wrong. I. J. Gelb, in his "Prisoners of War in Ancient Mesopotamia"(*JNES* 32, [1973], 71-2) pointed out that societies with an inadequate level of economic organization to utilize POWs as labor would kill them. This was true of Mesha at first, but he later achieved a sufficient level of organization to employ them, while Solomon's realm may have reached the peak of Israel's economic development. Religion and economics went hand in hand.

The scant use of deities in the MI (e.g. the absence of Baal), is presumably due to a desire to render Kemosh his due. It was Kemosh who was the national deity, i.e. the god of the ruling house, as Baal was the god of Jezebel's house. Also, many polytheists' texts are so centered around one deity that one would hardly believe that the author acknowledged the remaining deities of the pantheon.[54] Another possibility, given the equivalent status of YHWH and Kemosh visible from the MI and conceded, as we saw, in the Bible, is that Mesha's royal religion was significantly more centered around one god than the popular religion(s) of Moab.

Scholars have long searched for equivalents to the Moabite-Hebrew µrj. Parallels have been adduced from the ancient Celts[55] to Mari[56] and

---

[53] *CAD* I 271b. S. Segert, "Die Sprache," 232, speaks of a weakening of the name to an epithet; this is an extension of his argument. S H. Donner-W. Röllig in *KAI* III 196-7, begin their discussion of the problem with the assertion that the two must be seen as one despite the word dividers, yet they do not give this any support. In addition to the Ug. epithets, *ʿrẓ* and *lbu,* Ashtar of Arabia also has warlike attributes, as attested by the epithets *bʿsn, bʿl ṣnʿtm*, and *ʿzzm*, meaning 'the Bellicose,' 'Lord of Strength,' and 'the Mighty One,' respectively (W. Kaiser, *Ugaritic Pantheon,* 161).

[54] See, e.g., an Enlil hymn, *ANET* 576 (esp. ll.16-17), and an Inanna hymn, ibid. 578 (trans. S. Kramer).

[55] N. Lohfink, "Ḥaram," *TDOT* 5, (Grand Rapids, 1986), 191.

[56] A. Malamat, "The Ban in Mari and the Bible," in *Biblical Essays 1966 OuTWP* (Stellenbosch, 1967), 40-9.

elsewhere. Yet while there were evident similarities in practice--hardly surprising considering the nature of ancient war and religion--good parallels other than the MI are hard to find, especially from the ancient Near East.

An inscription of ^{d}Idi-Sin of Simurrum,[57] dated now conclusively to the early Old Babylonian period,[58] is obviously well removed in time and space from the period and place of the MI (and the Hebrew Bible). Yet it is easily more relevant to understanding the חרם than parallels drawn from the Celtic sphere. I excerpt starting from l.13, where the text, referring to a prince who was called either ^{d}Zabazuna, or Anzabazuna, reads as follows:

> awassu ^{d}Adad ^{d}Ištar ù ^{d}Nišba išmûma ālam uḫalliqma ana ilī šunūti uqaddissu ^{giš}BANŠUR-am=(paššuram) ša ^{d}Ištar bēltīšu iškun
>
> Adad, Ishtar and Nishba lent an ear to his word. He destroyed the city and dedicated it to those gods. He set up an offering table of Ishtar, his mistress.

It is suggestive that, as in the MI, it is the city itself which is dedicated to the deity. In the ^{d}Idi-Sin inscription, also, there is discrimination among the gods. The later section, devoted to curses, invokes, as is normal, many gods, including gods of the inscription proper. The dedication is restricted to two war deities and Nishba, a personal god. However, there exist three versions of the text, each of which relates an act of cultic dedication to one of the three gods (I shall return to this point shortly).

We may see then evidence of a common mentality at work. The ^{d}Idi-Sin text proves that the idea of consecration to destruction is very old. The inscription differs in some ways from the Bible and it reflects a reverse situation to that of the MI, that of an empire suppressing a revolt. It includes the setting up of a cult table to individual gods, an act that is different from the dedication of the city to the gods, ending with a section cursing any defacer of the text, using the first-person (the account of the war was told entirely in the third-person, since the king speaks of his son's exploits). Nothing is expressly said of the human lives involved in the attack on the city, which is not named in the crucial section just presented but earlier (l.6)--the city Kulunnum. There is nothing but the word *uḫalliqma,* "destroy," "annihilate," to go on, but it is not a word that bodes well for the population, especially since there is no account of spoils and captive-taking (as in the MI, which refers to Israelite labor, and which is typical in ancient inscriptions early on). Since the city was utterly destroyed, and dedicated to the gods Adad,

---

57 On Simurrum, as yet unlocated, see W. W. Hallo, "Simurrum and the Hurrian Frontier," *RHA* 36 (1978), 71-83. Also see M. F. Walker, *The Tigris Frontier from Sargon to Hammurabi--A Philologic and Historical Synthesis* diss., Yale (Ann Harbor, 1986), 170-191 and passim.

58 A. al-Fouadi, "Inscriptions and Reliefs from Bitwata," *Sumer* 34 (1978), 122-129. A brief discussion of dating comes on 124. However, Dr. D. Frayne (University of Toronto) has informed me that the ^{d}Idi-Sin texts may be definitely located in the Early Old Babylonian Period (as M. F. Walker also believes).

Ishtar, and Nishba (with their prior approval *awassu....išmû*), the parallel is an intriguing addition to those adduced by scholars previously.

The verb, *uqaddissu*, is of especial lexical interest since it serves here (augmented by *uḫalliqma)* as an Akkadian equivalent to Moabite/Heb. החרם. Akkadian *ḫarāmu* "to separate" has a different domain than the root קדש in Hebrew and Akkadian (cf. *qadāšu* in its metathesized forms), with two possible exceptions: *ḫamru* and *ḫarimtu* (see ch. 1).[59] Whatever one make of these possibilities, the main point is that the verb *ḫarāmu* is hardly attested in Akkadian. When we recall an admittedly far later Hebrew text, Lev 27:28, in which the roots קדש and חרם are explicitly equated, it is not surprising that in Akkadian the verb *quddušu* could be used to help express a concept similar to the חרם.

Consecration to/through destruction is the basic description of the חרם, and it is clearly attested in this relatively ancient inscription of ᵈIdi-Sin. I have introduced it here because it is relevant to the MI as well as to the biblical חרם. The way in which the deities are treated contrasts markedly in the two inscriptions. The latter half of the ᵈIdi-Sin inscription curses anyone who would deface it, invoking a total of nine gods. Three of these--Adad, Ishtar, and Nishba--are the divine actors of the first half. In the MI, however, the only divine actor is Kemosh. Yet this is not the whole picture. The same impulse to glorify one god above others comes to light in the publication of the ᵈIdi-Sin text, which has three editions. Each of the three primary gods is given special and separate consideration in the three; Adad and Ishtar are given a cult table in texts A and B, while Nishba is given a throne in text C.[60] Mesha has taken this even further. None of the other gods worshipped in Moab according to the various sources (Baal, Mother Goddess, perhaps Ashtar, etc.)[61] are seen in this text. Like YHWH in Israel, Kemosh is the one who listens (cp. *išmû* "they heard") and speaks, the one who feels for Moab or grows angry at it. The religion of Simurrum, a millennium earlier, shows such a tendency but in a less developed form. In relation to the vexed question of monotheism, Mesha's religion seems closer to biblical religion than that of Simurrum.

C. H. W. Brekelmans has suggested that the bloodthirsty character of the deity in the MI is a projection of the blood lust of the human beings who desire revenge on their enemies.[62] There is ample evidence that such a process occurred, although it comes not primarily through the ᵈIdi-Sin inscription, but through the Bible, in which such projections of human traits onto the deity, i.e. anthropomorphisms, are the norm. It should be noted in this connection that ritualized blood acts abounded in ancient religion and in ancient Israelite religion (in which the official cult, at least, seems to have drawn

---

[59] *CAD* H 89a-90b. Cp. *CAD* Q 46-50, with 146-47, 320.

[60] A. al-Fouadi, "Inscriptions and Reliefs," 124.

[61] See now W. H. Morton, "Summary of the 1955, 1956, and 1965 Excavations at Dhiban," *SMIM,* 245-6, M.-L. Mussel, "The Seal Impression from Dhiban," *SMIM,* 247-52. Also see G. L. Mattingly's overview, in same volume, 216-227.

[62] C. H. W. Brekelman, *De ḥerem* , 31.

the line at human sacrifice). To devote the enemy, by definition not of God's servants (hence the provisions of חרם for idolators in e.g. Exod 22:19, Deut 13:13-19), is to help maintain or restore the moral as well as physical order of the universe. Brekelmans' point applies especially to the term רית (see above). The theological impetus behind practice of חרם cuts deeper; the paradoxical idea of the bloodsome חרם--which involves the realm of the sacred--having an important ethical element helps explain its presence among more appreciated ethical texts like the decalogue.

One may rephrase this point by referring to the ancient theme of the deity slaying the monster of chaos. The ancients, whether Babylonians, Moabites, Egyptians, or anyone else, had good reason to fear disorder, which renders human calculation futile and life itself insecure. The hegemony of Israel over Moab conflicted with Mesha's sense that the Moabite gods, Kemosh above all, ultimately intended that Moab not be ruled by chaos. By defeating YHWH, Kemosh slew the chaos monster and restored the Moabite world order; which seems to be why the city of YHWH's shrine had to be put to the חרם. As O. Goelet pointed out to me, the Egyptian view of foreigners as the forces of chaos fits in well here. In wartime, this is especially natural, and of course Moab may have absorbed the notion while under Egyptian domination or through Egypt's influence after the retreat of the empire. In any event, the path from the thought to concrete action may be short, and the חרם is a practice which began in a mythic, polytheistic setting, as the ^{d}Idi-Sin inscription strongly indicates.

Much of the inscription is taken up with the rebuilding that followed the victories of Mesha over the enemy. The primary verb used is בנה, "build," although the verb עשׂה, "do, make" occurs (and other incidental verbs referring to construction). The verb בנה, "to build," occurs more often than any other verb in the MI. It is a verb of creation. It is used in *Enuma Elish* for the creation of the "black-headed ones."[63] Ugaritic *bn*y is used in an epithet for the god Il, *bny bnwt*, "Creator of creatures."[64] Also from Ugarit is the cosmogonic story of the building of Baal's house; at the end of the six days of fiery creation of his house, Baal exults, saying "I have built--*bnt*."[65] The Hebrew verb בנה is also used in Genesis 2:22, for the creation of woman--named "life"--out of Adam's rib (while עשׂה describes the whole work of creation in Gen 2:2-4). The emphasis on these verbs may therefore be due to the cosmogonic overtones which the root conveyed as Mesha worked hard to recreate the Moabite world order. The second Ugaritic example, assuming something like the Baal myth survived into the Iron Age (as a version of Aqht did, Ezek 14:14,20), was a good prototype for Mesha's building of shrines and his palace in particular (*imitatio dei*). In any case, the point is that the MI depicts the successful battle of Moab to overcome the forces of chaos such as Israel, Gad, and YHWH, and to restore order, re-creating a

---

63 VII.32 *ṣalmāt qaqqadi ša ib-na-a qātāsŭ CAD B* 87a; the entry supplies many other examples.
64 C. H. Gordon, "Glossary," *UT,* 373 cites 2 Aqht:I:25, etc..
65 Ibid., Text 51, VI, ll.1-34, 172b. Translated in *ANET* 134.

Moabite *Weltordnung*. The inscription pictures the restoration as a process first requiring the חרם, the defeat of the chaotic forces. Then came the process of restoration presided over by Kemosh (cf. ll.8-9, and l.33--in the latter line, if correctly restored, Kemosh is now dwelling in Horonaim), and put into practice by Mesha with his building program. All this positive activity, creative activity as it were, was made possible through the victory over YHWH and Israel (in the light of context and other ancient royal inscriptions of the area, the use of בנה at Ataroth and especially at Jahaz, which was close to Dibon, as Mesha annexed to its territory, must have been significant building activity, not just fortification, as is lexically possible).

R. Labat, in a penetrating chapter on "La Guerre Sainte," remarked that for the Assyrians every war was "sainte." An apt illustration of this and the idea of the fight against chaos is provided by J. J. Glassner in a recent essay entitled "Sargon, 'roi du combat:'"

> "...cette campagne est la dernière, l'ultime combat qui permet à Sargon de chasser de la surface de la terre le dernier représentant du désordre et du chaos. (Cités éloignées...) symbolisent l'extrémité de la terre, les conquêtes de Sargon ayant atteint à ses confins. Le commentaire néo-babylonien va plus loin encore, il donne à Sargon l'image d'un roi qui serait alle jusqu'a franchir l'Océan amer entourant la terre et...conquérir ..les limites du monde...."[66]

The Moabites were acting out of a general concept of holy war that was part and parcel of the heritage of many ancient peoples of the area, though expressed in their own way.[67] In the act of devotion of human spoils, i.e. the act of חרם as presented in the MI, the Moabites could take the step of foregoing plunder because of the deeper need to bring an end to the threat of continuing chaos, just as a late text depicted Sargon seeking to bring order to the earth's end.

The question must immediately be posed as to the place of the simple declaration (ll.5-6) that Kemosh was angry at his people (expressed here by ארץ; cp. Deut 11:17, Josh 23:16) when he allowed the Omrides sway over Moab. The specific cause of anger is left unstated; an important void. It raises the question, however, of whether the element of atonement is present in the MI. This element may have played a role in the devotion of Nebo and the ריה of Ataroth. It is not clear whether this role is etymological or merely logical. B. A. Levine has posited an analogy between the חרם and the BH cult term אשם, defined as "what the deity expected to be devoted to him if and when he was seriously offended,"[68] as Kemosh evidently was. Unfortunately, one can only assume from the MI that the Moabites had in some way not given the god his just due as incumbent on the people Kemosh had chosen (another 'biblical' concept clearly operational here as

---

[66] J. J. Glassner, "Sargon, 'roi de combat'," *RA* 79 (1985), 125-26.

[67] The Assyrians, for instance, an obvious example to focus on, behaved differently than kings of the dynasty of Akkad, for whom war was also 'holy.'

[68] B. A. Levine, *In the Presence of the Lord: A Study of Cult and Some Cultic Terms in Ancient Israel* (Leiden, 1974), 128-32.

elsewhere in the ancient world and later). There is no knowing whether the infraction was in the moral realm or in the more strictly ritual realm (although such distinctions were not always made). All one can say, then, is that the situation as given does not rule out the applicability of the idea of אשם. But as we shall see, it is only the concept that would apply, not the element of sacrifice. The idea of אשם might have played a role as a restorative element in the religious scheme of חרם as a way of restoring moral order. This scheme also applied, as with Sargon, to the world.

Atonement is not a discernable element in ^{d}Idi-Sin's terse inscription. Although the destruction-dedication of Kulunnum was followed by the erection of an offering-table to the gods, this was probably to thank, not to atone. Since the situation facing ^{d}Idi-Sin of Simurrum (and his son, the war leader) was the opposite of the MI, involving suppression of a revolt,[69] the lack of contrition may be natural. If the revolt was seen as a penalty for sin, the inscription does not mention it. Mesha, too, never described himself as the object of Kemosh's anger; rather, his references to Kemosh are triumphant. Yet one may infer from Kemosh's wrath (l.5) that Mesha viewed his actions as atoning for the sins of Moab against Kemosh. In any case, the MI well suits the conception of the war-חרם as a weapon against physical and moral chaos.

The fact that the crucial line containing the חרם is in the exact center of the MI indicates how carefully the Moabite scribes planned the text.[70] The exaltation of Kemosh is contrasted immediately after with the humiliation of the Israelite god YHWH. The furnishings of his shrine were looted and brought to Kemosh (even if the word כלי is wrong, the chances are good that a cult object was meant). E. Lipinski opposes the idea that an Israelite shrine existed in the Transjordan, basing it on the proposal that the lacuna usually restored as (ll.17-8) .א(ת.כ)לי.יהוה should be read as א(י)לי.יהוה,a reading which would change the import of the passage drastically.[71] Lipinski cites Jer 49:20 and 50:45 to show that סחב may be employed with a flock, while claiming that vessels could not be dragged. As the NJV translators have seen, צעירי הצאן refers to shepherd boys (cf. Zech 13:7), not to young sheep, who are routinely designated by one of several words for 'lamb' (צעיר is used only for humans in the other biblical occurrences). It is also clear that objects could be dragged about; cf. סחבה="rag, i.e. stuff dragged about"(*BDB* 695a). There is no reason to prefer "rams" to "utensils." In contrast to the dragged utensils of YHWH of the MI stand the proud "bearers of the vessels of YHWH," נֹשְׂאֵי כְּלֵי יְהוָה, of Isa 52:11.

---

[69] I owe my information of the situation to Dr. D. Frayne of Toronto.

[70] See P. Auffret, "Essai sur la structure littevraire de la stèle de Mesha," *UF* 12 (1980), 109-124, who shows just how carefully the text was structured. Also cf. J. C. de Moor, "Narrative Poetry in Canaan," *UF* 20 (1988), 160. Speaking of the MI, he says, "It might therefore well be that the structure of the complete text was much more systematic than many modern scholars tended to believe."

[71] E. Lipinski, "Notes," 335. Also, A. F. L. Beeston proposed אראלי ("prophets"--see above).

J. Blau's opposition to the conventional restoration stems from his analysis of the use of the direct object marker, את, in the MI. He theorizes that it is only used with persons (places he explains as extensions of people, viz. concentrations of people).[72] Since את followed by כלי would violate this rule, he rejects it without giving a plausible alternative. The rule cannot be proved from the MI alone; and surely כלי could also be viewed as an extension of the deity, as items intimately connected with the service of YHWH (such items often acquire sanctity, from the 'holy scepter of ᵈAššur' of Tiglat-Pileser I to the 'holy grail'). One wonders where the sheep of l.31 fit in Blau's scheme, assuming that the line is correctly restored. It would be surprising if at a time in Israel in which there was no bar to the multiplication of sanctuaries (to YHWH), that the whole of Israelite Transjordan held not a single temple to the god of Israel. Moreover, the Moabites plainly rejoiced in the victory of Kemosh over YHWH, and the sack of a YHWH-temple on Moabite soil was a fit topic for the MI. We know that David took implements of gold, silver, and bronze (2 Sam 8:10-11), which he dedicated to YHWH--some part of which came from enemy temples. This is clearly what is involved in the 'dragging' (perhaps implying that spoils were taken against the will of YHWH) of the temple vessels to the house of Kemosh.

These facts seem to warrant another attempt at a theory of the direct object in Moabite. L.18 .ואסחב.הם, an anomaly, has led to the assumption that the usage results from a lack of an attached 3 m. pl. suffix, necessitating a detached הם. This is hard to accept. Every other NW Semitic language has a full system of verbal pronominal suffixes. Linguistically, the MI does not provide proof that Moabite is an exception, especially as a system of such suffixes is plainly in use. In the MI and other Moabite fragmentary inscriptions, the direct object marker appears frequently, yet it is never inflected. Perhaps it cannot be, and in place of inflected את Moabite uses pronouns (possibly with different vocalizations) as objects as well as subjects, as in l.18 (cf. Akkadian, also Ugaritic). Then the use of the pronoun-object would not come because *אסחבם did not exist in Moabite, but in order to place emphasis on the dragging of the vessels (or other property) of the enemy god, YHWH![73]

A final point on the putative temple at Nebo: it is conceivable that Nebo was considered a good site for a sanctuary because of the tradition linking the last moments of Moses with Mt. Nebo, a tradition that probably existed by that time. This is speculative, since there is no means of verifying it, but it is nevertheless a point that should be borne in mind in assessing the likelihood of the existence of a Nebo sanctuary.

---

[72] J. Blau, "Short Philological Notes," 152-3.

[73] K. P. Jackson, "The Language of the Mesha Inscription," *SMIM* 116, points to Biblical Aramaic הִמּוֹ.It is used only once as subject but regularly as direct object. Difficult to explain is the absence of את in the building phase of the inscription (ll.21-29). Given the fact that Ammonite seems to lack את, perhaps this reflects a certain Ammonite linguistic influence on its next door neighbor. A regular feature of Ammonite became an option in Moabite. Even in Hebrew, the particle is usually omitted in poetry.

The question arises as to whether there was another shrine of YHWH besides Nebo. There is no ground to suppose so from the MI. Were there a temple at Ataroth, the most obvious choice, the lack of mention of YHWH is conspicuous--why would Mesha, in destroying a shrine of YHWH, have waited to mention YHWH until the second shrine, instead of exulting over YHWH's downfall (cf. Dagon's defeat in 1 Sam 5:1-5) at the first opportunityy? As mentioned above, although the phrase אראל דודה is difficult, it does not fit into any known cultic terminology and is susceptible to another explanation. A. Dearman raises and scants the possibility of the "levitical city" of Jahaz having a shrine.[74] A priori one may say that the idea of the Israelites calmly casting lots and distributing dozens of cities on both sides of the Jordan for settlement, as we find in Joshua 21, is unlikely to have occurred in Joshua's time, early in the history of Israel in Canaan. The chapter is clearly a projection backward, for whatever purpose (political, priestly, etc.). If the levitical city had any reality, it was that of a much later period. [74]

Since most probably the MI refers to the despoiling of an Israelite temple at Nebo, we must ask if the action that Mesha took with regard to the enemy's temple fits in with what is known of such behavior from the neighboring powers of the ancient Near East. This is potentially a vast subject, but for our purposes we do not have to go very far. Evidence comes from the Bible itself. The political dimension strongly obtrudes in the fascinating story of 1 Samuel 21-22. There an entire priestly house and town is depicted as having been caught up in the developing struggle between Saul and David. In the end, the king sacked the town (1 Sam 22:19). The text does not give the details of what happened to the temple, but it was plainly destroyed along with the priests.[75] It is intriguing that little or no censure of Saul is found in this account. Yet regardless of the theme of church-state relations in Israel which this narrative throws light upon, it is important to note here that if an Israelite king could war on a YHWH-temple and its city (Nob), so much the more so could a Moabite king. Nor is there much doubt that in his theological perception of Kemosh, which has great similarity to the theology of YHWH known from the Bible, he had a positive inducement to destroy the Israelite cult site. YHWH held no place in the Moabite pantheon. It is interesting that in this Moabite liberation account, YHWH is directly named. In contrast, the story of Israel's liberation from Egypt does not ever mention the Egyptian gods directly or portray a triumph over Egyptian gods, except obliquely in Exod 15:11.

---

[74] J. A. Dearman, "Historical Reconstruction," 184. However, cf. his cautious remarks in J. A. Dearman, "The Levitical Cities of Reuben and Moabite Toponymy," 276 (1989), 55ff.. On the basis of the archeological evidence, R. G. Boling assigns the levitical cities to the eighth century in his commentary with G. E. Wright, *Joshua: A New Translation with Notes and Commentary* (Garden City, 1982), 492-4. N. Na'aman, *Borders and Districts in Biblical Historiography* (Jerusalem, 1986), 233, prefers the end of the 7th century.

[75] Such is the plain meaning. Cf. J. Bright, in *A History of Israel* (2nd ed., Phila.,1975), 188.

We are brought now full circle, as it were, to the comparison of the MI and the MT. It is remarkable, though fairly unremarked upon, that this small stone should contain, besides the key word החרם, other key roots long familiar from their distribution in the Pentateuch and elsewhere, which serve as the linguistic matrix into which the word חרם fits. It is an axiom of modern linguistics that one cannot deal with a word in isolation. Each word is part of a semantic field. Such a field cannot be delineated with absolute precision, at least not in the case, as here, of a language that is both dead and almost entirely lost (Moabite). I will start with four important representative verbs, found both in the MI and in the Exodus-Conquest cycle, each with a claim to belonging to the semantic field of חרם; אחז,"capture," גרש, "expel," הרג,"kill," and ירש,"take possession, dispossess." All of these have some bearing on the חרם (note that רצח, "murder" is definitely outside the semantic field of חרם).

The first, אחז, is not used in describing the capture of cities in BH. The verb is used, *int. al.*, for attacks of fear, disease, and for taking up arms. BH uses a nominal form, אחוזה, which reflects its etymology as testified to in the MI. The noun is used differently in the main,[76] but traces of the MI's usage remain. In Num 32:22,29 and Deut 32:49, the אחוזה or "possession," the land, is acquired by military force applied according to the will of YHWH.

The verb הרג is one of the major indicators of battlefield killing in the MI. It is not often associated with the חרם in BH, but a comparison of Josh 8:24 and 8:26, verses which occur in the Ai narrative, is helpful:[77]

Josh 8:24:

וַיְהִי כְּכַלּוֹת יִשְׂרָאֵל לַהֲרֹג אֶת־כָּל־יֹשְׁבֵי הָעַי בַּשָּׂדֶה

As Israel was coming to the end of killing all the inhabitants of Ai....

Josh 8:26:

יְהוֹשֻׁעַ לֹא־הֵשִׁיב יָדוֹ... עַד אֲשֶׁר הֶחֱרִים אֵת כָּל־יֹשְׁבֵי הָעָי׃ .

Joshua did not withdraw his hand...until he had made the dwellers of Ai חרם (devoted to destruction).

Although the battle at Ai is described in an unusually lengthy and convoluted manner, the two verses do show a kind of organic relationship existing between the two verbs הרג and החרים in similar contexts, though the text is more straightforward in the MI. In contrast to חרם, there is no reason to see הרג as a religious term. In BH, it is one of the important ways the action of killing, so prominent a feature of the חרם, may be verbalized. The conjunction of the root הרג with the חרם in the MI thus speaks for itself. The MI uses הרג but twice (ll.11,16), although in significant places. It might have been

[76] On this verb, see B. A. Levine, "Late Language in the Priestly Source: Some Literary and Historical Observations," *WJCS* 8 (1983), 72-81.

[77] J. C.de Moor pointed to this in "An Incantation against Infertility (KTU 1.13)," *UF* 12 (1980), 306; the Ugaritic text in (see ch. 1) also associates Ug. *hrg* with חרם.

chosen an economical means of expression given the limited space on the stone (vs. such longwinded biblical expressions as 'smiting with a sword so as not to leave a survivor'). However that might be, it remains as a witness to the consonance of Moabite and Hebrew conceptions of the theory and the practice of חרם.

Of the four roots, the remaining two verbs, גרש and ירש, are of vastly more importance in the biblical (historical and religious) scheme than the first two, although it would be harder to assign relative values for the MI. The former of these verbs, גרש, is of especial interest in the context of חרם.

The situation in the Torah is quite interesting. The passages in Exodus which deal with the handling of the peoples of the land use the verb גרש. Corresponding passages in Deuteronomy do not, and the verb חרם, if it is not used immediately in relation to the peoples, soon follows. In fact, the verb חרם only appears once in Exodus, in another context (Exod 22:19, dealing with individual idolatry). Similarly, in Deuteronomy, גרש is only found in 33:27 (Blessing of Moses), well outside the main body of prose. This is not the product of chance. In three out of four passages from Exodus[78] dealing with the disposal of the peoples of the land, the important verb is גרש. In the fourth, כחד appears, a rather different word which is not used in the qal-stem, but in the hiphil may mean "efface, annihilate" (*BDB* 470b, cf. ll.2-3 of the Ammonite Citadel Inscription, Zech 11:9).[79] Parenthetically I may note that in the first three Exodus passages YHWH sends an emissary or agent for the task of dealing with the peoples; but that in all four it is understood that YHWH is the true actor, which is how Mesha evidently regarded Kemosh in the events recorded on the MI. In the corresponding deuteronomic passages גרש is altogether absent.[80]

The Exodus statements reflect an earlier stratum which as in other cases presumably provided prototypes for the deuteronomic equivalents. These verses reflect a concept that the creating of a ordered world is not to be left solely in the hands of the deity. Human action with the aid of the divine is the deuteronomic formula, and the חרם is the most dramatic example of it.[81] Yet while גרש is absent from these passages, a close equivalent is found in Deut 7:1. YHWH promises to bring the people to the land to possess it; he will clear the nations away (Heb. נשל). The next verse says that this is to be achieved by striking the enemy with the חרם. One may justly conclude that the concepts of גרש and חרם are not seen as contradictory in Deuteronomy, but complementary. The חרם is a way to realize the general goal of expelling the enemy nations.

The MI, too, combines the concepts and roots of גרש and חרם. I have argued that in l.7 the verb אבד means "to flee," as Mesha strove to drive

---

78 Exod 23:23,28; 33:2; 34:11.

79 Cf. F. Israel, "The Language of the Ammonites," *Orientalia Lovaniensia Periodica* 10 (1979), 154. In both places the root כחד is associated with the root מות.

80 Deut 7:1-2, 20:17.

81 This is only one level of meaning of the Deuteronomic passages. An exposition of the role of the חרם in Deuteronomy will be found in ch. 5.

away the Israelites. One is struck by l.19: ויגרשה.כמש.מפני "Kemosh drove him out (the king of Israel) from before me" (enabling Mesha to attack Jahaz). This is directly comparable to the Exodus passages using גרש with YHWH (or his agent) as the subject. Deut 7:1-2.'s combination of the concept of גרש with the חרם is also present in the MI, though not in one formula. It seems a safe conclusion that the Deuteronomy passages represent only a shift in emphasis from their Exodus predecessors and not a radical innovation. However, later the argument will be made that the change in terminology is (at least in part) a response to the historical circumstance of the Moabite חרם.

The last root, ירש, is of exceptional importance in BH. It is well known and no comprehensive overview need be undertaken here.[82] Ll.7-8 of the MI read in part: וירש.עמרי.את.א(ר)ץ.מהדבה,"Omri took possession of the (lan)d of Mhdb'." The important thing about this verb's appearance on the MI is that it affirms the presence of a certain concept at work in Moab and Israel. It is all the more interesting because in the biblical literature it is seen in the context of the Exodus and Conquest, whereas Moab presumably lacked at least the Exodus tradition. Deut 7:1-2, which I have just commented on, has ירש in addition to the important נשל and חרם. It is no accident that these roots cluster in both the Deuteronomy pericope and in the brief span of the MI. This parallel clustering suggests that the terminology relating to the Exodus-related Conquest found in the passages from Exodus and Deuteronomy, cited above, is rooted in the struggle of Israel to survive the encroachments of her neighbors--as opposed to their obstensible context of the Exodus or its aftermath.[83]

Another relevant passage is Jud 11:12-27, a pericope which has been judged harshly by modern scholarship. However, Jephthah's longwinded message to the Ammonites, while it may be an interpolation or a message originally addressed to Moab, is certainly relevant to the study of the MI, particularly with regard to this root. Jud 11:21-24 include eight uses of it, divided 5/3 qal/hiphil. In Jud 11:24, Kemosh appears in the role of the deity responsible for giving land to the Ammonites (and Moabites--much of the pericope deals with the Moabites), i.e. the same role he plays for the Moabites in the MI. This seems untenable to some, but Kemosh was worshipped widely in Syria--from 3rd millennium Ebla to LBA Ugarit, and Ammon could have shared in the worship of its neighbor's major deity, Kemosh. The state of our knowledge of ancient Ammonite religion is hardly so perfected as to allow us to draw the negative conclusions which some have drawn.[84] Although

---

[82] See N. Lohfink, "jarāš," *TWAT* III, 953-85.

[83] S.M. Kang, *Divine War in the Old Testament and in the Ancient Near East, BZAW* 177 (Berlin.1989), 164, concludes ch.V with a similar conclusion from different evidence and another viewpoint, "the war descriptions in the Exodus-Conquest traditions are cases of theoretical holy war which grew in the light of the traditions of YHWH war."

[84] See J. A. Soggin, *Judges: A Commentary, OTL* (Philadelphia, 1981), 211, J. van Seters, "The Terms 'Amorite' and 'Hittite in the Old Testament," *VT* XXII (1972), 77, among others.

Ammonite PN's do not feature Kemosh, as J. H. Tigay has pointed out, the "onomastic evidence does not always give a complete picture of the gods worshipped in a society,"[85] and other types of evidence should also be employed. On the other hand, 1 Kgs 11:5,7 distinguish between Milcom, the "Ammonite abomination" and Kemosh, "the Moabite abomination" (another Ammonite "abomination" is *mlk*, which may appear in the Ammonite PN *mlk'l*).[86] Alternatively, it is possible that in his recounting ot Israel's Transjordanian adventures, Jephthah, by lumping together the Moabites and the Ammonites (as he does in his speech), lumped together their gods under Kemosh, and botched his diplomacy. The Ammonite king was not impressed at hearing Kemosh referred to as his god, but pressed on with the war. The narrator wanted to make the point that these alien gods were interchangeable. Then when Jephthah had to fight, he straightaway vowed a vow worthy of the abominations of Ammon, not YHWH .

Regardless of whether this interpretation of the passage is correct, the Jephthah passage dealing with Kemosh exists in its own right as a witness to the existence of competing gods in their attempts to give their worshippers the land they crave. In Jud 11:24, just interpreted above, Jephthah appeals to Ammon. "Do you not possess what Kemosh, your god, has given you to possess? All that YHWH, our God, has given to us to possess, I shall take possession of." This is an interesting argument, and not one that Mesha would have accepted, any more than the Ammonite king did. It is a pacific theology, implying that one should accept the will of both one's god and the god of one's foe (and that their wills are reconcilable). According to MI ll.7-8, Omri took possession of (ירש) Medeba until after a generation, Kemosh returned it to Moab. Mesha thought that Kemosh--not YHWH--was the one who decided on who would dispose of land in Moab (and beyond, as Mesha expanded his domain, l.29, cp. Deut 12:20), just as the Bible depicts YHWH as the one with the power to determine possession of the land.

The cumulative effect of the use of these four roots, as well as others (לחם, אבד, and more) is impressive. It fixes the חרם more precisely in a matrix of terms having to do with the struggle for land and an ordered existence. Also, the term "YHWH-war" used by some is clearly of limited value when so much of the mentality of war was shared regionally, most of all by Moab and Israel.[87] This is what the common terminology teaches, and the most dramatic element held in common was the חרם.

The main object of this chapter has been to achieve an understanding of the mentality which produced the MI. It is not enough to say that it is part and parcel of a larger *Weltanschauung* known and analyzed for many years now in the framework of 'holy war.' Here I have attempted to apply the evidence garnered by close inspection of the Moabite Inscription, trying to go

---

85 J. H. Tigay, *You Shall Have No Other Gods: Israelite Religion in the Light of Hebrew Inscriptions, HSS* 31, (Atlanta, 1986), 20.
86 K.P. Jackson, *The Ammonite Language of the Iron Age, HSM* 27, (Chico, Ca., 1983), 96.
87 *Contra* Gw. Jones, "'Holy War' or 'Yahweh War?'" *VT* XXV (1975), 642-658.

beyond the philological minutiae and the historical details to arrive at a deeper understanding of the world view of the Moabites as reflected in particular by the חרם. The similarities between the MI and the MT, which I have tried to stress throughout this chapter, demonstrate the close linguistic and ideological ties of the two. The remarkable resemblance between the Israelite Exodus and Conquest ethos and the ethos of the MI has been given far too little attention, and its implications could and should be probed more deeply than possible here.

The Moabite חרם, involving as it seemingly did the slaughter of thousands, must be understood as an intensely moral-religious act, reasserting the rule of the god(s) and reflecting the victory of Kemosh and Mesha over the 'monsters of chaos,' i.e. YHWH and Israel. Moab was able to slaughter the Israelites without a qualm with the aid of this mythopoeic conception. The devotion of the city of Nebo to Kemosh seems uneconomical in secular terms but it probably went together with an inadequate degree of socio-economic organization to use POW labor (a lack which Mesha was able to remedy). It was seen by the Moabites as a cosmic act, designed to win the god's aid in the battle against the encroachment of chaos. On the positive side this involved the reestablishment of the land as a "sacred space" where the Moabite world order could rise again from the ashes. As Sargon's military career was thought of in these terms, so was Mesha's. In fact, the immediate economic equation was relatively trivial. It was vital to align oneself with Kemosh, the arbiter of destinies, who alone could guarantee economic prosperity, and the political independence which was a prerequisite for prosperity. Only independence could put an end to tribute paid to Israel,. give Moabite towns the liberty to build their vital water facilities, build roads and ply trade and farm for the benefit of the Moabites themselves. Failure to carry out the dictates of the חרם was therefore penny-wise and pound-foolish (cp. Joshua 6-7). Yet there was more to it than material or secular political considerations. The חרם was the centerpiece of the campaign to restore not only Moab's freedom and prosperity but the ruptured moral order of the universe. Mesha and Moab wanted harmony to reign throughout the realm of the crucial triangle of relationships of people/land/god which constituted *Weltordnung*.

Appendix: The Question of 2 Kings 3

I alluded above to the dubious nature of 2 Kings 3 (see n. 2). In view of the fact that, at present, the nature of the chapter is still a matter of lively debate, and some scholars stand on the historicity of the 2 Kings 3 account, I have chosen to state my own opposing view. Even without the evidence of the MI, the chapter poses obvious problems. One example is the appearance and role of Jehosaphat. According to the chronology of the Old Greek, Jehosaphat and Jehoram were not contemporaries. This cannot be easily waved aside, for as R. Klein pointed out, the OG is buttressed by 2 Chron 21:12ff. which presents a letter written by Elijah after the death of

Jehosaphat.[88] In 2 Kings 3, Jehosaphat is supposed to be alive while Elijah is dead (2 Kings 3:11). Then again, the chapter is said to be literarily dependent on 1 Kings 20; which has close similarities even without examination.[89] Some scholars have made a case for the events of 2 Kings 3 occurring at a later time.[90] I wish, however, to focus here mainly on the primary texts in question.

2 Kings 3:4 tells of Mesha as tribute-payer and herdsman. There is no reason to doubt its accuracy. Yet the Mesha of the MI never even begins to emerge in 2 Kings 3. 2 Kgs 3:21 portrays the panic-stricken Moabites massing at the border; the contrast with the normal language of the muster is starkly illustrated by 2 Kgs 3:6, in which Jehoram musters 'all Israel' (always a suspicious phrase). Mesha, on the other hand, is not even mentioned in connection with the muster of Moab. The king of Moab appears only at the end, 2 Kgs 3:26-7, first leading a vain charge (in an attempt to break through the weak point, the presumably reluctant Edomite contingent), and then (like Jephthah) sacrificing his offspring on the walls of Kir-Hareshet, the last remaining stronghold. Yet the Mesha of the inscription would have been in charge, and would have disposed of his men more ably. Why would Mesha stand on the border and wait for the enemy when Moab had advance notice (2 Kgs 3:21) and could easily have attacked when the allies were still organizing and thus vulnerable, in Edom? Or on the way, when Israel's line of supply was nonexistent? Nothing in the incompetent and passive behavior of the "king of Moab" fits Mesha, who was indubitably made of more enterprising stuff.

The magnitude of the disaster as portrayed by the biblical account is such that it is impossible to reconcile it with the MI. Mesha could not have left such an account of his accomplishments if he were the Moabite equivalent of Hezekiah after Sennacherib (the survival of his stele is a mute witness to this). Moab continued independent in Mesha's time and after. Furthermore, if victory was so complete that only one city was left resisting, a large part of the land of Moab would have passed automatically into Israelite control, since the Gadites were there. Yet 2 Kings 3 takes no account of the Gadites. The wholesale destruction in 2 Kgs 3:25 of cities, trees, fields, and water sources was in fact as inimical to their interests as to those of Moab. The strategy of coming by the south makes sense from neither Jehoram's point of view nor especially from that of the Gadites, who were the ones most in distress due to Mesha's rebellion. The Kings text portrays no knowledge of nor concern for their plight; it reflects instead an apology for the failure of Israel in the large sense to master the revolt. The MI in l..19 is

---

[88] R. Klein, *Textual Criticism,* 39.

[89] J. R. Bartlett, "The 'United' Campaign against Moab," 136f., following S. de Vries.

[90] J. M. Miller & J. H. Hayes, *A History of Ancient Israel and Judah* (Phila., 1986), 353, 259-262, G. Rendsberg, "A Reconstruction of Moabite-Israelite History," *JANES* 13 (1981), 67-73. *Contra*: S. Timm, *Die Dynastie Omri,* 177. Cf. also his concluding remarks on 180.

more realistic than 2 Kings 3 when it mentions Jahaz as the Israelite king's base for his failed counterattack, not a circuit to the south through Edom.

I have spoken of tendentiousness in the MI. The biblical text is full of tendencies. Its final form reflects a Judean point of view. The Judean king is a picture of piety, especially compared to Jehoram; in fact, as soon as Elisha has finished praising him (2 Kgs 3:14), Jehosaphat vanishes. Since Mesha's portrait of triumph over the entire house of Omri is accurate, the Israelites could not in the end win, despite the fact that Elisha had supposedly joined the army uninvited. Instead of the usual practice of consulting with God (or gods) prior to the battle, the three kings had to look about them for a diviner once they had already got into difficulties. The success which they enjoyed followed the mechanical pattern of the Book of Kings: what the prophet forecasts, must materialize, preferably sooner rather than later. The whole expedition would have failed were it not for Elisha's miracle. This alone indicates the unhistorical nature of the account. The figure of the prophet is far more important here than the real events, none of which are found in the chapter except the bare fact of a revolt. On the one hand, this fits into the pattern of mythicization of history pointed to by Eliade.[91] Whole epic accounts spring up from a historical core while the historical events leave little or no trace, even when the epic is contemporary with the event. On the other hand, what it adds up to then, besides the boosting of Jehosaphat and Elisha (the latter believed by some to be wholly secondary to the account, as he certainly was to the events), is an apology for the failure of Israel (in the large sense) to suppress the Mesha revolt.

Another important point was made by J. Bartlett, who observed that the geography of 2 Kings 3 is "quite unreal," and that the wandering in the desert of Edom and the need for a prophet to miraculously supply water are remarkably like Num 20:3-20, the story of which may have served as a model.[92] In contrast, the MI exudes familiarity with the Transjordan.

The final verses of 2 Kings 3 illustrate a known custom from the Canaanite world, that of sacrificing a child or children during a siege.[93] The author(s) have rounded out their tale with this particular custom, which

---

[91] M. Eliade, *Cosmos and History: The Myth of the Eternal Return* (New York, 1959), 38-48. He uses modern examples where the history is known and the myth reflects next to nothing of the history. He also gives the example of the Iliad.

[92] J. R. Bartlett, "The 'United' Campaign against Moab," 138.

[93] M. Cogan & H. Tadmor, *II Kings: A New Translation with Introduction and Commentary,* 47, cite classical sources on the Punic/Phoenician practice. They do not take into account all the evidence in A. Spalinger's article (which they also cite): "A Canaanite Ritual Found in Egyptian Reliefs," *Journal of the Society for the Study of Egyptian Antiquities* 8 (1978), 50, gives an example of a relief of Rameses II before Ashkelon where "the child is definitely being sacrificed." More examples follow. The Ugaritic text 24.266, was dismissed by Cogan and Tadmor as "disputed." A. Caquot & M. Sznycer, *Ugaritic Religion, Iconography of Religions* XV, 8 (Leiden, 1980), support the sacrificial interpretation without a shade of doubt. The reliefs prove the antiquity of the practice in any case.

serves to bring an unspecified wrath down upon the besiegers,[94] who otherwise would have subdued the last Moabite resistance. This does not explain, of course, why the Israelites never enjoyed the fruit of their victories but simply retreated, granted Mesha a total reprieve, and never regrouped and retook Moab.. In other words, the custom is used here as the basis of a literary construct. This construct, and the wrath of God, seem to be best explained as an application of the deuteronomic mandate not to dispossess the Moabites (Deut 2:9), since the desperate straits of the Moabite king in 2 Kings 3 and the devastation of the land wrought by the allies made that mandate relevant. The sacrifice of Moab's heir symbolized the destruction of Moab's inheritance, as portrayed in 2 Kgs 3. The situation naturally evoked the wrath of the God of Israel whose will it was that Israel should respect Moab's right to its inheritance. The use of קצף, "wrath," here without a subject is frequently held to be so unprecedented as to warrant the interpretation that the wrath was that of Kemosh (an interpretation which would have appalled the deuteronomists!). Yet this was around the time that Ahab was leading a large army against a far greater god than Kemosh, namely ^{d}Aššur, without fleeing in terror. In fact, as Y. Elitsur has seen, there are similarly constructed verses in the Bible (referring to YHWH), such as Num 1:33,18:5, the latter of which ends in the same language as that of 2 Kgs 3:27 :וְלֹא־יִהְיֶה עוֹד קֶצֶף עַל־בְּנֵי יִשְׂרָאֵל.[95] The correct answer is as mentioned above, that it was YHWH who was angry, and it was Israel's threat to blot out Moab's inheritance, which was God-given (Deut 2:9), that precipitated the wrath. Not only is the part played by the miracle-making prophet a literary 'embroidering' of events, but the more military aspects of the chapter have been given an extensive literary-theological treatment as well.

Both the revolt itself, the MI, and 2 Kgs 3:4 indicate that Israel had followed a policy towards Moab similar in conception to that of ninth-century Assyria towards its provinces; one of harshness and unrelenting economic exploitation.[96] The numbers of 2 Kgs 3:4 indicate the latter, and the virtual beggaring of a tributary was not unknown elsewhere in the ancient Near East. S. Dalley, for instance, cites an example from the Old Babylonian period where the tributary literally did not have enough shirts to give his overlord.[97] Such extreme exploitation was hardly calculated to foster a stable vassal-master relationship. I have already touched on the fact that one of the few things that the MI and 2 Kings 3 have in common is the water supply si-

---

[94] B. Margalit, in "Why King Mesha of Moab Sacrificed His Oldest Son," *BAR* 12/6 (1986), 62-3, notes the Ugaritic text's relevance, but sees the "wrath" as Kemosh's "bitter indignation."

[95] Y. Elitsur, "Problems of Historical Interpretation in 2 Kings 3," (Heb.) in B. Z. Lurya, ed., *Studies in the Book of Kings II* (Jerusalem, 1985), 226-8. He argues that "wrath" is the theological equivalent of "plague."

[96] S. M. Paley, *King of the World: Ashur-nasir-pal II of Assyria 883-859 B.C.* (Brooklyn, 1976) 3-5, H. Tadmor, "Assyria and the West: The Ninth Century and Its Aftermath," in H. Goedicke and J. J .M. Roberts, eds., *Unity and Diversity: Essays in the History, Literature, and Religion of the Ancient Near East* (Baltimore, 1975), 37-9.

[97] S. Dalley, *Mari and Karana: Two Old Babylonian Cities* (London, 1984), 40.

tuation. Mesha (ll.24-5) had to address the lack of cisterns in at least one town. In 2 Kings 3 it was Israelite policy to block up Moabite wells and waterholes. One can infer, therefore, that both texts reflect an Israelite policy of restricting Moabite access to water before the revolt; which was evidently a precaution to prevent Moabite cities from having the capacity to withstand siege. Such limiting of the most vital resource, even more than the exploitation of Moab's pastoral economy, must have engendered the kind of hatred of Israel reflected in the MI. The fantasy of Israel's near destruction of Moab, on the whole, is a reflection of Israel's frustration at the loss of dominion, and a response to the devastating success of Mesha, including the חרם of Kemosh, a theological challenge which resulted in 2 Kings 3.

Finally, K.-H. Bernhardt argues that Elisha's chronology has been tampered with to allow him a long enough life to participate in the campaign of 2 Kings 3, and that Jehosaphat of Judah was already dead according to 2 Kgs 1:17. Therefore he feels that the story has a much later provenance.[98] It is probable that this is true for the final form of the story. Originally, this story, which is patterned in some ways after 1 Kings 20, may have likewise featured an anonymous prophet. Also, it appears from the biblical and MI reference's to Omri that he probably encountered feeble resistance in what was surely a swift conquest. If so, 2 Kings 3 may preserve some elements from the campaign of Omri's conquest, such as possibly the alliance with Edom and Judah, the lack of an urgent need to help the tribe of Gad, and the inability of the Moabites to organize effective resistance. There is another point that is of some interest for the provenance of the chapter. I have touched on the anonymity of the kings of Moab and Edom in 2 Kings 3. This has its counterpart in the MI, where no king of Israel after Omri--a king Mesha did not fight--is mentioned by name. This more than any other indication suggests that at least the nucleus of the traditions which crystallized in 2 Kings 3 was contemporary with the aftermath of the Moabite war, the time when the need to invent apologies for the disaster was most acute. This may be true of other chapters in Kings which follow such a pattern.

In sum, the MI and 2 Kings 3 do not exist in the same plane. The MI (and archeology) proves that Mesha's revolt was not only successful, but that his reign was, too. His inscription, whatever its tendencies, is deeply rooted in the reality of Moab and shows a deep awareness of Transjordanian geography and history (e.g. Gad's being there from of old). The biblical account portrays a king of Moab who is a failure. Its disregard for the Gadites (who were a potential strategic asset, never utilized or mentioned in the biblical account) is damning; its dependence on legendary elements and miracles also contrasts badly with the MI.

THE MESHA INSCRIPTION IN TRANSLATION

---

[98] K.-H. Bernhard, "Der Feldzug der drei Könige," *Schalom: Studien zur Glaube und Geschichte Israels* [*FS* A. Jepsen], (Stuttgart, 1971), 11-12. S. de Vries, "Three Comparisons in 1 Kings XXII 4B and its Parallel and 2 Kings III 7B," *VT* 39 (1989) 283-306, retains Jehosophat.

*=discussed in body of chapter.

1. I am Mesha, son of Kemosh-yatti, the king of Moab, the
2. Dibonite. My father reigned over Moab thirty years, and I succeeded
3. my father. I erected this high place to Kemosh at QRḤH, high pla(ce
4. of sal)vation. For he saved me from all kings, he showed me (the defeat) of all my enemies (especially) Omri,
5. king of Israel. For he oppressed Moab for many years, because Kemosh was angry at his people.
6. His son took his place and he, too, said "I will oppress Moab." In my time he said s(o),
7. but I have seen (the passing) of him and his house; and Israel has surely fled* for eternity. Omri had taken possession of the l(an)d
8. of Mhdb' and he occupied it during his reign and [it was occupied] half the reign* of his son--forty years,*
9. but Kemosh restored* it in my reign. So I rebuilt Baal-meon, constructed a reservoir in it, and I rebu(ilt)
10. Kiriathiam. The men of Gad had dwelt in the land of Ataroth from days of yore.
10-11. A king of Israel had built Ataroth for himself. I attacked the city and I seized it and I slaughtered all the peo(ple
12. of) the city--satiation* for Kemosh and for Moab, and I dra(gg)ed back from there the chief* of the (clan of) Areli.*
13. And I dragged him before Kemosh at Kerioth, and I settled in it men of ŠRN and me(n) of
14. MḤRT. And Kemosh said to me, "Go, seize Nebo from Israel,"
15. So I went at night and I attacked it from the break of dawn until noon when
16. I seized it and I slew everybody (in it)--seven thousand m(e)n, b(o)ys,* ladies, gi(rl)s,*
17. and maidens*--for to the warrior* Kemosh I devoted them. I took from there
18. t(he vessel)s* of YHWH and I dragged* them before Kemosh. Now the king of Israel had built
19. Jahaz and he lodged there in his warring against me, but Kemosh drove him out before me.
20. I took from Moab 200 men (in) all its divisions* (and) I led them against Jahaz and I seized it
21. to add to Dibon. I rebuilt QRḤH, the walls of the park, the walls( ) of
22. the acropolis(?). I rebuilt its gates, and I rebuilt its tower,
23. and I built a palace and I built the retaining walls(?) of the resevoi(r at the spri)ng in the middle of
24. the city. There was no cistern in the middle of the city, in QRḤH, so I said to all the people, "Make
25. for yourselves each one a cistern in his house." And I dug pits(?) for QRḤH with

26. Israelite( )prisoners. I rebuilt (or fortified) Aroer and I constructed the highway by the Arnon
27. and I rebuilt Beth-bamoth because it was destroyed. I rebuilt Bezer because it was in ruins( )
28. (he) with 50 m(en) of Dibon because every Dibonite is (my personal) vassal.* I ru(le)
29. (over the) hundreds of cities that I added to the land. And I rebuilt
30. *even* Mhdb', and Beth-diblathaim and Beth-baal-meon and I brought there (my
31. shepherds to pasture) the sheep of the land. And there had settled at Horonaim (
32.) Kemosh (or)dered me, "Go down, fight at Horonaim." So I went down (and
33. I fought against the city and I took it and) Kemosh (dwelt) in it in my time (remainder unintelligible; it ended originally at 34).

* I.e. someone over whom the king exercises his own immediate personal authority.

CHAPTER 3

PREVIOUSLY PROPOSED PARALLELS TO THE BIBLICAL *ḤEREM*

The Mesha Inscription is both the best and the best known of the parallels that have been adduced to the biblical חרם. In the next two chapters we look at other, lesser parallels. This chapter is devoted to parallels which have been suggested in the past. Chapter 4 contains some parallels that are, with the exception of the Hittite, which in my view has been wrongly scanted in the past, completely new. The first previously proposed parallel is from Old Babylonian Period Mari, and it will be treated more fully in the analysis of Joshua 7.

A. *asakku* at Mari: In 1960, A. Malamat, who has devoted himself indefatigably to the examination of the Mari findings in order to shed light on the Bible, published in Hebrew (and later in English), "The Ban in Mari and the Bible."[1] In this article he proposed an equivalence between the Akkadian expression, *asakkam akālum* as employed at Mari and the biblical חרם. *CAD* A2 (326b) defines *asakku* as "something set apart (for god or king, a taboo)" and the combination with the verb *akālu* as "to infringe on a taboo." The peculiar character of the idiom thus employed is a result of straight translation from Sumerian.[2] The חרם terminology is rooted entirely in Semitic usage. Immediately we can sense that this parallel has built-in limitations. For one thing, unlike *asakku,* חרם is never used in relation to a king in the Hebrew Bible (e.g. "the חרם of David"). More significantly, though the semantic domain of *asakku* is considerably broader than that of the noun חרם and its uses, it never functions in a way analogous to the hiphil usage. Thus *asakku akālu* can never refer to the kind of phenomenon that occurs when booty and human lives are consecrated to destruction, as in the MI and the Bible, but only to an infringement on the proper sphere of king or god.

The strength of Malamat's Mari parallel lies predominantly not in its formal equivalency to Hebrew חרם, for in the abstract *asakku* seems no closer to it than any other Akkadian term for "taboo" or the like, such as *ikkibu.* Nor is there semantic identity. Statements like "the root hrm is the semantic equivalent of asakkum,"[3] are too sweeping. Thus the author of these words, A. Glock, immediately qualified his statement. What is truly impressive in the Mari material is the parallel between a Mari letter, and the Achan incident (Joshua 7), where the resemblance of the Mari account to the biblical story is undeniable, since both deal with stolen proscribed

[1] A. Malamat, "The Ban in Mari and the Bible," (Heb.), *Yehezkel Kaufmann Jubilee Volume* (Jerusalem, 1960), 149-58. Around the same time were C. H. W. Brekelmans, *De ḥerem in het Oude Testament* (Nijmegen, 1959), 138, and H. W. F. Saggs in *JSS* V (1960), 414.

[2] For the Sumerian, see, e.g. J.-M. Duand, "Une condamnation à mort à l'époque d'Ur III," *RA* 71 (1977),126, l. 12.

[3] A. E. Glock, *Warfare in Mari and Early Israel,* diss., University of Michigan (Ann Arbor, Mich., 1968), 206.

plunder.[4] Since *asakku* is used in a many more situations than חרם, and is clearly a more generic term, once can hardly speak of "semantic equivalency." Moreover, as was just noted, there is no "war-*asakku*." The *asakku* has bearing on the חרם, but it should not be exaggerated. Comparable notions of the inviolability of certain war spoils are found both in Mari and the Bible, which tends to support those, like Kaufmann, who already believed in the authentic nature and genuine antiquity of the type of situation described in Joshua 7,[5] but the war-חרם is not widely attested in among Israel's neighbors. In short, *asakku akālu* sheds indirect but welcome light on the war-חרם in its parallel to Joshua 7, the Achan story (see below), dealing with the aftermath of battle and the disposition of booty.

B. One of the most interesting parallels adduced heretofore comes from fourth century Athens in the oration of Aeschines, *Against Ctesiphon* 107-113.[6] The section, which deals with the sacrilege of two lawless tribes, the Cyrrhaens and the Cralidae who εἰς τὸ ἱερὸν τὸ ἐν δελφοῖς καὶ περὶ τὰ ἀναθήματα ἠσέβουν, "had profaned the temple of Delphi and its votive offerings." τὰ ἀναθήματα is often used by the LXX in its singular form (ἀνάθημα) or its equivalent (ἀνάθεμα), or as a verb, in its attempt at translating the Hebrew root חרם. Unfortunately, the precise nature of the offence to the gods is not stated directly, although it is natural to speculate on the basis of the indictment that these "lawless tribes" had gone so far as to rob the sanctuary at Delphi of votive offerings set up there. This could consist of a variety of objects, such as weapons. As the text continues by saying that the Cirrhaens and the Cragilidae also offended against the Amphictyons, these tribes may have gone on to raid the treasuries which the various city-states maintained at the site of the oracle. On the other hand, writing in the 2nd century A.D., Pausanias said that the Cirrhaens behaved impiously towards Apollo, particularly in taking some of the god's land, and this provoked the war against them.[7] Yet this account differs from Aeschines, which mentions sacrilege against the temple.

The account given by Aeschines is a part of a polemic, indeed a diatribe, against his most hated enemy, Demosthenes. The history which he goes on to relate is vouchsafed us as part of an elaborate rhetorical device (by current standards) designed to place Demosthenes in the same camp as the villainous Cirrhaens and the Cragilidae, as the denouement in §113 makes plain. Nevertheless. the story has a realistic dynamic, and though there may be distortions designed to enhance the orator's point of view, these are probably minor, since the facts were so well-known. Even were the

---

[4] A. Malamat, "The Ban in Mari and the Bible," in *Biblical Essays 1966, OuTWP* (Stellenbosch, 1966), 44f., C. H. W. Brekelmans, *De ḥerem*, 138, H. W. F. Saggs, Review of *ARM VII-VIII*, *JSS* V (1960), 414.

[5] Y. Kaufmann, *The Book of Joshua* (Heb.), (Jerusalem, 1966), 127, calls it "a most realistic story."

[6] N. Lohfink, "Ḥaram," *TDOT* V, 190-1 lists parallels.

[7] Pausanius, xxxvii. 5.

story a fabrication, it would still be an instructive fabrication and an interesting though, even if wholly accurate, incomplete parallel to the Israelite חרם.

The Pythian oracle decreed a harsh fate for the Cirrhaens and the Cragilidae, which was executed by the Athenians and their allies: their land, consisting of a plain and a harbor, was to be devastated, the population enslaved, and the land devoted to Apollo, Artemis, Leto and Athena Pronaea, to be left untilled for the future. This sounds very much like the later Hittite practice--the still more severe early Hittite practice will be dealt with in the fourth chapter. The curse is interesting in itself; it was designed to deter the utilization of the land devoted to the four gods and goddesses. The use of a curse in this situation is, of course, reminiscent of the one found in Josh 6:26. Here is the text of the curse in C. D. Adams's translation:

> If any one should violate this," it says "whether city or private man, or tribe, let them be under a curse," it says, of Apollo and Artemis and Leto and Athena Pronaea." The curse goes on: That their land bear no fruit; that their wives bear children not like those that begat them, but monsters; that their flocks yield not their natural increase; that defeat await them in camp and court and market-place, and that they perish utterly, themselves, their houses, their whole race; "And never," it says, may they offer pure sacrifice unto Apollo...and may the gods refuse to accept their offerings.[8]

By violating the sanctity of the gods in an egregious manner, whether by temple-robbing, treasury plundering or whatever, the two tribes brought upon themselves condign punishment in many respects worthy of comparison to the חרם; Lohfink points to Judges 21.[9] The collective action of the tribes, first against Benjamin (Judges 20-1) and then against a specific locale, Yabesh Gilead, is somewhat parallel to the war of the Amphictyons against the two tribes (however, see the treatment of Judge 20-1 below). The setting apart of the land is more akin to the setting apart of the land of Jericho and Ai, especially as this feature of the curse occurs in Josh 6:26.

One of the fascinating things about this incident of classical Greek history for the historian of the ancient Near East is the multiplicity of sources bearing on it, something lacking in any account involving the חרם. If it is hard to judge the accuracy of individual details of Aeschines account, as mentioned above, we at least know a sacrilege was committed, and that the punishment that followed resulted in rendering the Cirrhaen plain sacred to Apollo--hence fallow and not even to be used for grazing--for centuries. In Dio Cassius's *Roman History* (Epitome of LXII:14,2) he tells of the Emperor Nero taking away the sacred land of Apollo (Cirrha) from the god--truly a remarkable time span for the curse to have been in operation. Isocrates, a contemporary of Aeschines, alludes to it (Plataicus 32). Diodorus Siculus has an account of how someone set off a Sacred War. This occurred after the land was consecrated. The war involved the Phocians who were sacrilegiously cultivating the sacred land. The Phocians were heavily fined

---

[8] C. D. Adams, *The Speeches of Aeschines, LCL* (London and New York,1919), 393f..
[9] N. Lohfink, "Ḥaram," 191.

and there was also talk of cursing them. However, the Phocians were defiant and war resulted instead (Diodorus Siculus XVI 23, cf. also Pausanias 10,2,1 and 10,15,1; Justin 8,1).

The plenitude of sources, although they vary widely in date and in their general reliability, attest to the importance of the phenomenon in question. Nevertheless, the fact that the sources agree that the original population was not subjected to a large-scale massacre (in Judges 21, the virgin women were spared), but enslaved, makes this interesting sidelight of the religious history of classical antiquity only a partial parallel.

C. Old South Arabian *hrg*. N. Lohfink in his summarizing article (*TDOT* 5 180ff.) points to only one 'close parallel' other than the MI (and *asakku*), and this is from Old South Arabic. There seems to be no reason why this should be included. OSA *hrg* is equivalent to its Hebrew cognate, and means simply "to kill," according to A. Jamme, or "to kill enemies," according to H. F. Fuhs.[10] The Sabean inscription Lohfink cites provides no justification for citing this verb as a parallel to the חרם.[11] In the inscription, the verb appears thrice and a nominal form appears twice (A. Jamme's translation):

> 6. *wldhmw/w"nṯhmw/fhrgw/wsybw....* ...their children and their wives, so that they were either killed or captured.
> 7. *'wm/bhsm/whrg/whshtn...wyhrgw/bnhmw/mhrgm* *'Awwam is* cutting to pieces and killing and destroying...and they deprived them of a war trophy...
> 8. *yt'wlw/bwfym/whmdm/wmhrgm/wsbym*... they went back in safety and praise and (with) war trophy and captives....[11]

The last usage, in which *mhrgm* is understood by Jamme to mean "war trophy," is unattested in Northwest Semitic, and certainly far removed from the semantic domain of חרם. The element of consecration (to destruction) is absent, even in the full text of the inscription. It is therefore hard to see what, if anything, about OSA *hrg* compares well with the phenomenon of חרם: not even the sense which has been imputed to OSA *hrg* , that of "kill on account of a sworn obligation,"[12] comes close to the meaning of Hebrew or Moabite החרם. The fact that in Num 21:1-3 an oath was taken in connection with the חרם does not come into play here. The connection was not etymological but the result of circumstance. H. F. Fuhs's definition of Heb. הרג, as "kill enemies in battle or to carry out the ban" (*TDOT* III 451f.), does not hold water and was dismissed by N. Lohfink in his article from the same theological dictionary. A prooftext, Gen 49:5-7, in which Fuhs holds that the use of *hrg* in Gen 49:6.6 must mean "to kill to carry out the ban," since it must refer to the events of Genesis 34 (the rape of Dinah), rests on the

---

[10] A. Jamme, *Sabaean Inscriptions from Maḥram Bilqîs (Mârib), American Foundation for the Study of Man* 3 (Baltimore, 1962), 66 and passim. H. F. Fuchs, *TDOT* III "Haragh," 449f..

[11] A. Jamme, *Sabaean Inscriptions*, #575 (p.64).

[12] H. F. Fuhs, "Haragh," 447f..

unwarranted assertion that the חרם is at issue there, whereas both the word חרם and the act of consecration through destruction are absent.

D. Livy VIII. IX. Most of the proposed parallels remaining are found in Roman sources. The only exceptions come from the Arab ambit, although they are unconvincing and have never shed light on the חרם. The fact that "the Ghassanid prince Al-Harit ibn 'Amr is said to have burned his enemies to a man while invoking the gods," or that "the same was done under the aegis of Islam by the Wahabi Ibn Saud,"[13] is proof of a policy of religious extermination; which alone does not suffice for a true parallel to the חרם. If these latter cases were relevant, the Assyrian Holy War practices would be still more relevant.

In the history of Livy (VIII. IX) (c. 60 B.C.-17 A.D.), cited by K. Hoffmann in the article "Anathema" (*RAC* I 427-30), we have, however, a much more interesting parallel. In part this is because Livy wanted to explain a forgotten and disused practice. He describes a battle that took place between Rome and a Latin army (around 340 B.C.) in which the Romans began to fall back and were in danger of losing. A consul named Decius, with the aid of a member of the pontifical college to instruct him in word and deed, devoted (*devoveo*) the enemy soldiers and himself to the *Deis Manibus Tellurique*; to the divine Manes (the Shades) and to the Earth. Having altered his attire to suit his special role Decius plunged into the fray, *sicut caelo missus piaculum omnis deorum irae,* "just as one sent from heaven to expiate all the gods' wrath" (cf the tantalising reference to Kemosh's wrath at his people, MI 1.5). He soon succumbed, *omnes minas periculaque ab deis superis inferisque in se unum vertit;* having "turned all threats and dangers from the heavenly and infernal gods on himself alone." He died nobly. The Latin camp was taken and all found there were slain. As Livy sums it up:

> It seems proper to add here that the consul, dictator, or praetor who devotes the legions of the enemy need not devote himself, but may designate any citizen he likes from a regularly enlisted Roman legion; if the man who has been devoted dies, it is deemed that all is well; it he does not die, then an image of him is buried seven feet or more under ground and a sin-offering is slain.... But if he shall choose to devote himself, as Decius did, if he does not die, he cannot sacrifice for himself or for the people without sin, whether with a victim or with any other offering he shall choose. He who devotes himself as the right to dedicate his arms to Vulcan, or to any other god he likes. The spear on which the consul has stood and prayed must not fall into the hands of the enemy; should this happen, expiation must be made to Mars with the sacrifice of a swine, a sheep, and an ox. XI. These particulars, even though the memory of every religious and secular usage has been wiped out by men's preference of the new and outlandish for the ancient and homebred, I have thought it not foreign to my purpose to repeat, and in the very words in which they were formulated and handed down.[14]

Livy, in his charming prose, makes many interesting points. First, it is obvious that this parallel, too, is deficient. In this Roman practice, a

[13] N. Lohfink, "Ḥaram," 191.
[14] B. O. Foster, *The Histories of Livy, LCL* (Cambridge, 1957), 43.

"consul, dictator, or praetor" is required to devote himself, or another citizen to the divinities, and the devoted person's death is regarded as a desideratum. The devoted person must don a special garb and has the opportunity to dedicate his weapon to a god. All these things are absent from the חרם. It is interesting though, that an adept in sacred matters accompanied the army; that is vaguely reminiscent of the role priests sometimes play in biblical warfare. When one subtracts the many elements of Livy's account which diverge from the biblical picture, there remains a hard core of similarity. One should note the role the consul played, to expiate or avert the wrath of the gods. Although in the MI no note of expiation was overtly sounded, the wrath of Kemosh was in the background. It is unfortunately not specified at what stage the deity's anger was assuaged, although the MI makes it clear that after the חרם the situation rapidly took on a favorable hue and military action soon ceased or greatly moderated and Mesha could turn to works of peace. In Num 21:1-3, the people offered YHWH a חרם in order to propitiate the deity and solicit God's cooperation. More important still is the fact that the consul (Decius) devoted the enemy to the divinities, like Numbers 21 as a response to the fact that the battle was going badly. This is much closer to the concept of חרם than merely invoking the gods while slaughtering the enemy, as did ibn 'Amr, the bloodthirsty Ghassanid prince.

This practice had fallen into obscurity, yet Livy deftly portrayed the psychology involved. In speaking of the supernal and infernal powers whose threats must be dealt with, his narrative helps strengthen the argument that the mentality of חרם sprang originally from a polytheistic setting, from which it took root in the soil of the religion of Israel.

E. Other parallels from Roman sources. Lohfink cites a Roman practice of devoting criminals to the gods of the underworld, as reminiscent of Lev 27:29. However, as argued later on (ch.6), Lev 27:29 should not be subjected to the assumption that it forms part of the criminal law; it plainly deals with the vow and its most severe form involving the dedication of human life. The execution of miscreants for offenses is found elsewhere in relation to חרם, but always in cases of sacrilegious behavior. Hence this Roman practice can shed no light on the חרם of Lev 27:29, which takes its place in a different framework.

Another parallel frequently cited comes from Caesar's *Gallic Wars* (vi. 17). It is a somewhat problematic parallel because for the first time, the only record we have is that of a completely foreign observer, Caesar, who was not, of course, an anthropologist. It is hard to know how well his interpretation of events corresponded to Celtic notions. The crucial word, *devoveo*, the Latin "equivalent" of חרם, also appeared in Livy's account (as against, e.g. *devotio*), so it is possible that Caesar used the same or similar model as Livy's to interpret the Celts' actions. On the other hand, if one simply takes the report at face value, it does have some interesting elements: the devotion of spoil before the important battle (to 'Mars'), and the destruction of all enemy life after, as well as careful adherence to the principal of keeping hands off the devoted spoil. These are the chief features of the Celtic practice as described by Caesar. If the interpretation Caesar gives, viz. the idea of devoting booty to the god of war is correct--along with the report of the mass destruction of all enemy life, then we have more evidence that a polytheistic milieu was instrumental in producing a phenomenon similar to the חרם.

In the final analysis, Caesar's observations might just have value for the study of Roman attitudes towards their enemies, were they not buttressed by similar observations of Tacitus of a German parallel to the חרם. Tacitus (born c. 56) records in his annals (xiii. 57) a war between two German tribes, the Hermunduri and the Chatti, the outcome of which was bound to be deadly:

> *quia victores diversam aciem Marti ac Mercurio sacravere, quo voto equi viri cuncta occidioni dantur. Et minae quidem hostiles in ipsos vertebrant.*

> "...in that both sides consecrated, in the event of victory, the adverse host to Mars and Mercury (=Tiu and Woden); a vow implying the extermination of horses, men, and all objects whatsoever. The threat of the enemy thus recoiled upon himself."[15]

The word *sacravere* is stressed here as it is not the same word used by Livy and Caesar, viz. *devoveo*, which a priori might be thought to have a more negative connotation than Tacitus's usage. But the two mean the same thing in the light of the context. However, *sacravere* is closer to the Hebrew root קדש (and to חרם) than *devoveo*. The war itself, according to Tacitus, broke out over a desire of the two tribes to control a river which had hitherto marked their respective boundary line, and which abounded in salt. This is, of course, a rather different *casus belli* than anything one encounters in the biblical חרם stories or in the MI. However, although Tacitus gave what may be a purely secular motivation priority in his account, he goes on to mention that the area in question was also held to be a place special to the gods where prayer was held to be more efficacious than in other areas. This may well have been a powerful motivating force for a sort of Germanic 'Holy War.'

The translator of the passage just quoted draws a comparison between the biblical חרם and the German practice described there.[16] Yet in the citing of Joshua 6 and 1 Samuel 15, prominent biblical examples, there is an element missing. For in those passages, it is not by vow that the חרם is unleashed, but by virtue of prophetic transmission of God's will. This element is lacking in all parallels cited heretofore, if one distinguishes between a cultically-based oracle such as the Pythia and the less constricted and more powerful prophetic figures of Joshua and Samuel (a Mari parallel treated below has a 'prophet').

Yet if we take Tacitus at face value as a reliable reporter of the German view of their practice, we find a certain similarity to the חרם, especially in the consecration by destruction of the enemy, including their horses, which reminds one of deuteronomic prescriptions calling for slaughter of livestock

[15] J. Jackson, *The Annals of Tacitus* IV, *LCL* (Cambridge, 1937), 101.
[16] Ibid. 100, n. 2.

reminds one of deuteronomic prescriptions calling for slaughter of livestock (also in 1 Samuel 15). Yet I can say little of the world of thought that brought about this behavior in the case of the German tribes, and this limits the usefulness of the parallel for this study, except to note once again that it adds another page to the body of evidence that the חרם most naturally originated and developed in a polytheistic milieu.

In addition to this partial parallel drawn from Tacitus, Lohfink cites another putative parallel drawn from the Germanic sphere, this appearing in the *Geography of Strabo* 7,2. Strabo, a historian and traveler who flourished in the last half century B.C., recorded a peculiar practice of the Cimbri. The priestesses of this once well-known tribe would greet prisoners-of-war with wreaths, conduct them to giant kettles, slit their throats, and then practice divination with their entrails. While this is interesting in its own right, it does not compare to the חרם. As I. J. Gelb noted, it was standard procedure in many societies on a low-grade economic level to execute prisoners, especially the most uncontrollable ones, the young males (soldiers).[17] Not every ritual slaughter of POWs, as this example indicates, is to be put in the same category as the חרם.

Some have also compared the חרם with the account of the 5th century A.D. Christian writer Orosius (*History* v. 16,5):

> The enemy seemed driven by some strange and unusual animus. They completely destroyed everything they captured, clothing was cut to pieces and strewn about, gold and silver thrown into the river, the breastplates of men were hacked to pieces...the horses themselves were drowned in whirlpools and men...were hanged from trees. Thus the conqueror realized no booty, while the conquered obtained no mercy.[18]

This example, stemming also from a Germanic milieu, was capably analyzed by F. M. Abel as reflecting a real fear of the conquerors for the "objects of defeat."[19] Yet while some peoples may have been afflicted with this fear and so driven to destroy the booty, this was not the motivation of the חרם. There are, firstly, the many places in the Bible and the ancient Near Eastern sources where the taking of booty is the object of the exercise and a matter not of fear but of great joy. Then there is the fact that even when חרם had been declared in all its gravity, we have the stories which show how the attraction of the spoil for Israel remained great--the stories of Achan (Joshua 7) and of Saul (1 Samuel 15). In Israel (and Moab) the חרם was a special act of dedication and never the norm. Hence, the Orosius account, while again worth studying on its own merit, diverges sharply from anything we may reasonably term חרם.

It should be clear from the above that only some of the parallels previously adduced hold water or shed light on the Israelite-Moabite practice

---

[17] I. J. Gelb, "Prisoners of War in Early Mesopotamia," *JNES* 32 (1973), 71-2.
[18] Translation provided by N. Lohfink in "Ḥaram," *TDOT* V, 191.
[19] F. M. Abel, "L'anathème de Jericho et la maison de Rahab," *RB* 57 (1950), 323.

said and done it provides only a limited model from which to understand the war-חרם. Within its limitations, which are easily discernable, it is important. The only other parallels drawn from the ancient Near East--the Arab ones--have received short shrift here. The parallels from the Greco-Roman writers are mixed; it is hard to understand why some of them, such as that of Orosius just cited, should have interested biblical scholars at all in connection with חרם. Others, such as Livy's account discussed above, are valid parallels or partial parallels. Yet few conclusions have been drawn from them. We can only say that they enhance the historical plausibility of the biblical accounts which picture the חרם as an actuality of Israel's warfare. This, if paid attention to, should help counter those who would prefer to see the חרם as unreal, viewing it as a practice too horrible to contemplate. The other conclusion we have drawn is that those parallels drawn from the polytheistic world help place the origin of the חרם, not in a peculiarity of Israel's (which may have later spread to Moab), but in a pagan world view which was adapted or inherited by Israel, along with so much else, and adjusted to Israel's peculiar religion.

APPENDIX: A PROPOSED ARCHEOLOGICAL PARALLEL

According to the eminent archeologist, E. Stern, there is no purely archeological evidence bearing on the subject of the חרם, or any reason to expect to find such evidence in the future, given the nature of the phenomenon[20] His point is that written testimony is all that can differentiate between the חרם and a more ordinary destruction. However, there is a Palestinian find which has been so interpreted. The find is described as follows:

> In a pit on the plain west of Tell al-'Ajjul, (Sir Flinders) Petrie discovered an im mense quantity of black ash, the remains of burnt garments. Amid this ash was goldwork which had obviously been most carefully destroyed. Bracelets had been cut into scraps, and the terminals, in the shapes of serpents' heads...had been severed. (...) Found together with the gold were two basalt tripod stands which had been smashed on the spot.... Many horses' teeth and chips of bone were also found. There must have been a complete destruction of property, gold and silver, at the spot.[21]

The authors go on to cite Petrie's dating of the find to the beginning of the 2nd millennium B.C., and evaluate it as a "remarkable Canaanite example illustrating the biblical ordinance of the חרם (doom)--the punishment of complete destruction."[22]

---

[20] Oral communication.
[21] W. G. Dever & S. M. Paul, *Biblical Archeology* (New York, 1974), 202.
[22] Ibid. 203.

ple illustrating the biblical ordinance of the חרם (doom)--the punishment of complete destruction."[22]

The find is indeed a remarkable one. If this definition of חרם were complete, the find might indeed "illustrate the biblical ordinance." Yet without epigraphic evidence, we can not know if the element of "consecration to destruction," which is essential to the חרם, was present or not. Also, Josh 6:19 allows for precious objects to be placed in the "treasury of YHWH" rather than be destroyed, as does the MI. Even if this verse from Joshua is an addition, it must have been a plausible addition. Another consideration is that this find seems to be close--in spirit if not in precise detail--to the account of the Christian writer Orosius mentioned above, where the warriors were seized with a frenzy of destruction (a different mode of operation from the pre-planned deliberation of the חרם). If F. M. Abel was correct, this stemmed from a fear of the objects associated with the enemy, quite a different motivation from that of the חרם.[23] The chances of this find being an actual illustration of the חרם, then, are slim. It does illustrate the fact that unusual acts of destruction on the scale of the חרם were not strange to the inhabitants of Canaan, at least at the beginning of the 2nd millennium. Nothing in the Bible or MI matches this kind of systematic and all-encompassing destruction. Even in the case of 1 Samuel 15, the prophet's instructions only dealt with living things, and these instructions were not adhered to. It is doubtful that the impulse behind this more complete and careful destruction of everything including material objects was that of the חרם. The remains may be better explained according to Abel's theory, or some third explanation.

---

[22] Ibid. 203.

[23] F. M. Abel, "L'anathème de Jericho," 323.

CHAPTER 4

NEW PARALLELS

I: A MARI LETTER

In this chapter, we offer new parallels from the ancient Near East, starting with Mari.[1] The best-known attempt to seek a Mari parallel to the biblical חרם is that of A. Malamat (see above), who adduced the Mari usage of the Akkadian idiom, *asakkam akālu*.[2] We have pointed to the fact that the Akkadian expression is never the functional equivalent of the hiphil usage common to Hebrew and Moabite. For that we shall direct our footsteps towards a Mari letter, published by G. Dossin and A. Finet as *ARM* X 8 (in the volume of women's letters). Although the letter is well known (translated in *ANET* 630), it has not been adduced in this connection, but I hope to show that the comparison is warranted.

The letter is by Shibtu, a wife of Mari's last king, Zimri-Lim. The transliteration we use here is that of W. L. Moran in *Biblica* 50 (p.31):

> [1]a-na be-lí-ia [2]qí-bí-ma [3]um-ma ^{mi}Ši-ib-tu [4]GEMÉ–ka-a-ma [5]i-na É Annu-ni-tim ša li-ib-bi a-lim [6]^{m} ^{mi}A-ḫa-tum SAL·TUR ^{d}Da-gan-ma-lik [7]imma-ḫi-ma ki-a-am iq-bi [8]um-ma-mi Zi-im-ri-Li-im [9]ù šum-ma at-ta mi-ša-ta-an-ni [10]a-na-ku e-li-ka [11]a-ḫa-ab-bu-ub [12]na-ak-ri-ka [13]a-na qa-ti-ka [14]ú-ma-al-la [15]ù LÚ·MEŠ Šar-ra-ki-ia [16]a-ṣa-ab-ba-at-ma [17]a-na ka-ra-aš ^{d}NIN-É-GAL-lim [18]a-ka-am-mi-is-sú-nu-ti [19]i-na ša-ni-i-im u_4-mi-im [20]^{m}A-ḫu-um ^{lu}SANGA ṭe-ma-am [21]an-né-e-am šar-ta-am [22]ù sí-is-sí-ik-tam [23]ub-la-am-ma a-na be-lí-ia [24]aš-pu-ra-am sar-ta-am [25]ù sí-is-sí-ik-tam [26]ak-nu-ka-am-ma [27]a-na ṣe-er be-li-ia [28]uš-ta-bi-lam

This translates as follows:

> To my lord, speak! Thus Shibtu, your servant: in the temple of Annunitum, which is in he heart of the city, Aḫatum, the young girl of Dagan-malik went into a trance. Thus she spoke, saying, "O Zimri-Lim, even if you scorn me, I will love you. I will put your enemies into your hand; I will seize the men of Sharrakiya and collect them for the annihilation of Bēlet-ekallim." On the following day, Aḫum the priest brought this information, hair (of Aḫatum) and the hem (of her garment). I have written to my lord; I have sealed the hair and hem and had them delivered to my lord.

The sentence beginning in 1.12, "I shall put your enemies into your hand," has been identified as 'holy war' language. This is not surprising, as G. von Rad, whose seminal work *Der Heilige Krieg* has affected the study of the subject ever since, took the equivalent Hebrew sentence for what was

---

[1] Cf. the statement of S.-M. Kang, *Divine War in the Old Testament and in the Ancient Near East, BZAW* 177 (Berlin, 1989), 81, "The idea of ban is not attested in the ancient Near Eastern context except in the Moabite stone and in the Bible."

[2] A. Malamat, "The Ban in Mari and the Bible," in *Biblical Essays 1966 OuTWP* (Stellenbosch, 1966), 40-9.

almost his point of departure.[3] This first sentence then, furnishes a holy war context for what follows, and so does the fact that the whole series of statements emanated, according to Shibtu, indirectly from God via the prophet.

The statement that brings us directly to the core of the matter occurs in ll.15-18: "I will seize the men of Sharrakiya, and collect them to the annihilation of Bēlet-ekallim."[4] In the ᵈIdi-Sin inscription, the destroyed city was dedicated first to a group of three gods, and then some form of cult observance to each individual god (of the three) was described in its three versions (dedication of a cult table or a throne). In the published version, the spotlighted deity was the goddess of war, Ishtar. Here it is interesting to note that Belet-ekallim, (written NIN-É-GAL-lim) is the same as the goddess Nin-egal, who, according to Jacobsen, is less a goddess than an epithet of the goddess of war Inanna (=Ishtar).[5] That may have been true elsewhere, but Bēlet-ekallim had her own temple at Mari.[6] Dossin refers to her as one of the great oracular gods; Dagan, Annunitum, and Itur-Mer were others.[7] Moran believes that she protected the dynasty of Mari, a role Nin-egal apparently played in the Syrian town of Qatna.[8]

E. Noort follows Moran in seeing Bēlet-ekallim as the only war goddess at Mari, and he cites *ARM* X 4:32, where she is on the march.[9] We may add to this citation our letter, and *ARM* X 50, where an ominous dream disappearance of Bēlet-ekallim is interpreted as a reason for Zimri-lim to refrain from campaigning. Thus, whatever her other traits, Bēlet-ekallim was definitely a war goddess at Mari.

The prophet's mode of expression as reported in ll:15-18 is significant; for she did not have to put it in quite that way. If, by way of comparison, we turn to the (Old Akkadian) inscriptions of Rimush, son of Sargon (2278-2270), we find a number of short, fairly stereotyped descriptions of his victories. The salient portion of one should suffice. The lines come from Rs. b 1. Col. 3=17, ll.17-30, published by H. Hirsch:[10]

> [17]5700 [18]eṭlutim (GURUŠ.GURUŠ) [19]in âli (URU.KI URU.KI) [20]šu-me-ri-im [21]u-šu-z(i-a)m-ma [22]a-na [23]ga-ra-si-im [24]iš-KUM(=kùn) [25]ù [26]âli(URU.KI

---

[3] J. G. Heintz noticed this language in "Oracles prophétiques et 'guerre sainte' selon les archives royales de Mari et l'AT," *SVT* 17 (1969), 120ff., G. von Rad, *Der Heilige Krieg im alten Israel* (Zurich, 1951), 7ff..

[4] On *karašû* see *CAD* K 214. Cf. I. J. Gelb "Prisoners of War in Early Mesopotamia," *JNES* 32 (1973), 73-4.

[5] T. Jacobsen, *Treasures of Darkness: A History of Mesopotamian Religion* (New Haven, 1976), 37, 140

[6] G. Dossin, *ARM* X:50.

[7] Idem "Sur la prophétisme à Mari," in idem. ed., *La Divination en Mesopotamie ancienne et dans les regions voisines* (Paris, 1966), 86.

[8] W. L. Moran, *ANET*, 630 n. 82, M. Hörig, *Dea Syria: Studien zur religiösen Tradition der Fruchtbarkeitsgöttin in Vorderasien, AOAT* 31 (1979), 186.

[9] E. Noort, *Untersuchungen zum Gottesbescheid in Mari: Die 'Mariprophete' in der alttestamentlichen Forschung, AOAT* 29 (1977), 55.

[10] H. Hirsch "Die Inschriften der Könige von Agade," *AfO* 20 (1963), 53.

URU.KI)-su-nu [2] [7]in'ar(SAG.GIŠ.RA) [28]ù [29]dûri̅(BAD.BAD)-šu-nu [30]I.GUL.GUL

This reads as follows:

> 5700 men out of the cities of Sumer he caused to leave, and gave them to (lit. placed them for) annihilation; and their cities he conquered and their walls he destroyed.

In this text the physical side of חרם is present, though the devotion of the city and/or its inhabitants is lacking. This does not mean that Rimush was not pursuing a holy war. Elsewhere in the text (Rs. Col. 4) he mentions erecting a statue and dedicating it to Enlil. It was the statue he dedicated to the god, not the city. This reminds us of the ^{d}Idi-Sin inscription. There the victors dedicated cult tables to the war deities and a throne to Nishba, the personal god, after dedicating the enemy city to the gods. This illustrates the narrow dividing line between חרם and massacre under the aegis of the gods.

The important point here, however, is to contrast the usage of *karašû* in the inscription of Rimush with the usage in the Mari letter transliterated above. In the Rimush text, the formula *ana garašîm iškun,* which recurs with each account of a battle, never ends the way the Mari letter does, with *karašû* in construct with the name of a war deity. This is a significant distinction, for the Rimush text presents us with a situation, one aspect of which is not far removed from the events portrayed in the MI, where there was a mass slaughter as well. The missing link to the חרם--the view of the slaughter as a consecration to or through destruction, is supplied by the insertion of Bēlet-ekallim, the war goddess. If a concrete word to mean "dedicate, devote, proscribe," specifying that the enemy has been consigned to a wholly other realm (i.e. that of חרם), is lacking in the Mari letter, this merely shows that the parallel is imperfect. However, the idea of separation which is basic to the root חרם is found in the Akkadian expression used here, although *karašû* per se lacks the idea of the sacred. Yet that element is supplied by the DN. The idea of something very close to the חרם seems implied by the phrase *karaš Bēlet-ekallim*, which as we have seen, is a usage that need not have occurred.

The practice of taking the seer's hair and the fringe of his garment and sending them to the object of the prophecy (in this case Zimri-Lim), makes an interesting sequel to the prophecy. Commentators to date seem content with rather matter-of-fact explanations to the phenomenon, but it is hard to imagine in this context that there is no magical element. The *CAD* suggests as much (s. v. *sissiktum*). There are indications of the magical significance of hair in biblical Israel (Num 6:5-7, Jud 16:17, Deut 21:12, and so on). The items sent under seal were not only used as a means of identification, as Moran states (*ANET* 623 n.10) but probably also to assure the king that, possessing these personal objects he had the magical means to check the power of the *muḫḫu* ecstatic. In short, it was also a security matter or a matter of insurance.[11]

We do not know the motives for calling for the destruction of this obscure city. In the context of this letter (and *ARM* X 81) one can only conjecture that Sharrakiya had encroached on Mari or on territory which Zimri-Lim could regard as traditionally within its sphere of influence (within his world order), in order to merit the closest approach the Mari texts have to the war חרם.

II: THE UTUḪEGAL INSCRIPTION

The text of the inscription is known to us only through copies. The question as to whether the copies accurately reflect a historical inscription has been debated, but in the main, scholars agree that the contents are authentic.[12] The inscription has been published many times, most recently in *Or* 54 (1985) by W. H. P. Römer, the title of whose article describes it as a *Siegesinschrift.* Even if it were a purely literary invention, it would still be of interest to us, just as the Jericho story is indispensable to study of the חרם in its present (literary) form. The relevance of this inscription to the חרם may be established on the basis of its contents.

The basic historical situation described by the Utuḫegal Inscription, henceforth UI, resembles that of the Mesha stone. The king of a subjugated territory, here Utuḫegal of Unug (=Uruk), describes the events that led up to the defeat of an occupier (Guti). The Utuḫegal era was, of course, much earlier than Mesha's time-- it goes back to around 2110 B.C.--and the text is not Semitic but Sumerian. Nonetheless, the UI illustrates certain typological features which show up as important aspects of the later חרם.

The first item which is interesting for the study of חרם is the command of Enlil to destroy the name of Gutium. This is a formula not much different from that of the instructions in the Torah with regard to Amalek, which has a חרם tradition associated with it (1 Samuel 15). The association of the biblical injunctions regarding Amalek, i.e. to wipe out the name not "memory" which makes nonsense of the idiom) of it (Exod 17:14, Deut 25:19) with the חרם becomes more meaningful in the light of this text. The UI, as it were, acts as an ancient precedent to the biblical texts dealing with Amalek. Given the perceptions of the enemy expressed similarly in the UI and the Torah, severe measures had to be taken. Utuḫegal's actions were on a par with the חרם in severity. It is also significant that Enlil's command

---

[11] Cf. *ARM* X 7 8 50 81 (E.T. *ANET* 630ff.). All involve conflict or something ominous involving the king.

[12] See the positive study of H. Sauren, "Der Feldzug Utuḫengals von Uruk gegen Tirigan und das Siedlungsgebiet der Gutäer," *RA* 61 (1967), 75-9. See discussion with citations in W. H. Ph. Römer, "Zur Siegesinschrift des Königs Utuḫegal von Unug (c. 2116-2110 v. Chr)." Or N.S. 54 (1985) 274f.. Also, A. L. Oppenheim, *Ancient Mesopotamia: Portrait of a Dead Civilization* (Rev. ed. E. Reiner, Chicago, 1977), 155, 417, lends his support.

mentioned the name of the people as a whole, as in the Bible, and not an individual king. For the language is that of treaty curses and could have been used against the person of the king.

The UI and the MI both reflect bitter revolt against a foreign occupation, while the use of the formula "to erase the name of," in the MT (reflecting the cuneiform world, since the language goes back to curse formulae and to erasure of a clay tablet) also is a reaction to foreign oppression. Gutium is also known as "the snake and the scorpion of the mountain who lifted his arms against the gods."[13] Remember that in 1 Sam 30:26, David called the Amalekites the "enemies of YHWH." This degree of chaos in the life of a people is the precondition for חרם.

Utuḫegal's commission to fight the Gutians came from Enlil, "Lord Wind," who raised up kings and elevated generals above the ranks. In addition, his role as the power behind the fearsome storm made Enlil, in common with other storm gods such as Adad, a perfect embodiment of that unnatural tempest, war. Utuḫegal went on to seek the assistance also of Inanna, addressing her (A I 27) as "lioness of battle." Then he sought the aid of Ishkur, another storm god, and lastly, of Utu, the sun god. This last may have been merely to assure that justice would be done (although it is hardly surprising to see a man of the name 'Utuḫegal' invoking the aid of the sun god Utu). However, the characterization of Gutium as a snake and a scorpion, images of chaos, symbolizes Gutium's dangerous role as a force against the world order, as does the image of the raised arm against the gods. Utu was especially involved in maintaining order, like Re in Egypt.

The UI says little about the actual battle, and not all of that can be read with certainty. According to one of the translations--by E. Sollberger and J.-R. Kupper, "Utu-ḫegal, l'homme fort, fut vainqueur (et) 'fit prisonniers' ses généraux."[14] The rest of the tablet is mainly devoted to the description of the undoing of Tirigan, king of Gutium. From this we see that the UI is not in fact identical to the חרם. It describes, however, a similar type of phenomenon. The fact that only 'generals' were taken indicates a great amount of carnage. The king himself fled to Dubrum, alone and unaccompanied, which also indicates the magnitude of his defeat. The inhabitants of Dubrum wisely gave Tirigan up. It looks like Utuḫegal, after the ceremonial laying-on of his foot on the neck of the enemy king, disposed of Tirigan, as in Josh 10:23-27.[15] The destruction of the Guti people is symbolized in the UI by the subjection of Tirigan. Finally, although the text does not appear to offer us a verbal (Sumerian) equivalent to the *uqaddiš* of the ^{d}Idi-Sin or the חרם in biblical Hebrew, the pietistic element is similar in character to that of the ^{d}Idi-Sin inscription. When we take all the elements common to the UI and

---

[13] S. N. Kramer, *The Sumerians: Their History, Culture, and Character* (Chicago, 1963), 325.

[14] E. Sollberger and J.-R. Kupper, *Inscriptions royales sumériennes et akkadiennes* (Paris, 1971), 131.

[15] Prof. William W. Hallo informs me, however, that another source (an omen) gives a different version.

previously mentioned texts, we conclude that although the parallel is again imperfect, it comes intriguingly close to the חרם.

Whatever the fate of the king of Gutium, it is unlikely that the other prisoners lived long.. Of course, even in the most paradigmatic application of the biblical חרם, Joshua 6, it was possible to exempt those who deserved it (Rahab and her kin). Here it seems unlikely that there would be any reason to allow the prisoners to live. They were an ambassador and two officers, none of whom are said to have rendered special service to Utuḫegal. The impression that the UI conveys is that Utuḫegal gave no quarter. The notion of consecration is implicit. By destroying those the gods hate, one makes the world a holier place.

Three important items are found in a similar form in the UI and in the Bible: a) the divine proscription for erasing the name of the enemy b) the harsh measures taken c) the enemy is characterized as an enemy of the god(s). In addition, both Tirigan of Guti (at least following the scenario envisaged by this text) and Agag of Amalek died "before god."

The appearance of the god of justice, ^{d}Utu, occasions a last word. It is frequently the case that a people or polity should attribute a moral character to its war(s). ^{d}Utu is not only a judge, but in the UI he is entreated to assume an active role in assuring justice for the people of the Uruk area. This moral component appears also in the MI. In the, UI, too, the moral order is restored through intervention of war gods and the god of justice, ^{d}Utu. The UI affords scope for a very rich and significant comparison to the biblical and Moabite חרם.

III: HITTITE

In his able summary treatment, N. Lohfink adduces a number of the standard parallels to the חרם. At one point he says, "in order to find more precise parallels to the OT חרם we must go beyond the geographical and chronological boundaries of the ancient Near East...."[16] We have tried to find new parallels from the ancient Near East. Of course, the Hittites' have been investigated by those seeking parallels to the חרם. Lohfink did not treat the Hittite evidence, possibly because of C. H. W. Brekelmans negative judgement of it.[17] But while he is correct in drawing distinctions, the Hittite evidence appears to offer good material for comparison with the Bible. In fact, the Hittites--at any rate of the Old Empire--did follow a practice similar in many ways to the חרם. As A. Goetze put it:

> Sometimes selected conquered territory was emptied of all its inhabitants and consecrated to the gods. It was, e.g., dedicated as pasture to the bulls drawing the Storm God's chariot. A solemn curse was inflicted upon anybody who resettled such towns and thereby withdrew them from the god's use. Also, it might have

[16] N. Lohfink, "Ḥaram," *TDOT* 5 190-1,

[17] C. H. W. Brekelmans, *De ḥerem in het Oude Testament* (Nijmegen, 1959), 128-34, esp. 133f..

been sown with salt in a symbolic ceremony. It is a curious fact that Hattusa itself had been subjected to such treatment by Anittas of Kussar; nevertheless it had been rebuilt and in fact became the capital of a prosperous empire.[18]

In addition, the Hittites shared with many ancient peoples the tendency to ascribe military victory to the intervention of the gods. In the Hittite texts the most important god to whom warlike activities are attributed appears in cuneiform script as ^{d}IŠKUR, and is known in the literature simply as the storm or weather god. The role the god(s) played resulted in the practice of placing "precious things or statues of the gods of defeated towns...in the temples of the gods at home (cf. Mesha placing the furnishings of the YHWH shrine before Kemosh)"[18] These comments of Goetze show that the Hittites did engage in practices rather like those of the war-חרם; it would be foolish to expect actual identity.

One of the best texts for comparative purposes is that of the annals of Hattusili I, known from a colophon as "the manly deeds of Hattusili." The major points of interest are summed up by H. A. Hoffner:

> The cities of recalcitrant foes could expect only the direst of fates. The city would be burned (§ 19) with the smoke ascending to the storm god, and/or the entire terrain surrounding the city, where crops would normally be cultivated, would be sown with salt and/or cress (Akkad. *saḫlu*).
>
> The king as pious servant of the gods is depicted as dedicating the more impressive items of booty to the temples of the state deities (so §§ 2-3, 6-7, 12-13, 17-18), who in this text are the sun goddess of Arinna, the storm god of heaven, and the goddess Mezzulla.
>
> Common in later annals are the deportees (Sum. NAM. RA. Hitt. *arnuwalas)* which the Hittite king carries back to Hattusa. They are conspicuously lacking in texts from this early date. Also missing from this text, but found commonly in later ones, is the permanent subjection of foes, the imposition of regular tribute, and troop levies.[19]

The "manly deeds" of Hattusilis I, as described above, along with the Anittas text mentioned by Goetze, constitute the basis from which to compare Hittite practice with the חרם. As Hoffner indicated in his last paragraph above, major changes occurred over the course of time. The later annals of Suppiluliumas, for example, lack material for comparison. This is unsurprising, not because of the 'primitive' character of the חרם--the Assyrians, for instance, were utilizing barbaric techniques in warfare much later in the day--but because such customs, as with the Romans and Hebrews, tend to fade out as time passes and circumstances change. As an extraordinary practice among the Hittites, too, it was the easier to abandon. One generation sowed

[18] A. Goetze, "Warfare in Asia Minor," *Iraq* 25 (1963), 129.

[19] H. A. Hoffner, Jr., "Histories and Historians of the Ancient Near East: The Hittites," Or N.S. 49 (1980), 298. Hoffner highlights the importance of the Hattusili I Annals and the Anitta text for our purpose also on 292. For the former see H. Otten "Keilschrifttexte," *MDOG* 91 (1958) 73-84. Also see E. Neu, "Der Anitta Text," *StBoT* 18 (1974),1-15.

weeds over Hattusas (the Anitta text), another rebuilt the city which became, of course, a metropolis (cp. Jericho).

Several aspects of Hittite practice in war thus seem to shed light on the biblical practice of חרם. One aspect of the biblical practice is that of consecrating a city to destruction, and leaving it an eternal ruin mound; תל עולם. This aspect is almost identical to the Hittite practice we have just been discussing. The best biblical example is the account given in Josh 8:24-28 of the חרם of Ai. Upon devoting to destruction the inhabitants of Ai in v.26, the Israelites sack the city and burn it. As in the Jericho narrative, this is accompanied by an element of the working of the supernatural, viz. Joshua's symbolic use of a sicklesword. Joshua then makes it into an eternal ruin-heap: וַיְשִׂמֶהָ תֵּל עוֹלָם שְׁמָמָה עַד הַיּוֹם הַזֶּה The vague phrase וַיְשִׂמֶהָ תֵּל עוֹלָם has been too much taken for granted to mean that Joshua accomplished an act of destruction. Actually, in the light of the Hittite texts as well as the MT, which does not assign Joshua as active a role as usual, a different reconstruction should be considered. Ai was already ruined by sword, looting, and fire. Other verses with similar phraseology are Deut 13:17 and Jer 49:2, the relevant parts of which read as follows:

וְשָׂרַפְתָּ בָאֵשׁ אֶת־הָעִיר לַיהוָה אֱלֹהֶיךָ וְהָיְתָה תֵּל עוֹלָם לֹא תִבָּנֶה עוֹד

Deut 13:7: ...You must burn with fire the city...to YHWH your God: it will be a perpetual ruin-mound; it must never be rebuilt.

וְהִשְׁמַעְתִּי אֶל־רַבַּת בְּנֵי־עַמּוֹן תְּרוּעַת מִלְחָמָה
וְהָיְתָה לְתֵל שְׁמָמָה וּבְנֹתֶיהָ בָּאֵשׁ תִּצַּתְנָה

Jer 49:2: ......I will make heard the alarm-signal of war to Rabat-Ammon; it will become a mound of desolation and its daughter-cities shall go up in flames.

The point that immediately calls attention to itself is the fact that both passages, employ the verb הָיְתָה: here, 'becomes.' In both verses it is fire which is the agent which turns a city into a tell, and the city *becomes* a tell. To understand Josh 8:28 as saying that Joshua burnt the city of Ai and Joshua made it into a perpetual ruin-mound, as natural as it may seem, is actually a non sequitur. The flames made the city into a ruin without Joshua's help. Nor could he make it stay that way. Jer 49:2 does not prophecy the eternal damnation of the city, but Deut 13:17 prescribes that fate for the city without specifying how it was to be done. The vague וַיְשִׂמֶהָ of Josh 8:28 may best be understood as "designated," thus reading Josh 8:28 as: "Joshua burnt the Ruin and designated it a perpetual ruin-mound, desolate until today." Contrast this with Josh 6:18: וְשַׂמְתֶּם אֶת־מַחֲנֵה יִשְׂרָאֵל לְחֵרֶם, in which a group of people can achieve an object in "real time." Yet the language is very close in the two verses from Joshua. This closeness, and the obscurity of this practice and the many meanings of the verb שים made it easy for the versions to miss this nuance. By "designation" I mean a symbolic or ritual act such as the Hittites practiced by the sowing of weeds on the tell or by sowing it with salt (like Abimelech, though the root חרם is not used in Jud 9:45--or Deut 29:22).[20] It may be that the practice found in Josh 6:26, namely, cursing the person who would rebuild the burnt city, was all that Joshua contemplated for Ai. Such is the least we could expect in the case of Ai, and perhaps also a procedure such as the strewing of salt; something like this is what is expressed, however obliquely, through וַיְשִׂימֶהָ. Presumably, if this line of thought is correct, the original audience knew which ritual act or acts was or were intended by וַיְשִׂימֶהָ. A ritual to give a tell this special status would set the site apart, for the normal course of action was not to render the enemies' cities sacrosanct, but to prepare, as in Jer 49:2, for a take-over of territory (ירש). In any case, both the early Hittite evidence and the example from Josh 6 of תל עולם occur, understandably, in the teeth of an enemy's obstinate resistance.

To sum up the common elements between the חרם and Hittite practice discussed so far, we have the destruction of a city by fire, the consecration of the land, and the designation of the ruined mound as perpetual. An important element as yet undiscussed is the fate of the inhabitants of the city. This is actually laid out by Hoffner in the paragraphs cited above: "the cities of recalcitrant foes could expect only the direst of fates. The city would be burned...."[21] He further specifies that only in the later period do the texts speak of deportees. In the period of Hattusili I, clearly there was an attempt to massacre the enemy; and since the precious spoils (including gold-plated(?) statues of gods) were dedicated to the "temples of the major state deities,"[20] it becomes clear that the early Hittite practice of war included a special option against a stubborn foe, as opposed to meeting a more tractable or fearful enemy (cf. Deut 20:10-12, which draws an operational distinction on the same basis), and this option bore a remarkable resemblance to one form of the Israelite חרם.

O. R. Gurney takes note of a "unique ceremony" in which devotion of human life to a deity plays a role. The rite was enacted at an unlocated city called Gursamassa, and it consisted of the following:

> The young men are divided into two groups and receive names: the one group they call 'men of Hatti,' the other group 'men of Masa' and the men of Hatti carry weapons of copper, but the men of Masa carry weapons of reed. They fight with each other and the 'men of Hatti' win; and they seize a captive and devote himto the god.[22]

The god in this case is the god of pestilence, Yarris. One cannot make too much of this interesting and deadly 'ceremony,' but it does seem to show the principle of the חרם operating on a small scale, in a battle situation that

---

[20] H. A. Hoffner, Jr., "Histories and Historians," 289.

[21] W. R. Smith in *The Religion of the Semites: The Fundamental Institutions* (repr. New York, 1972) observes that while most see the sowing of salt in terms of infertility of soil, salt may also be a sign of consecration (Ezek 43:24). One might add also Lev 2:13, Num 18:19, 2 Chr 13:5, and Deut 29:22, where *KBL* sees salt "strewn on devoted (gebanntes) land" (528b), as another indication that salt sowing was not foreign to Israelite tradition.

[22] O. R. Gurney, *The Hittites* (Baltimore,1962), 155.

is only partly simulated, since it results in the death of at least one of the participants. It may therefore offer indirect support for the larger thesis of the affinity of the Hittite practice of reducing a city by fire with Israel's. The smoke goes up to the storm god, which reminds one of the pleasure other gods take in the scent of burnt offerings, including the god of Israel. The main point here is that the principle of devotion to a deity was part of the cult of at least one Hittite deity.

We turn now to the problem raised by S. Gevirtz in his article "Jericho and Shechem: A Religio-Literary Aspect of City Destruction," in which he concludes that:

> the interpretation of the salting of a devastated city as a procedure intended to purify the site as a preparatory or concomitant act of consecration remains the most probable hypothesis.[23]

This conclusion does not fit the Assyrian evidence. In reference to Tiglathpileser's scattering of the mineral *ṣ̄ipu*, the *CAD* (Ṣ 205b) observes:

> Instead of *saḫlu*-seeds and *kudimmu,* alone or with salt, the symbolic act signifying the annihilation of the destroyed settlement is described here as performed by scattering over the ruins a mineral called *ṣ̄ipu*.

There is no consecration involved in the Assyrian practice, just as no consecration takes place in biblical practice, except beforehand in the חרם. The key to the Hittite practice may be found in the older version of the Myth of Illuyankas (*ANET* 126a):

> (ii) Thus spoke Ina(ras to Hupasiyas): "Thou shalt (not) open the (window again)!" She (killed him) in the quarrel and the Storm-god sowed *saḫlu* (over the ruins of the house). That man (came to a) griev(ous end).

A. Goetze added to this one very practical annotation, in which he defined *saḫlu* as "a weed commonly found on ruins." For obvious reasons, the commonly found weeds were deemed by the Hittites to be the work of the Storm-god. While the sowing of these weeds may have partaken of *imitatio dei*, there is no reason to attach to it either a meaning of consecration or preparation for it. In the annals of Mursili, he disposes of the city of Timmuḫala, destroying it by fire, and then declares it sacrosanct and not to be rebuilt. It is the city most awkwardly located from his point of view, so the king may have had more incentive to dispose of it for good than with other cities. Gevirtz cites this example,[24] which is close to Jericho and Ai, but, while Mursili made the area sacrosanct, he did not sow *saḫlu* or spread salt, as he should have done according to Gevirtz's hypothesis.

---

[23] S. Gevirtz, "Jericho and Shechem: A Religio-Literary Aspect of City Destruction," *VT* 13 (1963), 62.

[24] Ibid. 59.

Although Hittite culture and religion were radically different from ancient Israel's, another parallel between Hittite and Israelite practice is worth mentioning. We know that soldiers had to maintain a certain ritual purity from some biblical texts. Deut 23:10-17 deals with a nocturnal emission in the war camp, and aims to maintain ritual purity inside the camp. That this law is not merely a theoretical product of a redactor or the unrealized dictat of a lawmaker but reflects reality is assured by the role of ritual purity in 1 Samuel 21. In Deuteronomy 23 the term for purity is the usual one (favored in the priestly legislation) of טהרה; in 1 Samuel 21, David's men are judged fit to eat food that was קדש of the sanctuary, because they withheld themselves from women (1 Sam 21:6-7) for a time. Later in the book, Uriah the Hittite is portrayed as withholding himself from his wife so as to emphasize his readiness to return to the front (2 Sam 11:6-26, esp. vv.8-11). David's invitation to Uriah to go down to his house and wash his feet in 2 Sam 11:8 implied all the things of which Uriah speaks in 2 Sam 21:11--eating, drinking, and "lying with his wife," but Uriah the (Neo?)-Hittite refused to do these things, as his mind was on the other soldiers and on the ark, all encamped in makeshift housing on the field. It seems probable that Uriah had in mind to preserve his ritual purity so that he could make haste to return to war. In any case, in the example from 1 Samuel 21, the concept of ritual purity for warriors is explicit.

The immediate relevance of this is that Hittite soldiers were also required to be ritually clean.[25] Since ideas of purity and danger (taboo) are intimately related,[26] we are probably safe to say that the presence of two such systems in the two cultures is not fortuitous, but the result of a common approach from which the two cultures worked out similar practices, although history, environment and culture then led them on different routes. The creation of a sacrosanct area is a form of purification, which is ipso facto acceptable to the powers above and/or below. When a purified area is respected or left unprofaned, the community's safety is secured. In the case of Hattusa, a later dispensation of which we are ignorant allowed normal habitation again.

Despite differences in outlook between the Hittites and Israelites (expressed, e.g. in the allocation of the ruined tell for pasturage of the Storm-god's bulls), the case of the Hittites sheds light on the חרם and its world view. A range of evidence shows that the Hittite concept of warfare and the place of the gods in it were closer to Israel than one might have thought, at least in the early period of Hittite warfare. The 'war game' involving the devotion of one 'player' shows that the Hittites partook of a "חרם-mentality."

---

[25] A. Goetze, "Warfare," 128-9.

[26] Cf. M. Douglas, *Purity and Danger: An Analysis of Concepts of Pollution and Taboo* (London, 1970).

IV: THE ᵈIDI-SIN INSCRIPTION

We utilized this inscription in connection with the MI (ch. 2). It was published originally in *Sumer* 34 in 1978, by Abdul-Hadi Al-Fouadi, and republished by M. F. Walker in a Yale dissertation.[27] There is therefore no necessity to reproduce the document beyond the immediately relevant material found in the Mesha Inscription chapter.

In his article on Simurrum, W. W. Hallo has gathered many threads together to give something of a picture of Simurrum in the Ur III period.[28] The city or locality, as we noted, has never been definitively located. Speaking of a kingdom whose king took the title "king of Urkiš and Nawar," Hallo narrows the location of Simurrum down considerably: the kingdom's "southeastern half included the cities or districts of Gumarši, Šašrum, Šetirša and Hibilat, all on or near the Lower Zab, and Simurrum at its southernmost end."[29] From the Mesopotamian point of view, then, Simurrum was located on one of the margins, just as Israel was found on a margin on the other end of the Fertile Crescent. Simurrum was conquered repeatedly in the Ur III period,[30] but in the period preceding the inscription, Simurrum asserted itself and become the center of an empire, about which little is known.[31]

The events of the inscription are straightforward. The city of Kulunnum mentioned was a subject city of Simurrum that revolted against its overlord. This differentiates it from the MI and UI, but puts it with the Egyptian text dealt with below. As we know from the ᵈIdi-Sin inscription, the king sent his son to lead the army against Kulunnum, a mission blessed with the approval of the gods. The son's name may be read either as ᵈZabazuna or possibly Anzabazuna, since it would be surprising if the son were accorded divine honors in the father's lifetime, unless there was a coregency.[31] In Babylon, Hammurapi (1792-1750) was the first to stop using the DINGIR-sign with his name; this text dates to the 20th century.[32]

The main interest of the inscription is its similarity to the חרם. It involves, as was noted earlier (ch. 2), the intertwined themes of destruction (*ḫulluqu*) and dedication/consecration to the godhead (*quddušu*). Although neither Al-Fouadi nor Walker adopted this translation, the *CAD* Q 46b rendering, which is one of a number of instances the dictionary adduces, is that of "to dedicate/consecrate." Another way to translate the verb is by 'purification' (a notion discussed briefly in the Hittite context above), which can be an aspect of consecration, although this concept does not adequately express the action here; it is hard to see how "purified to those gods" makes

---

[27] M. F. Walker, *The Tigris Frontier from Sargon to Hammurabi--A Philologic and Historical Synthesis* diss. Yale 1985 (Ann Arbor, 1986).

[28] W. W. Hallo, "Simurrum and the Hurrian Frontier," *RHA* 36 (1978), 71-83.

[29] Ibid. 72.

[30] Ibid. 74, 77-9.

[31] I base this on an oral communication from Dr. D. Frayne; he is naturally not responsible for my emphasis or any errors.

[32] Dr. Frayne on philological grounds dates the ᵈIdi-Sin inscription to the period between Ishme-Dagan (1953-1935) and Bilalama of Eshnunna (c. 1980)

much sense either by itself or in the historical context, especially when the *CAD* has provided a better alternative.

This parallel arises unexpectedly from an obscure corner of the Semitic world, if one may so describe a city which spent many years under Hurrian hegemony or influence--though this inscription is free of any noticeable Hurrian stamp. It is a fine example of a practice typologically similar to the חרם, although the cultural differences in outlook between Simurrum and Israel--such as the ascription of divine honors to the king--are considerable. Nonetheless, it is fair to say that this inscription, if it does not go far to validate W. F. Albright's claim that the חרם "was apparently universal among the early Semites,"[33] gives every ground for belief in the oft repeated conclusion that the origins of the חרם are to be found in the pre-Israelite world and world-view.[34]

V:UGARIT

In the philological chapter, we dealt with a text which J. C. de Moor classified as a fertility incantation from Ugarit which used the root חרם in a way comparable to the usage of the Hebrew Bible. Some remarks on the meaning of this passage are in order, even though the passage does not deal with actual warfare, nor does it prove that the war-חרם ever was practiced at Ugarit. Here again is the revised version of the text:

(1) [ ]xx (2)[ ]	
[ ]	
[r]ḥm. tld (3) [ibr. lbʿl .]	may the Dam(sel) bear (a bull to Baal)
(2) ḫrm. ṯn. ym(4)m.	Devote to destruction in(?) two days,
š[kl. ṯlṯ] ymm. lk.	Annihilate in(?)(three} days. Go,
(5) hrg .'ar[bʿ.] ymm . bṣr.	kill in (fo)ur days....[35]

Our interpretation depends on retaining J. C. de Moor's classification of the text as an incantation. Other treatments, including a new treatment by

---

33 W. F. Albright, *From the Stone Age to Christianity: Monotheism and the Historical Process* (Garden City, N.Y., 2nd ed. 1957), 279-80.

34 Cf. N. K. Gottwald, whose sociological analysis of the Israelite חרם offers a theory of how the חרם was integrated into an Israelite "socio-economic program." *The Tribes of Yahweh: A Sociology of the Religion of Liberated Israel: 1250-1050 B.C.* (Maryknoll, N.Y., 1979), 543-550.

35 The last.word *bṣr* seems to go with the next clause.

A. Caquot and J.-M. de Tarragon, do not; the latter team deems it a hymn.[36] However, hymns are not characterized by series of imperatives aimed at the deity, as in these lines, indicating that the person has a specific need the writer/reader desires the deity to fill. The first line as restored by de Moor and Spronk strengthens this interpretation,[37] for the restored first line fits the incantation genre exactly. It constitutes what Egyptologists call, a "mythical antecedent," a mechanism by which invoking a mythic paradigm enacting a scenario with a desirable outcome is supposed to be reenacted or actualized by the human sufferer resorting to the magic. This incantation technique is found also in Mesopotamia, and doubtless in other cultures. Thus, Anat's fertility is to be a model for human fertility. The bull itself is a symbol of fecundity (cf. the well-known Ugaritic depiction of "Bull El," as the "progenitor of creatures"), so that the child, too, is to be fecund. Then come a series of imperatives addressed to Anat in her capacity as war goddess. The objects of her fearsome attack are not stated, but for now it suffices to say that whomever they were precisely, they doubtless represent all those chaotic forces that oppose childbirth (e.g. demons). Thus the link between Anat, the goddess of love and her seemingly opposite side is made explicit here: Anat the Divine Warrior must exterminate the forces that lead to chaos and nonexistence and help bring the desired result of love, children, into the world. This is brought about by the triple invocation of verbs of destruction, starting with the חרם. Interestingly enough, one reason for beginning with the word *ḫrm* seems to be the word's close resemblance to *rḥm* (cp. in a different genre, MI ll.16-7). In the philological chapter, I pointed to biblical evidence that here the sacral connotation of the word is present, as de Moor thought. The desire to tap into the holy was probably a second reason the writer opened with the verb. The play on *rḥm* may well have had magical value as well, reinforcing the plea of the person using the incantation.

It should be emphasized, however, that this is only the beginning of a longer text, much of which is quite obscure or else damaged.[38] The incantation technique of mythical antecedent is fleshed out and treated at greater length in the remainder of the poem, which, as should be fairly obvious, also contains hymnic elements. A recently published Akkadian fertility incantation features a dialogue between Adad and his sister, just as this Ugaritic text later stresses Anat in relation to El and also to Baal.[39] The essential thing here is that these few lines, assuming the general correctness of the restored text (especially l.2), seem to have direct bearing on the prehistory of the Israelite חרם, giving it an 'ancestor' in the area of Syria-Palestine.

---

[36] A. Caquot and J.-M. de Tarragon, *Textes ougaritiques II: Textes religieux, rituels, correspondance, Litteratures anciennes du Proche-Orient,* 19-27, with bibliography.

[37] J. C. de Moor & K. Spronk, *A Cuneiform Anthology of Religious Texts from Ugarit* (Leiden, 1987), Semitic Study Series 6, 58.

[38] J. C. de Moor, "An Incantation against Infertility (KTU 1.13)," *UF* 12 (1980), 305-10, J. C. de Moor & K. Spronk, *A Cuneiform Anthology*, 58-9.

[39] A. Livingstone, *Court Poetry and Literary Miscellanea, State Archives of Assyria,* III (Helsinki, 1989), 118. There are other points of comparison as well.

VI: EGYPT

In the search for parallels to the חרם, ancient Egypt has not taken pride of place,[40] for although the Egyptians, like other great powers, were quite capable of cruelty on a mass scale (cf. their behavior at Megiddo, *ANET* 234ff.), one would not expect the חרם to be a characteristic of the Egyptian mode of war. The Egyptians enjoyed the most favorable economic conditions in the ancient Near East; Herodotus's famous statement, "Egypt is the gift of the Nile," puts it in a nutshell. Therefore the Egyptians were in a good position, at least in theory, to utilize captive slave labor. As I. J. Gelb pointed out,[41] a society had to have a certain level of economic organization to be able to utilize POWs as slaves. In general, the Egyptians took prisoners, who would become either the slaves of the temple/state or end up in private hands.[42] When prisoners of war were sacrificed to the gods, as was not uncommon, they were brought to Egypt to be sacrificed at a temple by the king, as in the Medinet Habu inscriptions of Rameses III. He sacrificed, among others of his enemies, representatives of the Sea Peoples to Amon-Re.[43] This practice of selective sacrifice differs essentially from the חרם. The reliefs of Pharaoh smiting his enemies with a god watching over him also raise the possibility of an Egyptian parallel. However, in all the Near Eastern cultures we have encountered, the idea of divine intervention in war on behalf of the "good" side is present. The idea of consecration to the god through destruction, which is peculiar to the חרם, leaves no trace in these reliefs.

Three thousand years of ancient Egyptian history cannot be reduced easily to any one mode of behavior. Mr. Paul O'Rourke of the Brooklyn Museum has drawn my attention to a text which has חרם-like traits. It comes from the inscriptions of Osorkon, the governor of Upper Egypt and also the High Priest of Amon-Re. Osorkon, a contemporary of Mesha of Moab, left a long, autobiographical portrait on the walls of the Bubastite Portal at Karnak.[44] The latter half of the ninth century was a fairly chaotic period in

---

[40] C. H. W. Brekelmans, *De ḥerem,*139-40, found no Egyptian parallel.

[41] I. J. Gelb, "Prisoners of War in Early Mesopotamia," *JNES* 32 (1973), 71-2.

[42] A. Bakir, *Slavery in Pharaonic Egypt, Supplement aux annales du service des antiquities de l'Egypte* 18 (1952), 109-113.

[43] For Medinet Habu, see W. F. Edgerton & J. A. Wilson, *Historical Records of Ramesses II: The Texts in Medinet Habu: Vols. I & II Translated with Explanatory Notes, Studies in Ancient Oriental Civilization* 12 (Chicago, 1936). Plate 44 (pp.46-8) is an example of a victory over the Sea Peoples. More generally, see *Lexikon der Ägyptologie*, s.v. "Kriegsgefangene," and, recently, A. R. Schulmann, *Ceremonial Execution and Public Awards: Some Historical and New Kingdom Private Stelae, OBO* 75 (1988).

[44] K. A. Kitchen, *The Third Intermediate Period in Egypt (1100-650 B.C.),* (Warminster, England, 2nd ed. with supplement 1986). On 467, Kitchen dates the reign of Takeloth II (Osorkon's father) to 850-825, and Shoshenq, Takeloth's successor, from 825-773. On 88, n.18 he dates Osorkon's active years from year 11 of Takeloth "right through to Year 39 of Shoshenq III." This makes him a rather younger contemporary of Mesha.

Egyptian history, with no one pharaonic line in uncontested ascendency. It was the middle of Third Intermediate Period, in the days of the 22nd Dynasty.[45] The country was wracked by civil war, and secessionist tendencies were rife. Osorkon's high position was due to the fact that he was the crown prince of King Takeloth II, though he never lived to be king. Early in his career he suppressed a revolt in or around Thebes, Upper Egypt's capital. It is his account of the punishment of the rebels, suffering from lacunae, which is of interest in connection with the חרם:

> 35) Thereupon (the governor of) Upper Egypt said, 'Go and bring to me every (case of) transgression against him and the records of the ancestors. . . . . the Eye of Re. Then the prisoners were brought in to him at (once) like a bundle of pinioned ones(?). Then he struck them down for him causing (them) to be carried like goats the night of the feast of the Evening Sacrifice in which braziers are kindled. . . . . . like braziers (at the feast) of the Going Forth of Sothis (i.e. the New Year). Everyone was burned in the place of his crime . . . . . .Thebes.[46]

Here, as in the cases of Mesha, [d]Idi-Sin and Utuḫegal, we are dealing with a revolt,[47] although like the [d]Idi-Sin text, Osorkon's chronicle deals with a revolt's suppression, not with its success. A major difference is that the revolt here did not involve a foreign power, although in that period it might have involved foreigners. Nevertheless, it was a revolt from within the borders of the land, and so the rebels' activity is labeled a crime. But it was no ordinary crime.

The event portrayed in the above text possesses traits comparable to the practice of חרם. For instance, R. A. Caminos says, "It is obvious that Osorkon himself strikes the blow, and that the prisoners are immolated to Amen-Re."[48] Although this does not take place on the battlefield, the last intelligible line ("Everyone was burned with fire in the place of his crime"), indicates that a connection was preserved at least in theory between the site of the rebellion and the execution. Unlike many biblical instances, we are not dealing here with the consecration to/through destruction of any city, but as a city is not involved in the חרם of 1 Samuel 15, no problem arises from that direction ('revolt' from within is envisaged in Deut 13:13-19). The element of consecration through destruction appears to be present in the immolation to Amon-Re. This impression is strengthened by the heavily religious language, e.g. the sacrifice metaphor and the invoking of two different cult practices.

---

45 B. G. Trigger, et al., *Ancient Egypt: A Social History* (Cambridge, 1983), 235-241. See also, of course, K. A. Kitchen's treatment in *The Third Intermediate Period*.

46 R. Caminos, *The Chronicles of Osorkon, AnOr* 37 (1958), 48. A. Gardiner, *Egypt of the Pharaohs: An Introduction* (Oxford, 1961), 332 says of Caminos that he "has extracted as much of the historical gist as is humanly possible."

47 R. Caminos, *The Chronicles*, 48, titles the text, "Osorkon punishes the rebels." This understanding is strongly defended (against an astronomical interpretation of a phrase) by K. A. Kitchen in *The Third Intermediate Period*, 546-550, and its correctness is not in doubt

48 R. Caminos, *The Chronicles*, 50.

The French scholar J. Yoyotte has helped to explain the background to this text. He first introduces it as a ritualization of capital punishment,[49] and, after a translation of the text, then continues:

> Les adversaires vaincus que le texte stigmatisait plus haut comme des perturbateurs de l'ordre divin et royal sont donc tués "pour" le dieu thébain et brûlés comme on le fait de victimes animales en certaines fêtes.[45]

The imagery of the 'goats of the Evening Sacrifice' draws the comparison to sacrifice while indicating that the writer does not perceive what is going on as a sacrifice. This device is reminiscent of the use in Deut 13:17 of the sacrificial term כליל, 'whole offering,' which is surely used in a metaphorical sense there. More important is that Yoyotte's focus on the "ordre divin et royal" directs us to the whole raison d'être of the חרם as we have understood it; the fight to fashion or to keep a livable order in the face of the forces of chaos, personified by one's enemies. Yoyotte then goes on to make another important point for my argument:

> Le principe d'une justification de l'homicide légal par des considérations mythologiques était d'ailleurs de tradition.[45]

The mythological justification of annihilating one's enemies works by placing them on a nonhuman plane (after all, it is not only permissible but laudable to slay the dragon). Yoyotte pointed out that mythological justifications for killing were traditional. The question then may be asked in this connection: given this kind of *Weltanschauung*, why was this חרם-like practice not 'traditional' in Egypt as it was in Israel? There is no absolute answer to this question. Indeed, it may have been practiced before or since Orsokon's time (mid-Third Intermediate Period), though evidence is lacking. Even given the underlying world view that made such a behavior possible, it took the extraordinary disorder of the circumstances to bring out what was normally latent in Egypt. The Bible portrays the חרם as a means of creating a settled order which could be used against chaos from within or without.

A function of mythology which Yoyotte spells out in the above quotations is this: myth helps justify behavior that would otherwise, in normal circumstances, be 'simply not done'; in this case, by invoking the basic need of the community to maintain the world order against the forces of chaos.

It may be worthwhile to probe a little deeper. D. Lorton's study, "The Treatment of Criminals in Ancient Egypt from the Old Kingdom through the New Kingdom,"[50] gives not a single instance of execution of criminals by fire. Why then did Osorkon choose this mode of executing the malefactors?

---

[49] J. Yoyotte, "Héra d'Héliopolis et le sacrifice humain," in *École pratique des haute études V section--sciences religieuses Annaire: Résumés des conferences et travaux , (1980-1)*, (Paris, 1981), 99.

[50] D. Lorton, "Treatment of Criminals in Ancient Egypt from the Old Kingdom through the New Kingdom," *Journal of the Economic and Social History of the Orient* XX, Part I (1977), 3-64.

For one thing, he wanted to protect himself from the complaints of the dead by placing the onus of his acts onto the goddess Sekhmet (="the Eye of Re"), just as Rameses III sought to distance himself from the death of the plotters against his life.[51] This motive is not found in the same form in Israel, but the חרם was always executed under YHWH's aegis, so that bloodguilt was not in question.

Unfortunately, the phrase "Eye of Re" is isolated from its immediate context. Still, the use of the Eye is significant, especially in view of the simile referring to the New Year festival, called the Going Forth of Sothis. The goddess Sekhmet (still identified with the Eye of Re) played a major role in the effort to maintain order and fight chaos.[52] In particular, she played a large role in the New Year's festival.[53] A good example of this is a magical text translated by J. F. Borghouts entitled "(Book) of the last day of the year."[54] It begins by invoking Sekhmet (others, too, but Sekhmet is mentioned repeatedly, by name and as Eye of Re). It is an attempt to ward off enemies and the plague. Sekhmet is in effect asked to prevent the triumph of chaos over the individual. This expresses the concept that continuation of life depended on the ritual observance of the New Year. In these ceremonies Sekhmet played an instrumental role. One such ceremony, according to P. Germond, was the "rite of conferring the heritage." The New Year was a dangerous transitional time of disequilibrium, and in order to protect the king (who embodied Re), the "litany of the New Year and of Sekhmet" was recited.[55] Also, on New Year's Eve, a mock cosmic battle was enacted, in which chaos in the form of the snake Apophis was defeated. H. Frankfort cites a relevant Egyptian curse:

> It must be remembered that the sun-god Re had been the first ruler of Egypt and that the pharaoh was, to the extent that he ruled, an image of Re. The verse says of the enemies of the king: 'They shall be like the snake Apophis on New Year's morning.' ...Apophis is the hostile darkness which the sun defeats every night.... But why should the enemies be like Apophis on New Year's morning? Because the notions of creation, daily sunrise, and the beginning of the new annual cycle coalesce and culminate in the festivities of the New Year...(which is) conjured up, to intensify the curse.[56]

In my view, the myth of the New Year acted as a model for Osorkon. Like Re, he engaged in combat with the darkness or chaos that threatened him. By putting his enemies to death by fire (Eg. *rkḥ* is used in mythological contexts, e.g. a battle in the underworld)[57] in this ritual and myth-based way,

---

[51] J. Yoyotte, "Héra d'Héliopolis," 98-9. D. Lorton, "Treatment of Criminals," 28-30.
[52] P. Germond, *Sekhmet et la Protection du Monde, Aegyptiaca Helvetica* 9 (1981).
[53] Ibid. 194-212.
[54] J. F. Borghouts, *Ancient Egyptian Magical Texts* (Leiden, 1978), 12-14.
[55] P. Germond, *Sekhmet,* 204.
[56] H. Frankfort in H. Frankfort et al., *Before Philosophy: The Intellectual Adventure of Ancient Man* (Harmondsworth, England, 1949), 33-34.
[57] J. Zandee, *Death as an Enemy According to Ancient Egyptian Conception: Studies in the History of Religion* V (Supplements to *Numen*) (Leiden, 1960), 137.

Osorkon succeeded in reasserting order over chaos. We noted that his use of fire did not fit into established criminal procedure. It fits well with his invocation of the Eye of Re, Sekhmet. She was known as "the devouring flame," and "the Lady of the Flame,"[58] among other things. Osorkon's actions were predicated on something akin to what J. F. Borghouts terms a "mythical antecedent" in magic. According to him, "the earthly 'case' is similarized to a mythical antecedent by way of association, completely...or by way of allusion."[59] A single purpose moved the Egyptian magician and Osorkon; to thwart chaos and make life possible.

The word "crime," shows an Osorkon eager to minimize the danger that he faced (earlier on his mere appearance drew admiring crowds); his actions spoke otherwise. His use of fire shows that he felt impelled to take urgent measures; calling on the Eye of Re he used myth and ritual as a model to follow to protect himself. This analysis coheres, but as the Egyptologist O. Goelet reminded me, caution is in order due to the Eye's lack of context (cf. bottom of 123).

The question arises as to whether there was a specific mythical antecedent connected with the Israelite חרם. Information on this subject is meager, but to a limited extent there was. The stories which gave Israel title to Canaan prior to the Exodus may have played such a role, although they would have applied equally to the other actions associated with conquest. Mythic traditions like the Song of the Sea may have played a broadly similar role, as will appear from the treatment of 1 Samuel 15 below.

While this parallel may not be the closest of the parallels adduced here, it is not as distant as it appears on first sight. The Egyptian religion had its own special character. However, that did not prevent it from being cross-fertilized by Semitic religions e.g. by adopting deities such as Anat, or from influencing other religions, like that of the Phoenicians. Here we are dealing with a small and rarefied area of religion. Whereas previously we spoke of the need to overcome chaos and establish an order sufficient for human beings to flourish in Mesopotamia and elsewhere, in Egypt a rather subtle but similar concept, that of the 'nonexistent' held sway.[60] The 'nonexistent' preceded the creation of the universe but never wholly vanished, and in war the Egyptians fought the forces of the 'nonexistent,' to which they also consigned their enemies, e.g. in Merneptah's words about Israel "his seed is not."[61] Such a concept of a pervading negative force--if that is an adequate way to epitomize it--is not to be simplistically equated with the notions of chaos found in other places in the ancient Near East or in the ancient world in general. Yet it may have functioned in the same way in this instance of

[58] P. Germond, *Sekhmet,* 122,208.
[59] J. F. Borghouts, *Ancient Egyptian Magical Texts,* ix.
[60] E. Hornung, *Conceptions of God in Ancient Egypt: The One and the Many* (Ithaca, N.Y., 1982), 172-184. Also, B. J. Kemp, "Imperialism and Empire in New Kingdom Egypt (c.1575-1087 B.C.)," in P. D. A. Garnsey & C. R. Whittaker, *Imperialism in the Ancient World* (Cambridge, 1978), 8.
[61] J. A. Wilson, *ANET*, 378a

Osorkon's revolt. The ideology of fighting chaos formed a part of the early *Weltanschauung* from which acts like the חרם could be derived, in ancient Egypt (cf. the Execration texts)[62] and Israel. Another point in favor of drawing on this text is its emphasis on the use of fire. As we have seen, in the first chapter and in this, there is a frequent association of fire with the root חרם in usages linked one way or another to the חרם Also, the coincidence that Osorkon was a younger contemporary of Mesha adds to this text's appeal. The most significant point to bear in mind, though, is that this Egyptian parallel stems from a mythologizing order/chaos *Weltanschauung* similar to that of Israel, which appears to be the conceptual underpinning to the חרם.

In the light of this parallel, it is fair to ask why did not mainstream cultures of Mesopotamia, especially that of Assyria, practice something like the חרם, given the ideas held in common about chaos and holy war? Such questions are ultimately unanswerable. Human behavior is a riddle, and the behavior of societies in antiquity is not easy to fathom, much less the absence of a given behavior. The words of H. W. F. Saggs, not intended, naturally, for this particular context, do supply part if not all of the answer:

> Thus, although there is no static difference of basic principle between Mesopotamian and Israelite religion, there can be seen a dynamic difference in the way in which religious concepts could develop. The difference was that whilst the traditions of Mesopotamian society tended to permit an accretion of religious concepts, even though logically non-compatible, Israelite society was, because of the forces which had moulded it, much readier to reject, and, because of the pressures upon Israel threatening her very existence in her early stages, Israelite society was, both for good and for bad, basically less tolerant than Mesopotamian.[63]

Saggs has shed light on the absence in Assyro-Babylonian culture of a חרם, despite a view of chaos close to Israel's. This distinction, that Mesopotamian (and Egyptian) polytheism was less exclusive, more 'accretive,' than Israel's religion, is obvious, but this 'intolerance' was apparently true as well of Moabite royal religion, as we have seen (ch.2). Saggs's observations buttress the position that the connection between the חרם and Israelite anti-iconicism (iconoclasm) is primary, not secondary.

The survey of previously proposed parallels to the חרם showed that because of the tendency to identify the חרם with destruction pure and simple, or other mistaken identifications with the חרם, many of them should not be used in discussions of חרם (e.g. OSA *hrg*). The most interesting, that of *asakku*, is of restricted application. It was my aim to make up for the paucity of parallels from the ancient Near East with new proposals, such as the

---

[62] For more on the Egyptian view of war, cf. the references given in n.59. The Execration Texts witness to this mentality, especially the smashed or burnt figurines of enemies (foreign and domestic). However, since they rely on curse (and sympathetic magic), not deed, they are only tangentially related to the object of this study.

[63] H. W. F. Saggs, *The Encounters with the Divine in Mesopotamia and Israel* (London, 1978), 185.

Egyptian text just discussed. The Hittite is exceptional, in that I have tried to make a case for a parallel which Brekelmans in his monograph on the חרם strongly rejected.[64] None of the parallels are perfect, not even the MI, for no two cultures can be expected to produce facsimile copies of such complex behavior. Even if one (or more) of the parallels just proposed is unsound, we have seen that the ancient Near East is the best area to look for new parallels to the חרם, and that the last word on ancient Near Eastern parallels is still unsaid.

The aim here was not to prove truisms like "extreme situations call for extreme measures," although this certainly was a factor in the incidence of חרם. I have tried to show that a specific cast of mind that was responsible for the חרם was also present at varying times and places elsewhere in the ancient Near East. Given the right circumstances, practices parallel to the חרם did in fact occur. Since the mentality involved (as well as most of the examples) was already ancient when Israel appeared on the map, it is certain that Israel borrowed the חרם from abroad, perhaps directly from Moab, and then adapted it to fit its own peculiar religious needs.

---

[64] C. H. W. Brekelmans, *De ḥerem*, 134. His basic argument is that the Hittite practice lacks strong religious motives, and the actual motives are not those of the חרם (132). I hope that this presentation overcomes these objections. While it is not surprising that a Hittite curse would read very differently from a biblical one, as Brekelmans points out (curses vary greatly according to the individual culture--cf. the Egyptian curse cited by Frankfort, and the Greek curse against violaters of the sacred plain of Cirrha (ch.3)--but they remain curses). But the curse is not a necessary feature of the חרם. The fact that both Hattusa and Jericho were both rebuilt despite the curse is more significant, underscoring at least for the Bible how secondary the curse was in the scheme of the חרם.

CHAPTER 5

THE BOOK OF DEUTERONOMY

I: THE DEUTERONOMIC *ḤEREM* AND THE LISTS OF NATIONS

We begin our survey of the חרם in relationship to the biblical text with the Pentateuch (Torah), naturally enough. Deuteronomy is a good starting point because the book holds the bulk of the Pentateuchal material referring to the חרם. In contrast, Genesis is the only book of the Torah in which the חרם is lacking.

In his commentary on Deuteronomy, S. R. Driver judiciously characterized the lists of peoples to be subjected to expulsion and חרם by the word "rhetorical."[1] Subsequent writers--among them, A. C. Welch, J. van Seters, and G. Schmitt--have come to similar conclusions.[2] These are the lists of Deut. 7:1 and 20:17:

7:1 Hittites, Girgashites, Amorites, Canaanites, Perizzites, Hivites, Jebusites
20:17 Hittites, Amorites, Canaanites, Perizzites, Hivites, Jebusites

The two lists are nearly identical except that the Girgashites have been inserted into the second list, a fairly insignificant peculiarity. Since we have in the case of the Moabite stone an instance of the חרם in the real world, we shall assume here from the start (unlike many) a real connection to that world in these two chapters.

After all, the widely accepted northern provenance of the Book of Deuteronomy and its terminus ad quem in the seventh century, at least for the bulk of it, show that the Mesha stele and Deuteronomy are not far removed either in geographical space or in time. In particular we may cite the fact that Deuteronomy has special affinities with the 8th century prophetic Book of Hosea, as M. Weinfeld and H. L. Ginsberg have pointed out most recently, drawing far-reaching conclusions from it.[3] Thus, it may be that the chapters which mention the חרם are composed with the direct assistance of living traditions from the Northern kingdom, from a time when the North was itself sufficiently strong to apply the חרם. If this is correct, it would imply the relatively early dating of at least one of the two chapters. The problem at hand, then, is to reexamine Deuteronomy 20 and 7 in order to see what light they throw on the חרם. We shall start from the above lists of nations.

---

[1] S. R. Driver, *A Critical and Exegetical Commentary on Deuteronomy, ICC* (Edinburgh, 1895), 97.

[2] A. C. Welch, *Deuteronomy: The Framework of the Code* (Oxford, 1932), 70 and passim, J. van Seters, "The Terms 'Amorite and 'Hittite' in the Old Testament," *VT* 22 (1972), 68, G. Schmitt, *Du sollst keinen Frieden schliessen mit dem Bewohnern des Landes* (Stuttgart, 1970), 8.

[3] M. Weinfeld, *Deuteronomy and the Deuteronomic School* (Oxford, 1972), 366-370, idem "The Deuteronomic Movement" in N. Lohfink, *Das Deuteronomium: Enstehung, Gestalt, und Botschaft, BETL* 68, 76-96, H. L. Ginsberg, *The Israelian Heritage of Judaism* (New York, 1982), 20-24.

As noted above, the six or seven member lists of nations of which we speak have elicited a good deal of skepticism. The overall extremes are represented by G. Mendenhall's approach which takes the lists as being of historical consequence,[4] as against that of M. Liverani, whose evaluation is that the lists "show substantial ignorance of the ethnic and political situation in pre-Israelite Palestine."[5] It seems to me that a certain caution is warranted. Thucydides, for example, mentions a plethora of small, local Greek peoples otherwise lost to history. Most interestingly, as the Egyptologist, O. Goelet, pointed out to me, the Egyptians, too, had a traditional repertoire of enemies, some of whom were invoked long after their departure from the scene.

Liverani's remark could be substantially true and still be beside the point. It remains the case that this concatenation of nations had meaning for Deuteronomic Israel as well as earlier sources such as J and E which utilized the same stock of nations to construct lists. In fact, these same nations appear in some twenty lists scattered from Genesis to Nehemiah (and Chronicles). This has prompted T. Ishida to "assume that independent material such as the lists of nations was transmitted on its own."[6] If the lists were truly a self-subsisting entity, a source independent of the traditional major Pentateuchal strata (JPED), then this might vitiate any attempt to seek any significance from the juxtaposition of the חרם with the 'stereotyped' lists of nations in Deuteronomy 7 and 20.

However, this assumption cannot be maintained. Other scholars who have subjected the lists to scrutiny have demonstrated the need to analyze them in relation to the different strata in which they are embedded, such as F. Langlemet in his two-part study of Exod 34:11-16.[7] It has also been observed that there is a correlation between the order of the lists and the stratum to which they belong. Thus, typical of J is the following order: Canaanites, Hittites, Amorites, Perizzites, Hivites, and Jebusites.[8] Deuteronomy (as may be seen from the lists cited above) goes by a different order, and so do D's lists in the Book of Joshua. Hence, source criticism is actually indispensable.

Ishida's idea is a natural one, however, and it is not surprising to find something similar as early as F. Böhl (1911).[9] His observation was that the lists had more in common than not. Böhl inferred that therefore, the lists derive from a common *Grundform* or source. It is not the former possibility

---

[4] G. Mendenhall, *The Tenth Generation: The Origins of the Biblical Tradition* (Baltimore, 1973), 144-5.

[5] M. Liverani, "The Amorites," *POTT*, 124.

[6] T. Ishida, "The Structure and Historical Implications of the Lists of the Pre-Israelite Nations," *Bib* 60 (1979), 490.

[7] F. Langlamet, "Israel et 'l'habitant du pays' Exode XXXIV 11-16," *RB* 76 (1969), 321-350, 481-507, M. Caloz, "Exode XIII 3-16 et le Deutéronome," *RB* 75 (1968), 5-62.

[8] See F. Langlamet, *Gilgal et les routes de la Traverse du Jourdain, CRB* 11, 196.

[9] F. Böhl, *Kanaanäer und Hebräer* (Leipzig, 1911), 64f..

which we quarrel with, although the matter is more complex than the one German word suggests, but the latter. To back up this deduction he cites the list that appears now in Josh 24:11, as the work of a later interpolator (so too BHK, BHS). In support of this one might add that the order of names in the list is unique, although closest to that of Exod 23:23. However, on further examination, the list appears not to be interpolated, but merely displaced from the following verse. As in Exod 23:28 and Deuteronomy 7:20, the surprising image (or perhaps not so surprising in view of YHWH's weaponry in the ten plagues) of the צרעה should appear to expel the peoples of the land, not the two Amorite kings of Transjordan, whose place is back in Josh 24:8. However, once the displacement occurred, secondary changes followed in its wake, and any attempt at further restoration of the original would be bootless, especially as the LXX reflects MT. Nevertheless, we see that a more conventional source criticism would link the passage with Exod 23:23ff., or with less likelihood to Deuteronomy 7.

It is necessary, then, to investigate the deuteronomic lists in the historical and literary context in which they are found. It is certain that in the Northern Kingdom in the eighth-seventh centuries, the memory if not the practice of חרם was alive and well. Although no account of Mesha's חרם appears in the Bible, this is unsurprising considering the selectivity of the annals contained within it. This resulted in the omission of many important events, such as the Battle of Qarqar (which was undoubtedly treated in the lost annals of the kings of Israel).

In addition, Mesha's version of events was peculiarly ill-suited to the theological tendency of the biblical writers. There can be little doubt, however, that Mesha's obliteration of cities built or fortified by the Omrides and his enslavement and massacre of Gadite populations must have reverberated widely and long both in Israel and in Judah, helping to pave the way for Jehu. The primary effect, consequently, must have been upon the North (although fellow-feeling in Judah should not be discounted). No literary prophet commented on Mesha's חרם. Only in 2 Kings 3 does the Bible give any account of the Moabite king, although this account is flawed and has little to do with the reality of Moabite success (cf. appendix to ch. 2).. Therefore we turn elsewhere for help, to the oracles against the nations of Amos. In Amos 2:1-3, the prophet condemned Moab because it had defeated Edom, a country that Judah had always sought to dominate. In fact, Amos cursed Moab in more detail for turning the bones of the Edomite king into lime than he did Edom for its pitiless warfare against its 'brother' Israel (cp. Am 1:11-12 and 2:1-3). Although objections to the authenticity of the 'Edom' oracle are still raised, S. Paul's literary analysis of how the links between the oracles create an organic whole should eventually settle the matter in favor of the oracle's authenticity.[10] One may add a couple of general

[10] S. Paul, "Amos 1:3-2:3: A Concatenous Literary Pattern," *JBL* 90 (1971), 397-403. V. Fritz, "Die Fremdvölkerspruche des Amos," *VT* 37 (1987), 26-38, dates the oracles after Amos, but cf. B. Gosse, "Le recueil d'oracles contre les nations du livre d'Amos et l''histoire deutéronomique'," *VT* 38 (1988), 22-40.

considerations against jumping to the conclusion that Am 1:11-12 comes from a later pen. In principle, it is hazardous to throw all references to what was obviously a longstanding feud into a single (post-exilic) period without good reason; cf. the material in Genesis, e.g. Genesis 27. An oracle on Edom in Amos's scheme would be mandated, so that some hidden hand would necessarily have deleted a genuine prophecy of Amos; moreover, the terse, telling language fits in perfectly with that of the accepted oracles. If K. Schoville is correct, the Edom oracle preserves an echo of an event from Mesha's day.[11] The Moab oracle itself can be said to refer to the brief period of Moabite power, which began with Mesha's revolt, and hence very possibly to the actions of Mesha himself. Parenthetically, we might compare Israel's rivalries with Edom and Moab to the Anglo-French hatred, which goes back to the Hundred Years War and yet exists, though muted, today. Similarly, the Bible repeatedly traces the enmity of the Moabites to the days of Balaam and Balak (e.g. Josh 24:9-10), when Israel was emerging as a nation.

What then is the historical referent of the Amos Moab oracle? The Moab oracle indicates that Edom, having a king, had some degree of autonomy. I would follow the approach of M. Haran in dating the Amos oracles regarding the neighboring countries and Judah and Israel to the period before the Transjordanian campaigns of the second Jeroboam, early in his reign.[12] This would make the reference to the taking of Moabite towns in Am 6:13 subsequent in history as well as in the text. The Moab oracle reflects the chagrin of a prophet who resented the successful intervention of a rival power in the sphere of influence which Judah had long claimed for its own. The reference to Moab's reducing the king of Edom's bones to lime speaks volumes. Amos refers to a known battle or war. Fire was a potent weapon in the warfare of ancient times (especially in a siege) as well as one of the common Holy War motifs (for the connection with חרם, see ch. 1).[13] Yet this has only secondary significance here. Ordinarily, monarchs did not reduce their 'brother' monarchs to ashes. Ahab was quick to spare his 'brother' Ben Hadad, who had caused him so much despondency (1 Kgs 20:31-34). Nebuchadnezzar spared Jehoiachin after besieging Jerusalem (2 Kgs 24:12). Most significantly, Saul wished to spare Agag of Amalek but in this he violated the חרם (1 Sam 15:19-33). This suggests that Amos, by using this one figure of the burnt king, the representative of the people (cf. 1 Kgs 20:42), may have chosen to focus on a characteristic feature of the חרם, the devotion of the brother monarch to the deity (cf. the disposal of kings in Joshua 10-11,

---

[11] Cf. K. N. Schoville, "A Note on the Oracles of Amos against Gaza, Tyre, and Edom," *SVT* 26 (1974), 61-3, dating the oracles events to 841.

[12] M. Haran, "Amos," *EM*, 273.

[13] J.-G. Heintz, "Le 'Feu Devorant' un symbole du triomphe divin dans l'ancien testament et le milieu semitique ambiant," in *Le Feu dans le proche Orient antique: aspects linguistiques, archéologiques, technologiques, littéraires, Actes du colloque de Strasbourg 9 et 10 juin 1972* (Leiden, 1973), 63-78.

Deuteronomy 2-3, esp. 3:6).[14] This allusion sufficed to inform his listeners, who knew of the event. If, as mentioned above, Mesha was the king of Moab who did the deed to Israel's vassal and ally, Edom, it may be that Amos was referring to the last, southern campaign of Mesha (MI 32:ff). 2 Kgs 3:26 probably reflects with accuracy the enmity between Moab and Edom at the time (especially since of the kings mentioned in 2 Kgs 3, Israel, and Edom are undoubtedly two of the enemy kings of MI 4). Although Mesha did not execute the חרם against Horonaim, he may have done so against another Edomite controlled town, probably one he considered to be in Moab.. Another possibility is that Amos refers to an incident in the period following Mesha. As Aharoni pointed out, the oracles of Isaiah 15-16 and Jeremiah 48 list Moabite cities not mentioned in the MI, indicating further Moabite expansion.[15] In this case, one may assume that at some point--perhaps while Moab was dominated by Israel--Edom, Judah's pawn took advantage of Moab's weakness, perhaps by encroaching on Moabite lands, as it was to do with Judah. Such behavior would have given Moab provocation--as Amalek's injuries of Israel engendered the prophet Samuel's call for the חרם (1 Samuel 15). However, since Moabite expansion was "always directed northwards,"[16] the first hypothesis is preferable. We know for sure, that Mesha, the Moabite Moses, applied the חרם against Israel (an event not mentioned in the Bible), and that he had the wherewithal to do it against Edom. If Aharoni was right that Moabite expansionism was directed solely to the north, than the probabilities favor Mesha and not a successor. Mesha was primarily concerned with his triumph over Israel in the stele and the southern campaign is almost an afterthought.

The event alluded to in Amos may have influenced those involved in the early formulations of Deuteronomy 7 and 20, especially the latter. The chapter lists which nations must undergo the חרם as well as strictly defining the circumstances under which a city of a non-listed nation could suffer its rigor. The nations who might be subject to the חרם were none of them a factor by the 8th century. Whatever the intent, the effect of the laws was to prohibit or discourage a king such as Jeroboam II from retaliating against Moab by using the חרם as the Moabites did in Edom (if my theory is correct), as well as against the Israelites of Transjordan under Mesha. Yet even if this attempt at historical reconstruction based on the Amos oracle on Moab is, like all reconstructions of ancient history, uncertain, the fact remains that the events of the Mesha period most probably influenced the aim of legislation of Deuteronomy 20 with regard to the חרם.

---

[14] B. Lurya, "The Prophecies against the Nations from a Historical Perspective," in *Studies in the Twelve Prophets* (Heb.) ed. B. Lurya (Jerusalem, 1981), 212-3, assumes Amos refers to an ancient practice dealing with dead kings' bones. This runs counter to his citation (Isa 33:12) which refers to the living, and does not account for this peculiar oracle, in which Israel does not appear.

[15] Y. Aharoni, *The Land of the Bible: A Historical Geography* (Phila., 1979), 340.

[16] Ibid. 206.

Only timidity could account for failure to draw the conclusion that Amos was referring to a war between Moab and Edom in Am 2:1-3 (a war otherwise unmentioned in MT). Am 2:.2b indicates that the fire of God shall descend at a time of war, i.e. "Moab shall die in the din (of battle) and in the blowing of the (war) horn (cp. NEB)." Even the next verse, translated by the NJV, "I will wipe out the ruler within her/And slay all her officials along with him--said the Lord," could be translated more in keeping with the martial context. Heb. שופט, used so often to denote a military deliverer in the Book of Judges, probably stands for something similar here (with a touch of irony). Heb. שׂר often has a military connotation, as in the passage where the שַׂר־צְבָא יְהוָה appears to Joshua with a drawn sword (Josh 5:13f.). Thus it seems clear that Am 2:2b-3 speak of Moab's military might and YHWH's dealing with it. To understand these lines differently would only vitiate the prophet's point and do violence to the context.

If the Book of Amos can shed a certain light on Deuteronomy 20's approach to the חרם, it also leads us back to the question of the lists of nations by another route, the intriguing passage of Am 2:9-10, which reads like this:

> 9. And I destroyed (השמדתי) the Amorite before them,
> whose height was as the height of cedars,
> and who was sturdy like oaks.
> I destroyed (אשמיד) his boughs[17] above, his roots below.
> 10. I led you forty years in the wilderness
> to possess (לרשת) the land of the Amorite.

This passage from Amos can best be understood in the framework of the lists of nations, as found in, e.g., Deuteronomy 7:1. Uniformly, writers who have dealt with the 'stereotyped' lists of nations have selected those lists which are most stereotyped, i.e. the six or seven member lists (with few additional lists). Actually, as has generally been ignored, the lists range from one to ten.[18] This is not to deny the existence of conventional lists of traditional enemies (consisting of six or seven nations). This phenomenon has a counterpart in Egyptian conventional terminology for its enemies, such as the ubiquitous "Nine Bows." In Egyptian writings, the enemies continue to be mentioned, long after their departure from the world scene, as is the case in biblical writings. In fact, in the Hittites, the Egyptians and the Israelites share a nation in common in their anachronistic listing of enemies.[19] However, that is not the whole of the story, at least not as we can see from the biblical evidence. The table below shows that to advert to the "stereotyped lists" alone is to see only the narrow picture. Here are some selected citations which do not fit the stereotype:

---

[17] Following NJV.

[18] As in R. North, "The Hivites" *Bib* 54 (1973),43-59. T. Ishida, "Structure and History," &c..

[19] I owe my knowledge of this to Prof. Ogden Goelet.

THE 'SEVEN NATIONS' OUTSIDE THE 'STEREOTYPED' LISTS

A=Amorites G=Girgashites C=Canaanites J=Jebusites P=Perizzites H=Hittites and HV=Hivites.

Gen 10:15-18=1 Chr 1:13-17	C,Sidon,H,J,A,G,HV,Ark-Sin-Arvad-Zemar-and Hamathites
Gen 13:7	C,P
Gen 15:19-21	Kenites, Kenizzites, Kadmonites, H,P, Raphaites, A,C,G,J
Gen. 34:30	C,P
Exod 15:14-16	Philistia, Edom, Moab, 'dwellers in Canaan'
Num 13:29	Amalek, H,J,A,C
Num 14:25,43,45	Amalek, C
Josh 17:13	P, Raphaites
Jud 3:3	Philistines, C, Sidon, HV
2 Sam. 24:6-7	Sidon,Tyre, HV, C
1 Kgs 11:1	Egypt, Moab, Ammon, Edom, Sidon,H
2 Kgs 7:6	Aram, H, Egypt
Ezra 9:1	C,H,P,J, Ammon, Moab, Egypt, A, Sidon, H

This table contains not only lists proper but also groupings of names. Clearly the 'stereotyped' lists of six or seven are not the whole story. Especially intriguing is 2 Sam. 24:6-7, where the reference to the Hivites and the Canaanites comes in the middle of a realistic chapter, which depicts events and places in a manner similar to that of the MI (neglecting David's encounter with the angel later on which is standard ancient Near Eastern fare, too) In any case, the table does provide a good background to Am 2:9-10. These two verses use the term "Amorite" as a poetic summary designation for all the pre-Israelite peoples of the land, just as Gen 13:7 seems to use just the Perizzites and the Canaanites for the same thing. The language Amos applied to the Amorites is--apart from the similies--found also in Deuteronomy and in allied literature (e.g. Jeremiah). For example, Amos uses the term 'Amorite' in a way similar to that of Josh 7:7, which speaks of the inhabitants of Ai as Amorites, who (without YHWH to prevent it) were in a position to put Israel to flight (האביד) and force them take refuge across the Jordan, and perhaps the five Amorite kings Joshua meets up with in Joshua 10. This use of the Amorites goes back to the time of Amos, and he is unlikely to be the inventor of this traditional terminology (it may have had its source in the kingdom of Amurru of the LBA). The threat that the Amorites represented to Israel's establishing its world order--as summarized in Josh 7:7 made them and the city of Ai candidates for the חרם in Josh 8:26.

The roots שמד and ירש are basic to the vocabulary of Deuteronomy. The former root is of interest in itself, however, because it sometimes appears in Deuteronomy with a force slightly different from that of its conventional English equivalent, 'destroy.' This is illustrated by Deut 4:26-27. The language of Deut 4:26 seems to speak of destroying the people as individuals and collectively, but the actual destruction is of the people as an entity subsisting on the land, for the continuation speaks of the Lord scattering the supposedly annihilated people hither and yon (cp. Deut 9:3-4). This is worth stating because it applies also, we believe, to the peoples of the land. The law does not envision wholesale physical annihilation. The major clue to this is found in Deuteronomy 7:1, where the main verb is נשל, here equivalent to גרש, "to expel."[20] The חרם is subordinate to the expulsion, and functions as an aid to expelling, rather than as the uniform practice (see ch. 2). After all, the universal application of the חרם was never credibly demanded or claimed (see below on Joshua). It would neither have been possible nor desirable (given the lust for spoil, and even the fear of the reclaiming of the land by wild beasts!). Thus Deuteronomy 7:2 immediately goes on to forbid treating with the seven peoples, and places a ban on intermarriage. These were steps intended to preserve the threatened national identity. The ban on intermarriage must have only applied to such marriages as Ahab and Jezebel or Samson and Delilah where the bride retained her identity as an alien, and hence as a worshipper of a foreign god (as a ban on marriage with nonexistent peoples it would have been irrelevant). Deut 21:10-14 deals with the case of the captured woman who is inducted into Israel and treated as an Israelite bride. Deut 7:2 reflects the point made above that the חרם was never intended as the sole mode of operation (i.e. genocide), Along with the separation of the חרם, which according to Deut 20:18 was aimed at idol worship, the legislator aimed at separation of Israel from marriages that would lead to idolatry.

The oratory of Amos in 2:9 uses the image of the dwellers of the land as powerful giants; an image Deuteronomy also employs in Deut 9:1-6 with reference to the Rephaim. Although the unity of the Israel oracle in Am 2:6-16 has been the object of suspicion, it seems most probable that J. L. Mays was correct in his defense of the passage.[21] Its affinities with D as mentioned above are at least partly due to their geographical and chronological proximity.

---

[20] M. Greenberg, "Ḥerem" *EJ*, ad. loc., endorsed by J. Milgrom in *Numbers: The Traditional Hebrew Text with the New JPS Translation, JPS Torah Commentary* (Philadelphia, 1990}, 429 derives Deut 20:16-17 from a deuteronomist who melded Exod 22:19, 23:20ff.. Although something like this has occurred, our argument is that it happened early in the writing of D, not in Dtr-istic times. Milgrom observes that the phrase in Deut 20:17 "as the Lord your God has commanded you" indicates the writer's sense of conveying old news. The link with the past (and its repetition) gives the command a timeless quality and authority dear to the religious mind.

[21] *J. L. Mays, Amos: A Commentary, OTL* (Philadelphia, 1969), *ad loc.*

Interestingly enough, in its use of the verb העלה in connection with the Exodus, Am 2:10 resembles, in Deuteronomy, only Deuteronomy 20:1, one of the two חרם chapters of the book. The balance of the time (inc. ch. 7), Deuteronomy employs the verb הוציא, a strikingly disproportionate distribution which may have significance. An investigation into the anomaly is in order. Most of the ground for this has been covered by J. Wijngaards, who has analyzed the differences in usage of העלה and הוציא.[22]

The key to the matter is the distribution of the two verbs. Wijngaards makes three important observations: 1) (of הוציא) "*that the formula lies embedded particularly in the legislative parts of the Old Testament.*" 2) "Another striking feature of the הוציא formula is *its absence among the early prophets....*"[23] and in addition, 3) "Contrary to הוציא, the העלה formula *is well attested in the pre-deuteronomistic and early prophetic texts* (emphases original)."[24]

The ancient Israelite authors viewed going to Egypt as a going down (=going south); hence, the most frequent verb used in the Bible for travel to Egypt from Canaan was ירד, "to descend" (Gen 12:10; 26:2; 42:2,3,38; 43:3,15; Deut 10:22; Josh 24:4; Isa 30:2 &c.). In Gen 39:1, when Joseph is taken to Egypt as a slave, the hophal of ירד is employed.

When God brings Israel out of Egypt the opposite verb העלה naturally expresses bringing the people to the land. This also shows why הוציא, the later of the two, is so uniformly adopted in the law codes. Its relative lateness is supported by its ubiquity in late Hebrew. The codes posit the law-giving of Moses, who never reached the land. Whether the site of the law-giving was Sinai (Exodus-Leviticus) or in transit (Numbers-Deuteronomy), the verb העלה was not applicable.

If this is so, why was the rule broken in Deut 20:1? Consider the text: Deut 20:1b

כִּי־יְהוָה אֱלֹהֶיךָ עִמָּךְ הַמַּעַלְךָ מֵאֶרֶץ מִצְרָיִם.

For YHWH your god is with you, who is the-one-causing-your-going up from the land of Egypt (cf. LXX).

The use of the participle in a circumstantial clause reflects the situation which Deuteronomy has posed; that the people are not yet in the land. They are about to enter it and (Deuteronomy 20:1a) they had to be prepared for battle. In reality, of course, the author of the passage is thinking of a rather different situation, as appears from the course of the chapter--the Israelites had no newly planted vineyards at the time of entry, for example. The point is that a relatively early author (for he uses העלה in contrast to הוציא), stemming probably from a prophetic circle, used the construction and the verb form that he did to harmonize it with the kind of text he was writing,

---

[22] J. Wijngaards "*hwṣiʾ* and *ʿlh*: A Twofold Approach to the Exodus," *VT* 15 (1965) 91-102.

[23] Ibid. 92.

[24] Ibid. 99.

the Mosaic law code. This also points to the relatively early date of the laws of חרם found in Deuteronomy 20 (Deuteronomy 7 is apparently another, perhaps later production of the same or similar school). So points the consonance between Deuteronomy 20 (and 7) and Am 2:9-10.

We will now look at two previously proposed solutions to the problem of the provenance of Deuteronomy 20.

The problem of determining the provenance of passages from Deuteronomy in general is a difficult one. The task of finding a place in history for a given text, especially a text artificially projected back to an idealized past, is not solved by the generally accepted correlation of a newly-discovered scroll of law in Josiah's day (2 Kings 22) with the Book of Deuteronomy in some form. This only establishes a terminus ad quem (neglecting the exilic component). Part of the difficulty is that we know relatively little of the history of Israel in the period preceding this terminus.

E. Junge long ago made an ingenious attempt at finding a plausible historical setting for Deuteronomy 20, an attempt endorsed by G. von Rad.[25] He relates the chapter to a situation in which Josiah sought to reconstitute the army of Judah, which had been stripped of its useful fighting force of mercenaries by the Assyrians. It was therefore necessary to recruit, in effect, the old-fashioned peasant militia. As Junge understood it, "the population capable of bearing arms had to be called up for military service. Such service could be demanded of every subject as a civil liability...."[25]

Yet looking at Deuteronomy 20, it is hardly possible to envision it arising from the desperate situation of the kingdom of Judah as it finished the seventh century, even without going into the matter of the northern provenance of Deuteronomy's core. The overall mood of the chapter is a serene confidence that with the aid of YHWH any war could be won, even against an overwhelming numerical superiority of the enemy. The chapter does not seek to draft the entire "population capable of bearing arms," or demand service "of every subject as a civil liability," but lays out categories of exemption with a liberal hand. We know from the Keret epic what could happen: all categories of the population might be forced into action. Krt 98-103 lists categories of usually exempt people whom the king drafts for his mighty army, including (Krt 100-3),

> wyṣi. trḫ. hdṯ. yb'r.lṯn. aṯth. lm. nkr. mddth Verily, even the new bridegroom goes forth (to battle; cp. Deut 20:1a). He sends his wife to another man, his beloved to a stranger.

The Ugaritic text uses a root *b' r* in a sense that is rarely attested in BH (cf. Exod 22:4).[26] The context here is helpful. The analogy to Deuteronomy 20:7 is twofold; the Ugaritic text implies that normally, newlywed husbands were exempt from war, and it speaks of the remarrying of widows after the

---

[25] E. Junge, *Wiederaufbau des Heerwesens des Reiches Juda unter Josia* (Stuttgart, 1936), quoted by G. von Rad in *Studies in Deuteronomy* (London, 1953), 61.
[26] Prof.. B. A. Levine pointed out this Hebrew cognate usage to me.

husband's death in battle. This parallel with Deuteronomy 20:7 (and with 24:5, as H. L. Ginsberg noted in *ANET* 143 n.11)), does not aid the case for a Josianic provenance of Deuteronomy 20; on the contrary, it aids the case for the probable antiquity of the legislation.

The Ugaritic passage shedding light on Deuteronomy 20:7 is well known. I am not aware if this is also true of a parallel to the exemption of Deuteronomy 20:6, which occurs in the Hittite Laws §56 (trans. A. Goetze *ANET* 192a):

> No one of the metal workers shall be freed from participating in a royal campaign in a fortress, (and) from cutting a vineyard. The gardeners shall render the full services (cf. §§100, 107-8 which indicate the great value of vineyards as opposed to other fruit production (orchards), and §113 which indicates the difficulty of viticulture).

It is clear from this law that viticulture was regarded as a strategic industry by the framers of the Hittite laws, not to be suspended even in wartime.[27] The Israelite framers of Deuteronomy 20:6 shared in this ancient perception. For this reason the law is placed with the marriage exemption, which also had the strategic purpose of perpetuating the community even as it stood to lose valued members. Therefore the law provided that the viticulturist who had only begun his planting be sent to his vineyard to tend this most important fruit. Wine was a necessity in water-poor ancient Israel. The antiquity of this Israelite law is not proved by the existence of the much older Hittite law, but it is certainly consistent with the thesis that the laws of war, at least as revealed in Deuteronomy 20 and 7, should not be pushed forward to the Josianic period. The Hittite law dovetails nicely with the parallel from Ugarit, and indicates that the legal material is very early. The formulation, while much later, is best assigned to the period and place of the Kingdom of Northern Israel, which was so influenced by Canaanite (i.e. Phoenician) culture, which in turn was impacted by such cultures as the Hittite culture far more directly and forcefully than provincial Judah was ever likely to have been. Of course, it is both unnecessary to assume and impossible to prove that there is an actual line of cause and effect between Hittite Laws §56 and Deuteronomy 20:6. The Hittite law certainly demonstrates that the deuteronomic exemption is a not at all quixotic, but a practical and prudent idea, rooted in the reality of viticulture in biblical times, and hence not a new idea.[28]

Further, a recently discovered, short booty inscription of Hazael, the Aramean usurper and king (who assumed power in 842 B.C.), has been

---

[27] This is true even though the Hittite Laws were "academic." See R. Westbrook, "Cuneiform Law Codes and the Origins of Legislation," ZA 79 (1989), 204ff..

[28] An article offering a parallel from the Code of Eshnunna and other Akkadian sources, as well as a Hittite parallel to Deut 20:10 has now appeared. See E. Otto, "Die keilschriftlichen Parallelen der Vindikatsformel in Dtn 20,10," *ZAW* 102 (1990), 94-96. This cannot weaken the argument for an older setting for the formulation of these laws.

compared with Deuteronomy 20:14 by I. Eph'al and J. Naveh.[29] The verse speaks of the "spoil of your enemies," while the inscription refers to the piece of booty which bears the inscription:

> Deut 20:14 אשר נתן יהוה אלהיך לך (spoil)...which YHWH... has given you.
> Hazael inscription זי נתן הדד למראן חזאל (spoil) which (the god) Hadad gave to our lord Hazael.

This kind of evidence does not prove by itself that the chapter is early, but it certainly places a heavy burden on those who would make it as late as Josiah. In conjunction with the other evidence (e.g. Am 2:9-10, see above), the case for an earlier provenance is a strong one.

In addition, Junge's proposed scenario fails on technical grounds, as noted by N. K. Gottwald.[30] A recent writer on this subject, A. Rofe, has also treated the laws of war extensively. Only that part of his work which deals with the material under discussion will be considered here. Rofe takes as starting point for his analysis the centralization of the cult. In making his case for the lateness of the code, he makes a threefold argument: he argues that Josiah made his cult reform on the basis of Deuteronomy, but that Hezekiah, whose centralization of the cult came earlier, did not do so at the instance of a book. This dates the book to the interval between Hezekiah and Josiah, i.e., the seventh century. Secondly he argues, that if the legal reform of the Book of Deuteronomy was composed in the 7th century, it was not a utopian vision--it had a real precedent that had made an impression on the author and on his contemporaries.[31] He continues, "Recently, some parallels have been recognized in subjects, ideas, and style between the Book of Deuteronomy and the inscriptions of the Assyrian kings of this period (my translation)."

The first argument is unconvincing. The biblical text may not ascribe Hezekiah's reform to the same cause as that of Josiah, yet his reform could have been influenced directly by Deuteronomy (so Ginsberg),[32] or indirectly; in which case, the book might not have traveled to Judah from the north by Hezekiah's time. Any number of possibilities exist which could explain why a northern book failed to have a recorded impact on Judah before Josiah. Rofe's argument is essentially an argument from silence.

---

[29] I. Eph'al & J. Naveh, "Hazael's Booty Inscriptions," *IEJ* 39 (1989), 194. They also cite Neo-Assyrian parallel language.

[30] N. K. Gottwald, "'Holy War' in Deuteronomy: Analysis and Critique," *Review and Expositor* 61 (1964) 306 n. 14. Dr. Gottwald kindly sent me a copy.

[31] A. Rofe,"The Laws of War in the Book of Deuteronomy: their Origin, their Purpose, and their Compulsoriness," (Heb.) in *Introduction to the Book of Deuteronomy: Additional Chapters* (Jerusalem, 1982), 17.

[32] Consider H. L. Ginsberg's penetrating remarks in *The Israelian Heritage of Judaism* (New York, 1982), esp. on p.38; "The Torah which had been adopted by Hezekiah was forgotten until, seventy years later, there arrived a moment when it was opportune for it to be discovered, in a somewhat updated form." See further ch. IV, "The Josian Reformation," 39ff..

The second argument is merely a rhetorical statement, almost a wish. It may be that the centralization of worship belongs to a late, 7th century stratum of Deuteronomy, but that does not affect the laws of war. Neither does his third point, the Assyrian parallels, affect the status of the laws of war, because neither he nor anyone else alleges that there is anything in the neo-Assyrian corpus comparable to Deuteronomy 20 and 7.[33]

Rofe also concludes that the verb, החרים merely means to destroy, due to the lack of ליהוה following the verb.[34] When the "voice of YHWH" is speaking, as in 1 Sam 15:1-2 (through Samuel) and in Deuteronomy 20 and 7 (through Moses), the ליהוה may be seen as superfluous, as there was no possibility of the חרם being directed to another god. Just as Deuteronomy 13 deals with a 'real' חרם, i.e. something homologous to that of Mesha, so do the laws of חרם in Deuteronomy 7 and 20. Nor does the context favor the 'desacralization' of חרם here. One final remark: Rofe places Deuteronomy 20:7 in the later stratum of laws, which as we have seen is unlikely to be the case.[35]

Having looked at two alternative theories of the provenance of the laws of war, a summary of my own approach and the conclusions which flow from it is now in order:

a) The prophet Amos's oracles on Moab (Am 2:1-3), Edom (1:11-12), and Israel (2:6-16, esp. vv.9-10) were used as a (second) starting point for this inquiry because their contents seem to have direct bearing on the חרם or its background, and on the peoples of the land, subsumed here under the name of the Amorites.

b) In language and concepts Am 2:9-10 resembles the war passages in Deuteronomy, with closest ties to the first part of Deuteronomy 20 and Deut 9:1-6. The oracle of Moab (Am 2:1-3) combines Holy War and חרם motifs in the image of the destruction of the enemy king by fire. It may very well have been the prophet's trenchant way of using the image to denote the operation of the Moabite חרם. Thus the oracles of the nations in Amos 1 as well as Am 2:9-10 are both relevant to the חרם and to Deuteronomy 7 and 20. I have suggested also that the חרם executed by Mesha long played a part in Israelite thinking, and along with the later depredation mentioned by Amos against Edom, materially affected the authors of Deuteronomy 20 and 7. They wrote at a time when Ephraim was in a position to retaliate against Moab for her

---

33.Cf. par. 45 in the (earlier) "Middle Assyrian Laws," T. Meek *ANET* 184a, a contrast to Deut 20:7,24:5. A woman whose husband is captured may wait two years and remarry. R. Frankena, "The Vassal Treaties of Esarhaddon," *OS* XIV (1965), 148, gives a parallel to the negative of 20:7, viz. Deut 28:30: You will betroth a woman, and another man will lie with her. ND 4327 428-30 reads: May Dilbat...make your wives lie in the lap of your enemy before your eyes.... M. Cogan & H. Tadmor in *II Kings: A New Translation with Introduction and Commentary, AB* (Garden City, 1988), 238, relate the Deut 20:19-20 law to Assyrian habits of "intentional devastation of enemy countryside," but this is not an imitation of the Assyrians but a reaction to them, assuming their reasonable assertion is true.

34 A. Rofe, "The Laws of War," 19 (see esp. n. 14).

35 Ibid. 27.

past depredations, the time of Jeroboam II. Whereas Amos's prophecies against the nations were before Jeroboam's period of success, the deuteronomic laws were a response to the real possibility that an Israelite king might wish to retaliate against Moab with an Israelite חרם. As Amos's poetry shows, the figures of the "Amorite" and the aboriginal race of giants were alive (and united) at his time (see below).. The authors of the chapters (or the bulk of the material in them), probably moved in similar (prophetic) circles. In any case, the age of Jereboam called for legislation on the subjects of war and חרם far more than the age of Josiah, when the incentive to practice the חרם was small compared to the period following Mesha's successful exercise of it against Israel.

As pointed out (ch.2), the Deuteronomy passages using חרם against the nations (Deut 7:1-2, 20:16-18) "replace" earlier passages from Exodus (23:28; 33:2; 34:11) which employ גרש although in the immediate overall comparison this amounts to but a shift in emphasis (cf. Exod 23:23}. This shift fits in with the hypothesis just outlined. The terminological change can be seen as flowing from the historical context of the Moabite use of the חרם, not just as a theologizing of some redactor called D or Dtr. The Deuteronomic writers restricted the use of the חרם to the primordial nations. The only Transjordanian חרם applied to the Sihon/Og traditions which, at least according to Numbers 21, originally lacked the חרם altogether. This set of traditions is dated prior to Israel's settlement in the land. It is easier to see a deuteronomic addition of the חרם than a Numbers stripping the story of the חרם, especially as Deuteronomy 7 and 20 correspond to Exodus passages there the verb is lacking.

There is unanimous agreement that at the time of the war legislation, the six or seven candidates for the חרם were not in the picture, whatever the case had been in the past. Since the חרם was directed to these peoples, it is quite clear that--for reasons we are unable to determine given the lack of evidence--the framers of the laws wanted to eliminate the possibility of using the חרם against others. Despite Moab's historic wrong against Israel and against Judah's coveted neighbor, Edom, the חרם was not by its nature the proper vehicle for pure revenge, unaccompanied by considerations of achieving *Weltordnung*, which was not at stake in the land of Moab (except in the conditions before Israel's settlement in Canaan, when Sihon and Og threatened Israel's very access to the land where it sought to achieve *Weltordnung*). Nor was Moabite Transjordan part of the 'Holy Land,' so that the sacral dimension of the חרם was lacking as well. Thus, the seemingly anomalous use of the lists of nations in Deuteronomy 7 and 20 becomes a key to understanding the חרם legislation in both Deuteronomy 20 and in Deuteronomy 7, which is influenced by ch. 20. Indeed, Deuteronomy 7 fits in well with Deuteronomy's Sihon-Og narratives, with its references to the Exodus from Egypt (reminding one of Moses, the leader at the time of Sihon and Og). These references provide a similar context to Deuteronomy 2-3. In addition, Deut 7:24 speaks of destroying enemy kings. Deuteronomy 2-3 does, too, using the חרם, while avoiding it against the "brother nations" of

Moab and Edom. This reflects a historical tradition that Israel had never used the חרם against these nations at the time; Deut 20:16-18 is against it, Deuteronomy 7 follows in its wake, and Deuteronomy 2-3 fits in with Deuteronomy 7 in this respect.

All this is not inconsistent with the historical narratives in which Joshua or Samuel call for the חרם. When the divine call came for such measures, the measures had to be taken. Then it was a matter of establishing the order ordained by the ruler of the universe. We merely suggest that the author of the legislation of Deuteronomy 20 and 7 saw no divine mandate to take the kind of measures demanded by the חרם against Moab, and this is the typical biblical attitude (see ch.2). However bitter Israel became, YHWH had given Moab land as a possession, which could not be חרם without dispossessing Moab from its ancient inheritance. Deuteronomy 20 thus fits the historical situation of Jereboam II much better than any subsequent era, while Deuteronomy 7 appears to be a repetition and elaboration from a later date, possibly the time of Uzziah's Transjordanian conquests. This does not mean that individual laws or verses may not go back further or come from a later time. However, this dating seems much preferable to a Josianic provenance. By placing this in the structure of Mosaic legislation, the deuteronomic authors of these chapters suffered a loss of the flexibility that goes with, for example, parliamentary legislation. Yet they clearly had an eye on more than one evanescent time, which farsighted observers knew could not last. The reference to nations stronger and more numerous than Israel (Deut 7:1) probably brought to mind in their contemporaries only the image of Assyria, Egypt, Aram, et. al.. Yet these 'lawmakers' did not mention the contemporary threats, but rose above their immediate time, for they were writing for future generations as well. They accomplished this by harnessing the mythic--the lists of primordial nations--in the way indicated above. A. F. Stewart, speaking of a different culture and a different medium, made this important point for the understanding of the function of the lists of nations in Deuteronomy 20 and 7:

> As anthropologists have long recognized, such memory-images [here: the lists]...implicitly function not not only to validate but to eternalize and mythicize the values of the present by taking them 'out of time' as it were.[36]

Rather than producing a short-lived political cautionary document, the authors of Deuteronomy 7 and 20 expressed their convictions in a way relevant to their time and to their posterity and they may have achieved their purpose, or else altered circumstances in the direction they desired: subsequently, prophets would sometimes speak of YHWH employing the חרם (in figurative language), but not Israel (e.g. Isa 34:2,5; 43:28, Mal 3:24).

---

[36] A.F. Stewart, "History, Myth and Allegory in the Program of the Temple of Athena Nike, Athens," in H. L.Kessler & M.S. Simpson, eds., *Pictorial Narrative in Antiquity and the Middle Ages, Studies in the History of Art* v.16 (Washington, D.C.), 63-4.

II: DEUT 13:13-19

Deuteronomy 13 provides our discussion, DEUTERONOMIC ḤEREM AND THE LISTS OF NATIONS with a useful appendix and our general inquiry with invaluable additional material for understanding the conceptual underpinnings of the חרם. As an adjunct to the chapters dealt with in the above (20 and 7), it demonstrates that the idea of the חרם as a consecration (through destruction) to the deity still was in the mind of at least the earlier writers composing the core of Deuteronomy. This is spelled out in one sentence in Deut 13:16-18, where the whole operation is also characterized as כליל ליהוה (on this, see below). Yet Deuteronomy 13 differs greatly from chapters 7 and 20, in that it deals with the חרם not in relation to foreign nations but in relation to large groups of Israelites.

The relationship between the חרם and idolatry has been held by some scholars to be an artificial or secondary development, a view that goes back many years.[37] There are, of course, a number of passages that relate the two in Deuteronomy aside from ch. 13, such as Deut 7:1-6, 25-6, 20:17-18. These have been dismissed as secondary by the school just mentioned. Yet Exod 22:19, which proscribes the individual who sacrifices to any god but God, if not aggressively emended (see below, ch. 6), is among the oldest, perhaps the oldest of חרם passages. That being so, there is no reason to look at Deuteronomy 13 askance, as it is merely an expanded version of an early tradition.

In other words, the association of חרם with anti-idolatry, while not invariably expressed, was integral to the Israelite concept of חרם, and not incidental to it. The חרם partakes of a dual nature; so that it may manifest itself at one pole as the "most holy" (Lev 27:26) and at the other pole as an "abomination." (Deut 7:25-6), which God appropriates to himself into the sphere of חרם. The seemingly all-destructive חרם unites both poles by removing abomination and creating holiness. This being the case, the place of idolatry in Israelite conceptions of the חרם can by no means be the result of secondary juxtaposition by late schools of deuteronomists or deuteronomistic theologians; the place of idolatry in these texts flows from the sacral nature of the חרם itself.

The Mesha Inscription provides evidence to the same effect. The חרם of Kemosh takes place at YHWH's sanctuary town, and YHWH's sanctuary is not spared. Mesha evidently held the conception that the temple of YHWH, identified with his Israelite foes, was a תועבה or abomination that had to be removed. Mesha, with the help of Kemosh, restored his land to its pristine ("holy") state by following the god's commands and consecrating Nebo to the deity.

It may perhaps be possible to go further on this question of idols by considering it in the context of Israelite monotheism. Much ink has been spilled on the subject of Akhenaton's supposed monotheism and its possible

---

[37] A. C. Welch, *Deuteronomy: The Framework,* 73, and citations there.

influence on ancient Israel. The worship of the sun disk, the Aten, even were it exclusive of all other worship in *Amarnazeit* Egypt, was the worship of something visible and in a sense tangible. The cult of YHWH, however, was aniconic from an early period, as the descriptions of the ark in the Book of Samuel show, even though other images, such as those of the cherubim and seraphim, might be associated with it. (pagan processionals involve images of the gods, or the Assyrian kings chase peoples carrying their gods, but in the Bible, at least, YHWH's image is never on parade, just the ark, at least until the creation of the golden calves of the Northern Kingdom..

Since alien peoples brought with them alien gods, one of the root anxieties in dealing with alien peoples was, for the devotee of YHWH, that idolatry and syncretism would result. It is this not only aniconic, but anti-iconic strain--best known from the Ten Commandments--that goes back far into Israel's past, which informs the deuteronomic חרם in all three chapters (7,13,20) of legislation. It partly accounts for the religiously motivated xenophobia of Deuteronomy 7 and 20. There was also the belief that Israel owed its possession of the land to divine favor. This anti-iconic stream of thought is highly developed in Deuteronomy but does not begin there.

An excellent illustration of the dangers of a simplifying evolutionism in Israelite religion--which from its beginning stood at the end of a long religious evolution--is provided by the example of early Roman religion, as portrayed by R. M. Ogilvie:

> Early Roman religion is extremely shadowy. As far as we know it was ani conic...and certainly not anthropomorphic. ...the primitive Romans worshipped Mars as their chief deity. ...But Mars remained indistinct. ...The Etruscans brought with them more vigorous ideas. They personalized their gods,they thought of them visu ally and they housed them in temples instead of merely dedicating altars to them.[38]

In other words, early in Rome's history the coming of the Etruscans brought with it worship of images, and in this case the 'higher' form of religion was superseded by a 'lower,' which was precisely what the writers of Deuteronomy feared.

H. W. F. Saggs sketched the development of Israelite religion in this way:

> In Mesopotamia, it is likely that each of the original Sumerian city-states had a sin gle city god. As the city-states came into political relationship, they brought their gods into corresponding relationship, creating a pantheon. (...) The pre-settlement group of Israelites associated with Moses began, like any Sumerian city-state, with one god.... Other Israelite groups had other gods, the patriarchal numina. These were not placed alongside the Mosaic god in a pantheon, but identified with him, avoiding a clash of claims. Other tribal groups, contemporary with early Israel, had yet other gods, and the Israelite showed their distinctive reaction to these. Instead of following the accretive principle of Mesopotamian civilization, they exercised selectivity and rejection. They first

---

[38] R. M. Oglivie, *Early Rome and the Etruscans, Fontana History of the Ancient World* (Glasgow, 1976), 35-7.

> ignored those other gods and later denied their very existence. Thus, what began as monolatry in both Sumerian city-states and Israel developed on one side into polytheism and on the other into monotheism.[39]

We have here an account, necessarily speculative, of how worship of one deity could have occurred in Israel at an early stage. It complements the Roman example of primitive aniconicism. Together with our other arguments, it helps make the case that Israelite iconoclasm and the חרם were wedded early; for 'other gods' could not be "accreted" as easily in Israel as in Sumer. Furthermore, it is the way that the חרם could be both adopted from the polytheistic environment and adapted as an expression of early Israel's anti-iconicism (cf. Exod 22:19) that may well have provided the ideological impetus for the initial Israelite borrowing of the term. The early legislation of Exod 22:19 employs the hophal of the verb instead of using the noun (like Deut 7:25-6 or Joshua 7), suggesting that its authors were already familiar with the hiphil, which I have suggested deals with establishing world order. Of course, "holiness" and "*Weltordnung*" are separate categories in our minds, but the verbal form of חרם shows how one they were in the mind of those who clung to the biblical faith. Out of destruction would come a world order in which YHWH would reign in his holiness. The Israelites who adopted the term from outside did so because they saw it as a word with which to express certain aspects of their faith. It filled a perceived gap in the religious vocabulary and helped create--by the power inherent in words--an enduring reality in the religious life of ancient Israel. On this theory, the usage of Exod 22:19 was derived and made possible, by the hiphil החרים, yet simultaneously this usage was a major reason that the term was borrowed at all.[40]

Returning to Deuteronomy 13, we will not deal with redaction or literary critical issues here. For it is pretty generally agreed that the חרם passage (Deut 13:13-19) is--at least in the main--a unit, and a unit belonging to an early stratum in D. It is obvious why this חרם law is found in its present setting, as it would be highly incongruous in either ch. 7 or 20. In opposition to those chapters, it deals with the internal Israelite application of the חרם. The description of the act of חרם is interesting. We find it in Deut 13:16-18:

> You shall utterly smite the dwellers of that city by the sword, devoting it and all in it and its cattle by the sword; and all its booty you shall gather in the middle of its square, and then you shall burn in flames the city and all its booty, כליל ליהוה and it shall become a ruin (tell), never to be rebuilt.

---

[39] H. W. F. Saggs, *The Encounter with the Divine in Mesopotamia and Israel* (London, 1978), 286.

[40] C. H. W. Brekelmans, *De ḥerem in het Oude Testament* (Nijmegen,1959), 146-152, reviews a number of theories of origin, from Bedouin greed for loot arousing revulsion, to canabalism to human sacrifice to taboo (among others), all of which he gives good reasons to reject. While he did not offer a theory of his own, he did note that the "origin of the חרם must be sought in the pre-Israelite period" (my translation).

There are two basic meanings of כליל, both of which are well known: the first is whole (or wholly), the second a sacrificial term for a holocaust or whole offering. In Jud 20:40b we have the interesting passage:

וְהִנֵּה עָלָה כְלִיל־הָעִיר מִן־הָעִיר הַשָּׁמַיְמָה.

This is translated by sources as disparate as Boling-Wright and the NJV almost identically: Boling has "there it was, the whole city going up in smoke."[41] NJV has "there was the whole town going up in smoke." Both translations supply the word "smoke," which is not in the text. Although the word does mean "whole" here, both the ambiance of the event and the wording (עָלָה evokes עולה, "holocaust" again), suggest to the Hebrew reader that the writer has deliberately evoked the second meaning of כליל i.e. the whole offering, and for more than literary effect.[42] In Deuteronomy, this need for holocaust is a reaction to the תּוֹעֵבָה or abomination practiced by the city. The holocaust normally atones for sins against God. It is a grim reference to an entire city's sacrificing the wrong way instead of the right way, perhaps a direct reference to the verse, "Whoso sacrifices to a god aside from YHWH alone, shall be devoted" (Exod 22:19).

It should also be understood that in כליל ליהוה of Deut 13:17, which is translated--again with technical accuracy--as "whole-offering"[43] or "holocaust" (NJV), the other meaning, "wholly" is implied, too. However, another important question here in Deut 13:17 is the meaning of the use of a sacrificial term, "whole-offering," in this context. Does the writer of this passage view the חרם as a sacrifice? Kapelrud and Driver, among others, view it as figurative.[44] At the least then, the writer of the passage drew an analogy between the חרם and the whole-offering; but it may be that the special circumstances of the idolatrous city were such that the חרם was literally viewed as a sacrifice. It has long since been pointed out, however, that a sacrifice is a free-will offering.[45] The categories may be fixed as to what is acceptable (cow, sheep, bird), but within the categories, the sacrificer may choose which animal or bird to offer, an element lacking in the חרם. The possibility that the חרם was viewed as a type of sacrifice was first raised (ch. 2) in connection with the אשם, and it cannot be dismissed on the basis of this chapter, but it will be dealt with further below (see ch. 6, II).

The passage Deut 13:13-19 thus raises profound issues regarding the nature of חרם. As noted above, it shows that the view that the deuteronomic use

---

[41] R. G. Boling, *Judges: A New Translation with Introduction and Commentary, AB* (Garden City, 1975), 283.

[42] S. R. Driver, *Deuteronomy,* 155, cites Jud 20:40; "the same sense of the word is at least alluded to." A. Kapelrud calls it "Wortspiel," in "Kalil," *TWAT* III, 194, among others.

[43] S. R. Driver, *Deuteronomy,* 155.

[44] S. R. Driver, Ibid., A. Kapelrud, "Kalil," 195.

[45] C. H. W. Brekelmans, *De ḥerem* , 149, following E. Mader, *Die Menschenopfer der alten Hebräer, Bibl. Studien* XIV, (Freiburg, 1909), 3-6.

of חרם is simply an ordinary act of destruction are mistaken . Its reference to כָּלִיל shows the absolute nature of the חרם. This is illustrated by the use of the 'short form' of כָּלִיל, כֹּל, "all, everything" in relation to the חרם. S. G. Dempster has pointed out, that כֹּל appears 29 times in all, and that it is "usually employed to govern the objects of the war practice in question."[46] He points to עִיר, נפש, נשמה, as well as to the phrase כָּל אשׁר לו, which together add up to 20 of the 29. And as he observes, MI 16, speaking of the inhabitants of Nebo, is another instance. In Deut 13:16-19, כֹּל is used like a drumbeat, emphasizing the will of YHWH. It is used twice in Deut 13:17, "with all the spoil," a phrase which in the repetition is juxtaposed with כָּלִיל for super-emphasis. Finally, it appears in a wholly different and somewhat climactic manner in the last verse of the pericope (i.e. Deut 13:19), which adjures Israel to obey all of God's commandments and to do what is right in the eyes of YHWH. This is the recipe for avoiding the wrath of God and the necessity for חרם. (cp. Deut 6:23).

Along with the other passages in Deuteronomy, this passage shows that the deuteronomic חרם is more than mere theory,[47] While much of the attention of Deuteronomy to the חרם is concentrated on seemingly theoretical aspects of the practice, there is more than one type of theory. One is completely abstract, the other is a more 'applied' theory, designed with real situations in mind. The deuteronomic חרם writers had the horrible example of Mesha before them. Given that the prophets of old (e.g. Samuel) approved the חרם, these later writers were cognizant of its religious content and historical role and use, and not least of its anti-iconic aspect. They took no interest in propounding theories for the sake of theories. In fact, M. Weinfeld has pointed to certain resemblances between Hittite and Assyrian treaty language and Deuteronomy 13.[48] Thus he says:

> The religious treason is here described and combated just as if it were political treason. Inciting an entire community to adopt foreign worship (13:13-19) implies no less than its delivery into the hands of the enemy. It is precisely for this reason that the punishment is so severe.[49]

---

[46] S. G. Dempster, *The Prophetic Invocation of the Ban as Covenant Curse: A Historical Analysis of a Prophetic Theme* (M.A. thesis, Westminster Theological Seminary, Chestnut Hill, Pa., 1978), 51. He goes on to speak of the desolation associated with the חרם, a desolation which in the view propounded here is the necessary antecedent to the cosmogonic goal of the חרם. Or, it is the returning of the enemy to the non-existent which allows world order to begin or continue.

[47] E.g., C. H. W. Brekelmans, "Le ḥerem chez les prophètes du royaume du Nord et dans le Deutéronome," *Actes du Congres international catholiques des études bibliques* (1958), (Louvain, 1959), 377-383.

[48] There are also differences: e.g. one doubts that kings incited their subjects to rebel as a test of their loyalty as YHWH does in Deut 13:4.

[49] M. Weinfeld, *Deuteronomy and the Deuteronomic School* (Oxford, 1972), 92. I owe this reference to Prof. S. G. Dempster.

The analogy between ancient Near Eastern treaty language which Weinfeld has raised is good, but it may only go so far. For the same kinds of language, even the same terminology, may appear in ancient Assyrian or Hittite treaties and this pericope, but their ultimate import has been transmuted in the alchemical furnace of Israelite religion. For neither the Assyrians nor the later Hittites had any analogue to the חרם, which brings about through the idea of 'consecration through destruction' the related ideas of establishing God's holiness on earth and bringing about Israel's world order. Though I will discuss the topic of the lack of association between the term for covenant, ברית, and חרם. in the logical place, Joshua 7 (where the two terms are, for once, found together), it is worth pointing out here that the word for covenant does not appear in Deut 13:13-19, nor anywhere in the chapter. In contrast, the in many ways parallel passage, Deut 17:2-7, does use ברית, while the word חרם is absent. Ezekiel 14, in a sense the prophet's personal treatment of the same material as Deuteronomy 13, lacks both terms. He uses למעל מעל, "to sin against God," which occurs in connection with חרם in Joshua 7. This direct-to-God terminology (vs. resort to the historically determined mediating factor of the Covenant) supports the view that the near total lack of contact between the term "covenant" and the חרם and, in particular, the non-juxtaposition of the two terms in Deut 13:13-19 and Deut 17:2-7, must be considered deliberate. חרם reflects a more fundamental religious idea than covenant. does, i.e. holiness, a word which attempts to convey the sense and the feel of the inexpressible but most fundamental nature of God.

Deuteronomy 13 is preceded by a short sermon, warning against idolatry and against the other abominable practices of the nations, especially human sacrifice (Deut 12:29-31). There the victory of Israel against the natives of the land is portrayed in terms of YHWH the divine warrior, destroying the enemy peoples. This is a conventional Near Eastern portrait of a warring god. It stands in a certain contrast with the חרם idea, which is similar to the idea of the psalmists who sang of Israel's feats of arms while God defeated the enemy (Ps 60:14=108:14). Deut 12:29-31 is relatively restrained, merely ordering Israel to beware and to refrain from committing alien abominations. It is in Deut 6:14-15 that YHWH threatens Israel with destruction as YHWH's response to an unfaithful nation (judging by the verb, השמיד, "destroy," the same fate visited on the nations in Deut 12:29-30 is to descend on Israel, where the same verb appears, along with "extirpate," הכרית). It is that ultimate fear, as in the Achan story of Joshua 7, that Israel will perish, that is at stake in Deut 13:18, which speaks of God's wrath turning back, thus saving Israel from major disaster, if the people keep to the rules of חרם. As observed earlier (ch.2), from this verse it follows that the חרם is to be employed to avert the wrath of the deity (as was the same no doubt with Kemosh). Deut 6:14-15 speaks of destruction of a people gone bad; Deut 13:13-19 offers an escape hatch for mass apostasy at a lesser, more local level of individual towns. The book seeks to emphasize in many ways the danger inherent in idolatry. The חרם passages are set apart only by their use of a special language of holiness outraged and danger looming as a result. While Israel is forbidden to put God to the test (Deut 6:16), God may even try the faith of Israel by sending false prophets to seduce them into idol worship (Deut 13:4). Many passages scattered throughout the book emphasize the reward for not succumbing to these blandishments: life, health, prosperity (the standard Egyptian wish for their pharaohs), or in other words, world order.

To conclude, the biblical writers thought that the חרם as ordained by YHWH was an expression of the fundamental role of the deity in the creation of order--divine order--out of chaos in partnership with human beings--Israelites--who worked with YHWH; cf. Ps 60:14=108:14; "With God we will perform feats of arms and he will defeat our enemies." In idolatry the worshipper served something that was no thing. Hence the idolator created an image that was not a mirror of the divine, but reflected another reality altogether, one of "non–existence" or chaos and not the supreme force for order in the world, which could not be reduced to a wooden or metal image. (Cf. Isa 44:29ff., Jer 2:5ff.) Circumstances and ideology combined to cause the deuteronomic writers to attach a special significance to the חרם--more than in any other stratum of the Torah--and their concern with it was not as a literary device or affectation. One can only believe so by standing without the thought world of the intensely religious biblical writers.

III: DEUT 7:25-6

Our study of the deuteronomic חרם, in which idolatry plays so integral and prominent a role, leads us next to Deut 7:25-26. These two verses have been declared an addition to the chapter.[50] A reason for taking the position is that the text of Deut 7:25f. is not prepared for in any way in what precedes it, critics averring that it is, rather, a *Nachtrag* to Deut 7:5. The connection between the two verses is clear enough; the last three words in the Hebrew of Deut 7:5, "their idols you shall burn with fire" are the same as the first three words of Deut 7:25.[51] Here are the words of G. Schmitt:

> Die Warnung vor dem Gold der Götterbilder is ein singulares Motiv, und zwar eins, von dem man sich fast noch schwerer als von den anderen Motiven des Kapitels vorstellen kann, dass es reine Theorie sei. Eigenartig, dass es gerade in einer Interpolation steht.[47]

Schmitt makes two basic claims with regard to Deut 7:25-6: a) they encapsulate a motive which is both singular in itself and hard to fit in with the other motives of the chapter. He sums it up with the last sentence quoted above. In his opinion, Deut 7:25-6's very singularity convicts it of being an

---

[50] For such a view, see N. Lohfink, *Das Hauptgebot: Eine Untersuchung literarischer Einleitungsfragen zu Dtn 5-11, AnBib* 20 (1963), and G. Schmitt, *Du sollst keinen Frieden schliessen mit dem Bewohnern des Landes, BWANT V 11* (1970).
[51] Ibid. 132.

interpolation! And b) he claims in passing that, in contrast, as it were. to the rest of the chapter, these verses are "pure theory."

Yet. Deut 7:25-6 are so not violently at odds with the remainder of the chapter as all that. The theme of a warning against utilizing the precious metals stripped from idols may only appear this once in the Pentateuch, but that does not mean that such warnings were not a feature of other and earlier traditions that are preserved in the Torah either in part or not at all. Moreover, if one were to attribute every apparent innovation in Deuteronomy to the work of some glossator or interpolator, then a vast proportion of Deuteronomy--a third or more--would have to be interpolated, and the originators of Deuteronomy deemed a priori as incapable of originality and innovation--or even unable to preserve ancient traditions which had otherwise fallen through the cracks.

Even from the literary standpoint, it is hard to accept such a verdict. If we permit the deuteronomic writer the power to speak in ways we could not predict from the so-called Tetrateuch, the introduction here, following Deut 7:23f.'s sketch of victory against the enemy nations, of how to treat captured idols, is not so out of place, even in and of itself. It is a continuing topic of interest both inside the Bible and out, as to how the victor treats the gods of the conquered (who are mentioned in Deut 7:3f.). Further, the three beginning words of Deut 7:25 are more likely to be a literary device, a resumption intended by the original writer, than a gloss. It seems persuasive to posit that the writer had two lines of thought; a main branch taken up by the immediate continuation "You are a holy people" in Deut 7:6, and the adjuration in Deut 7:25-6., which expresses an application of the same idea! Actually, both lines of thought are taken up at the same time, which makes for a rather brilliant literary device. Were the latter verses merely a gloss to Deut 7:5, we might expect the interpolation to follow immediately on its heels. As it is, the use of such a device is not unknown in Deuteronomy. It is even known with regard to the other text with which I have paired Deuteronomy 7, viz. ch. 20, or more precisely, Deuteronomy 20-21. The heading of the section beginning with Deut 21:10 is similar to 20:1, thus raising the possibility in the mind's eye, that the law of the captive woman was originally attached to ch. 20.[52] Yet the links between the end of Deuteronomy 20 and the onset of Deuteronomy 21 are not hard to find. Deut 21:1 begins with the use of the Heb. word, חלל="pierced (by a sword)," the regular Hebrew word for a casualty of war, e.g. its repeated use in the much older poem of lamentation in 2 Samuel 1. It does not matter whether this word is being used here differently or not; associations do not follow Euclidean logic, and the associations of the word חלל are primarily with war casualties. This is one connection with the preceding. The second one, which has gone unnoticed, is between the law of war relating to fruit trees and the circumstances of the case, as they are worded in Deut 21:1-9.

Deuteronomy 20:19 forbids the cutting down of fruit trees during a siege. It then asks if tree of the field is a man that may retreat before you (Israel)

---

[52] S. R. Driver, *Deuteronomy*, 244.

in a siege, in this language: כִּי הָאָדָם עֵץ הַשָּׂדֶה לָבֹא מִפָּנֶיךָ בַּמָּצוֹר Obviously, the answer is that the tree will remain to fall under the axe (the peculiar language was probably meant to play on the wooden siege ladder which was also "to come before you in the siege"). Then, shortly afterwards (Deut 21:1), we have a case where

כִּי־יִמָּצֵא חָלָל בָּאֲדָמָה אֲשֶׁר נֹפֵל בַּשָּׂדֶה לֹא נוֹדַע מִי הִכָּהוּ׃

a dead man is found in the country which YHWH has given to possess, fallen in the field (whose killer is unknown). There is a clear analogy between the fruit tree of Deut 20:19-20. and the man of Deut 21:1, and the language indicates the connection (cf. also the use of אדמה instead of ארץ in Deut 21:1 and the use of האדם instead of איש in Deut 20:19). Neither the tree nor the man are supposed to be cut down. A final similarity is that both deal with the felling or falling of life in relation to the proximity to a city.

Were there a radical difference in the language of the two chapters (Deuteronomy 20-21), one could still hold that Deut 21:1-9 represents an interpolation, but in the light of these connections between the two segments, any such argument must fail. It is far more probable that the same writer deliberately phrased the law of Deut 20:19-20 to anticipate what was to come, and then, in Deut 21:10 used the resumption for the return to the war matter of dealing with captive wives. This would imply larger scale structures in the Book of Deuteronomy than some scholars seem willing to accept. However that may be, this example is designed to show that the original writer, and not an interpolator, may sometimes be postulated in these cases. This would then apply to the case of Deut 7:25-6, as well.

One should also consider that the third pericope, Deut 13:13-19, uses a resuming device similar to that of Deut 7:5,25. Both the first and last verse begin with the words כי תשמע, "when you hear." The progression is from hearing the evil words of the sons of Belial to the Lord's commands. This is clearly a purposeful, theologically motivated, heuristic repetition. The use of such a device in connection with each of the three legal chapters which deal with the חרם is more likely to be the result of authorial choice rather than redactional handling, since such a device is not used in D in dealing with a single theme. It gives a sense of (literary) wholeness to go with the subject of holiness.

The characterization of this chapter as "pure theory" is too severe. Naturally, Deuteronomy 7, which represents itself as a pre-conquest document, is in one sense nothing but pure theory. On the other hand, if our dating of chapters 7 and 20 is correct, then Deuteronomy 20 dates to the Jeroboam II period, and Deuteronomy 7 drew inspiration from it; i.e. Deut 7:25-6 could have had an earlier form (see below). Thus this little treatise on how to treat idols may well have been quite relevant once. Otherwise, why would it exist at all? Such a characterization seems overdrawn from a חרם-oriented perspective, especially as the verses in question are, by the nature of the law code, detached from their original historical context (cf. the similar case of Gideon, the gold, and the 'ephod' idol he made, in Jud 8:22-27).

We turn now to the work of N. Lohfink, which contains an extremely ambitious attempt to analyze the origin of Deuteronomy 7, basically on the grounds of its structure. It is unnecessary to enter here into all the intricacies of his work. His most interesting contribution for our purposes is to be found in his idea of *chiastische Stichwortverknüpfungen* or chiastic combinations of key-words.[53] He produces two charts, one taken from Deut 7:6-7:14; the second contains phrases from Deut 7:2-5 and Deut 7:25-6. All of these possess to some degree *chiastische Stichwortverknüpfungen*. Lohfink's demonstration is impressive. The grounds on which he goes on to relegate all of Deut 7:7-24 to a "second hand" are not as convincing, though in regard to Deut 7:17-24 he speaks only of a shaping of the material.[54] For example, it is true that some of the chapter is a "new interpretation" or at least is derived from the decalogue, but since "both (authorial) hands" would have been well after the time of the decalogue, this is hardly a criterion to fixing relative dating by layers.[55] His charts disclose that the material covered by them must surely be assigned to the earliest layer, as the structure Lohfink reveals is basic to the chapter. Yet it should be noted that a given failure to adhere to the chiastic structure does not prove that it must be a later addition. Only if it could be shown that the Book of Deuteronomy purposely subordinated content to form would this argument be convincing. Deuteronomic prose is not subject to so rigid a formalistic prescription. When such a loose structure as Lohfink has found does exist we must not assume that all of the writer's output necessarily stuck strictly to that structure. The content was crucial, the structure secondary. We have here the kind of structure that can arise through the normal process of composition, i.e. an intuitive structure without the enforced, almost geometrical rigor of an Elizabethan sonnet or the metrics of Greek poetry. This structure is not a staple or a standard.

However this may be, I see in this no impediment to assigning Deut 7:25-6 to an early stratum of tradition. One more view should be mentioned, that of G. von Rad. In his commentary to Deuteronomy he gives as his view that both Deut 7:5 and Deut 7:25-6. are interpolated by the same hand.[56] He based this on their use of plural forms, but this is better understood as a stylistic device of Deuteronomy. Surely an interpolator would have the sense to adjust his text in such an elementary way, if this were the case, so as to prevent his addition from sticking out in so conspicuous a manner. Also, both Deuteronomy 7, 13, and 20-21 all use a resumptive device (see above).

The preamble to Deut 7:25-6. is now concluded, and it is time to examine the passage itself. It reads like this in English:

---

53 N. Lohfink, *Das Hauptgebot,* 182-3.
54 Ibid. 186-7.
55 Ibid. 187.
56 G. von Rad, *Deuteronomy: A Commentary* (Philadelphia, 1966), 68-9.

25. You shall burn the images of their gods with fire; you shall not desire (any) gold and silver upon them and take for yourself lest you be ensnared by it for it is an abhorrent thing to YHWH your God 26. You shall not bring an abhorrent thing (=idol) to your house, and thus be an object set apart for destruction (חרם) like it, you shall detest it as unclean[57] and treat it as abhorrent for it is an object to be dedicated to destruction (חרם).

This passage lacks, despite its rather liberal use of emphatic verb forms, the verbal form of the root (החרם), but prefers the noun, which is twice repeated for emphasis. The reason for this appears to be the writer's desire to define the legal status of the item, i.e. the idol and especially its covering of precious metal, as חרם. The way in which it is to be treated is defined by other nouns and verbs: שרף, "to burn," a familiar associate of the root חרם, שקץ and תועבה, similar words for "abhorrent thing, abomination," and the denominative verbs deriving from them meaning "to abominate." As in Joshua 7, which as we shall see, has a genuine historical typology, the person who encroaches with malice aforethought on objects YHWH designates חרם acquires that dangerous status.[58] In Deuteronomy, it was not necessary to add that becoming חרם brought with it a death sentence. A related idea is found later, in a historical context: Ezek 23:7 cites the Northern kingdom's whoring after Assyria, and "being polluted (נטמאה) by their idols," one of the circumstances which doomed Israel.

A clarification of what I mean by "legal status" is necessary. M. Noth pointed out a long time ago that Deuteronomy was not designed as a state code.[59] Yet we are dealing here with a legal code, nonetheless, though one we may term, broadly, as a religious code. Its authors obviously hoped to exert a beneficial influence in a host of ways on both the populace at large and the behavior of the state and its monarch. Like earlier law codes of the Torah, it appealed directly to YHWH as the source of its authority. It apparently influenced Josiah greatly. The place of the Book of Deuteronomy as a reformist document--illustrated in the case of the חרם by the laws of Deut 20:15-18, 7:1-5 in my interpretation--and in the history of ancient Near Eastern law codes, has been illuminated recently by R. Westbrook, who argues that the law code in the modern sense first appeared in Greece.[60]

This passage is remarkable in its use of the term חרם. It presents it as a consequence of engaging in a practice labeled three times as a תּוֹעֵבָה or abomination (of YHWH). There is much written on the subject,[61] but per-

---

57 *KBL* 1009a.

58 People could touch the objects Achan stole with impunity, as their intent was innocent. Innocence was no defense in 1 Samuel 15 because it was plain to all that they had disregarded the words of YHWH's edict.

59 M. Noth, *The Laws in the Pentateuch and Other Studies* (London, 1966), 14, 18f., 34ff., 48f..

60 R. Westbrook, "Cuneiform Law Codes and the Origins of Legislation," *ZA* 79 (1989), 201-222.

61 See W. Pickett, *The Meaning and Function of T'B/TO'EVAH in the Hebrew Bible diss. HUC-JIR* (Cincinatti, 1985), with bibliography.

haps most useful for understanding this passage is the article of W. W. Hallo, in which he utilizes what he calls the contextual approach, a form of the comparative method which focuses not only on similarities but takes into account differences as well.[62] He surveys a range of mostly Mesopotamian texts which include the formula "X is an abomination/taboo of DN." We excerpt here from his concluding remarks:

> All this evidence leads me to conclude that the concept of a divine taboo or abomination, so widespread in the ancient Near East, embraces two widely divergent realms. One involves the infraction of ethical norms.... But the other realm evoked by the concept is more profound, *touching on the sacred and inviolable nature of deity* (emphasis mine). In this meaning, the expressions are used by the Babylonians with reference to those acts which, while innocent enough in themselves, become taboo on unfavorable days; by Israel, with regard to acts enjoined by alien cults but anathema to god.[63]

Much of this paragraph fits Deut 7:25-6 nicely (note that 'taboo' is not used here in the ordinary English sense, not the Polynesian way). The precious but tainted metal is neither to pollute the "treasury of the Lord" (Josh 6:19), nor is it to be used to violate the prohibition of images, as Gideon collected captured gold (although not actually from idols) for construction of an ephod (a term never so used in Deuteronomy) which became a מוקש or snare in Jud 8:24-27; cp. Deut 7:26, פֶּן תִּוָּקֵשׁ "lest you be ensnared." The writer is trying to protect "the sacred and inviolable nature of deity," with the heaviest verbal ammunition available, including the enforcement provision of חרם, viz. a removal into a wholly other realm, in which the holiness of the deity makes it impossible for human beings to exist--therefore all those foolhardy enough to enter it must die. This passage thus follows a long and widespread ancient Near Eastern tradition, and so is not as peculiar as it would appear (see above). In fact, from the conceptual point of view this passage fits in perfectly with the חרם-writings of Deuteronomy 20 and the rest of Deuteronomy 7. The fact that one may feel, as scholars have often in the past, that these verses constitute an appendix to the bulk of the chapter, does not mean that they are a late addition. As I hope to have shown in two ways, their presence here is far more integral to the chapter and to the theme of חרם than has been assumed.

There are a number of reasons to assign these חרם passages a northern, fairly early provenance. These included the ancient Near Eastern parallels to verses from Deuteronomy 20, the affinities with passages from Amos, the likelihood that Mesha's חרם haunted Israel in the years and decades following (among other reasons, such as the long established northern provenance of Deuteronomy). Historians have generally sought to see the man of the חרם in Deuteronomy as Josiah. It is hard to see why. Jereboam had the power and the motive to use the חרם in his campaign across the Jordan. If Deuteronomy

---

[62] W. W. Hallo, "Biblical Abominations and Sumerian Taboos," *JQR* 76 (1985), 34f..
[63] Ibid. 38.

20 had been aimed at Josiah, it would have urged him who had no reason to use the חרם, not to.

IV: THE LAST BATTLES OF MOSES; SIHON AND OG

This survey of the references to חרם in Deuteronomy ends with the occurrences of the root early in the Book. Much thought has been dedicated to the subject of the varied traditions relating to the two kings of Transjordan, as found particularly in Numbers 21, Judges 11, and Deuteronomy 2-3.[64] There is no end of literature analyzing the place of the 'historical prologue,' Deuteronomy 1-3 in terms of its origins, and in the days since Noth, its place in the "deuteronomistic history."[65] In fact, the term "history" seems peculiarly ill-advised in relation to the Book of Deuteronomy (or any of its posited *Vorlagen*). In particular, it is dubious in relation to the traditions which have crystallized around Sihon and Og.

It is not strictly accurate to characterize the Numbers account as "historical" and the deuteronomic account as "theological" (hence late!), as some scholars have done. The Numbers account appears fairly matter of fact in isolation, but in context the theology informs all the action. No one involved in the putting together of Numbers 21 thought that victory was won independently of or against God's will. The prologue, Num 21:1-3, makes that point emphatically (even if these three verses are from another source, certain basic beliefs are common to all sources). And if theologizing is a criterion of lateness, then the Stele of the Vultures must be re-dated to a later epoch. What sets the deuteronomic account apart from Numbers is not merely a more overt presence of the deity, but also the fact that the writer utilizes mythic thought to produce a more powerful effect. This use of myth includes not only the mention of the various mythic predecessors of the Ammonites, Edomites, and Moabites, but the Rephaim. The use of the term חרם itself fits perfectly into a context such as this in which the Israelites had to push aside the forces of chaos in order to reach the safe harbor of the divinely promised *Welt*, the place of a promised Israelite *Ordnung*.[66] We

---

[64] Cf. W. A. Sumner, "Israel's Encounter with Moab, Ammon, Sihon and Og," *VT* 18 (1968), 216-28, J. R. Bartlett "Sihon and Og, Kings of the Amorites," *VT* 20 (1970), 257-77, idem "The Conquest of Sihon's Kingdom; A Literary Examination," *JBL* 97 (1978), 347-51, J. van Seters, "The Conquest of Sihon's Kingdom: A Literary Examination," *JBL* 91 (1972), 182-97, idem "Once Again--The Conquest of Sihon's Kingdom," *JBL* 99 (1980), 117-19. None of these articles deals with the חרם, surely a factor in any 'literary examination.'

[65] For an excellent bibliographical essay which includes such matters see H. D. Preuss, *Deuteronium, Erträge der Forschung* Bd. 164 (Darmstadt, 1982), 75-84.

[66] This agrees with the views of V. Maag in "Kosmos, Chaos, Gesellschaft und Recht nach archäisch-religiösem Verständnis," *Kultur, Kulturkontakt und Religion: Gesammelte Studien zur allgemeinen und alttestamentlichen Religiongeschichte* (Göttingen, 1980), 329-41. For a somewhat different view, see E. Wurthwein in "Chaos

should not fall into the snare of assuming that the only sources of importance are the few we happen to retain, when it is a near certainty that we have only in the Bible only a distillation of a larger group of Sihon-Og myths and traditions (cf. Homer's brief references to myths). It is thus impossible to arrive at a full source analysis of this story with its three major variants, but it is likely that the mythic portrayal in Deuteronomy results from drawing on an ancient source rather than literary creation of an author, redactor, or glossator. S. R. Driver characterized the references to primordial peoples and Rephaim as "antiquarian," while Von Rad saw it as an indication of Israel's interest in history.[67] Actually, they represent primordial chaos that was put in order in Transjordan, by the will of YHWH--just as the "seven nations" of Deuteronomy 7 and 20 represented the enemies who embodied the chaos Israel had to face to gain its own territory. Chaos was similarly present in the case of Israel's wars against Sihon and Og "of the remaining Rephaim." These wars, as YHWH's work, accounted for the otherwise anomalous Israelite presence on the east bank of the Jordan despite the opposition of the legendary Amorites of Transjordan, who play an analogous role to the Emim &c..[68]

The Ugaritic texts have given us much information about the Rephaim in particular,[69] which shed light on the indication the Og belonged to their number (Deut 3:11). Some dismiss this indication as an obvious example of a gloss. If this is a gloss, it is a very suggestive gloss, not to be completely disregarded.. As has long been known (*BDB* 952a.), the Rephaim take on two mythic roles in the Hebrew Bible; one in the form of gigantic long-gone inhabitants of the land and secondly as shades of the dead. Clearly, the two notions are in some way connected,[70] and in the person of Og, both are united in one person. The association of Rephaim with kings is known from the Bible and Ugarit.[71]

One may reasonably conclude that while there may be a historical kernel to the story of Sihon and Og, it has been overlaid with myth, and that the text is less historical than religious. Into this, the term חרם fits perfectly, although not, as some believe, in a partly or wholly secularized meaning.[72] As we showed above, such a secularized meaning is inappropriate, and is perhaps even more so in the context of Israel's search for an end to its wanderings. As M. Eliade put it:

---

und Schöpfung in mythischen Denken und in der biblischen Urgeschichte," *Wort und Existenz* (Göttingen, 1970), 28-38.

[67] S. R. Driver, *Deuteronomy,* 40. G. von Rad, *Deuteronomy,* 43.

[68] S. R. Driver, *Deuteronomy,* 36,37,40. G. von Rad, *Deuteronomy,* 43.

[69] A. Caquot, *DBS* fasc. 54 (1981), "Rephaim," 344ff., and J. C. de Moor, "*Rap'iuma*-Rephaim," *ZAW* 88 (1976), 323-345.

[70] So S. R. Driver, *Deuteronomy,*40.

[71] Cf. B. A. Levine & J.-M. de Tarragon, "Dead Kings and Rephaim: The Patrons of the Ugaritic Dynasty," *JAOS* 104 (1984), 649-659..

[72] C. H. W. Brekelmans, *De ḥerem,* 74, idem "Le ḥerem chez les prophètes du royaume du Nord et dans le Deutéronome," *Sacra Pagina I, BETL* 1 12/13 (1959) 277-283, idem *THAT* I, 635ff..

> (As we saw) to settle in a territory, to build a dwelling, demand a vital decision for both the whole community and the individual. For what is involved is *undertaking the creation of the world that one has chosen to inhabit* (emphasis his). Hence it is necessary to imitate the work of the gods, the cosmogony.[73]

In these few lines Eliade sums up a great deal. It should be clear that our emphasis in the treatment of the cosmogonic nature of the חרם in the MI is reinforced by these words (striking, considering Eliade was not coming from the ancient Near Eastern side of religion, though he knew a good deal about it): for the Moabites were trying to create their own world or to re-create it in their struggle against Israel. Eliade's words are, if anything, more illuminating in relation to the use of חרם in the context of Sihon and Og. In this context, too, we see that to deny the sacredness of the land in Deuteronomy,[74] goes too far, for it is actually implicit in the endless reiteration of and variation on the expression "the land which YHWH swore unto your forefathers." The land was consecrated--set apart for Israel--by YHWH's oath.

Let us return to the question of glosses for a moment. A typical comment is that of J. Leclerq, speaking of Deut 2:10-12, who expunges it in this manner:

> Les vv. 10-12 forment une note qui, par son style impersonnel, est etrangére au récite.[75]

The idea is that the biblical author must display an utter uniformity of style; any variation must be the result of another hand. Yet in reality an intelligent glossator would try to see to it that any addition conformed exactly to the style of the text. However, B. A. Levine has pointed out to me a good solution of the literary problem; the "antiquarian" passages are ancient, and used in a way analogous to the old poetic passages quoted from sources like the Book of Jasher.

The passages referring to the Rephaim and other shadowy giants in D's already distant past play an indispensable role in the deuteronomic version of the Sihon-Og story. These mythical beings symbolize the forces of chaos which had to be overcome in order to enable peoples to dwell in the land, and attain to *Weltordnung*, to life in a world order--as against, to give one possibility, a life of wandering in the chaotic wilderness. This is perfectly illustrated by Amos 2:9, a passage utilized previously in this chapter. It, too,

---

[73] M. Eliade, *The Sacred and the Profane: The Nature of Religion* (E.T.; San Diego, 1959) 51; see also 29-36.

[74] M. Weinfeld, *Deuteronomy and the Deuteronomic School* (Oxford, 1972), 225-32. In an attempt to distinguish between P and D he goes too far, drawing an absolute dichotomy between concepts of 'holy land'=P and 'holy people'=D. Actually, the two concepts, while expressed differently in both, are certainly present in D, not only as complementary to each other but indissolubly connected: YHWH has chosen a 'holy land' where his 'holy people' can reside.

[75] P. Buis, *Le Deutéronome, Source bibliques* (Paris, 1963), 45.

represents a break from the style of what precedes it (the oracles against the nations). It uses the term "Amorite" to characterize the primordial giants who preceded Israel in occupying the land. Amos characterizes the result of YHWH's destruction of the Amorites as Israel's entrance to the land. In 2:11 Amos envisioned a new generation of prophets and people consecrated to God (נזירים)[76]--people firmly rooted in YHWH's world order. Thus, the claim that we have in Deut 2:10-12 a conventional (late) gloss does not do justice to the text. When we add חרם to the picture we see that it is the perfect verb to indicate the human action of "building the world," because החרים combines the notions of destruction (of chaos) and consecration (of the world) at once. Amos did not use it here, but this may be due to a wish not to focus on any human share in the takeover of the land or found the word inappropriate for his poetic diction.

These peoples also act as "mythical precedents" for Israel. As YHWH enabled the Ammonites to dispossess the Zamzumim in primordial times, so Israel would dispossess the Amorites--the same people at issue in Deuteronomy 2 and Am 2:9-10.[77]

It is universally thought that the Sihon and Og stories are part of the deuteronomistic framework of the book, not the work of the authors of chapters 7 and 20, although in terms of content it has already been observed that the stories fit in more closely with Deuteronomy 7. The question of the relation between the versions found in Numbers and Deuteronomy must also be asked. U. Koppel has addressed it with a good deal of perspicacity, and makes the following points, in my summary:

1. The peace offer of Deut 2:26ff. stems from 20:10f..[78]

2. Sihon is termed king of Heshbon in these verses instead of as before, king of Amorites, in order to make the story fit the law of ch. 20 which deals in terms of war against cities.[79]

3. Koppel notes that in Deut 2:28-9, in opposition to Deut 20:10ff., Israel makes no demand of submission but makes requests, including the request to be allowed to pass through.[80]

4. The execution of the חרם without an expressly reported command from YHWH is due to the fact that the Israelites were seen as obeying the command of 20:10ff., Koppel infers that the whole Sihon narrative is based on

---

[76] Cf. the remarks of G. A. Smith in *The Book of the Twelve Prophets: Vol. I--Amos, Hosea and Micah, The Expositor's Bible* (New York, n.d.), 138.

[77] Cf. M. Eliade, *Cosmos and History:The Myth of the Eternal Return* (New York, 1959), 33. There are some similarities between the biblical portrait of Rephaim, Amorites, etc., and the way the Karuk Indians of California picture a primordial people, the Ikxareyavs.

[78] U. Koppel, *Das deuteronomische Geschichtswerk und seine Quellen: Die Absicht der deuteronomischen Geschichtsdarstellung aufgrund des Vergleichs zwischen Num 21, 21-35 und Dtn 2, 26-3,3 .Europäische Hochschulschriften,* Reihe XXIII, Bd. 122 (Bern, 1979), 84.

[79] Ibid. 85.

[80] Ibid. 89.

the laws of ch. 20. The חרם follows simply from an application of the law of Deut 20:10ff. once the message of peace has been refused.[81]

5. Deut 3:2 is a back-reference to 20:1ff..[82]

It seems evident that point three cancels out point one entirely. In Deut 2:26ff. the object is to avoid hostilities because control of the second party was not what was desired, while in Deuteronomy 20:10ff. conquest in one form or the other is a desideratum. His fourth point, that no express command for the חרם was given but it was nonetheless executed may be merely an indication of the deuteronomic author's understanding of the meaning of the root ירש in a Holy War or חרם context and what it entails. Yet the absence of a command for חרם does not justify the idea that Deuteronomy 20 comes into play in these narratives, since the author of the passage has done nothing to put his audience in mind of Deuteronomy 20:10ff., and the unstated command may have been understood. Koppel's fifth point is that Deut:3:2 refers back to 20:1ff. Deut 3:2 conveys YHWH's encouragement to Israel for the forthcoming battle with Og, including a reference to the successful battle against Sihon. The language of reassurance from the deity is classic Holy War language, which was familiar in Mari and throughout the ancient Near East. It is unnecessary to relate this verse to the beginning verses of Deuteronomy 20.

Only point two remains, which is indeed cleverly made, but it cannot stand up by itself. To do Koppel justice, he does not urge that the relation he sees between ch. 20 and the Sihon-Og narratives is one of slavish dependence on the part of the latter; he says at one point that "In Dtn 2,26ff. einen Mittelweg wählt zwischen den diviergenden Gesetzen in Dtn 20,10ff."[83] The narrative does have in common with Deuteronomy 20 and 7 the use of the ban, but it is unlikely that a redactor reshaped the Sihon-Og traditions in their light. If such reshaping had taken place, the story would have diverged more radically than it does from Numbers 21, e.g. by giving a siege account.

According to J. van Seters, the Sihon-Og cycle in Deuteronomy is in fact the source, along with Jephthah's speech, for the Numbers account.[84] Koppel follows the more conventional line of reasoning by deriving Deuteronomy from Numbers.[85] Although van Seters makes many good observations, he omits the matter of חרם. Num 21:1-3 is a brief חרם-account. One would doubly expect that, if Deuteronomy were the source for Num 21:21-35 of the same chapter, the חרם would also appear. It seems that the conventional view is the more probable one, although at least one additional source (the "antiquarian"} was available to the writer(s) of Deuteronomy 2-3. In the final analysis, then, it seems that any similarity between the Sihon-

---

[81] Ibid. 95.

[82] Ibid. 100.

[83] Ibid. 96

[84] J. van Seters "The Conquest of Sihon's Kingdom: A Literary Examination," *JBL* 91 (1972) 182-97.

[85] U. Koppel, *Das deuteronomische Geschichtswerk,* 83-105.

Og narratives and Deuteronomy 20 is due to their emanation from similar circles, or from similar subject matter. The writers of Deuteronomy 20, 13:13-19, and 7 had more important aims in mind than to serve as a source for the Sihon-Og traditions or for redactional shaping of narrative traditions (but if any of these had a direct influence on their formulation, it was Deuteronomy 7 in a general way).

According to my reckonings, the primary aim (in the short term) was to exert influence on Jereboam II on the eve of his campaign into the Transjordan. I argue that the Mesha affair and the Moabite חרם must have scarred the collective memory of Israel. Jereboam's campaign would have afforded the chance of getting an "eye for an eye." A court prophet with an ear for public sentiment, who had the thought *vox populi vox dei*, could have given an oracle calling on the king to retaliate against Moab with the חרם.

In one respect the Sihon-Og stories seem to go against the grain of Deut 20:16-18, 7:25-6. In Deut 2:34, which is almost the same as 3:7, the Israelites take away cattle and the "spoil of the cities," a somewhat lenient form of the חרם. A distinction is that in Transjordan they are not dealing with the homeland (Deuteronomy 20:16 נחלה), but a land of lesser status to which they are "sanctifying" their claim by reason of conquest of mythical inhabitants, like the Ammonites' defeat of the Zamzumim, and the Moabites of the Emim.

The writers of the laws of חרם were imbued with a deep YHWHism. They understood that the sacral nature of the חרם was not to be tampered with. Only if YHWH willed it could the חרם be put into operation. They transformed earlier traditions (e.g. Exod 23:27-33) for these and doubtless other reasons, introducing the חרם in a way that expressed their metaphysical appreciation of it as a weapon against chaos (as represented by the autocthonous nations), but in a way that would impede its improper use, in a vengeful crusade against Moab. The legislators of Deuteronomy 20 utilized other, ancient traditions as we saw above. Thus Deuteronomy 20 is as a consequence well-placed in the early period of Jereboam II. The other חרם traditions must date from various periods; Deuteronomy 7 draws directly on it for inspiration. Deuteronomy's חרם legislation stands revealed as more remarkable a religious document than at first sight meets the eye.

CHAPTER 6

THE "TETRATEUCH"

I: EXODUS 22:19

Exod 22:19 reads in MT: זֹבֵחַ לָאֱלֹהִים יָחֳרָם בִּלְתִּי לַיהוָה לְבַדּוֹ, "Whoever sacrifices to the gods shall be יָחֳרָם, except it be to YHWH alone." The question as to whether the יָחֳרָם is original to the verse has been raised by A. Alt. Using the Samaritan Pentateuch and the LXX Alexandrian codex (and the capital punishment formnula of the Covenant Code) as a starting point, he arrived at the following 'reconstructed' text: זֹבֵחַ לָאֱלֹהִים אחֵרִים מוֹת וּמָת,[1] or, "Whoever sacrifices to other gods shall be put to death." In other words, were we to follow Alt, we would then be in a position to dismiss this verse from consideration. More important, however, is the significance such a dismissal would have for the history of biblical religion and the חרם. For even a passing mention in the the oldest legal collection in the Torah, the Book of the Covenant, would be sufficient indication of חרם as a living practice from an ancient period. As such it would function as a precedent and basis for the laws of Deuteronomy regarding חרם, especially in Deuteronomy 13:13-19 (the existence of which mitigates in favor of the MT here). It would also offer indirect support for the antiquity of the חרם-narrative found in 1 Samuel 15. As discussed in the previous chapter, this verse, if not in need of reconstruction, has profound implications for understanding why the terminology of חרם was borrowed from polytheism.

It would seem that in this instance Alt, a scholar of undisputable brilliance, went beyond the evidence. The weight of his reconstruction is too heavy to be supported by the versions. In the first place, neither the Samaritan pentateuch nor the LXX^{A} are to be considered textual witnesses of the first order of reliability. R. Weiss has pointed to the numerous variants made by Sam. in the Covenant Code in particular, and has demonstrated their secondary character (e.g. changing שור, "ox," to בהמה, "cattle").[2] The same writer attributed the addition of אֲחֵרִים "others," to the ideological preference to refrain from using the plural form of god, אֱלֹהִים for any god other than YHWH, and judged the MT form of Exod 22:19 to be the original.[3] The second witness, the A codex of the LXX, was once considered suitable for a critical edition of the Septuagint, but Rahlfs's demonstration of the error of this view has been accepted.[4]

Apart from these caveats, another and more serious difficulty with Alt's proposal is that even the textual traditions which Alt cited, while they featured אחֵרִים, also included יָחֳרָם. or its equivalent in Greek.. מוֹת יוּמָת doesn't occur at all, and in the case of Sam. the word יָחֳרָם appears after אחֵרִים. It

---

[1] A. Alt, "The Origins of Israelite Law," in his *Essays on Old Testament History and Religion* (Garden City, N.Y., 1968), 144, n.73.

[2] R. Weiss, "Concerning One Type of Revision in the Samaritan Pentateuch," (Heb.), *Studies in the Language and Text of the Bible* (Jerusalem, 1981), 199-205.

[3] Ibid. 170.

[4] S. Jellicoe, *The Septuagint and Modern Study* (Ann Arbor, Michigan), 17f..

thus appears that if we take the nature of the two variant versions into account, the MT is in fact defensible. The substitution of אֲחֵרִים for לַיהוָה לְבַדּוֹ בִּלְתִּי may represent either a homogenization by Sam. or more likely, the desire to avoid the use of אלֹהִים for other gods mentioned by Weiss, and this tradition could have influenced LXX^{A}.[5] From a literary point of view, the wording of the pericope of Exod 22:17-19 is unusual (cf. v.17 לא תחיה) and Alt also tried to adjust v.18 to fit his conceptual scheme, but this emendation, too, has been shown to be unnecessary.[6] בִּלְתִּי לַיהוָה לְבַדּוֹ is thus more likely, in my opinion, to represent the original; it would be much harder to account for as a gloss than the conventional אֲחֵרִים, which would be a more natural choice of words for a glossator. However, from the point of view of the study of חרם, it makes no real difference. The important thing is that there is no textual tradition which does not feature the חרם. Its excision from the text must then, in the final analysis, rest on extrinsic grounds which lack sufficient weight. Moreover, the deuteronomic legislation on idolatry in Deuteronomy 13 is clearly an expansion of this ordinance; from what we have seen, there is no reason to suppose that Deuteronomy invented the idea of connecting idolatry with the חרם.

There is one more consideration in favor of retaining the MT, and that is a similar verse in 2 Kgs 5:17, the relevant part of which reads as follows:

כִּי לוֹא־יַעֲשֶׂה עוֹד עַבְדְּךָ עֹלָה וָזֶבַח לֵאלֹהִים אֲחֵרִים כִּי אִם־לַיהוָה׃

For your servant will not make holocausts and sacrifices to other gods but only to YHWH.

The verse bears an obvious resemblance to Exod 22:19. In fact, the use of the word אֲחֵרִים might even seem to strengthen Alt's argument, except that the above evidence already shows the MT is sound. What is interesting is the style of the verse, which is third person and which reads awkwardly to modern readers, especially the last clause, כִּי אִם־לַיהוָה, which has something of the same quality as the final clause of Exod 22:19. In other words, both cases were perfectly normal ways of expressing what they meant to say by the standards of biblical Hebrew.

The question that then arises is, what does יָחֳרָם mean in the context of this verse? According to Noth, it means exclusion from the community, hence inevitable death.[7] Yet death was not the unavoidable concomitant of exclusion from the community in the ancient world. The most famous example is that of Socrates, who in the *Crito* declined the opportunity to escape Athens and live elsewhere. Another example is that of Jereboam, who lived to return and rule the Northern kingdom. Moreover, the חרם is in every instance associated with some form of active intervention to bring about death.

---

[5] Ibid. 244f..

[6] A. Alt, "The Origins." 144. n.72, J. G. Williams, "Concerning One of the Apodictic Formulas," *VT* 14 (1964), 484-9.

[7] M. Noth, *Exodus: A Commentary, OTL* (Philadedphia, 1962), 186.

The exception, Ezra 10:8, comes from another period and situation not at all comparable to that of the Covenant Code. The LXX translations as "destroyed," "be utterly destroyed" are nearer the mark. It is unlikely that the penalty for sacrificing to strange gods would be less than that of cursing one's parents (Exod 21:14), for example.

There is a common thread between this verse and Deut 7:25-26. One makes an offering at a cult site, which in a pagan temple would involve the gods' images. The use of the term זֹבֵחַ in this verse, incidentally, is interesting. Since sacrifice was a universal form of worship from Mesopotamia to Rome and beyond, although the concept behind it varied, the use of the term here is a good, concrete way of expressing the idea of "thou shalt put no other gods before me." More than that, a major function of ancient sacrifice was to propitiate the gods and thus help maintain the world order of the individual and the community. The use of the word יָחֳרָם in relation to what the biblical author(s) saw as a major deviation from the proper mode of sacrifice (which had to be to YHWH alone), demonstrates one again the close relationship between the חרם, the respect for the sacral nature of god, and the consequent assurance of world order. The line that moderns draw between monolatry and monotheism can be, as this verse shows, exceedingly fine, if visible at all, since if there are gods that exist but should not be sacrificed to, they are superfluous to the world order, and are otiose at best.

This verse, like Deut 7:25-6, thus expressed the idea of an absolute prohibition of associating with idols which, if transgressed, put one beyond the possibility of atonement and with it, reintegration into the world order. The consequence would be simply to be devoted to destruction. We may well contrast this verse with Lev 27:29, "every human object of devotion that is devoted can not be redeemed; he shall surely be put to death." "Shall be put to death" is added because the context is more benign--it deals with vows--so the necessity for death is not as obvious. Also, it comes from a later age, perhaps the period of the non-lethal חרם found in Ezra 10:8. In Exodus, as the LXX translations attest, the addition of a מוֹת יוּמָת clause would not only have been superfluous but even weakened the sense. The crime was no ordinary one and the law called for no ordinary response. The idea of YHWH as a jealous god is expressed here in its intensity. To invoke a foreign god was to ascribe to an illusion the power to order the universe. The idolatrous sacrificer actively attempted to sanctify the unholy. This is stated in Deut 32:17; "they sacrificed to demons, non-god(s)." This impinged on YHWH's exclusive sanctity, which manifested itself throughout the world (Isa 6:3), a dangerous way to behave.

II: PRIESTLY WRITINGS AND THE ḤEREM

In the writings of the priests (including Ezekiel) we find the חרם in a peaceful, cultic setting, nestling amid the minutiae of the cultic regulations. The war-חרם has been somewhat 'civilianized,' and it has been reduced to a technical term among other technical terms. The theory behind the usage in

the priestly writings is not perfectly clear. The חרם still reflects its etymology
as a form of separation, inviolability, and holiness. The element of
destruction is also still present. The concept has been of necessity
reinterpreted to fit its new context. The idea of dedicating booty to YHWH
has been extended in the cult to include the priests, as with animals in
certain sacrifices (cf. Num 18:14, Ezek 44:29b). Yet while the superficial
character of the חרם is still to be seen, these few verses tell us much less
than we would like to know about the religious value the cultic חרם had for
the priests and the religious thinkers among them. All these passages,
whatever their history, date in their present form from the post-586 period.
Leviticus 27 seems to reflect a time when the sacrificial cult was again
active.

The relationship between Num 18:14 and Ezek 44:29b is of immediate
interest, and narrowly defined, is easily clarified. We say 'narrowly defined'
because we do not wish to enter here into the larger question of the blocks of
material in which they are embedded, which also have a certain relationship. Ezek 44:29 reads:

הַמִּנְחָה֙ וְהַחַטָּ֣את וְהָאָשָׁ֔ם הֵ֖מָּה יֹאכְל֑וּם וְכָל־חֵ֥רֶם בְּיִשְׂרָאֵ֖ל לָהֶ֥ם יִהְיֶֽה׃

"They (the priests) shall consume the grain offering, the sin offering, and the guilt
offering; and all חרם in Israel shall be theirs."

This is the equivalent of Num 18:9,14, which is addressed to Aaron as
follows:

9 כָּל־קָרְבָּנָ֡ם לְכָל־מִנְחָתָם֩ וּלְכָל־חַטָּאתָ֨ם וּלְכָל־אֲשָׁמָם֙ אֲשֶׁ֣ר יָשִׁ֔יבוּ
זֶֽה־יִהְיֶ֥ה לְךָ֖ מִקֹּ֣דֶשׁ הַקֳּדָשִׁ֑ים מִן־הָאֵ֛שׁ לִ֥י קֹ֣דֶשׁ קָֽדָשִׁ֖ים לְךָ֥ ה֖וּא וּלְבָנֶֽיךָ׃
14. כָּל־חֵ֥רֶם בְּיִשְׂרָאֵ֖ל לְךָ֥ יִהְיֶֽה׃

9. "This shall be yours from the most holy, from the fire; all the offerings
(including) all their grain offerings, all their sin offerings, and all their guilt offerings, which they give to me (ranking as) most holy, shall be yours and your descen-
dents. (14) All חרם in Israel shall be yours.

This is a case in which there can be little doubt that the Ezekiel text is
the secondary rendering. It has conflated two verses which stand well on
their own and in so doing, it has substituted חרם for the second קֹ֣דֶשׁ הַקֳּדָשִׁ֑ים
of Num 18:9. This is especially interesting, because it evinces the same
view of חרם as Lev 27:28d: "All חרם is most holy (קֹ֣דֶשׁ הַקֳּדָשִׁ֑ים) to YHWH." I
spoke of the חרם as a technical term in the priestly writings: it appears to
denote, in a scale of cultic value which (neglecting the negative side)
ranges from "profane" to "holy" to קֹ֣דֶשׁ הַקֳּדָשִׁ֑ים ("most holy"), something on
the plane of the latter. This helps shed light on why in the priestly writings
the connection of חרם and death is maintained (Leviticus 27, see below).
Both Ezekiel 44 and Numbers 18 stress the dangerous aspect of the holiness
of God when not correctly approached (cf. Num 18:1-5, Ezek 44:1-3); all the
more so when the "most holy" aspect is invoked via חרם (Lev 27:28-9). The

question arises as to whether this equation of קֹדֶשׁ הַקֳּדָשִׁים and חרם is an innovation of late priestly circles. It is almost certainly not an innovation. The reason why may be demonstrated from 1 Samuel 21, where the fleeing David arrives at Nob, seeking among other things food and weapons. When Ahimelech has only holy (קֹדֶשׁ) bread to offer, David assures him that he and his men have abstained from women the requisite length of time, curiously enough, and that the ritual precautions would be observed.[8] Hearing this, Ahimelech released the bread from the sanctuary. It is striking how easily the bread made the transition from קֹדֶשׁ to what was really the profane sphere. Had the bread been "most holy," i.e. קֹדֶשׁ הַקֳּדָשִׁים or חרם, Ahimelech could scarcely have given David the bread. In other words, both חרם and its 'equivalent,' קֹדֶשׁ הַקֳּדָשִׁים are irreversible in their sanctity and inviolability alike. The fatal quality of that which is קֹדֶשׁ הַקֳּדָשִׁים is brought out in Num 4:19, and in Lev 27:28-9, where the inviolability of קֹדֶשׁ הַקֳּדָשִׁים is equated with the חרם, with death the projected result. However, whereas the execution of the person who is חרם is left to human agency (cf. Joshua 7), the violation of קֹדֶשׁ הַקֳּדָשִׁים involves such an immediate infringement on YHWH's 'person,' as it were, that God's immediate intervention was the consequence (so 2 Sam 6:7f., implied in Num 4:19).

Leviticus 27 is a unique chapter in the book and in the Torah. It is a self-contained unit appended to the Holiness Code (Leviticus 17-26). It has some connection both to H, e.g. in its references to the Jubilee Year (featured in H in Leviticus 25), and to the Priestly Code of the first section of Leviticus (particularly, as Noth pointed out, to the אשם-section of Lev 5:14-6:7).[9] Therefore the chapter is in all likelihood latest as well as last.

While the chapter thus constitutes something of an anomaly, it also has the appearance of a purposeful, organized unit composed at a single time by an author or authors who participated in the traditions of Leviticus as a whole, though perhaps standing outside the immediate circles of the authors of Leviticus 1-26. At the same time, it is hard to date the practices prescribed in the chapter as opposed to the--presumably late--form in which they were distilled in order to fit into this chapter. We must first look at the chapter's beginning--in some measure its self-definition--and then analyze the passages which refer to חרם (Lev 27:21,28-9) in the light of their context and each other. I shall not attempt to define more narrowly the provenance of the chapter as a whole, as such a difficult undertaking would lead us too far astray.

The chapter begins in this way: "The Lord said to Moses thus: 'Speak to the Israelites and say to them that a man who makes a vow of separation to the Lord of the value of human lives....'" The translation of the rare expression הפלא נדר, which occurs only here and in Num 6:2, I owe to B. A. Levine, who derives the apparent root פלא from פלה, "to divide, separate," an idea

[8] There is a risk in treating of texts from different periodz "synchronically," but there is a high level of conservatism in these matters (cp. Ugaritic and even Hittite ritual texts), and the paucity of biblical material makes such a procedure unavoidable.

[9] M. Noth, *Leviticus: A Commentary, OTL* (Philadedphia, 1965), 203f..

that fits in perfectly with Num 6:2, which deals with another type of vow of separation, that of the Nazirite. None of the other renderings of the verb, e.g. the *BDB*'s rendering, "to make a difficult vow," make as much sense of the verb as this construal. The verses which employ the piel form of the vow (Lev 22:21, Num 15:3,8) denote a special votive offering as opposed to a voluntary offering (נדבה), which is basically a matter of routine in the life of the cult. This looks like a related idea, but different enough to require a different verbal stem.

In Leviticus 26, as v.2 indicates, things of the highest value are at stake, including human life. At issue are vows (נדר) of setting things apart, meaning not only by the milder form of dedication (הקדש) but also the חרם. In Numbers 6, we have yet a different mode of setting apart and of dedication, that of the Nazirite, who must accept the responsibility of certain special restrictions on his conduct for the rewards of the especially sanctified life. Thus, although it cannot be pressed too far, there is something of a parallel between the two chapters, and the use of the expression, הפלא נדר "to make vow of separation," in both could hardly be more appropriate.

This way of headlining the two chapters, as it were, with the conspicuous use of הפלא נדר is also important in another way. In Numbers 6, no one would question that the separation vow is the theme of the entire unit, in modern days called a chapter. In Leviticus 27, amid the technicalities, it is easy to lose sight of the fact that, whether the individual cases involve property redemption or lack of same, each case must be understood primarily in terms of a vow of separation (temporary or not). Any other concept not mentioned explicitly, such as punishment, should be introduced only if the sense requires it. This is important in dealing with the חרם. The three germane verses read as follows:

וְהָיָה הַשָּׂדֶה בְּצֵאתוֹ בַיֹּבֵל קֹדֶשׁ לַיהוָה כִּשְׂדֵה הַחֵרֶם לַכֹּהֵן תִּהְיֶה אֲחֻזָּתוֹ׃

27:21 The field shall become holy to the Lord when it is released in the jubilee year, like a(n irrevocably) devoted field; it shall become the priest's property.

אַךְ־כָּל־חֵרֶם אֲשֶׁר יַחֲרִם אִישׁ לַיהוָה מִכָּל־אֲשֶׁר־לוֹ מֵאָדָם וּבְהֵמָה וּמִשְּׂדֵה אֲחֻזָּתוֹ לֹא יִמָּכֵר וְלֹא יִגָּאֵל כָּל־חֵרֶם קֹדֶשׁ־קָדָשִׁים הוּא לַיהוָה׃

27:28: But every devoted thing that a man devotes to the Lord from all that he has, from man and beast and from his inherited land, shall not be sold or redeemed; especially, all that is (irrevocably) devoted is most holy to the Lord.

כָּל־חֵרֶם אֲשֶׁר יָחֳרַם מִן־הָאָדָם לֹא יִפָּדֶה מוֹת יוּמָת׃

27:29 : Every human object of devotion that is devoted cannot be redeemed; he shall surely be put to death.

Each of the verses poses problems and/or possesses peculiarities, which make it difficult to arrive at a definitive interpretation. C. H. W. Brekelmans, in attempting to solve the enigma of these verses, began by examining the relationship of Lev 27:28 to 29, and concluded, as have others before him, that Lev 27:29 should be regarded as an interpolation.[10] However, I believe that methodological considerations require that one should first compare Lev 27:21 and 28, and then consider Lev 27:29. This flows from the understanding that these three verses--or at least two of them--are organically tied to the surrounding material, and that to begin by treating any of these verses as originally separated from the immediate environment is a dubious procedure (even if it should turn out to be correct in the case of Lev 27:29).

Lev 27:21, in any case, cannot be read in isolation. Indeed, it is an integral part of what may rightly be called a paragraph, which begins in Lev 27:16. The topic of the paragraph is the consecration of land, its valuation, and possibilities of selling or redeeming it. The mention of חרם in Lev 27:21, in this context, appears as passing and almost incidental. It is, however, noteworthy, that the verse explains the lighter, and hence presumably more usual case by likening it to the case of the חרם-field, which must have been the most stringent case. This apparent paradox can easily be resolved on examination of the particular case. A landowner consecrated his land, did not redeem it, but then sold it to a presumably unsuspecting buyer. The end result is the logical one that the unredeemed, consecrated land should end up as part of the sacred holdings. The most important consideration here is that the sale, itself a form of separation, was illegal. The case, which involves apparent dishonesty on the part of the seller, must have been relatively infrequent, but at the same time, extremely frowned upon, which accounts for the almost casual use in passing of the technical usage of כִּשְׂדֵה הַחֵרֶם here. But it is also important to notice that some sort of equivalence between קדש and חרם is posited in Lev 27:21. This anticipates the more obvious connection drawn in Lev 27:28. The focus of the law of v.21 is on the disposition of the land, not on the punishment of the dishonest seller whose fate is left open. We see that this chapter is not focused on punishment. This contrasts with the seventh law of the Code of Hammurapi, which calls for the death penalty in such a case. However, Lev 27:21 does assume, in accordance with Num 18:14 (=Ezek 44:29b), that an object classified as חרם, here a field, belongs to the priests. The exact disposition of such a field has been something of an enigma. It is possible that the example of the Greek parallel cited in ch. 3, drawn from the speeches of Aeschines, holds a clue. The land devoted to Apollo, Artemis, Leto and Athena Pronaea was to be left untilled, as in the manner of some early Hittite texts and indeed Joshua 6, where Joshua curses those who would rebuild on the site. If so, this land would lie fallow. The priests would thus 'own' the land, but not benefit from it. This seems unlikely. More probably, as devoted cities became grazing grounds for the sacred bulls of early Hittite religion, so *mutatits mutandis* YHWH granted the priests the right to use the field of חרם of Lev 27:21 in Num 18:14, but such land was inalienable and could not be sold to

10 C. H. W. Brekelmans, *De ḥerem in het Oude Testament* (Nijmegen, 1959), 59-66.

any secular interest (cf.. Lev 27:28). This is the best reconstruction the meager evidence seems to allow, but it is necessarily incomplete at best.

The next step is to compare Lev 27:21 to 28 in order to see prepare the ground for testing the claim that Lev 27:29 is an interpolation by seeing just what the content of the levitical חרם is. Upon examination it becomes apparent that it is best to use not Lev 27:21 alone, but Lev 27:20 as well, for this is a case where too slavish a dependence on the verse divisions obfuscates the actual relationships of the clauses, which should not be severed so absolutely. This gives the following, much improved grounds for comparison, starting with Lev 27:.20-21:

20 וְאִם־לֹא יִגְאַל אֶת־הַשָּׂדֶה וְאִם־מָכַר אֶת־הַשָּׂדֶה לְאִישׁ אַחֵר לֹא יִגָּאֵל עוֹד׃ 21 וְהָיָה
הַשָּׂדֶה בְּצֵאתוֹ בַיֹּבֵל קֹדֶשׁ לַיהוָה כִּשְׂדֵה הַחֵרֶם לַכֹּהֵן תִּהְיֶה אֲחֻזָּתוֹ׃

Lev 27:28

28 אַךְ־כָּל־חֵרֶם אֲשֶׁר יַחֲרִם אִישׁ לַיהוָה מִכָּל־אֲשֶׁר־לוֹ מֵאָדָם וּבְהֵמָה וּמִשְּׂדֵה
אֲחֻזָּתוֹ לֹא יִמָּכֵר וְלֹא יִגָּאֵל כָּל־חֵרֶם קֹדֶשׁ־קָדָשִׁים הוּא לַיהוָה׃

It does not require a very close examination to see that with the addition of Lev 27:20, the two passages take on a much closer resemblance than would otherwise be the case. Although they make different points, there is a striking overlap of vocabulary and concepts. There is a total of eight words or roots which occur in both, which is remarkable in two such brief passages, which as can easily be seen, are of nearly the same length. Beyond the arithmetical considerations is the conceptual congruity if not identity of the two passages. Here are the eight:

אֲחֻזָּתוֹ / חרם / קֹדֶשׁ לַיהוָה / מכר / לא יִגְאַל / איש / שָׂדֶה

a man's field / not be redeemed /sell / (most) holy to YHWH / חרם / his holding.

Most of the chapter's leading themes are reflected here, with the exception of the jubilee year. Still, most of the other important motifs are present. The triple axis of land-man-god, which is absolutely essential to Israel's history, is found here. That triple relationship is most intensely figured in the Exodus-Conquest sequence, but it appears as a theme of other types of literature as well. In these verses, the lawgiver is treating of questions of individual land possession and its relation to the deity who gave the land (and all property) as an אֲחֻזָּה (= נחלה) to individual Israelites, who might then dispose of it in one way or another, either in ordinary ways such as selling, or in extraordinary ways so that the land ends up as "belonging to YHWH," by the interpretation of Num 18:14, i.e. the property of the priests. The matter is quite complex, and the possibilities include redemption, or contrariwise, חרם (= קֹדֶשׁ־קָדָשִׁים!) where the land or other property becomes irrevocably devoted to the deity. Does Lev:27:29 fit into this matrix, or not?

Lev 27:29:

כָּל־חֵרֶם אֲשֶׁר יָחֳרַם מִן־הָאָדָם לֹא יִפָּדֶה מוֹת יוּמָת

In fact, the terminology fits well into that of the chapter and the surrounding verses, as evidenced by the use of the roots חרם and פדה, and the word אָדָם. In fact, the latter two are found only in the immediate vicinity of Lev 27:27 and 28 respectively. While this may not be a decisive consideration, it should not be ignored either, for it is typical of the associational principle of the chapter's organization, which is a natural principle in this kind of legal document.

In the light of these facts, a more decisive proof is not necessary, since the burden is on those who hold to the interpolation theory to disprove the prima facie case against it. Yet clearly, Lev 27:29 fits well into a chapter dedicated to separation oaths (הפלא נדר) dealing with human life, which ordinarily is to be redeemed (so Lev 27:3-8). Finally, Lev 27:28 would be incomplete without it, since otherwise one would not know the disposition of the person of חרם.

Nonetheless, scholars who have studied this verse have been hard put to account for the harsh verdict. M. Greenberg sums up the matter pithily:

> The situation envisaged by the law of Leviticus 27:29 is obscure. Some take it to refer to a person condemned for idolatry...others, to the victim of a public vow (cf. the case of Jephthah's daughter).[11]

The suggestion that the case of Jephthah's daughter could be routinized by the law cannot be entertained. The narrative itself (Judges 11:34ff.) portrays the situation that arose in the story as grotesque and as the occasion for a special mourning observance--giving the story an element of etiology. Moreover, in the Jephthah story the gruesome outcome of the vow flowed from the vow's open-ended nature which made it impossible to predict what would be necessary for its fulfillment. No such irresponsible vow is made here. Any vow made in this context of priestly supervision must be seen as a sober and responsible act. The Jephthah vow occurred in a time of war, not (as here) peace. The randomness of the choice of the victim (who was sacrificed, not 'banned') goes against the grain of the חרם, since unlike Achan (see our treatment below), Jephthah's daughter had done nothing to infringe on the divine sphere or to endanger the world order of Israel. The case of Jephthah's daughter seems altogether too distant and too problematic to help with the priestly חרם.[12]

The other explanation is, that Lev 27:29 reflects, like Exod 22:19 and Deut 7:25-6, 13, the association of idolatry with חרם This would be consistent with what we know from elsewhere, and is much to be preferred to relat-

---

[11] M. Greenberg, "Ḥerem," *EJ* H, 345.

[12] However, Prof. Jacob Milgrom informs me that he disagrees on this point; it should be interesting to see his comments in the second volume of his *AB Leviticus II* commentary, now in preparation.

ing the passage to the story of Jephthah. Nevertheless, this explanation does not account for why this verse appears in its present context (a problem for the interpolation theory as well), of vows of separation, nor the lack of explicit connection between the חרם and idolatry or even contact with idols.

It is on the subject of who can be devoted that the connection between vv.28 and 29 assumes importance. Lev 27:28 carefully limits vows of חרם to the property of the man devoting. This property includes "all that is his, from men and cattle and from the field of his inheritance." Since we know from Lev 27:29 that the fate of the human being devoted is death, it is clear that a principal purpose of Lev 27:28 is to prevent the powerful landowner from devoting people other than those under his ownership, such as relatives or other freemen. In other words, his power to devote people was limited to slaves. Furthermore, we can assume that the slaveowner was not in a position to devote his Israelite slave. The latter had a special status and was to remain enslaved for a limited period of time--six years--according to the legislation of Exod 21:1-12 (cp. Deut 15:12-18); the fact that this legislation was sometimes honored more in the breach than in the observance (cf. Deut 15:18, which tries to coax the reluctant slaveowner into freeing his Hebrew slave and Jer 34:9ff., wherein an attempt is made to put Deuteronomy's legislation into effect), is immaterial to the intent of the lawgiver. The slave to be devoted must have been a foreigner. This would not in itself have acted as an incentive for making such a vow, as there are ways of showing one's piety other than depriving oneself of productive labor. Foreign slaves would have been viewed as more expendable, and less (potentially) a part of society--even possibly a threat to it. and its world order. Again, one might point out that if the case in question related to idolatry, it would not be placed with vows of separation, the subject of this tightly-knit chapter. The evidence from Deuteronomy, at any rate (and Exod 22:19 is consistent with it), indicates that the execution of an individual is a communal matter; it was not the job of the individual to eliminate his compatriots when he suspected them of worshipping alien gods.

The idolatry theory has another weakness. Lev 27:28 deals with a situation in which the animals and the property of the man as well as his human property can be devoted to the Lord and one assumes from the wording that this devotion is out of the free will of the landowner, unlike the case of idolatry (Exod 22:19).

If we put the matter into the framework provided by Num 21:1-3, where a vow of חרם was made by the embattled community in order to receive in return the aid of YHWH against the enemy, we see that we may have here, in altered form, the same mechanism at work. A landowner, despairing of his prospects, might be moved to devote irrevocably his property--from his land to his slave--hoping for YHWH to respond favorably and restore him to prosperity. Just like an average person who impinges on YHWH's immediate vicinity, the "most holy" or קֹדֶשׁ־קָדָשִׁים, a person devoted to חרם, as a result, not of war, but because of his or her status as a slave, would have to die. In this stratum of writings, then, the חרם continued to preserve something of its original force, though formulated in a hierocratic way, i.e. it has been placed at a remove from its "Holy War" origins and formulated as part of the priestly code of technical expression.

The use of the terms גאל and פדה in Lev 27:28-9 shows that the lawgiver is still thinking in terms of the "vow of separation" (הפלא נדר), for it is the same terminology used throughout the chapter. In the case of idolatry, the חרם stipulations are absolute, and there could be no question--especially in the priestly circles from which the text of Leviticus 27 emerged--as to whether the חרם could be mitigated by paying an equivalent sum of money. After all, many lesser offenses merit death according to Torah law. The point that emerges from Lev 27:28-9 is not that the slave has done something to set off the immutable workings of the חרם, for the whole tendency of the Torah in treating capital punishment indicates that the law itself would contain a justification or explanation of the nature of the offense (where it was not self-explanatory). Rather the slave has been set apart, devoted to YHWH because the master hoped for something in return, in a way close to that of Num 21:1-3 (where the spoils certain to accrue in victory had to be devoted to God instead). Once that had been done, it became irrevocable (לא יִפָּדֶה) since the matter had been translated to the highest sphere ("most holy"). This illustrates what was said above, viz. that the חרם had become part of the technical vocabulary of the priests.

One aspect of Lev 27:29 is surprising in the light of Num 18:14 (=Ezek 44:19b), which places the spoils of the חרם under the exclusive control of the priests. It would have suited the interest of the priests to take such devoted slaves and employ them on the temple estates, as they did, for example, in ancient Mesopotamia.[13]

Yet despite the 'secularization' that Noth saw in this chapter,[14] there still remained, for the framers of these laws of חרם, an overriding religious priority. The priests of all people entertained seriously and benefited personally from the idea of holiness, and they ranked חרם with its idea of consecration by destruction, as we have seen, with the highest degree of holiness. The classification was in keeping with the general notion that YHWH was the arbiter of destinies and that even animal blood was not to be consumed by humans, while human blood was not to be shed without YHWH's sanction. On the other hand, they had their avenues of recruiting temple labor, while they preserved, at least in the letter of their laws, the dreadful aspect of חרם.

A wholly different question is addressed by Ezek 44:29b in conjunction with Num 14:9,14, as to whether the אשם sacrifice has properties analogous to חרם. It is clear that these texts differentiate between the various offerings, including אשם, and חרם. Numbers treats of them in different verses while establishing that all of them are assigned to the priests. The Book of Ezekiel

---

[13] Cf., e.g., J. Oelsner, "Erwägungen zum Gesellschaftsaufbau Babyloniens von der neubabylonischen bis zur achamenidischen Zeit (7.-4 Jh. v. u. Z.)," *AOF* IV (1976), 131-49. Also, for an earlier period, cf. I. J. Gelb, "The Arua Institution," *RA* 66 (1972), 1-21.

[14] M. Norh, *Leviticus*, 203f..

combines Num 18:9 & 14 into one verse. But it differentiates חרם from the sacrifices; the חרם is clearly not one of them. This does not mean that the חרם was never used as a means of atonement--this would have been a usage of the vow-חרם just mentioned, since the landowner would have probably attributed his failing fortunes to his failures in religion (at least some of the time)--but it does mean, as already suspected, that the two terms could not be simply be identified with each other.

After all that has been said, the question Greenberg raises as to what situation was envisaged by Lev 27:28-9 has not been fully answered. My argument was that the laws of these verses applied only to foreign slaves, and was only for times of acute distress when the owner sought help from YHWH in this manner. Lev 27:21 shows that property could be irrevocably willed to the deity (שְׂדֵה הַחֵרֶם), thus coming under the management of YHWH's representatives on earth, the priests (Num 18:14, Ezek 44:21b). What is implied by the use of the term חרם in the first connection, and probably in the second as well, is that the deity, i.e. the priests (representing YHWH), had the right of refusal, just as YHWH did in Num 21:1-3. A misfortune-maddened landowner could scarcely be in a position to devote at will dozens of slaves or herds of valuable cattle. Thus in this model, there would be strong disincentives at both ends. The legislation of Lev 27:28-29 was not devised in order to create a bloodbath, nor should transactions involving the "most holy" take place as a matter of routine. The priests had nothing to gain by approving human slaughter; only real distress allied with true piety could have justified a man of property's devotion of a human being meeting with acceptance from YHWH or his priests. Furthermore, the priests could not--no bureaucracy could--allow the devotion of properties into their jurisdiction to occur in a way completely outwith their control. According to Lev 27:21,28, the שְׂדֵה הַחֵרֶם became part of the priests' holdings, and came under their management; hence they had to have control over what would come under that heading. As Leviticus 22, a chapter which deals with the lower level of "sacred donations"[15] or קֹדֶשׁ, illustrates, these donations were highly regulated to screen out the unacceptable. Using the Talmud's logical principle of going from the "light" or lesser case to the "heavy" or graver case (known as קל וחומר), this must also have occurred at the "most holy" level. The dynamics of the vow of חרם as well as the practicalities of the situation thus unite to show that the priests had the right of refusal, which kept the vow-חרם under control. The priestly right of refusal is implicit in the nature of a vow. YHWH had to agree to cooperate in Num 21:1-3 or victory would have been denied Israel. The vow does not accomplish the votary's will by compulsion of the divine, but is a bargain which can be declined by the party of the second part, here represented by the priests.

Whatever the date of Leviticus 27 (and the other passages), the priestly חרם is evidently a later adaptation of the war-חרם. That the priests could not let the חרם die in the period after its application in warfare ceased is an im-

[15] See now B. A. Levine, *Leviticus: The Traditional Text with the New JPS Translation, The JPS Torah Commentary* (Philadelphic, 1989), 147-52.

pressive indication that the חרם was closer to the heart of biblical religion than moderns have wanted to accept (another indication is the group of passages, beginning with Exod 22:19, that relate to the anti-iconic nature of YHWH).. Josh 7:1, 22:24, which in speaking of the חרם use the priestly term for a sin against the divine, מעל, also attest the degree of the priestly investment not only in the peacetime חרם, but in the war-חרם as well. Most significant, perhaps, is that Lev 27:28's יָחֳרַם אִישׁ לַיהוָה מִכָּל־אֲשֶׁר־לוֹ echoes the language of 1 Sam 15:3, וְהַחֲרַמְתֶּם אֶת־כָּל־אֲשֶׁר־לוֹ, which helps explain the former verse's peculiar formulation. It reflects an effort, despite the difference in situations, to establish continuity with the war-חרם, which was ultimately the source of the priestly חרם 's legitimacy.

The retention and institutionalization of the חרם envisaged in Leviticus 27, and the equation of the חרם to the קֹדֶשׁ־קָדָשִׁים or "most sacred,"[16] unite to show the positive light in which those most involved in maintaining the daily practice of YHWHistic religion, the priests, viewed it. The equation just alluded to is evidence the term חרם was preserved because it reflected a core conception of the holiness of God, which the priests were reluctant to discard. Indeed, although the prophets criticized the institution of sacrifice, we have no prophetic denunciation from any period which criticizes any aspect of the חרם any more than the prophets denounce holiness in general. Due to the unsystematic nature of the ancient Near Eastern law code, we may safely guess that we have in these few passages only the surviving remnant of a much more multifaceted priestly תורה or "teaching" on the subject. But we cannot know from these indications whether the priests applied Exod 22:19, the law against idolatry, to choose the most obvious example. Nevertheless, enough remains to us to characterize the priestly חרם as an expression of the ancient perception of the essential nature of the חרם, which the priests were able to express in their own language and in almost physical terms by giving it equivalence to the "most holy" or קֹדֶשׁ־קָדָשִׁים, also a name for the holiest place found in the sanctuary of YHWH.

III: NUMBERS 21:1-3

This pericope has been thought to be either awkwardly placed, or out of place, by the vast majority of scholars, although it is not easy to pinpoint the 'correct' place into which it would fit. An alternative theory would be that Num 21:1-3 was part of the core material, but that through the activity of one or more redactors new sections were added and the original structure changed to accommodate them. If we look at Numbers 20-21 and delete the story of Aaron's death, as well as the "brazen serpent" account, what would remain would resemble nothing so much as Exodus 16-17, which also contains "complaint material" climaxing with battle. Here, should this hypothesis be worth considering, the battle account has ended up being <u>prefixed</u> to a

---

[16] For a contrasting view, see J. Milgrom in *Numbers: The Traditional Hebrew Text with the New JPS Translation, The JPS Torah Commentary* (Phila., 1990},151-2, 429.

'complaint section' because the latter had been displaced by another account, possibly that of the serpent. Originally (according to this hypothesis) the loss in battle was as a result of the people's complaint at either Meribah or the Reed Sea Road. The reference to the Reed Sea seems designed to remind the reader or listener of the people's conduct after the crossing of the Sea (i.e. Exodus 16-17), assuming that Num 21:4a belongs to the same source as 1-3 (generally attributed to JE),[17] or, if it doesn't, as seems more likely, that it still reflects an equally old tradition. It is important to notice that, as things stand now, there is no reason given for the success of the King of Arad against Israel in Num 21:1.

Another way of looking at it is that of A. M. Goldberg, who says that the pericope is a piece of a broader framework; the victory is a counterpart to the defeat at the same site in Num 14:45, and is completed by the victories over Sihon and Og.[18] This leaves the question just posed unanswered as to why the initial defeat occurred. It is interesting that the final shape of the chapter includes no less than three etiologies; that of Hormah, the bronze serpent, and Beer (v.16). If my hypothesis outlined above is correct, however, the etiological principle of organization of the chapter--assuming it is not just incidental--is due to a secondary redaction.[19]

We come then to the next problem, that raised long ago by G. B. Gray, namely the question of whether the phrase, "king of Arad" represents a gloss, as he suggested.[20] Indeed, the reading "The Canaanite, the king of Arad, inhabitant of the Negeb," is unusual and looks awkward--at least to us. Yet it is perfectly good Hebrew. Gray said that once Arad is mentioned, the last clause becomes redundant,[15] but that is not convincing in context, especially as redundancy was a highly valued trait in ancient Near Eastern literature. The sense of the phrase becomes clear from the mention of the cities put to the חרם in Num 21:2. The king's base or capital city was Arad, but he sojourned in other places as well, a practice attested among later monarchs, such as the English Tudors (who called it a "progress"), for highly practical reasons. Whatever the case was in the LBA, in biblical times there were dozens of cities in the Negeb, including the Arad area, which doubtless gave the writer the idea of the additional cities (beyond Arad).[21] However, the presence or absence of the king of Arad in this pericope is not a matter of the first importance for our subject, while the question of the חרם in this passage is.

Following Num 21:1, in which a Canaanite king attacks Israel and defeats it, taking prisoners, Israel makes a vow (Num 21:2) in which it swears

---

[17] So S. R. Driver, *An Introduction to the Literature of the Old Testament* (repr.; New York, 1956), 66, and most commentaries.

[18] A. M. Goldberg, *Das Buch Numeri, Das Welt der Bibel, Kleincommentar* (Dusseldorf, 1970), 94.

[19] For a new redaction-analysis of Numbers 20-1, see J. Milgrom, *Numbers:*, 463-7.

[20] G. B. Gray, *A Critical and Exegetical Commentary on the Book of Numbers, ICC* (Edinburgh, 1903), 273.

[21] Cf. Z. Herzog, "Enclosed Settlements in the Negeb and the Wilderness of Beer-Sheba," *BASOR* 250 (1983), 41-50.

that upon YHWH's giving the enemy into Israel's hand, it would devote (החרם), i.e. consecrate to destruction, the enemy cities. The second verse reflects the situation of the first, that Israel does not stand well with YHWH, for otherwise it would not have to bargain for YHWH's help. It is notable that Moses does not intercede for Israel here. In fact, with the exception of the serpent episode, Moses's role in this chapter is either strikingly absent or quite perfunctory (as in Num 21:17), until the last episode of Og, which is viewed by most scholars as derived from Deuteronomy.[22] Num 21:21, "Israel sent messengers to Sihon, king of the Amorites," contrasts with Num 20:14, "Moses sent messengers from Kadesh to the king of Edom." This odd feature of Numbers 21 may be a secondary consequence of the kind of reshuffling postulated earlier. It is reasonable to infer also that Num 20:1-3 is either a version of an actual historical event that was projected back into Moses's time or of a type of event that occurred more.than once.

In considering the חרם in and of itself, this passage is of prime importance, quite aside from the historicity of the event, which is impossible to prove or disprove.[23] According to E. Stern, the archeologist, no excavational evidence shedding light on the חרם exists.[24] What is important here is the concept of applying the חרם as a result of a vow, which C. H. W. Brekelmans rightly takes as evidence of the 'positive quality' of the חרם. (see above. II). Despite the fact that the חרם involves refraining from plundering, it should be understood, as the same author says, as placing the spoil in God's sphere (thus putting it positively).[25] Brekelmans' point is that the חרם is not understood as an אסור, i.e. vow of restriction, or negative vow.

Two remarks immediately suggest themselves. The first is that the possibility of a war-חרם vow makes the idea of a peacetime חרם-vow plausible, and this applies to Lev 27:28-9. Secondly, the Bible portrays two possible ways of initiating the war-חרם; either as commanded by deity, as exemplified by the חרם in the Book of Joshua, or by a vow of the community, providing that YHWH has decided to accept it. Once YHWH has accepted it, then victory is assured. One reason why Moses could not be the initiator here, is that in general the חרם is utilized for conquest traditions, in which Moses could have no part (except in Transjordan). In this pericope, Moses is still active, but it was felt unsuitable to give Moses the role of either intercessor (see above) or generalissimo, if only as a concession to the fact that the Arad area was to come to have a place in

---

[22] According to S, R. Driver, *A Critical and Exegetical Commentary on the Book of Deuteronomy, ICC* (Edinburgh, 1895), 47, the idea was A. Dillman's in his commentary *Numeri, Deuteronomium, und Josua, Kurzgefasste Exegetische Handbuch zum A.T.*.

[23] For a sense of the discussion, see R. C. Boling and G. E. Wright, *Joshua, A New Translation with Notes and Commentary, AB* (Garden City, N.Y., 1982), 326-7. A. Aharoni, *Land of the Bible: A Historical Geography* (Rev. ed., Philadelphia, 1979), 201, M. Naor, "The Problem of Biblical Arad," *Proceedings of the American Academy for Jewish Research* 36 (1968), 95-105.

[24] Cf. the appendix to ch. 4.

[25] C. H. W. Brekelmans, *De ḥerem* , 69-70.

Israel's *Weltordnung* (in a way Transjordan could not). But this is not a conquest pericope in the strict sense, as G. W. Coats has pointed out,[26] and Israel did not take possession of the cities, which is one reason the war-חרם of Num 21:1-3 fitted into the schema of the chapter.

An important feature of Num 21:1-3 is the etiological dimension of the passage, as evinced in the word play of חרמה/חרם. C. H. W. Brekelmans thought v.3b an addition, which solved the problem of the nature of the etiology; it was secondary.[27] Yet the grounds on which he defended this are questionable--his reasoning involved some dubious considerations of an Arabian locale for Atharim.[28] On the other hand, B. O. Long, who devoted a book to biblical etiologies, saw this etiology as part of the integral literary structure of the passage while still taking it seriously as a battle report.[29] The biblical narrative abounds with small passages leading up to an etiology, which to the writers was the raison d'être of the individual passage. This pericope falls in that pattern. If one subtracts the etiology, too little foundation remains to be built upon.

There is no reason to doubt that, the archeology of Arad aside, this practice of a vow to put to the חרם in return for YHWH's support was an actuality in ancient Israel. This is the strictly historical importance of the pericope, and for the understanding and history of חרם the considerations adduced above regarding the use of the vow in peace add to this unique little section's importance. One might add that, in a previously discussed parallel of Livy, in which he (IX:7-X:11) described an outmoded Roman practice, the initiator of the vow is, along with the enemy, dedicated to the gods. No one would be likely to initiate such a vow, except in such a case as Livy expounds, where the legions were in deep trouble in the battlefield. A similar dynamic is found here. Israel was in trouble, and it resorted to a vow of חרם in order to retrieve the situation. Lives were at risk, so the price of divine aid, forfeiture of booty, was easy to pay.

The Torah contains a full range of uses of the חרם, from the legal subtleties of Deuteronomy and Leviticus to the war-חרם of Deuteronomy 2-3 and Num 21:1-3. The legal material has presented the greater challenge, because it is necessary to try to uncover the agenda of the legislators from the meager remains of their work as it has come down to us. The incident of Num 21:1-3 is a good lead-in to the Book of Joshua, which uses the root חרם more than any other book in the Bible. It presages the events at Ai (Joshua 8), which also began with disaster and ended with a successful חרם. It is now time to turn to the most eventful of books from the point of view of the חרם.

---

[26] G. W. Coats, "Conquest Traditions in the Wilderness Theme," *JBL* 95 (1975), 182-3.

[27] C. H. W. Brekelmans, *De ḥerem,* 68.

[28] Ibid. The NJV notes that the meaning of the word is doubtful and that it may not even connote a place name.

[29] B. O. Long, *The Problem of Etiological Narrative, BZAW* 108 (1968), 48-9. J. A. Seligman, "Etiological Foundations in Biblical Historiography," (Heb.) *Zion* 26 (1961), 144-5, points out that many ancient etiologies were historically accurate.

CHAPTER 7

JOSHUA-JUDGES

I: JOSHUA 6

Joshua 6 is a spectacular chapter, replete with what would today be called “special effects.” It is unique, and celebrates a unique occasion; the first conquest of a city on the soil of the land west of the Jordan River, the “Promised Land.” It contains many supernatural, mythic elements, too many to be explained away by positivistic reductionism. In addition, the archeological picture has been sufficiently clarified so as to rule out the possibility that the account before us has a strictly historical basis.[1] Therefore both M. Noth, in his well-known *History of Israel,* and J. M. Miller and J. H. Hayes, who recently collaborated on *A History of Ancient Israel and Judah,* were correct in dismissing the battle of Jericho from consideration in trying to reconstruct the actual course of the Israelite settlement in Canaan (which they do in virtually the same language).[2] R. de Vaux's effort to find a historical kernel in the story of Jericho is heroic, but not convincing.[3] However, questions of the Israelite conquest can be dealt with only incidentally here.

Nonetheless, even if Noth's position is correct, the chapter is an invaluable source from the point of view of the historian of Israelite religion. In fact, taking it in conjunction with ch. 7, the story of Achan and the חרם, it would seem that we have here material of great historical importance as well--provided we are willing to allow that the location (Jericho) was not chosen for reasons of accurate military history. As Y. Elitsur has pointed out, the entire conquest narrative in the Book of Joshua is a highly abbreviated schema.[4] Since the archeological/military historical approach has not unlocked the text's secrets, it is better to try to understand the chapter in its own terms, which are primarily religious in orientation. The excavator of Jericho, J. Garstang, understood this,[5] although many of his successors have become bogged down in attempts to reconcile the tell with the Jericho of Joshua 6.

---

[1] A. Negev, ed., *The Archeological Encyclopedia of the Holy Land* (Nashville, 1986), 196a. "...this site was inhabited after the beginning of (the 14th) century, but deserted again by the second half." It then hypothesizes that LBA II may have been conquered by Joshua; but this is too early. Cf. P. Bierkowski, *Jericho in the Late Bronze Age* (Warminster, U.K., 1986), 156, Jericho was abandoned in early LBIIb, and not resettled until the 11th cent.. J. A. Soggin in "Jericho: Anatomie d'une conquête," *Revue d'histoire et de philosophie religieuses* 57 (1977), 1-18 ,sees Joshua 6 as part of a liturgy. No one has explained away the combined evidence of desolation of Jericho and Ai in the period.

[2] M. Noth, The History of Israel (2nd ed. N.Y., 1960), 149, n.2, J. M. Miller & J.H. Hayes, *A History of Ancient Israel and Judah* (Philadelphia.,1986), 94f..

[3] R. de Vaux, *The Early History of Israel* (Philadelphia, 1978), 606-8.

[4] Y. Elitsur, "The Plan of Conquest in the Book of Joshua," (Heb.) in B. Lurya, ed., *Studies in the Book of Joshua, Ben Gurion House Bible Group*, (Jerusalem,1960/61), 1-7.

[5] J. Garstang, *Joshua, Judges* (London, 1931), 140.

Another pitfall has been the analysis of sources. Oesterly and Robinson, although sharing the now unpopular view that the chapter was divided between J and E, remarked that "exact disentanglement is practically impossible."[6] This caution has not been much heeded: a recent attempt traces eight or more sources with absolute precision.[7] I shall rest content for this analysis with two; one which is a "חרם source," and the other a priestly (though not necessarily P) source. It is not necessary for the purposes of this study, to multiply sources, since in this case the individual approach of each of the sources seems to complement that of the other (putative) sources; in other words, the sources are basically compatible in outlook, and that this is more important than any of the discrepant details. This should emerge in the course of my exposition.

C. H. W. Brekelmans has already constructed a case for the antiquity of the חרם passages in this chapter, with the exception of Josh 6:19, in which precious metals are dedicated to the treasury of the Lord. This he believes is an interpolation.[8] There seems to be no reason to follow this line of reasoning, however, since the MI offers a good parallel in that, almost certainly, cult vessels of YHWH (which would have included objects of metal) were dragged to Kemosh after the חרם of Nebo. The חרם plays a key structural role in leading to the story of Achan, where the חרם is at the heart of the events, and hence onward to the Ai episode (which is initially a disaster because of the infringement of the חרם), as well as linking backward to the old spy narrative of Joshua 2. De Vaux noted the geographical incongruity of the Valley of Achor in relation to Ai and Jericho, and concluded that the Achan story was originally independent of its present setting.[9] In fact, this makes too much of a detail. The authors and redactors of Josh 6-8 were well aware of the location of Achor, but they wished to use the name through typical biblical wordplay as a heuristic device (which the Chronicler later spelled out for all to see). The especially severe nature of the חרם at Jericho makes it clear that the חרם of Jericho and the Achan episode are organically connected. Brekelmans points out that the exceptionally thoroughgoing form the חרם assumes in Joshua 6 has no structural function, but relates rather to the circumstances at hand at Jericho. If in Num 21:1-3, the difficulty of the situation led to an invocation of the חרם, the conquest of a seemingly impregnable Jericho led to the חרם in its most extreme form.[10] The procession he interprets as a way of indicating the dependence of the people on YHWH to come to their aid.[11] Leaving this last point open, the other two points he makes are important: a) the structural function of the חרם in Joshua 6 is such that without it the Book of Joshua could not exist in anything faintly re-

[6] W. O. E. Oesterly & T. H. Robinson, *A History of Israel* v.1 (London, 1932), 123.
[7] L. Schwienhorst, *Die Eroberung Jerichos: Exegetische Untersuchung zu Joshua 6, Stuttgarter Bibelstudien* 122 (Stuttgart, 1986).
[8] C. H. W. Brekelmans, *De ḥerem in het Oude Testament* (Nijmegen, 1959), 91.
[9] R. de Vaux, *The Early History,* 612f..
[10] C. H. W. Brekelmans, *De ḥerem* , 88f..
[11] Ibid. 91.

sembling its present form and b) the exceptional way the חרם is presented is best explained by the circumstances of the chapter and cannot just be attributed to last-minute redactional tinkering.

There is more to be said on the subject of the second point. It bears on a basic question which has seldom been fruitfully addressed: what is going on? J. Garstang advanced the idea of a "first fruits" hypothesis, in which Jericho represented the first fruit of the Israelite conquest, and so was offered to God.[12] This idea cannot be accepted because of the lack of any real correspondence between the events of Joshua 6 and an offering of first fruits. It does seize, however, on an important datum; this is the first city that Israel is depicted as attacking on the west side of the Jordan. Now M. Eliade has pointed out that for any people, to settle into a new territory is a cosmogonic event; a new world is created and consecrated.[13] In a biblical context, W. Brueggemann has linked the creation theme and the land restoration theme in Deutero-Isaiah and in P, concluding that "creation then is restoration to the land."[14] Here, when dealing with the first takeover of the land, creation is no less present. Thus the length of time, seven days, is divided into a period of six and a single climactic day in Genesis 1, though more clearly in Exod 20:9f.: "Six days shall you work and do all your assigned tasks, but the seventh day is a sabbath to YHWH.... For six days YHWH made the heavens and the earth, the sea and all therein, and he rested on the seventh day...."

In the myth of Joshua 6, creation was only possible through destruction of the walled city. Hence the seventh day involved not rest--for this was war, Holy War par excellence--but a special heightening of activity (sevenfold!) which resulted in the collapse of the forces resisting the new world order promised by YHWH (while Holy War need not imply חרם, it certainly is compatible with it). In this context of war as creation of a new world order, the war-חרם, fit exactly, since according to our understanding it represents the purposeful destruction of the forces of chaos in order to bring about world order. In this way the priestly or so-called liturgical segment of the account may be seen as requiring the חרם in as absolute a form as can be imagined. It is true that the number seven's ubiquity in the Bible (and the Near East) makes it hazardous to read too much into it, but here the context of creation and the way the division is made between the first six days and the final day seem to point to the analogy of Creation. So does the example from Ugarit of the creation of Baal's house in six days of fire; on the seventh day the house cools into its final shape. Since the creation of a palace for a deity of Baal's importance is cosmogonic (dealing with the construction of order in the universe), and is preceded by fire and flames, the myth depicts a creation which arises from forces of destruction. It seems highly probable that this twin conception of creation through חרם had a part in "the Urtext" of Joshua 6. The miraculous power of YHWH, then, made possible the con-

---

[12] J. Garstang, *Joshua Judges,* 143.

[13] M. Eliade, *The Sacred and the Profane: The Nature of Religion* (San Diego, 1959), 29ff., 32ff..

[14] W. Brueggeman, "The Kerygma of the Priestly Writers," *ZAW* 84 (1974), 410.

secration of Jericho to destruction; thus in effect acting in concert with the miracle-making God to create and consecrate (via the חרם) the new territory. It thus becomes more apparent as to why the situation called for the חרם in such an absolute form. The mythic character of the chapter lends itself to the "pure" form of the practice. One might add that the saving of a select group of people from the holocaust is a widespread motif in biblical literature, so that it scarcely seems necessary to follow J. A. Soggin in separating the reference to Rahab in v.17b from the חרם of 17a[15]. In the light of the effort to separate out the Kenites from the Amalekites in 1 Samuel 15, such notices take on the cast of a deliberate attempt of the author(s) to emphasize the distinction between the just and the damned.. The disjunctive use of רק, "only" commonly introduces a qualifying phrase, and critics often pronounce such phrases additions (so with the law of חרם in Deut 20:16-18, cf. vv.14,20!) as if the people (esp. lawmakers!) of the biblical period never felt the need to qualify their statements or to draw distinctions. In fact, as the text stands, the חרם represents the strand of Joshua 6 most closely allied to the old spy story, since both assume that human exertion will be needed to deal with the enemy.

The "chaos to order" theory of the war-חרם thus has utility for deepening our understanding of texts like the Mesha Inscription and Joshua 6. The above lays out my basic interpretation of the חרם's role in the chapter. I shall conclude with some additional questions this chapter raises, as well as comment on one or two points raised in recent scholarship.

The section comprising Joshua 6-7 is the only one in which the חרם and the ark coexist in the same context. Critics have raised the question of the ark from the literary critical point of view, and to some the ark is secondary.[16]

P. D. Miller has addressed the question judiciously:

> There are numerous references to the Ark in the conquest narratives of Joshua 3-6, but these chapters are regarded as quite expanded and heavily oriented to the cult, and so may be dubious sources when dealing with such a matter as the Ark. ...noting the association of the Ark with the holy wars of Israel in all other relatively early texts, one is forced to see that same association here. ...it can hardly be doubted, contra Noth, that the Ark played a central role in the earliest level about the march around the city, although the very numerous references to it are the result of expansion.[17]

The last point about the central role of the Ark is well taken. Little of the narrative would stand up if the ark were deleted entirely. Moreover, there is a consistent pattern in Joshua 3-4 and 6. The language relating to the ark in Joshua 6 is the same as that of Joshua 3, but it is unlike the language used in connection with the ark in both the Torah and the other historical books. This is true of the verbs used (e.g. Josh 3-4. 6's נשא vs. Kings' עלה), of

---

[15] J. A. Soggin, *Joshua: A Commentary*, *OTL* (Philadelphia.,1972), 88.

[16] Cf. J. Dus, "Die Analyse zweier Ladeerzählungen des Josuabuches (Jos 3-4 und 6)," ZAW 72 (1964), 107-121.

[17] P. D. Miller, *The Divine Warrior in Early Israel* (Cambridge, Ma.,1973), 150f..

the terms for the ark personnel, and the precise designation of the ark. The implication of this observation for source analysis is to distance the ark references from any of the conventional sources to which literary critics are wont to resort, and tends to confirm the position that the ark is not secondary to the narrative.

Joshua 3-4 and 6 involve not only similarity of language with regard to the ark; each features a cultic procession and a miracle as well. Thus the web binding chapters 2-8 (at least) is rather more formidable than microanalytical studies could suggest. Together, the חרם source and the (priestly) source mentioning the ark connect to every chapter of Joshua 2-8.

The implications of a stimulating study by G. del Olmo Lete comparing Joshua 6 and the Keret epic[18] have not affected literary critical study of the Jericho story in any detectable way. Del Olmo Lete's citation of Canaanite epic style with its chronic repetitions and the specific resemblances between Keret and Josh 5:13-6 is significant in helping to assess the kind of text Joshua 6 is, and the place the חרם has in it. In all probability the Jericho story must in its main lines have a unity (even if the product of a sort of collaboration) and antiquity usually denied by the critics. R. Boling's remark "this is a highly polished story which became peculiarly stylized long before it was taken into the Dtr-history"[19] therefore hits the mark. This chapter still reflects the early concept of חרם found in the MI. Brekelmans sees here a refinement of the Moabite conception of חרם, since no conception of satiating the deity is present.[20] However, this element is still present in the later text of Isaiah 34.

In connection with Jericho, a school of thought has arisen which sees the origins of the חרם in terms of a medical model; i.e. as a response to plague or unhealthy conditions.[21] In line with this is 2 Kgs 2:19, which characterizes Jericho as an unhealthy spot. The Mesha Inscription itself proves that medical matters have nothing to do with it, and none of the biblical חרם texts sustain such a possibility, not even Joshua 6. The חרם comes out of a type of ancient religious thought manifested in a type of warfare known as Holy War, although as appears from the Assyrian example, the חרם is not integral to Holy War, but merely compatible with it. The חרם is a religious practice in which the people and deity interact in a certain way; in the חרם some or all of the spoils of the god's victory are are inviolably reserved to him. Medical explanations are an attempt to rationalize a practice based not on modern medicine but on ancient ideas of the world. Israel was Mesha's plague, against which he needed an army, not a clinic or a hospital bed. In general, attempts to sanitize the Bible are doomed.

---

[18] G. del Olmo Lete, "La conquista de Jerico y la leyenda ugaritica de KRT," *Sefarad* 25 (1965), 3-15

[19] R. G. Boling & G. E. Wright, *Joshua: A New Translation with Notes and Commentary, AB* (Garden City, 1982), 204.

[20] C. H. W. Brekelmans, *De ḥerem* , 92.

[21] R. G. Boling & G. E. Wright, *Joshua,* 214 with literature.

The canonical text of Joshua 6 raises complex questions; no definitive literary-critical solution has been sought, although some observations made might contribute in a small way to clarifying this murky area. More relevant to the topic is the idea that the war-חרם in Joshua 6 functions mainly as part of a process of creation in which the new territory was consecrated (through destruction) and made suitable for the community to dwell in.

As an afterword let us consider Josh 24:11. Deleting the list of the seven nations, which as I pointed out in the section entitled "Deuteronomy and the Lists of Nations" is not simply a gloss (which fills in the blank in Jericho's ethnic composition in rather a comprehensive fashion!); the list is displaced from Josh 24:12 (and the reference to the Amorite kings should be shifted to Josh 24:.8 accordingly). It reads: "You crossed the Jordan and came to Jericho; the masters (בעלי) of Jericho fought with you and I gave them into your hand."[22] As Wright-Boling point out, this בעלי יריחו expression is found in connection with Shechem (Jud 9:2), and Keilah (1 Sam 23:11-12).[22] The LXX translates the first as "men of Shechem" but omits it in the second, and in Joshua 24 it translates "residents of Jericho." The LXX reading of MT בעלי יריחו as (according to the team of Wright-Boling)[22] ישבי יריחו is not a textual variant but a contextual reading of a somewhat difficult phrase. It is not surprising that the LXX had trouble, for only recently has it been explicated in the light of similar ancient Near Eastern social terminology, as referring to groups of elders or others who held a high position in the community social structure.[23]

This leads us to an important point: Joshua 6 lacks any mention of ethnic terms in referring to the inhabitants of Jericho (the anonymous character of the enemy is Joshua 6 has a resemblance to the MI, which does not name Mesha's antagonist).This is the case likewise of Joshua 2, which makes repeated reference to the terror caused by Israel's bursting upon the scene, and concludes with a general reference to the "melting before Israel" of "all the inhabitants of the land" (Josh 2:24), placed this time in the mouth of Joshua. The fact that the חרם appears in Joshua 6 totally without reference to any of the six or seven autochthonous peoples demonstrates that the חרם tradition in the chapter, which I have already, following Brekelmans, seen as ancient, is certainly powerful evidence that the chapter is pre-deuteronomic.[24] Only in Joshua 7 is there talk of the Amorites and Canaanites (cf. the clearly

---

[22] J. A. Soggin, *Joshua,* 234 notes it as a late gloss, but the list appears there due to disarray in the text. One error led to another. Soggin says that the Amorite kings of MT v.12 are not Sihon and Og. Boling & Wright, *Joshua,* 536, accept MT, according to which the seven nations lived at Jericho together.

[23] J. M. Grintz, "The Treaty of Joshua with the Gibeonites," *JAOS* 86 (1966),119 esp. n.28. E.g. *b'ly PN* is translated "citizens" and "landlords" in a trilingual mid-fourth century text. See J. Teixidor, "The Aramaic Text in the Trilingual Stele from Xanthus," *JNES* 37 (1978), 181-5.

[24] M. Ottoson sees a deuteronomistic hand in the Rahab section. of Joshua 6, but sees the Jericho story of Joshua in the main as pre-Dtr in "Rahab and the Spies," H. Berhrens, et. al., eds. *DUMU-E$_2$-DUB-BA-A* [*FS* Ä. Sjöberg] (Phila., 1989), 426, 426 n.20.

deuteronomistic Josh 7:7-10), while Josh 2:10 reflects the deuteronomistic tradition of the חרם of Sihon and Og, which in other strands of tradition (Num 21:21ff., Jud 11:19ff.) does not appear.

One exegete has seen in the name Jericho the name of the moon god Yariḥ, whose cult or that of another lunar god has been documented in Palestine as well as Ras Shamra.[25] He has therefore interpreted the Jericho story as a theomachy. This interpretation does not have enough evidence to support it: Yariḥ is not explicitly mentioned any more than Amon-Re at the Reed Sea, although at least the Song of the Sea praises YHWH above other gods. However, it should not be ruled out either. Any interpretation that emphasizes the religious approach of the text over the search for military-historical truth has something to commend it. Joshua 6 expresses in a powerful way the belief that YHWH's power alone was ultimately responsible for the Israelite occupation of the land. The חרם does not contradict it; for the historical truth that real human beings fight the battles is combined in the חרם with the saving prowess of the warrior deity.

This idea is not limited to the חרם--cf. the psalmist's words in Ps 60:14, "through God we will fight valiantly and He will defeat our enemies." The ancients saw no contradiction, for this is classic religious logic, practiced by other ancient peoples such as the Assyrians. Furthermore, it is only by recognizing this kind of ancient religious reasoning that the criteria which the literary-critical method utilizes for its judgements can be most fruitfully selected. The wild divergence between the results of the various literary critics who have analyzed Joshua 6 is a good indication that a realistic set of criteria has yet to be developed for this kind of text (the comparison of Joshua 6 with KRT mentioned above has yet to affect the criteria).

II: JOSHUA 7-8

Joshua 7, the story of Achan, is undoubtedly one of the crucial texts for the study of the biblical חרם. That would be the case even on its own merits, but it is still more true on account of A. Malamat's groundbreaking utilization of Mari texts offering a parallel to the kind of חרם.[26] This places the chapter, in contrast to its predecessor, on a relatively firm footing. Whether a man named Achan lived or not, the stealing of plunder designated for the deity as חרם and the consequences are vividly depicted here in accordance with ancient practice. The term used in the Mari texts adduced by Malamat is *asakku*, and the action is denoted by *asakkam akālu*, "to eat the *asakku*." As pointed out above in the discussion of proposed parallels to the חרם, this

---

[25] J. Heller, "Die Mauern von Jericho," *Communio Viatorum* 1969, 205. Heller goes on to interpret Joshua 6 as a parody of the Akitu Festival. For more evidence of Palestinian lunar cults cf. A. Spycket, "Le culte du dieu-lune à Tell Keisan," *RB 80* (1973), 385-395 Cf. also E. Puech, "L'inscription de la statue d'Amman et paléographie ammonite," *RB* 92 (1985), 22-3.

[26] The English translation of A. Malamat, "The Ban in Mari and the Bible" is now conveniently available in *Mari and the Bible: A Collection of Essays* (Jerusalem, 1977), 52-61.

is radically different from the linguistic usage in Hebrew,[27] and it does not function as an equivalent to the Hebrew verb החרים. *asakku* is defined as a kind of taboo,[28] and Malamat in his article illustrated diverse ways in which it was employed in Mari documents. In contrast, the root חרם is not used in a wide range of applications in the Bible, although we may surmise that it had wider application than is evidenced therein. The Nabatean usage, to indicate reserved seats in the theater, seems to hint at that possibility. However that may be, it is a desideratum in considering this chapter that we examine the proposed equivalence not only of *asakku* and חרם but of חרם and taboo.

The idea of חרם as "taboo" long antedates Malamat's discovery. W. R. Smith spoke briefly of the חרם as a taboo; this goes back at least as far as 1891, but he was not innovating.[29] Writing much later, A. C. James depicted it as "the savage taboo carried to the extreme degree."[30] However, this understanding of חרם did not bear the weight of the thesis. The חרם was scarcely the "primitive taboo" with which James identified it;[31] it was not a mere survival from a 'savage' past but a practice conditioned by civilization. Without it, the organized warfare which served as the חרם's *Sitz in Leben* could not exist.

The tendency of earlier scholars to abstract the term 'taboo' from its cultural matrix is a methodological problem. If taboo were a self-subsisting entity it would be justified. But it originally was a part of a system of Polynesian thought, with relation to other ideas without which taboo itself becomes unintelligible (except in colloquial parlance, where it has taken on its own meaning). Two key terms are *noa* and *mana*. R. Wagner says of them:

> *Tapu,* as a state of sacred interdiction stands in contrast to the neutral, or common state *noa* (whatever is free from *tapu* restrictions).
> The cosmic principle or force behind the restrictions and prohibitions of *tapu* is conveyed in the general Polynesian conception of *mana*. *Mana* is invisible and abstract, knowable only through its efficacy and through its manifestation in things, yet it is universal.[32]

If חרם is a Hebrew equivalent to taboo, what is the Hebrew equivalent to *noa*? The only word that suggests itself is חול, but this is easily dismissed, for חול stands in a reciprocal relationship with קדש, and has no direct connection with חרם. In fact, one of the functions of *noa* is that it describes the condition of something after the removal of taboo, while the חרם could

---

[27] Further limiting observations are found in J. Milgrom, *Cult and Conscience: the ASHAM and the Priestly Doctrine of Repentance, Studies in Judaism in Late Antiquity* 18 (Leiden, 1976), 25-7.
[28] *CAD* A2, 325bf.
[29] W. Robertson Smith, *The Religion of the Semites: The Fundamental Institutions* (rep. N.Y.,, 1972), 454.
[30] A. C. James, *Taboo among the Ancient Hebrews* (Phila., 1925), 52.
[31] Ibid. 54.
[32] R. Wagner, "Taboo," in M. Eliade, ed., *The Encyclopedia of Religion,* v.14 (New York, 1987), 233f..

not ordinarily be removed once it has been incurred, and certainly there was no routine ritual to reverse it, as in Polynesia.[30] In Joshua 7 the people fall under the חרם in a secondary way which is resolved by the execution of Achan, but he as the person who brought the חרם upon himself could not reach a state like *noa*. The second word, *mana*, which is used to denote a universal, impersonal force serving to back the taboo has no analogy in the biblical concept of חרם. The very personal force of YHWH ordains the חרם[33] and sees to its enforcement.

The taboo is a system or method of internal social regulation which helps delimit the behavior of everyday life. In this, it differs from the חרם in general and the war-חרם in particular. The idea of "consecration through destruction" has nothing to do with taboo in its original *Sitz*. It thus becomes evident that, while the חרם has certain features in common with taboo which have led observers to equate them, even a cursory examination is enough to prove that the חרם is not really a taboo: for taboo involves *noa* and *mana*, concepts lacking Hebrew equivalents. Further, taboo is really a 'system' for regulating selected social behaviors in a peacetime setting, while the "peace-חרם" of the priests can only be a sublimation of the war-חרם, i.e. a secondary application of the concepts involved to a wholly different situation. In dismissing taboo, Brekelmans pointed to still other features of taboo, such the fact that taboo is applied to time among other things.[34]

With this in mind, we may now turn to the question of Joshua 7 and *asakku*. The standard lexica do not distinguish between three Akkadian words, *asakku*, *ikkibu*, and *anzillu*, defining them indifferently as 'taboo.' Fortunately for the non-Assyriologist, a recent work devotes some space to defining *asakku* and distinguishing it from its near equivalents. Here is K. van der Toorn's characterization of *asakku*:

> The Sumerogram for *asakku* is KU.AN (read AZAG), combining the ideogram for "holy" or "precious metal" with the ideogram for "heaven" or "god." Originally denoting the temple treasures, it has come to designate something sacrosanct, *consecrated to the deity and withdrawn from profane use* (emphasis added). InSumerian texts the only verb it appears with is GU_7 (KU_2) "to eat." A legal record from Nippur, dating back to the third dynasty of Ur, shows that "eating the sacrosanct substance" originally referred to the profane consumption of consecrated food. In Akkadian texts *asakku* can appear in combination with *akālu* "to eat," as well as *šarāqu* "to steal," both of which will at least originally have been used in their literal sense. Unlike Hebrew, *lāqaḥ min haḥērèm*, the Akkadian *asakka akālu* came eventually to be used for crimes connected with family, tribe, or warfare, all of them considered equivalent to sacrilegious actions.[35]

[33] This last point has been pointed out before; so C. Sherlock, "The Meaning of ḤRM in the Old Testament," *Colloquium* 14 (1982), 17, he cites Brekelmans in the *Theologische Handwörterbuch der alten Testament* I col. 638, and remarks that the חרם has destruction built into it, but taboo does not.

[34] C. H W. Brekelman, *De h\erem*, 149.

[35] K. van der Toorn, *Sin and Sanction in Israel and Mesopotamia, Studia Semitica Neerlandica 22* (Assen/Maastrict, Netherlands, 1985), 42.

As observed in the more general discussion of the Mari parallel, *asakku* came to its significance in the Old Babylonian period by a very different etymological route than Heb. חרם. Moreover, the objection to equating חרם. with taboo applies at least partially to *asakku*. Occasions in which *asakku akālu* occurred could be dealt with by regular judicial processes. No mana-like force was expected to enforce the *asakku*.prohibition in these cases.

In speaking of לקח מן החרם as the "Hebrew counterpart to" *asakka akālu*, van der Toorn makes the point that it is as idiomatic expressions that they are equivalent: the verbs are obviously incommensurable, while *asakku* is a more general term than חרם, and has a much different etymology The different units add up to equivalent sums, at least in the limited sphere of reservation of the spoils of war. In this sphere the Akkadian expression is functionally analogous to חרם. This brings us back to the Book of Joshua.

In what I have called the "חרם-source" of Joshua 6, Joshua foreshadows the action of Joshua 7 by explicitly warning the troops against any looting (Josh 6:18) of devoted or sacrosanct goods. Joshua produces a sentence which is quite complex and which has been emended. In my opinion that approach fails to take the structure of the verse into account and thereby eliminates a unique and rather interesting use of the hiphil:

וְרַק־אַתֶּם שִׁמְרוּ מִן־הַחֵרֶם / פֶּן־תַּחֲרִימוּ / וּלְקַחְתֶּם
מִן־הַחֵרֶם / וְשַׂמְתֶּם אֶת־מַחֲנֵה יִשְׂרָאֵל לְחֵרֶם / וַעֲכַרְתֶּם אוֹתוֹ׃

This is not an easy verse. The use of the hiphil in the second part is unique, as it lacks a direct object. Boling and Wright prefer to emend it, following the LXX, to "covet,".[36] It is hard to believe that the LXX text represents a better text, even given the difficulty of MT. The verb "covet" also requires an object. Josh 7:21 lists the booty Achan had stolen. He says of the objects "I desired them and I took them." Here we have the same two verbs that would transpire from the emendation (which may have been made on the basis of this verse), but חמד is supplied with a direct object, just as it is in the other uses of the verb, which is rare. It takes its own direct object in all the dozen instances of the qal-stem in the Bible (the rarity of the verb makes it a less likely candidate, even without looking into usage). Deut 7:25-6 is the only case where MT uses חמד in connection with חרם, although not in the same verse. It may be seen that this is not the most fertile ground on which to sow an emendation. The emendation would only create the need to explain the anomalous usage of חמד in the verse. It would also weaken Joshua's warning, since חמד is so much milder a verb than החרים.

There is also positive evidence which argue in favor of the MT. Neglecting the last two words, a prophetic pun, the verse as divided up above breaks into two parallel sets of phrases, AB//A'B' which read: "Keep yourselves from what is proscribed (חרם) / lest you spread חרם...../ Should you take from

---

[36] R. G. Boling & G. E. Wright, *Joshua,* 203. The proposed emendation is more remote from the MT than they indicate, although it does follow LXX.

what is proscribed / you will make of the camp something proscribed." This two-part structure in which each part has two sections (e.g. AB) once understood, the meaning of the hiphil is clear; failure to keep from the חרם will cause the proscribed state to come into being, to spread in the camp, among the people. A hiphil verb does not always take a direct object. Sometimes it is omitted when it is supplied elsewhere or understood, as in this verse. In this context, the above translation fits perfectly, reflecting the actual intent as revealed by its structure, obviating the need for emendation. The hiphil is more truly denominative here than in its regular use (which also accounts for the lack of a direct object), which reinforces the argument for a more complicated history of the verb than derivation from the basic stem, given in ch.1 on the basis of the Ugaritic evidence. Interestingly, the חרם is not "contagious" in the sense that one becomes proscribed if one has touched someone who has touched a proscribed object--nor do Joshua or his messengers fear to touch the proscribed objects Achan stole (Joshua 7:23-4). On the other hand, a person who infringes on the divine sphere has entered an area which is fatal, for there deity and human cannot coexist.

As we know from elsewhere, the חרם had to be declared and defined in advance of battle. Distribution of spoil was always vital; thus the only legislation of David which the Bible reports deals with the division of booty (1 Sam 30:24-5).

The basic plot of the Achan story is simple: a man named Achan disregarded Joshua's warning and took and his some of the plunder that was חרם. As a result the first Israelite assault on Ai went awry. By lot Achan was found out, encouraged to confess, and executed. Malamat brought to bear two letters from Mari on this incident. The first one, ARM V 72, is addressed to Yasmaḫ-Addu, the feckless younger son of the energetic Assyrian ruler, Shamshi-Adad I (1869-1837 B.C.), whose viceroy he was in Mari.[37] The letter is unfortunately damaged in a way that lessens its importance, but it is worth reproducing the parts of most interest:

Obv. 9) i-nu-ma da-WI-di-im (š)a La-ri-im-nu-ma-a
At the time of the defeat of L.
10) ša šarrum i-du-ku-ma a-na A-ḫa(
whom the king slew and to Aha.(...
11) a-na GAL.KUD ù labuttê^{meš} dan-na-t(im) (aš)-kun
I spoke harshly to the 'section chief' and his officers
12) um-ma-a-mi a-sa-ak ^{d}Addu ù (^{d}Šam)aš
saying "Whoever takes of the booty
13) ša su-uḫ-ṭam i-l(e-qú i-ka-al)
shall have eaten[38] the *asakku* of ^{d}Addu and ^{d}Shamash.
14) šu-u 2 ru-uq-qa-tim (

[37] S. Dalley, *Mari and Karana: Two Old Babylonian Cities* (London, 1984), 30ff..
[38] Following A. Malzer, "Mari Clauses in 'Casuistic' and 'Apodictic' Styles (Part I)," *CBQ* 33 (1971), 339. "Shall have eaten" is better than the simple future.

He, two bronze containers...[39]
15) kaspam ù ḫurāṣam
silver and gold.
16) ki-dam ki-it X X (
Outside justice (kittum?)[40]
17) iš-tu ša-al-(la-tim il-qé)
From the booty he has taken.
....
Rev.1'} (l)i-(d)u-ku (
Let them kill...
2'} ḫa-al-qú awīlum (šu-u)
Have perished. This man
20'} (ki)-ma a-sa-ak ᵈAddu
According to the sacrilege of
21' (a)-sa-ak ᵈŠamsi-ᵈAddu
Addu and of Shamshi-Addu and of
22'} (u) I(a)-ás-ma-aḫ-ᵈAddu be-lí-ya
Yasmaḫ-Addu, my lord
23'}(X-X)-X-ti awīlim ša-a-ti
the...of this man
24'}(x šiqlu kas)pum ú-lu-ma 15 še'u (ḫurâ)ṣum
Ten shekels in silver or 15 gold grains.

It should be easy to see why A. Malamat singled out this letter, even though due to its fragmentary state (the lines I chose to omit on the reverse side are in fairly good shape, however). As Malamat understands its contents, the writer of the letter is accusing someone of appropriating articles despite the fact that a tribal chief has issued an order to the effect that anyone taking of booty would have eaten of the *asakku* of Adad and Shamash (i.e. the war god and the god of justice).[41] He then says that due to the fragmentary nature of the text, it is impossible to know whether the word *lidūku,*which we translate as "let them kill," "relates to the accused or not."[37] He goes on to conclude that "from the last line of the letter it would appear that the accused was compelled to pay a mere fine." He then relates it to Joshua 7:

> The resemblance of this case to that of Achan at Jericho is striking (Josh VII). Despite variant details, the basic element is the same in both: enjoying the

[39] Following G. Dossin's translation in his *Correspondence de Iasmaḫ-Addu, ARM V* (Paris,1952), 101. *ruqqātum* may well be a cognate of Heb. רקע, which can refer to the beating of metals.
[40] *kittum* would seem to be the perfect word for the context, and there is space for it according to Dossin's markings (i.e. ki-it-ti-im). However, it is only a conjecture, and there may be objections to it of which I am not aware (e.g. in Akkadian usage)..
[41] A. Malamat, "The Ban in Mari," 55.

spoils of war, in particular circumstances, was considered a violation of the taboo.[42]

If Malamat is correct in his conclusion that the penalty for the miscreant amounted to only a fine, then the proposed analogy is actually weak. The death of the miscreant is an absolutely crucial element in Joshua 7. Mari practice would then be closer to the practice of modern armies than to Israelite practice. In my opinion, Malamat was unduly cautious in his assessment. After all, although the letter has lacunae, it is clear, even from the excerpts given above, that it treats of but one subject; the stealing of proscribed spoils of war. From line 2', whatever one makes of the plural, it is clear that punishment has been exacted according to the injunction of *lidūku*. The letter provides no candidate for this death other than the stealer of the proscribed plunder. The final lines seem to reflect on the writer's claim for compensation, which has not received a good hearing in the judicial process which occupies most of the tablet's reverse. The mention of the man, or a man, in l.23' does not mean that the miscreant was still alive. The idea that in l.1' the death of people otherwise unrelated to the case is called for is not plausible, especially as the letter is the work of a man who has singlemindedly pursued his cause (justice with regard to the spoils).

Another text from the Old Babylonian period reinforces this interpretation. In a brief communication M. Anbar (Bernstein) draws attention to a partial parallel to the Achan story.[43] The text is a hepatoscopic text dealing with a high priestess who commits sacrilege. The operative line reads as follows:

ēnum asakka ištanarriq iṣabbatūšima iqallûšima

A high priestess continually stole the *asakku*. so they seized her and burnt her up.[44]

In other words, this text records the actual execution of the *ēnum*. He also cites a similar text, which does not end with a burning but simply ends in the death penalty--*iddâk*--familiar from the Code of Hammurapi.[45] As Anbar points out, the penalty of the first text has much in common with that applied to Achan.[40] Furthermore, in a Mari letter to Yasmaḫ-Addu cited by J. Oates, an underling urges his lord to have a criminal's head cut off to use to frighten people into joining in a muster of the army--a tactic very like to that of the man in Judges 19:29 who cut up a corpse and used the pieces to muster the tribes against Benjamin.[46] The letter is relevant because it reflects the contempt for the lives of criminals in Mari at that time. All these

[42] Ibid. 56.
[43] M. Anbar (Bernstein), "Le châtiment du crime de sacrilège d'après la Bible et un texte hépatascopique paléo-babylonien," *RA* 68 (1974), 172-3.
[44] Ibid. 172.
[45] Ibid. 173.
[46] J. Oates, *Babylon* (New York,1979), 58.

considerations unite to contradict the conclusion that the violator or "eater" of the *asakku.* escaped with only a fine.[47]

Malamat cites another letter, ARM II 13, in which a high-ranking officer complains that he has not received his fair share of the spoils and, having established that *asakka akālu* is at stake, seeks redress.[48] However, it does not deal with the issue of the penalty.

Returning to the first letter, which as Malamat himself noted, is the closest parallel to Joshua 7, it is of interest to compare the stolen items. It is also interesting that the writers of both texts, so disparate in period, medium, and history, knew exactly what was missing, In both cases, the looter chose a small group of items, principally silver and gold, and a third item of lesser value--an exotic garment for Achan and a pair of bronze vessels for his predecessor from Mari (who may have taken another item, judging by a lacuna in the text). Of course, the "exotic garment," here actually a Babylonian cloak, may have carried a message to its original audience, since Babylon was so closely associated with idolatry in the eyes of religious biblical writers. Thus the item may have emblemized Achan's faithlessness to God--a nuance presumably lacking in the Mari letter.

There are major differences between the Mari letter and the chapter in Joshua. One is that the expression *asakka akālu* can apply also to the king and his viceroy (Shamshi-Adad and Yasmaḫ-Addu), whereas חרם in the Bible relates only to YHWH. This attests to a fundamental difference in outlook between the two cultures. Another crucial difference that, unlike the first, has never to my knowledge been remarked upon, is the fact that in Joshua 7 the violation of the חרם had bad and potentially catastrophic implications for the whole people, making successful warfare impossible until the evil has been extirpated. There is nothing in the Mari documents to suggest any such concept. A third difference related to the last is that in these Mari letters the spoils are to be divided among the soldiers, not consecrated to deities, nor was a sacred lottery used. to catch the perpetrator. Yet another difference is the confession Achan makes, clearly far from the intent of his counterpart(s) at Mari. For all the differences, Malamat made an important contribution to biblical studies with his study of the Mari material. It provides context for Joshua 7 and at one remove it lends reality to the war-חרם (החרים).

In the Achan story his breach of the חרם has the effect of endangering the whole *Weltordnung* or social order of Israel. Chaos, in the person of the enemies of Israel--"the inhabitants of Ruin," the Ai--had consequently a chance to erupt. I have described the events of Joshua 6 as a mythic depiction of the conquest as creation. As Creation in its second unfolding wit-

[47] J.M. Durand, "Une condamnation à mort à l'époque d'Ur III," *RA* 71 (1977),125-9 discusses a neo-Sumerian text in which someone is condemned to death for sacrilege. He believes the condemnation to death to be genuine, but he "hopes" that the king spared the defendant, as Durand believes was possible. This is interesting, coming from an earlier period, but in no way proves that there was no death penalty in the case discussed above. Prof. Ira Spar informs me that the death penalty was carried out.
[48] A. Malamat, "The Ban in Mari," 56

nessed the eruption of the forces of disorder in the person of the serpent, leading to fatal consequences (the creation of death), so here Achan's fall into temptation brings the rout of the first assault on Ai. The rationalist may argue that the failure of the assault was due to poor intelligence, and the subsequent muster of too few troops to meet the need of the assault; but this would be an impoverished reading of the text, unintelligible to the biblical writers, to whom no number was too few to prevail if YHWH was present (cf. 1 Sam 14:10). The biblical view is that because of Achan's trespass, YHWH was furious. The tenfold increase in the number of soldiers only succeeded because YHWH intervened, as the byplay of the sicklesword signifies. Yet before that could happen, the breach in the moral order had to be healed.

The Achan story is unique among חרם narratives in centering on the proscribed object (the nominal form), and so serves as an excellent test of the working theory that understands the חרם as stemming from a common ancient Near Eastern paradigm of warfare as a contest between the forces making for chaos and the forces which seek to establish the *Weltordnung* (a deity or deities and human beings such as the ruler). The story of Achan and its sequel at Ai as presented by the biblical writers bolsters this hypothesis, which seeks to understand the world-view behind the חרם; the question as to "what really happened" at a certain time and place is another question. The evidence seems to show that the Achan story must be viewed, at least in its essentials or typology, as firmly rooted in actual practice in antiquity.

M. Noth held the view that Joshua 7 is a unit essentially independent of its surroundings, and especially of Josh 8.[49] This view has been elaborated in a recent study by Z. Zevit.[50] However, from the חרם-oriented perspective, the debacle at Ai is tied theologically to the Achan story and serves, from the literary point of view, to introduce it as the occasion of the debacle. It was a commonplace in the ancient Near East when trouble struck to ask the question, "why are the gods angry?"[51] This is the question asked in the Book of Jonah which results in the prophet's unceremonious transfer from the ship to the sea and the interior of the great fish (examples could be multiplied). Nothing could be more typical of ancient Near Eastern thought (as well as other ancient thought, such as Greek) than this theological pattern, as found in Joshua 7. There is no reason to doubt that it belongs here.

It is clear from Joshua's and the elders' lament in Joshua 7:6-7 that he had fully approved the operation, and that he had acted on the recommendation of the spies (Joshua 7:3-4).[52] Certainly he does not reprove the people

---

[49] M. Noth, *Das Buch Josua, HAT* (Tübingen, 1938), 43.

[50] Z. Zevit, "Archeological and Literary Stratigraphy in Joshua 7-8," *BASOR* 251 (1983), 23-36.

[51] E.g. *ludlul bēl nēmeqi* which in lines 43ff. states that the sufferer's god, goddesses, and guardian spirits have all deserted him, leaving his vulnerable to enemies. See W. G. Lambert, *Babylonian Wisdom Literature* (Oxford, 1960), 32,33.

[52] Z. Zevit, "Archeological and Literary Stratigraphy," 23, points out that Joshua and YHWH do not "explicitly" order the first attack on Ai, but the order is implicit; the idea

for attacking on their own initiative. Therefore Joshua turned to YHWH to find the reason for the grievous setback so soon after the (miraculous) crossing over the Jordan. Since the successful attack on Ai of Joshua 8, which included the חרם, was conditioned on the successful handling of the crisis of the חרם in Joshua 7, it should be clear that no account of Joshua 7-8 can neglect the חרם as a religious or theological factor. Moreover, Z. Zevit makes an important contribution when he shows from topographical considerations that Et-Tell was the site that generated the Ai story, but that the archeological evidence militates against the historicity and makes clear the story's mythic character.[53] It follows the way of the Jericho story, despite its relatively sophisticated tactics and the impression it thus gives of historical plausibility,[54]

An important theological term introduces Joshua 7:1 and recurs in Josh 22:20, viz. מעל . Defined by J. Milgrom as simply "a sin against God,"[55] the word often takes YHWH as an object (Lev 5:12, Num 5:6, &c.), while in Joshua 7:1 it takes the חרם instead. The term is used here to indicate the nature and the seriousness of the offense; for disregard of his inviolable sancta is a special kind of rebellion which threatens the community's viability. The term constitutes a link between the war-חרם and the priestly חרם of Leviticus 27, since it is from the priestly material that the nature of the מעל emerges. In fact, it shows that the inviolability of banned booty is a precursor to the institutionalized stewardship of the priests of things חרם in Leviticus 27, Num 18:14. It is probable that this link is historical in nature, reflecting a genuine development, rather than redactional, since the link is only implied, and never made the subject of a *Tendenz*. The use of this term, again according to Milgrom, always relates to sins against God, even where obstensibly the object is human.[56] The use of the word מעל thus shows the sacrality of the חרם no less than the classification of the חרם as "most holy" in Lev 27:28. It is dangerous to infringe on God's holiness, but one cannot define God's sacral nature as negative--it is the humans who dare to rebel against it who are seen negatively. One is again led by the use of the term מעל to see why the חרם itself was seen positively, as reflecting of divine nature.

In Josh 22:20 Achan's sin against God is cited to indicate the gravity of the situation, i.e. the sin of building of an unauthorized altar. Interestingly, the חרם never comes into play in the dire threats that loom against the Transjordanian tribes. Instead, there is the specter of direct divine warfare (Josh

---

that a 'rogue army' attacked Ai does not fit well with Joshua's plea to God, for it shows that he had thought that YHWH was with the attackers.

[53] Z. Zevit, "Archeological and Literary Stratigraphy," 24b-34.

[54] J. Callaway, the excavator at Ai, took the position that the Ai story was basically historical in "New Evidence in the Conquest of Ai," *JBL* 87 (1968), 312-20, and has maintained it, according to Zevit, in subsequent publications (through 1980). Note the tie-in to the miraculous crossing of the Jordan in Josh 7:7, here described as the result of divine action.

[55] J. Milgrom, *Cult and Conscience,* 16ff.

[56] Ibid. 17-21.

22:31) and an army to destroy (לשחת) the territory involved. The entire chapter reeks of the aroma of priestly language and the sacerdotal agenda (Pinchas the priest appears at the head of the assembled princes and leaders of Israel at chapter's end), to a much greater extent than Joshua 7. The plot of this short story seems to involve an instance of how something like the scenario of Deut 13:13-19 (and Exod 22:19) almost came to pass. It also reflects a certain lingering uneasiness with Transjordanian Israel, which was not living on actual "promised land."

Another important theological term used twice in the Achan story is ברית, "covenant." This is the only place where חרם and YHWH's covenant connect, although, in Deut 7:3, the חרם is coupled with a warning against forming compacts with the peoples of the land (in Deut 7:9, a verse which quotes from the Ten Commandments, the covenant is mentioned, but as in the source, it is not connected with חרם).Yet a recent investigator, C. Sherlock, has concluded that the covenant is "the key aspect for Israel" of the חרם.[57] He argues:

> From the point of view of the covenant, however, חרם posed a wider significance. Not just what 'belonged' to other gods, but *anything* opposed to Yahweh's purposes was, ultimately, חרם.[58]

According to this view, any covenant violation would be "ultimately, חרם." Any covenant violation or transgression against YHWH's will in any other fashion is a matter of חרם; i.e. any trespass of YHWH's will in *any* respect would result in the person's becoming חרם and hence doomed to die! This is why the חרם could not act as the everyday enforcement agency of the covenant (YHWH does not rule out repentance and expiation in most matters). Deut 13:13-19 makes it clear that listening to and obeying God (stressed also in 1 Sam 15:22-3 in poetic form) and upright action in God's eyes are what is at issue; in neither of these crucial passages does the term occur. The evidence shows that it should no more be subsumed under 'covenant' than the other term for holiness, קדש.

Putting Joshua 7 in perspective, Achan's trespass is viewed as a covenant violation in Joshua 7, but the underlying significance of what he has done reflects the overall concept with which we have been working (see above). The חרם stems ultimately from a foreign milieu where the Hebrew concept of covenant was not operative. There is no hint of it in the Mesha Inscription; nor had it a place of importance in the Mesopotamian world of thought which led to *asakka akālu*.[59] The notion of חרם flows from more fundamental religious conceptions than the covenant. As the root implies,

---

[57] C. Sherlock, "The Meaning of ḤRM," 15.

[58] Ibid. 16. On a larger scale, S. G. Dempster propounds a different covenant theory. See S. G. Dempster, *The Prophetic Invocation of the Ban as Covenant Curse: A Historical Analysis of a Prophetic Theme* (M.A. thesis, Westminster Theological Seminary, Chestnut Hill, Pa., 1978).

[59] K. van der Toorn, *Sin and Sanction*, 52. "It cannot be said that the covenant category was a central notion in Mesopotamian religion."

the חרם is a form of holiness, and flows from the immediate nature of the divine, while the covenant is an external result of YHWH's action in history. The connection between חרם and the covenant between YHWH and Israel, mentioned in Joshua 7 alone, is not the key to understanding the חרם. The connection is a natural one but it is tertiary at best, and of no importance in the larger biblical picture outside this chapter; for otherwise the covenant would come up again and again in connection with חרם, which it does not (nor does it occur in the MI).. Similarly, Achan's action is branded a נבלה, an act of scandalous folly, often associated with sexual outrages. A נבלה it was, as well as a covenant violation, but neither description of Achan's trespass explains the essence of the חרם for Israel. It relates to a specific situation in which Achan's folly threatened the very operation of the covenant by endangering the community.[60]

In sum, the Achan story proves to be testing ground for ideas of the חרם. Taboo dates back to a long obsolete anthropology, and has been discarded in the sociologically oriented treatment of N. K. Gottwald.[61] We have seen that taboo exists in relation to other concepts, like *noa* and *mana,* which are absent in the Bible. Taboo acts in a pervasive way for the internal daily ordering of society, unlike the (war-)חרם. The Mari parallel, while far from perfect, puts the story of Achan in an historical framework. The use of מעל provides an indirect link to the peace-time, priestly חרם. The fact that the behavior of Achan endangered the whole community demonstrates the חרם's role in the preservation of *Weltordnung* or in its breach, the disintegration of the world order.

III: JOSHUA 9

Joshua 9 does not employ the word חרם, and on that ground would not rate mention in this study. However, we must give it some attention because of the fact that scholars have tended to relate the Gibeonite story to the laws of war in Deut 20:10ff. and Deut 7:1ff.. A recent example of this tendency is found in an article of C. Schäfer-Lichtenberger.[62]

She believes the action of Joshua 9 is conditioned and determined by the content of the deuteronomic laws of war.[63] It is strange then, that the חרם should never be mentioned in the chapter. The omission is especially striking in view of the fact that חרם plays a role in Joshua 6-8,10-11, but not in ch.9. In view of the concern with the חרם in Deuteronomy, it is hard to understand why anyone of the deuteronomic school would have omitted mention of it (as a threat, for instance, or in the introduction, as in Joshua 10).

---

[60] On collective punishment, see J. Milgrom, *Cult and Conscience,* 21.

[61] N. K. Gottwald, *The Tribes of Yahweh: A Sociology of the Religion of Liberated Israel* (Maryknoll, N.Y., 1980), 543-550, esp. 550.

[62] C. Schäfer-Lichtenberger, "Das gibeonitische Bündnis im Lichte deuteronomischer Kriegsgebote," *BN* 34 (1986), 58-81.

[63] Ibid. 58f.

Schäfer-Lichtenberger. believes that the deuteronomists were writing about a much later time. With diffidence, she associates the Gibeonite story with the events of Josiah's reign.[64]

J. Garstang pointed out some time ago the startling correspondence in Palestinian place names as found in Egyptian texts from the time of Tuthmosis III to Akhenaton (d. circa 1362) to those found in Joshua.[65] The map of Josiah's day had been transformed both by peaceful evolution and the depredations of foreign powers, especially Assyria. The Book of Joshua must preserve some ancient traditions.

J. M. Grintz has illuminated the chapter with a discussion using the evidence of Hittite treaties as well as various other pertinent ancient texts.[66] All the features that critics have attributed to the influence of Deuteronomy and its school are found *in situ*, as it were, in these documents. It thus becomes clear why the feature most redolent of the laws of חרם, viz. the distinction between how to treat foreigners from within and without the land, was mentioned without reference to the חרם. As Grintz points out, the distinction was a normal one.[67] An example appears in a Ugaritic omen, which C. H. Gordon cites in *UT* (glossary #391a): *hm qrt tuḫd(?) hm mt yʿl bnš*, which Virolleaud translated as, "either the city will be captured or Môt [the god of death] will go up against man." Thus the distinction made in Deut 20:15-18 with the חרם was in keeping with the older tradition as expressed also in Joshua 9 Just as the law of Deut 20:15-18 drew on an older tradition (as is demonstrable often in that chapter) so, too, did Joshua 9 (whatever its redaction history).[68] The writers of Joshua 9 did not lack for sources from which to draw the traditional distinction.

IV: JOSHUA 10-11

In contrast to Joshua 9, the חרם returns with a vengeance in the succeeding chapters. It occurs, always in the form of the verb, ten times in these two chapters, or nearly a quarter of the total attestations of the verb. I shall try to answer the question as to why the hiphil of חרם recurs so frequently as we proceed.

Josh 10:1 looks back to the past triumphs of Israel, portrayed in terms of the חרם of Jericho and Ai, as well as the Gibeonite episode. It says nothing of

---

[64] Ibid. 79.

[65] J. Garstang, *Joshua, Judges,* 53.

[66] J. M. Grintz, "The Treaty of Joshua with the Gibeonites," *JAOS* 86 (1966), 113-126.

[67] Ibid. 125

[68] See J. A. Soggin, *Joshua,* 112-13 and accompanying literature; he also believes in an "underlying account" going back to a "very early narrative relating to a covenant between the invaders and the Hivite tetrapolis" though he believes that a later elaboration has tried 'to justify the existence of a situation which was "a flagrant violation of the norms laid down by Deut. 20. 10-18." The lack of mention of חרם shows that any deuteronomistic redaction along such lines was executed an extremely gingerly fashion.

walls or processions led by priests, but focuses on the aspect of the חרם. The diction is stilted and noticeably redundant even by the standards of biblical Hebrew. This is an important observation if an obvious one, because it continues to characterize the chapter as a whole. The chapter is connected to Joshua 8, too. Joshua 10:8 compares with 8:1 in which YHWH addresses Joshua almost identically; Josh 6:1 is not quite as close. The expression עם המלחמה, "combatants" is peculiar to chapters 8, 10 and 11 of the Book of Joshua (8:1,3;10:7;11:7) The idea of Josh 8:2a, "you shall do to city B as you did to city A" is elaborated on not only in Josh 10:2, but becomes a refrain in the section of maximum repetition, Josh 10:28-38.

In Joshua 6-7, Joshua is eclipsed by the events (in Joshua 7 he faces a painful reverse), in Joshua 8 his star is ascending, but in Joshua 10, Joshua is in command as nowhere else. The main purpose of the citation from the Book of Jasher is spelled out plainly in 10:14, as adulatory a statement as can be imagined: "there was never like that day before or since, when YHWH listened to a man's voice; for YHWH fought for Israel." The voice was the voice of Joshua, and this verse compares him favorably to, among others, Moses. In this chapter, in contradistinction to Joshua 7 and 9, everything the great leader does or commands is blessed. We are dealing here not with history as such,[69] but with a type of hagiography, which glorifies the figure of Joshua.

Even before Noth's theory of the Deuteronomistic History became popular, the influence of Deuteronomy in Joshua 10 had been commented on.[70] Brekelmans focused on the deuteronomisms in relation to the חרם[71] and pointed out the unmistakable reference to the deuteronomic laws of חרם in Josh 10:40,[72] which rounds off repeated mentions of the חרם with "as YHWH, the God of Israel commanded." It should be noted that the locution "YHWH, the God of Israel," is not found in Deuteronomy itself. However, the introduction of the phrase "five Amorite kings" early in the chapter, as well as the schematic of the geographical distribution of the six nations (the Girgashites are wanting) in the continuation (Josh 11:3), as well as the use of the חרם against them, is sufficient to show that the phrase, "as YHWH, the God of Israel commanded," refers to Deuteronomy 20 and/or 7.

Whether or not Josh 10:35-42 is an addition or not is open to question; it seems to be part and parcel of a zealous deuteronomistic redactor's work.[73] It ends with the same line that followed the miracle at Gibeon (Josh 10:14c), "YHWH fought for Israel" (except that once again "the God of Israel" is appended in Josh 10:43). A satisfactorily close phrase is found in a passage usually considered deuteronomistic: Deut 3:22, "YHWH your God is he who

---

69 *Contra* G. E. Wright, "The Literary and Historical Problem of Joshua 10 and Judges," *JNES* 5 (1946), 105-14.

70 H. Holzinger, *Das Buch Josua* (Tübingen, 1901), 36-8.

71 C. H. W. Brekelmans, *De ḥerem,* 101-3.

72 Ibid. 102.

73 M. Ottoson, "Rahab and the Spies," 426b. "According to the Deuteronomistic opinion only the extermination of human life was included in the ban...." This is true of Deuteronomy 2-3, but not this chapter, where no remnant is left, nor spoil taken.

is fighting for you (Israel)." The (twofold) use of the phrase in Joshua 10 is unique to the chapter, however, and so may not be the result of the deuteronomistic redactor (it is found in Exod 14:5). It should be added to the items mentioned above that give the chapter a different literary character than, e.g. Joshua 6, which would have been an excellent place to employ the phrase. This deuteronomist has reworked older material. As Brekelmans says, the חרם here (Joshua 10-11) bears a much later stamp than the חרם of Joshua 6-7.[74] In fact, the contrast between Joshua 10 and the preceding chapter is one of the most telling arguments against the widespread school of thought that relates Joshua 9 to Deuteronomy 20 and 7. The deuteronomist employs the חרם in Joshua 10 with a heavy hand; there is not the slightest subtlety sought or achieved. Joshua 10-11 make it clear that if the same redactor had reworked Joshua 9, the חרם would have certainly been in evidence. The use the deuteronomizing redactor makes of Deuteronomy 7, 20 shows a definite remove in time from his source. This is indicated by the obvious fact that to the redactor, this material had divine authority (i.e. it was already part of the canon) and was to be consulted as an infallible guide to history. The redactor does so with every confidence in the veracity of this method, rather than act as a modern historian would in seeking documentary and other evidence on the conquest. Therefore this makes an additional argument against a Josianic dating of those deuteronomic chapters, since such a dating which would place this redactor at an extremely late date.

The treatment of the defeated kings is of interest. The placing of the feet on the captured monarch's neck (Josh 10:24) is a feature also of the vastly more ancient Utuḫegal inscription, which we have brought in (above, ch,4) as one of our attempts at adding some new parallels from the ancient Near East. According to this section, all kings were faithfully executed; this is of course necessary if only to keep up the shine on the image of Joshua the hagiographer wished to burnish (cp. 1 Samuel 15, and the trouble that results for Saul when he spares Agag).

J. A. Soggin draws a fundamental distinction between Joshua 10 and 11, citing especially the lack of a plausible rationale for the banding together of the kings of the North against Israel. He says that the redactor of Joshua 11 has remade old traditions in the image of Joshua 10, which flowed plausibly from its predecessor (ch. 9).[75] L. Hoppe points to Josh 10:40a, "Joshua defeated the whole land," as evidence that the conquest traditions of the book once stopped there, and that Joshua 11 was only added on later.[76] He also observes the lack of etiological motives in Joshua 11 in contrast to Joshua 10.[77]

What is important in terms of the study of חרם, however, is the use the redactor has made of Deut 7:1-4 and 20. Josh 11:3 lists the six nations, found

---

[74] Ibid. 103.
[75] J. A. Soggin, *Joshua,* 134
[76] L. Hoppe, *Joshua, Judges: with an Excursus of Charismatic Leadership in Israel, Old Testament Message* 5 (Wilmington, Delaware, 1982), 71.
[77] Ibid. 73.

in Deut 20:17 and Deut 7:1 (with the addition of the Girgashites), which is not so remarkable, especially as the order is not the same and the lists are found throughout the Bible. Yet Josh 11:4 goes on to speak of the great size of the enemy army and the profusion of horses and chariots in it, in language close to Deut 20:1 but even closer to Deut 7:1. Josh 11:4 follows Deut 7:1 in its repetition of the word רב, "many" (Deut 7:1 רבים), once in the middle and again towards the end of the verse (the omission by LXX of the first in Josh 11:4 is not preferable). Thus Josh 11:3-4 is culled directly from Deut 7:1. The wording of Josh 11:3-4 is certainly long after the fact and theologically colored.

In Josh 11:12 we have, as in Josh 10:40, a direct appeal to the חרם legislation of Deut 20:15-17, again as commanded by Moses, "the servant of YHWH." The following verses take pains to show that the letter of the law was followed. Only Hazor was put to the fire, but then the law does not specify fire here (only in Deut 13:13-19),[78] and booty was taken as in the early chapters of Deuteronomy. Not "a breathing body--כל נשמה was left alive" (Josh 11:11) as the legislation's language is referred to again (Deut 20:17: "do not let live כל נשמה"). The use of two of the roots for spoils (out of many such roots) is similar in Josh 11:14 and Deuteronomy 20. The use of the hiphil of שמד, understood conventionally as the equivalent to "destroy" is found here and in Deut 7:4, although in the latter verse it is used as YHWH's threat against Israel. Here it is used along with phrases like "to kill without leaving a remnant," as an equivalent to חרם--necessary because even the zealous deuteronomizing writer shied away from using חרם in every sentence. This usage is possible due to the context, although neither is used independently to refer to the חרם as such.

A final observation is that Josh 11:20 says that YHWH saw to it that there should be no mercy (תחנה) shown to them, which is an echo of the final adjuration of Deut 7:2 not to spare them (תחנם). In this the redactor fell into a small inconsistency, since he implied that the "peoples of the land" could have escaped their doom by behaving differently, which goes against the grant of the land to Israel of Deuteronomy 20. In practice, due to YHWH's hardening of their hearts, this submission was impossible and the conquest is portrayed as a long series of applications of the חרם in Joshua 10-11. In both chapters the military action of Israel, as expressed by above all the חרם, went hand in hand in with YHWH's fighting for Israel. The land had to be brought into the sphere of YHWH's world order to be made a fit abode for the people Israel to live. Such was the underlying conception that brought about the many reiterations of the חרם theme in Joshua 10-11.

V: THE BOOK OF JUDGES

In complete contrast to the Book of Joshua, the Book of Judges employs the root חרם only twice, at the extreme ends of the book (1:17, 21:11). The

---

[78] On the connection between the root חרם and fire, see ch. 1.

reasons for the relative absence of the חרם are a matter more of speculation than of certainty. In the present canonical form of the Bible, the abundant use of the חרם in Joshua would have obviated the need to explore the theme greatly; by and large the Book of Judges describes the early triumphs and misadventures of an Israel which has a foothold, however insecure, in the land. The first chapter, which presents a different view of the conquest than Joshua 10-11 in particular, features the חרם once, but only in relation to the city of Hormah. Jud 1:16-17 reads:

> 16. The descendents of the Kenite (who was) Moses's father-in-law ascended from the City of the Palms with the sons of Judah to the Judean desert (a clear anachronism!) that is in the Negeb of Arad....17. Then Judah went with Simeon his brother, and they smote the Canaanite dwelling in Zephath and they devoted it to destruction and called the name of the city Hormah.

This rather bare narrative contrasts with the account in Num 21:1-3, which does not mention the city of Zephath, but gives a fuller etiology for the name of an place or area, named Hormah, also in the Arad/Negeb area. The Numbers account is not, as mentioned above, a conquest tradition. Jud 1:17 is less a conquest tradition than a settlement tradition, which is historically rooted in the settling of the weak tribe Simeon in the area of Beer Sheba and the south.[79] The use of the verb here is motivated more by the biblical love of puns than any deep expression of *Weltanschauung*. If we accept the account at face value, the name Hormah was used in connection with more than one place in the Negeb; it probably reflected an alternative name to Kedesh for 'holy place' among the pre-Israelite dwellers, referred to in similar terms in both Numbers 21 and Judges 1 as "הכנעני הישב ב"[80]

More interesting is the appearance of the חרם in the concluding drama of the book chs.19-21. The word 'drama' is used advisedly here, because the literary character of the three chapters is clear. We have here a small novella which tells a complete story (rather like the Joseph story, or the Book of Jonah). The question is, is the story true or fiction (or a combination thereof)? This is not the place to investigate this problem anew, but an excellent treatment by B. Z. Lurya has been available, although perhaps overlooked, for over twenty years.[81]

In his paper, Lurya pointed to twenty examples of language and plot common to both the story of the concubine at Gibeah and the story of Lot and Sodom and Gemorrah, taking the resemblances out of the realm of 'motif.'[82] Furthermore, he points to numerous anomalies in Judges 19-21. For example, the anonymous Levite succeeds in mustering all the tribes (except

---

[79] Y. Aharoni, *The Land of the Bible,* 201.

[80] Similarly C. H. W. Brekelmans, *De ḥerem,* 41, contra Noth, who derived it from *ḥrm* II. Brekelmans adduces as well the example of Luz/Bethel

[81] B. Z. Lurya, "The Incident of the Concubine at Gibea," (Heb.) in idem ed., *Studies in the Book of Judges: Discussions of the Workshop at David Ben-Gurion House* (Jerusalem, 1966), 463-494 (including discussion).

[82] Ibid. 465-8.

Benjamin) bringing about a far greater unity than was achieved by the Judges themselves (cf. Deborah, Gideon, and Jephthah).[83] The idea of a vast army assembling, then making inquiry of the Levite as to what the matter was (Jud 20:3) is quite unreal. In any case, there was no such unity in the days of the Judges.

It may further strengthen Lurya's case to draw the comparison between Jud 20:18 and Jud 1:1-2a, which are practically identical. Judges 1:1 begins with the words, "After the death of Joshua," and it is clear that the beginning verses continue the Israel-as-a-body framework of the Book of Joshua (as well as Exodus-Deuteronomy), even if this does not continue for long in the Book of Judges. Indeed, the subsequent fragmentation of Israel found in Judges has a kind of explanation in the oracle of Jud 1:1-2; each tribe will wend its way in the direction of its own area. Jud 20:18 is surely a slight reworking of Jud 1:1-2a.[84] The story itself draws on the model of ch. 1 in its use of the tribes as the actors in the battle. Hence this comparison adds to the evidence that it is the story of Judges 19-21 which is derivative.

The episode of Yabesh Gilead must be seen in this light; it is also problematic from a historical point of view since the depopulated city drew the attention of Nahash the Ammonite not long afterwards, in the days of Saul (1 Samuel 11). Besides, the artificiality of the whole sequence of events connected with Yabesh Gilead is patent. We are supposed to believe that every town in Israel had sent troops except for Yabesh; that in the course of applying the חרם 400 marriageable virgins were found and spared and sent to the enemy who had defeated them in two previous encounters. Compare this to Numbers 31, in which the Midianite women were spared, and Moses angrily commanded that only the girl children be saved; here at least the sequence has more logic to it. Contrast this also to the MI, ll.16-17, where Mesha singles out as part of his consecration through destruction the young maidens (רחמת) of Nebo. Actually, in the context of Judges 20, this contrast might lend the story an added plausibility (of course however it was created, the story takes on its own internal logic), were it not for all the considerations briefly referred to above. In the final analysis, however, the חרם in this story is merely an adjunct to the plot device of an author who has written himself into a corner and needs a *deus ex machina* to extricate himself. It is interesting to see in this pericope the חרם, which we have called the stuff of myth, here serving the purpose of legend and song.

It is true that in the Song of Deborah (Jud 5:23), a curse is laid on Meroz and its inhabitants for failing to "come to the aid of YHWH." That is the only mention of Meroz in the Bible. We do not know what happened to it, but we can be sure that that curse did not issue in a חרם of the city, for the

---

[83] Ibid. 471.

[84] This near identity of a verse from this story to a verse from a historical narrative was, naturally, noticed long ago. A recent treatment is that of Sh. Talmon "In Those Days There Was No MLK," in *King, Cult and Calendar in Ancient Israel: Collected Studies* (Leiden, 1986), 45f.. He arrives at the old conclusion that the appendices of the Judges narratives originally were placed near the beginning of the book. He sees no implication, however, of the derivative nature of the narrative; his major focus is elsewhere

curse is a verbal invocation of supernatural agents--gods or demons--who execute the curse. Yet even here the חרם is used to restore order; because the males had offended, they and their wives died (like the family of Achan). The aim, too, of the sparing of the virgins for Benjamin was to re-create Israel's world order.

Jud 21:5's use of חרם is isolated, peculiar.[85] and is to be understood as a function of the drama. It is also fair to say that the commentators who say that the חרם was dead or all but dead in the period of the Judges are pronouncing the death knell of the חרם prematurely (cf. the MI, 1 Samuel 15).[86]

---

85 R. G. Boling & G. E. Wright, *Judges* , *AB* (Garden City, 1975) 288. Boling claims that Jud 20:48, which uses the typical language associated with the חרם in D, must therefore indicate the חרם. But destruction alone does not qualify as חרם, and a member of the deuteronomic school may not have considered Benjamin's offense to have come under that category, since the scope of what could require the חרם was quite restricted. It is very moot. Presumably there was nothing stopping a redactor from putting the word in with the rest of the verse, so in my view this verse does not alter the isolation of Jud 21:5

86 L. Hoppe, *Joshua, Judges*, 206.

CHAPTER 8

SAMUEL-KINGS

I: I SAMUEL 15

1 Samuel 15 is one of the most important chapters for the study of חרם in the entire Hebrew Bible. It begins with a speech by the prophet Samuel in which, after emphasizing that he is the holder of the prophetic office by virtue of which Saul was anointed king, Samuel delivers the order for the חרם to be executed in what is to us moderns a bloodcurdling fashion. The Amalekites of every age and all their livestock are to be חרם and therefore slaughtered (1 Sam 15:1-3). Nothing is said of the material booty, presumably because the chapter focuses so markedly on Saul's handling of the captured living. This is part of the economy of the Hebrew narrative, which as in the case of the narrative of the binding of Isaac (Gen 22), can be positively laconic.

Before dealing with the חרם, it is necessary to make a preliminary excursus on the provenance of the chapter. In a recent article on this chapter, D. Edelman writes:

> That v.2 alludes directly to Exod.17.8-16 and Deut. 25:17-19 is almost universally acknowledged, as is the indirect dependence of vv. 3, 18, and 21 on holy war prescriptions in Deut. 20.10-20. Treatment of the Amaleqites is to go beyond the special norms set out there.[1]

This approach, if correct, would rob this chapter of any significant new data for analysis, since it would not reflect the period of Saul or the years following his demise.[2] It would merely be a fresh instance of the deuteronmizing in Joshua 10. The חרם is the focus here as it seldom is elsewhere; is it an archaic account or does it rely on late deuteronomistic חרם traditions?

The consensus on the subject of the Book of Samuel in the 'deuteronomistic history,' is that this is the book most lightly touched by the hands of the deuteronomic school of redactors. In the introduction to his recent commentary, P. Kyle McCarter phrases it this way: "The most striking aspect of the Deuteronomistic redaction of Samuel, whether Josianic or Exilic, is its sparseness."[3] He then goes on to assign 1 Samuel 15 to a middle, though still pre-Deuteronomistic prophetic stratum.[4] Yet in contradiction to that position, he says in a comment on the commencement of the chapter:

---

[1] D. Edelman, "Saul's Battle Against Amaleq (I Sam 15)," *JSOT* 35 (1986), 75.

[2] Ibid. 80. Edelman sees no historical value in the chapter, but she does mention one crucial factor; that the central character (to the author) was not Saul or Samuel but YHWH.

[3] P. K. McCarter, jr., *I Samuel: A New Translation and Commentary, AB* (Garden City, 1978), 15.

[4] Ibid. 20.

"The phrasing of Saul's instructions points in detail to the passage...in Deut 25:17-19."[5] In fact, the phrasing in 1 Samuel 15:1-3 points to the opposite conclusion.

Under the influence of Noth's Deuteronomic History hypothesis, the Book of Samuel has sometimes been handled in a rather peculiar way. Yet one has but to turn to the first chapter of the book, and one is breathing a rarified and pre-deuteronomic air. The language in its diction, and idioms, and even in its subject matter which involves the shrine at Shilo, barely mentioned in the literature with affinities to Deuteronomy, is as unlike deuteronomic Hebrew as Hemingway's English is unlike Defoe's. Here, in a chapter dealing with warfare, a subject which tends to develop a vocabulary which is consistent over time (barring innovations in technology, formations, and so on, which came slowly in antiquity; cf. the phalanx, invented for the army of Philip II of Macedon in the mid-4th century, and smashed for the first time by the Roman maniple at Cynoscephalae in 197),[6] it may, in general, be more difficult to discover which source has the priority. But the narrative of 1 Samuel 15 uses a totally different vocabulary in describing the content of the חרם than any of the חרם accounts in books where the deuteronomic school has had a more marked sway. 1 Samuel 15 evinces nothing more than an acquaintance with the general tradition that Amalek attacked Israel shortly after the departure from Egypt; nothing marks it as dependent on the particular formulations of Deuteronomy 25 and Exodus 17. Of the sources dealing with Amalek found in Exodus 17, Deuteronomy 25, and 1 Samuel 15, the latter could be the earliest of the three. It very clearly is earlier than the passage from Deuteronomy from which it has been said to derive. Deut 25:17-19 itself supplies data not found in Exodus, which can be said to contradict it. For example, Exod 17:8-15. gives no account of Amalek's attacks on stragglers, which means that either D invented it, or had another source.

There is only one line that can be validly adduced for comparison between 1 Sam 15:1-3 and Deut 25:17-19, i.e. Deut 25:17-18a:

זָכוֹר אֵת אֲשֶׁר־עָשָׂה לְךָ עֲמָלֵק בַּדֶּרֶךְ בְּצֵאתְכֶם מִמִּצְרָיִם אֲשֶׁר קָרְךָ בַּדֶּרֶךְ

Remember what Amalek did to you on the way after you left Egypt, how it met you on the road....

It is similar to 1 Sam 15:2:

כֹּה אָמַר יְהוָה צְבָאוֹת פָּקַדְתִּי אֵת אֲשֶׁר־עָשָׂה עֲמָלֵק לְיִשְׂרָאֵל אֲשֶׁר־שָׂם לוֹ
בַּדֶּרֶךְ בַּעֲלֹתוֹ מִמִּצְרָיִם׃

Thus says YHWH of hosts: I seek vengeance for what Amalek did to Israel, that he attacked Israel on its way up from Egypt.

The verse from Deuteronomy is in its own typical style. The verse from 1 Samuel, on the other hand, expresses itself in a wholly undeuteronomic

[5] Ibid. 265.

[6] P. Ducrey, *Warfare in Ancient Greece* (New York, 1986), 84-5.

manner: כה אָמַר יְהוָה צְבָאוֹת. The familiar description of the deity as יְהוָה צְבָאוֹת is actually not found in the Book of Deuteronomy; it is basically the province of the prophets from Isaiah to Malachi. In the books from Deuteronomy to Kings, the warlike expression יְהוָה צְבָאוֹת rarely occurs; it is found only a few times in Kings (twice in the same formalized oath in 1 Kgs 18:15, 2 Kgs 3:14, twice in the self-same expression of zealousness for God: 1 Kgs 19:10,14; a fifth occurrence 2 Kgs 19:31=Isa 37:32). Of the historical books, Samuel is the one with the most variegated and alive usage, although even in the Book of Samuel יְהוָה צְבָאוֹת appears in a total of ten verses. The distribution clearly demonstrates that it is not the deuteronomic school which is responsible for the dissemination of "Lord of Hosts," but that the phrase was chosen by individual prophets and prophetic writers. As I read P. D. Miller, he considers it to be either part of the oldest divine name, of which YHWH is but a hypocoristicon, or an early epithet of YHWH.[7]

The same pattern obtains for the other phrases in which the 1 Samuel 15 verse differs from the deuteronomic phraseology. In the semantic field of punishment, the verb פקד occurs but once in the Book of Deuteronomy, namely in Deut 5:9--in the Ten Commandments. M. Sternberg translates פקד in 1 Sam 15:2 as "remember," which is logical, since the root is sometimes used in parallel with זכר, but this is not a possibility entertained by the lexica.[8]

The phrase or expression שם לו, which S. R. Driver pointed to as an example of military idiom,[9] is represented in Deut 25:18 by the more characteristically deuteronomic use of a suffixed participle, קרך. Driver's position has recently been attacked by P. K. McCarter, on the grounds that the supporting verse Driver cited, 1 Kgs 20:12, was "hopelessly corrupt."[10] This characterization is not obligatory. J. Gray in his commentary did not deem it so, but in support of Driver added yet another possible occurrence to 1 Kgs 20:12, namely Ezek 23:24, admittedly a difficult verse (Gray's idea was adopted, with diffidence, by the NJV).[11] Thus Driver's idea remains a lively possibility; whereas McCarter finds the MT's שם לו inexplicable.[12]

Another possibility for interpreting the expression שם לו is to work on the assumption that the idiom expressed is not complete in itself but abbreviated. In this case, the native Hebrew speaker would automatically supply the missing element. A. B. Ehrlich suggested supplying the word "sword" (חרב), drawing on Exod 32:27--surely an idea that should not be ignored.[13] Still

---

[7] P. D. Miller, *The Divine Warrior in Early Israel* (Cambridge, Mass., 1973), 153-55.

[8] M. Sternberg, "The Bible's Art of Persuasion: Ideology, Rhetoric, and Poetics in Saul's Fall," *HUCA* (1983), 49.

[9] S. R. Driver, *Notes on the Hebrew Text and the Topography of the Books of Samuel* (2d ed.; Oxford, repr. 1966), 122.

[10] P. K. McCarter, jr,. *I Samuel,* 260.

[11] J. Gray, *I And II Kings* (2d ed., Philadelphia, 1970), 424.

[12] P. K. McCarter, jr,. *I Samuel, 260.*

[13] A. B. Ehrlich, *Mikra ki-Pheshuto: Scholien und kritische Bemerkungen zu den heiligen Schriften der Hebraer: III Die prosaischen Schriften* (repr. New York, 1969), 136.

another idea, drawing on the LXX translation, would be to supply פניו, an idiom which can be used in a confrontational sense, as the *BDB* (q.v.) documents. A similar expression in Akkadian, *pānīšu šakānu,* meaning "to attack," adds indirect support.[14] This last suggestion has the advantage of according with the LXX without resort to the text of Deut 25:18 to fill in the "inexplicable" MT of Samuel, as McCarter does, although the Greek of Deut 25:17f. is not the same as the Greek of 1 Sam 15:2.[15] It is best to retain the 'difficult reading' as another example of pre-deuteronomic idiom. If deuteronomic language represents the latest stratum in the Hebrew of the Book of Samuel, then there is every reason to believe that non-deuteronomic idiom comes from an earlier era.

In speaking of the Exodus from Egypt, 1 Sam 15:2 uses the older form (as I have argued in connection with Deut 20:1) עלה, as against the later הוציא, found only once in the Book of Deuteronomy in ch. 20, which I placed in the time of Jereboam II. It should be clear that if a dependence exists here, it is to be found in the opposite direction; Deut 25:18 is, if anything, dependent on 1 Sam 15:2, not contrariwise. Nor, as pointed out above, is the wording of 1 Sam 15:3 describing the חרם related to the wording in Deuteronomy, Joshua, or Judges. Also, the injunction not to have pity (using the verb חמל) is not found with the חרם in deuteronomic texts, though it is found close by (Deut 13:9). The injunction does not appear in Deuteronomy 20 at all (except in the somewhat different form, "Do not let a soul live!"). It does appear in Deut 7:4, but with a different verb (לא תחנם) Moreover, there is nothing deuteronomic about 1 Sam 15:18,21. The sequence of phrases in v.18 is in fact unique. This is the one time in the Bible that the Amalekites are called sinners. 1 Sam 15:21 tells of an unprecedented event, and employs a unique expression ראשית החרם, "choice of the חרם." The dependence of these two verses on anything deuteronomic is impossible to sustain.

Additional considerations help demonstrate that the idea that 1 Samuel 15 is 'indirectly influenced' by Deut 20:10-20 does not do justice to the chapter. Deut 20:17 lists those nations to be subject (at least theoretically) to the חרם, among which Amalek is conspicuous hy its absence. Only in a rather distant pericope is the Amalek question addressed (Deut 25:17-19), and the solution to it, not to forget to blot out its memory from under the sky, is that of Exod 17:14. What that meant in practical terms was not stated, but only in 1 Samuel 15 is the ancient hostility towards Amalek put forth in terms of חרם. In the light of this the further point that in 1 Sam 15:19 the expression of "to do evil in the eyes of YHWH" is "typically deuteronomistic,"[16] has little validity. In fact, this is common biblical and Near Eastern (Egyptian, Sumerian and Semitic) usage, as can be seen in part from the *īnu* "eye" entry (*CAD* I/J 156a) which attests to similar expressions, e.g. EA 131:26 *mariṣ ana IGI^{II}-nu* "it is distressing to us." The

[14] See, for now *CAD* N1 249b.
[15] P. K. McCarter, jr,. *I Samuel,* 260.
[16] D. Edelman, "Saul's Battle," 79.

stipulated "indirect dependence" of 1 Samuel 15 on Deuteronomy does not work. In fact, it is only an impediment to fruitful exegesis of the chapter.

All sources agree that Amalek constituted a special case, a unique occasion for divine wrath. It is clear from the foregoing, however, that 1 Samuel 15, like 1 Samuel 1, breathes a different and older air than Deuteronomy 25 (or 20, as formulated), and that this is evidenced by a Hebrew which differs linguistically from D, but not in the direction of exilic or post-exilic Hebrew, both of which differ from early biblical Hebrew due to normal linguistic development, and in the late period, due to the growing influence of the Aramaic language.

C. H. W. Brekelmans pointed to another factor in attaining a more realistic assessment of the connection between Deuteronomy and 1 Samuel 15:

> We must naturally make plenty of room for an inner connection or memory of the prophetic movement, which flowed from Samuel and Elijah towards Hosea and Deuteronomy (my translation).[17]

In other words, without good evidence to the contrary, we may expect Deuteronomy to be dependent on earlier prophetic traditions. Jeremiah's pairing together of Moses and Samuel (Jer 15:1), "YHWH said to me, if Moses and Samuel were to stand before me...." indicates the high standing Samuel had with a prophet of a much later period.

The implications of the pre-deuteronomic dating of the 1 Sam 15 tradition of the חרם against Amalek are quite important for our study. The chapter is likely to stem back to the earliest part of the Samuel traditions, certainly no later than the ninth century B.C.. Moreover, as was the case in comparing the MI to 2 Kings 3, the MI account was straightforward and unmagical, while 2 Kings 3 was not. 1 Samuel 15 is like the MI in this respect. YHWH plays a role, as Kemosh did in the MI, but the narrative is straightforward and unmagical. In contrast, Exod 17:8-17, which has been supposed to be another source of this chapter, reduces the battle account to Moses's miraculous doings which determine the course of the struggle. One would as soon suppose that the present text of the MI is based on an account containing supernatural intervention like that found in Exodus 17.

Whether or not the events of 1 Samuel 15 occurred as exactly described, the חרם against Amalek seems to reflect an early stage in the adaptation of the practice from Israel's neighbors. The idea that spoils that were חרם were eligible for sacrifice reflects a certain confusion of the related ideas encapsulated in the roots קדש "to be holy," and חרם; the latter was never applied to cult worship in Israel. In any case, we certainly have here one of the earliest extant biblical narratives which portrays the חרם. In contrast to the lists of nations, which many scholars say have no relation to the population of pre-Israelite Canaan, no one doubts the existence of Amalek, and Amalek's depredations in every period made it a group that was extremely eligible for the חרם.

---

[17] C. H. W. Brekelmans, *De ḥerem in het Oude Testament* (Nijmegen, 1959), 112.

One of the most difficult tasks in biblical study is to attempt to transcend our own 20th century Western orientation in trying to assess biblical texts. In this respect, anyone viewing biblical material from the standpoint of חרם is privileged, since it is in itself a non-Western concept. The original audience for which this story was intended grew up in that non-Western culture, and so required much less persuasion as to the rectitude of Samuel's actions (cf. the esteem in which he was later held; Jer 15:1, Ps 99:6). Moreover, the fall of Saul in this context was from the start more explicable to the audience for which the chapter was written than that of the present day.

To understand why these things are so, we must revert to the original problem raised in the chapter, that of Amalek and the חרם to which it was condemned. Exod 17:8-15 and Deut 25:17-19 delineate the nature of Amalek's crime. Shortly after the deliverance from Egypt, Amalek attacked Israel when it was at its most vulnerable point in the wilderness, to which it was completely unaccustomed. Indeed, it could not even survive there without the continual assistance of YHWH. The anticlimax of the event, the attack coming so swiftly on the heels of YHWH's victory at and over the sea, is truly ludicrous, but one has to attempt to peer under the surface level of narrative to understand Amalek's role as the demonic people whom David called the "enemies of YHWH" (1 Sam 30:26, cp. the fate of YHWH's enemies in Ps 37:20).

Yet it is necessary to go back one step further still--to the Exodus itself. Only by placing the Amalekite crime in its full context can one hope to clarify anything. In his interesting book on the "theology of warfare in ancient Israel," M. C. Lind has focused especially on the Reed Sea 'incident' as a "paradigm for YHWH's saving action in Israel's difficult experiences of the future," and added that "later Old Testament writers follow the lead of the writer of this poem (i.e. Exodus 15) in viewing the sea and exodus as an archetypal event."[18] So far so good. However, he also seems to believe that Exodus 14-15 occurred basically as described, and therefore one should understand the exodus traditions as historically rooted in a battle of YHWH vs. Egypt![19]

As for a mythic explanation, he argues that there was an "early break with myth" followed by a later "remythologising" under David.[20] The fact is that myth permeates the Hebrew Bible from Genesis to Chronicles, but that it takes on a different appearance in relation to other Near Eastern mythologies due to its lack of divinities to populate the tales. Monotheistic myths may be more subtle than polytheistic myths, as Genesis 1 may be compared to *Enuma Elish*, but they remain myths. The Exodus as described in Exod 14-15 may reflect some historical relationship between Israel and

---

[18] M. C. Lind, *Yahweh is a Warrior: The Theology of Warfare in Ancient Israel* (Scottdale, Pa., 1980), 50, and see ch. 3.
[19] Ibid. 49-60.
[20] Ibid. 56f..

Egypt, but to deny its mythic *Gestalt* is to deny it its very essence and importance in the thought of ancient Israel.[21]

It is also important to recognize that myths were not objects that could be discarded like old clothes. Myths perpetually arose in human minds, as they do today.[22]

The Sea of Reeds narratives are, in fact, cosmogonic in character, and may combine two cosmogonic motifs: 1) the triumph of deity over chaos (*Chaoswasser*) as seen in the Ugaritic mythology, one exemplar of which is that of Baal's victory over Yamm.[23] We have a similar myth in much fuller form in *Enuma Elish,* which has a number of elements in common with Exodus 15, although humans had to be pressed into service to substitute for the good and the evil gods who serve in the Babylonian Creation Epic. Thus the Pharaoh and the Egyptian army play the role of Kingu and his demons, while Israel is the equivalent to Marduk's passive supporters. Tiamat (whose corpse forms dry land) is represented in Exod 15:9 by the 'congealing of the waters of the abyss (=chaos),'[24] which allows the people to cross the tamed chaos to dry land (Exod 15:16).[25] YHWH and Marduk both harness the wind; as fruit of victory Marduk receives his temple Esagila and YHWH his "sanctuary, the work of your hands" (Exod 15:17), i.e. there is no god of crafts like Kothar to construct it. I would scarcely deny the various differences between the two poems. The cosmogonic element in *Enuma Elish* deals with the creation of the world, Exodus 15 with the creation of the people Israel (15:16). However, both deal with the establishment of world order as epitomized by the housing of deity, a shared cosmogonic element of no little significance.

One should note that cuneiformists agree that *Enuma Elish* was written not to explain the creation of the world but to exalt the upstart Marduk and serve Babylonian political ends. Clearly this ploy succeeded, or Assyria

---

[21] For an interesting new discussion of Exodus 15 in relation to 'divine warfare,' see S-M. Kang, *Divine War in the Old Testament and in the Ancient Near East, BZAW* 177 (Berlin, 1989), 114-127.

[22] For a diametrically opposed view, see (among others) R. Bultmann, *History and Eschatalogy* (New York, 1957), 23-30 and passim.

[23] See N. Wyatt,"Who Killed the Dragon?." and literature cited there, in *Aula Orientalis* V (1987), 185-198.

[24] Cf. H. W. F. Saggs, *The Encounter with the Divine in Mesopotamia and Israel* (London, 1978), 54-63. He concentrates on the monster motif, without dealing at all with the idea of chaos.

[25] F. M. Cross, *Canaanite Myth and Hebrew Epic: Essays in the History of the Religion of Israel* (Cambridge, Mass., 1973). In a philological note on קפא (128 n.59) Cross attacks the traditional translation of the verb קפא, "to congeal" on comparative philologic grounds. He arrives at a translation of קפא "to foam." This is not satisfactory as it does not make a fitting conclusion for the third in the set of parallel units. "Congeal" is supported by LXX and Vulgate, so that in the absence of strong philological evidence it cannot be simply ruled out, especially as Cross cites the use with milk, where it can mean coagulate, curdle, or in other words, lose its character as a fluid. "Congeal" also fits the context far better, since part of the idea behind the waters being "piled up" is that their normal chaotic movement is being brought to a halt by YHWH's will.

would not have imitated it. This does not detract from the validity of the comparison I am making, for much the same may be said of Exodus 15. It is from first to last a hymn of praise and exaltation to YHWH--on this point, content and present context are agreed--who, if the Book of Exodus may be trusted so far, was equally an upstart, and in its references to foreign nations the Song of the Sea made an avowedly (Israelite) political statement.

2) The second cosmogonic element is that of the repelling of a human enemy into the realm of chaos, as exemplified by Exod 15:5, where the waters of the abyss cover the enemy and the threat is safely consigned to chaos. This is precisely the Egyptian view of warfare in which the enemies must be returned to a state of non-existence.[26] This allows the daily re-creation of the world to continue; human survival is thus assured, at least for the time being. All these elements, found elsewhere in the environment, are put together in an original way to meet the needs of Israel's religion; but to deny the mythic in Exodus 14-15 is to close the way to understanding the role of the Amalekites in the larger biblical scheme, as well as to leave unanswered many questions. F. M. Cross, in his well-known treatment of Exodus 15, does not denigrate the importance of the element of myth. He does deny, however, that there is a cosmogonic element in the first sense. He argues that there is no battle against chaos, since YHWH manipulates the sea without resistance.[27] However, in the Ugaritic text III A B A, in which Baal fights Yamm, he meets with no active resistance. Yamm reacts to both assaults in a completely passive way. Even fierce Tiamat does not really resist; her demise takes up only a few lines of text. Therefore the contrast is not as great as one might assume. The dramatic element in the Song of the Sea in its exposition of the Divine Warrior theme would be completely lacking were one to suppose the use of תהום and ים were entirely devoid of all reference to subduing chaos--chaos is just not personified. To suppose chaos is not a factor would strip an entire level of meaning from the poem.[28] Speaking of the Ugaritic poem of Aqhat, which is incomplete, S. P. Parker observes that:

> Assuming that the poem as a whole would have concluded with the establishment or restoration of order as understood as understood by the culture--and such a conclusion appears to be almost universal in ancient literary works....[29]

It certainly seems that both *Enuma Elish* and the Song of the Sea illustrate the idea of an "establishment,,, of order as understood by the culture." Perhaps this is why not only Moses and Miriam sing the Song, but the whole people (cp. Judges 5, sung only by Deborah and Barak).

---

[26] E. Hornung, *Conceptions of God in Ancient Egypt: The One and the Many*, (Ithaca, N.Y., 1982), 172-84.
[27] F. M. Cross, *Canaanite Myth and Hebrew Epic*, 131-2.
[28] Ibid.
[29] S.B. Parker, *The Pre-Biblical Narrative Tradition, SBL Resources for Biblical Study* 24 (Atlanta, 1989), 131.

No sooner had YHWH exercised his cosmogonic powers, allowing Israel to safely pass through the *Un-Welt* in two manifestations, Egypt and the Sea, then Amalek arrived on the scene to threaten Israel with non-existence, or in other words, with a return to the *Un-Welt* (which was also threatening Israel in the form of the desert, of which it might be said the Amalekites are a personification of its deadliest dangers)! It was the timing of this attack that rendered Amalek so heinous in the eyes of the biblical writers and of YHWH, so that Amalek became officially set apart as the "enemies of YHWH" and deserving of being fought against from generation to generation. It was the prophetic understanding of this sort of tradition, of which we surely have only remnants, that in the person of Samuel led to the call for חרם. It was the cosmologically required response to a people whom YHWH perceived as having no place in the world order. Therefore Saul's decision to spare Agag (and the booty) was unacceptable to Samuel, whatever his personal feelings, because he was, as it were, a member of YHWH's council.[30] The moral dilemma that moderns have in regard to this ruthlessness has been absurdly overemphasized, especially as the wiping out of the Amalekites in a body is rarely commented on in the same light. Yet given the Amalekites role as a threat to world order in the history of Israel--which is portrayed by the Bible as unremitting and unrelieved--and the conception of חרם I have been testing, the only surprising thing is how lightly Saul and the people were treated. Compare what happened to Achan! The reason for this may be that the motive was not to steal from the חרם, but at least obstensibly to sacrifice the proscribed cattle to YHWH. Also, the chapter lacks the same character imputed before to Joshua 6, that of "pure myth." Thus, at the end of the chapter, Saul might be doomed, but he was not ritually executed, nor was the doctrine of collective responsibility applied here (the Deuteronomistic historian not being in evidence). One might offer more suggestions, but they would be speculative in the absence of data. It is enough to note that King Saul offended less, and was treated more leniently than Achan, the peasant.

On the question of the spoil, the presence of Agag has the function of demonstrating that Saul's sparing of the cattle was not motivated by pious motives, as he claimed. In fact, no one who understood the term חרם could have so acted except, as in the case of Achan, out of greed. The idea that Saul was afraid of the people seems questionable in view of his previous dealings with them; cf. the episode of the eating on the blood, in 1 Sam 14:31ff., where he upbraided the people with the cry "Sinners!" Talk of sacrifice was mere pretext. He had failed to obey YHWH in this vital matter of

---

[30] J. Milgrom interprets 1 Samuel 15 so as to make Saul the hero who obeyed God, in *Numbers: The Traditional Hebrew Text with the New JPS Translation, JPS Torah Commentary* (Phila., 1990}, 430. However, on capturing a king during the חרם, it was incumbent on Saul to kill him, i.e. by hanging, as Joshua did, and which Saul did not do; Samuel had to do it. Saul clearly disobeyed YHWH (cf. 1 Kgs 20:42, which derives its bite from this circumstance. Milgrom's idea that Saul's actions against the Gibeonites (referred to in 2 Samual 2) were a "clear historical precedent" for the חרם of Deuteronomy is interesting.

the Lord's enemies (so 1 Sam 28:18, when the specter of Samuel relays God's verdict). For when in 1 Sam 15:3, YHWH of Hosts had commanded that Israel should have no pity on the enemy (וְלֹא תַחְמֹל עָלָיו), Saul and the people directly disobeyed. The same verb (וַיַּחְמֹל שָׁאוּל וְהָעָם) appears to signal his disobedience to everyone. Interestingly, there is a good likeness in tone and even in content between Saul under interrogation and Adam under interrogation. Each blamed a second party, and each was harshly punished but escaped immediate death.

M. Sternberg has pinpointed another reason for the harsh command to destroy the livestock of Amalek, in addition to YHWH's general discretion in these matters:

> Note the verbal analogy devised between Israel's coming revenge and Amalek's periodic invasions in the Gideon era: the prospective "both ox and sheep, both camel and ass" rhymes with the retrospective "they left no sustenance to Israel, neither sheep nor ox or ass...and their camels were without number" (Judges 6:3-5).[31]

As the writer goes on to remark, the relation between 1 Sam 15:3 and the Judges tradition is a good example of the biblical notion of divine retribution.[32] It also illustrates the feeling of endangerment which the Amalekites engendered in ancient Israel; it was their threat of chaos which resulted in the need for the חרם. Saul was only able to deviate from the "commandment of YHWH" because he had so far followed it so as to wipe out the mass of human beings.

C. H. W. Brekelmans felt that this chapter evinced a weakening or shift of the original sense of חרם to a seeking of the purity of the cult.[33] As cult purity, i.e. monotheism in this context, is not an issue in this chapter, the point does not seem to be well taken. Furthermore, if purity of the cult were at issue here, it would merely reflect what I have argued is an ancient facet of the חרם and inherent to it. In the chapter on the Mesha Inscription, I pointed out that Mesha acted with an exclusive devotion to Kemosh, treating YHWH as an enemy. In the light of this and of biblical religion, it is more likely that the חרם in Israel was associated with an exclusive YHWHism than not.

It is as a uniquely dangerous and perpetual challenger to the divine order of YHWH that the Amalekite nation appears in the Bible. One might add a small note on the use of ויזנב in Deut 25:18: this graphic verb, which could not but remind people of the Hebrew word, זנב, "tail," gives a suggestion of some monstrous animal (the Chaos-monster) pursuing Israel's stragglers (this is not the case in the other attestation of the verb in Josh 10:19, where it is Israelites who are the subjects of the verb, not the

---

[31] M. Sternberg, "The Bible's Art of Persuasion," 50.

[32] C. H. W. Brekelmans, *De ḥerem*, 114.

[33] Cf. our treatment above, which relied on an article which the author, Prof. W. W. Hallo kindly supplied me, "Biblical Abominations and Sumerian Taboos," *JQR* 76 (1985), 21-40.

objects). S. D. Sperling has pointed out to me that in *Enuma Elish* (V 59), Marduk twists the tail of Tiamat--Akk. *ēgir zib-bat-sa* (*CAD* Z 101a)--which adds to the plausibility of the suggestion. In any case, the biblical sources are united in promoting a ruthless end to the Amalekites; a people which had forfeited any place it might have had in YHWH's cosmic order.

A later biblical interpretation of the Amalekite threat appears in the Book of Esther, where Haman the would-be destroyer of the Jews is given the epithet, "Agagite" (Esth 3:1,10 and elsewhere). The epithet is best interpreted as a reference to the Amalekite king, Agag.[34] The scroll thus interprets Haman and Agag as having been among the greatest threats to the existence of Israel. As an aside, it is worth noting that, although the text of Esther lacks overt references to YHWH, by alluding to Agag, who died by the hand of Samuel "before YHWH," the scroll of Esther makes an indirect reference to past divine intervention against Israel's enemies.

It is evident that the debate between Saul and Samuel in the last section of the chapter, as Saul attempts to exculpate himself, revolves around the question of obedience to the Lord and around sacrifice. In the view of some scholars, Samuel's execution of Agag was a sacrifice. In Deut 12:31, human sacrifice is singled out as an abomination of the surrounding nations. The relevance of this may be limited in the present context, but there is nothing in the language used of the killing of Agag (1 Sam 15:33) which smacks of sacrificing Agag; indeed 1 Sam 15:20 explicitly delimits the sacrifice to the sheep and cattle. The expression "before the Lord" refers to the scene of Samuel's execution as being at a sanctuary or where god is present, as in other ancient Near Eastern contexts.[35] This does not make it a sacrifice, any more than when (be it a literary device or no) Utuḫegal brings Tirigan to the temple to die was his death was a sacrifice (cf. our treatment above, ch.2, of the MI's crux, אראל דודה, and Assyrian examples found under *CAD mašāru*}. For Samuel to turn around and sacrifice Agag would be to fall into the trap that Saul and the people fell into, for Samuel was complaining that sacrifice under the circumstances of חרם was the worst kind of disobedience,which would result in Saul's losing his scepter. The verb שסף mentioned in connection with the execution is not a verb used in the cult--if it were it would not be so obscure--but is apparently a verb of separation (*KBL* s.v.) and was therefore chosen to emphasize Samuel's fulfillment of the botched requirement--1 Sam 15:9 says that of the inanimate booty, only the worst was devoted of the war-חרם against Amalek, meaning that the requirements of the חרם were flouted in proportion to the people's desire for the spoils. All this would have merited an even more dire divine punishment than that which (quite literally) fell to the lot of Achan. Indeed, this punishment was effected. Just as Israel lost the first round at Ai due to Achan's sacrilegious behavior, this is precisely the reason why in biblical terms Israel suffered such a crushing defeat under Saul in his last battle.

---

[34] C. A. Moore, *Esther: Introduction, Translation, and Notes, AB* (Garden City, 1971), 35-6, discusses the epthet and arrives at a similar conclusion.

[35] Cf. Gilg. VI:154-5, for example.

In 1 Sam 15:32-3, there is an elaborate, if compact, "morality play" showing that Samuel indeed killed Agag out of retribution for his past depredations. It starts with a play on a toponym מעדנות, a name that has associations with earthly delights and a next-worldly paradise (Eden). Agag says that the bitterness of dying has left him, an evident word-play on מעדנות. Samuel reverses this sanguine attitude with his crisp evocation of the pain of bereavement which Agag had brought upon Israel. So would Agag's mother be rendered the most bereaved of woman, recalling the ending of the Song of Deborah (the blessed "mother in Israel" is contrasted to the unfortunate "mother of Sisera"). The verb Samuel uses, שׁכל, "render childless," may even link back to the previous verse through an unspoken play on שׂכל, a verb which can mean "to prosper" (1 Sam 18:30).[36] Thus the prophet executes a dialectical reverse of Agag's sanguine words in more than one way. Agag cannot expect an enjoyable death or afterlife.

The whole question of sacrifice is shaped so as to lead into the poetic oracle in which Samuel denounces disobedience (1 Sam 15:22-3), saying that obedience is better than sacrifice, a general sentiment echoed in the later prophets. The oracle condemned Saul to lose his kingdom in these terms. However, this is not to say that the whole matter of the sacrifice or the whole matter of the חרם is secondary, nor the poem--as much of the narrative has been structured to lead to just such an oracle-- but both matters have been artfully worked together from an early stage of composition into a theologically coherent narrative and cautionary tale. Not only Saul but Agag, too, is given the opportunity to speak and both show what manner of men they were, a device characteristic, too, of heroic clashes in Greek epic, e.g. Hector before his death in the Iliad, as elsewhere in the Bible. (Sisera in Judges 5). In this the text is far less slanted against Saul then it could easily have been (and this is partially evidenced by the large number of his adherents in modern scholarship; enough material exists to make his case). The narrative reflects not rabid Saul-hatred, but the historical fact of his fall, which had to be seen as first a fall from grace before his god. Not for the first time in the book, Saul is depicted in his complexity. He is a man who, like King Lear, imagines himself to be doing the right thing and learns differently too slowly, and loses a kingdom..

I would not claim to have penetrated every mystery contained in 1 Samuel 15. The analysis has produced some important gains, nonetheless. It was first shown, by a straightforward comparison of texts (aided by other factors such as distribution, e.g. יְהוָה צְבָאוֹת is not deuteronomic), that the widespread belief that 1 Samuel 15 is dependent on Deuteronomy is incorrect, helping to place its חרם account in its proper (relative) chronological place. I then brought into play the order/chaos paradigm to explain various ramifications of the unique treatment of Amalek in scripture, as viewed through the prism of the חרם. The mythic depiction of the eternal struggle against chaos served as a forerunner to the use of the חרם as an instrument

[36] *KBL* 922, wonders if it should be in hiphil like the other instances with this meaning, but this seems unnecessary.

in that struggle. Amalek filled the unenviable role of 'chaos' and so served as the object of the war-חרם. The exposition of the chapter ended with a glance at how the issues raised early in the chapter are worked through in ways that could not have predicted from any formula, deuteronomic or otherwise.

A NOTE ON EXOD 17:14 AND DEUT 25:17

Two verses in the Torah have related formulations relating to the fate of Amalek (see below for a comment on a third). The first comes in Exod 17:14:

כִּי־מָחֹה אֶמְחֶה אֶת־זֵכֶר עֲמָלֵק מִתַּחַת הַשָּׁמָיִם

This is customarily translated as, "For I will surely erase the memory of Amalek from under the heavens." The equivalent from Deuteronomy is this:

תִּמְחֶה אֶת־זֵכֶר עֲמָלֵק מִתַּחַת הַשָּׁמָיִם לֹא תִּשְׁכָּח׃

This is normally translated along these lines, "You must erase the memory of Amalek from under the heavens, you must not forget." The seeming incongruity between the two statements, viz. that YHWH is to be the actor in Exod 17:14 and Israel is assigned the task in Deut 25:19 follows the line of the passages in Exodus which spoke of YHWH or his agents's intervention to expel (גרש) the primordial peoples, the equivalents of which in Deuteronomy employed the חרם, which required human participation.

It is clear that these basically identical formulations come from the world of Near Eastern antiquity. This has already been pointed out above in relation to the Utuḫegal inscription (c. 2110 B.C.), which contains Enlil's command to destroy the name of Gutium. The wording closely resembles that of an Assyrian treaty curse adduced by R. Frankena:[37]

> May Zērbanītu, who gives name (and) seed, destroy your name and seed from the land.

W. W. Hallo informs me that the Akkadian equivalent of the Hebrew expression מחה שם, "erase the name," is *šuma pašāṭu*. Von Soden (*AHw* 844b) gives a nice example from a middle Babylonian *kudurru* or boundary stone (in the D-stem): *ša ... šum ili u šarri ... uptaššitū*.Here the writer does not expect the miscreant's activity to wipe out 'god and king' But the transition to the treaty curse (cf. Deut 29:19) and to the Biblical Amalek passages which partake of their character is a slight one, given the way the name of a person was often identified with that person in antiquity in what would today

[37] R. Frankena, "The Vassal Treaties of Esarhaddon," *Oudtestmentliche Studien namens het oudtestmentisch werkgezelschap in Nederland* 14 (Leiden,1965) 147. The author treats the treaties as essentially one, since they differ only slightly from each other.

be regarded as a magical form of identification of name and person. In treaty curse language, to erase or destroy the name is to destroy something, whether Gutium or Amalek. Although this is not the place to launch a full scale philological investigation of the biblical phraseology in its Near Eastern context, it seems clear that this is a case of זכר, "memory," acting as an equivalent to cognate Akkadian *zikru*, "name," as it seems to act elsewhere.[38] Therefore the translation "memory" misrepresents the idiom and obscures its background and true meaning. It makes little sense to give an order not to forget to erase the memory (Deut 25:19), since it is the Bible which has in fact perpetuated the memory of Amalek. The writers of Deut 25:19 and Exod 17:14 were not interested in memory but in Amalek's existence as a fighting force. Thus, the Hebrew formula was a wish to return Amalek to a state of non-existence, like that depicted in the first line of the Babylonian Creation Epic in similar language, *enūma eliš la nabû šamāmu, šapliš ammatu šuma la zakrat* ("when heaven on high was not named--the earth below not called by a name")[39]

The link between the language of the Torah's Amalek passages and that of 1 Samuel 15 becomes clear. Both are speaking in terms of world order, in the Torah passages in simple negative terms. Amalek is to be drummed out of the world order. The use of the חרם in 1 Samuel 15 is another, practical way of expressing the same thing, except that it reflects the continuing struggle to build an Israelite *Weltordnung* worthy of the name. If the Torah passages reflect neo-Assyrian influences (as the vassal treaty parallel to Deut 25:19, Exod 17:14 may indicate), this would be another reason to see 1 Samuel 15 as as the oldest source on the "war against Amalek from generation to generation."

II: 1 KINGS 20:42

The root חרם appears only three times in the Book of Kings; 1 Kgs 9:21, 1 Kgs 20:42, and 2 Kgs 19:11. 1 Kgs 20:42 will be first.. It is the most interesting of the three occurrences, as it poses a problem of interpretation.[40] 1 Kgs 20:42 reads as follows:

וַיֹּ֣אמֶר אֵלָ֗יו כֹּ֚ה אָמַ֣ר יְהוָ֔ה יַ֛עַן שִׁלַּ֥חְתָּ אֶת־אִישׁ־
חֶרְמִ֖י מִיָּ֑ד וְהָיְתָ֤ה נַפְשְׁךָ֙ תַּ֣חַת נַפְשׁ֔וֹ וְעַמְּךָ֖ תַּ֥חַת עַמּֽוֹ׃

> He (the prophet) said to him: thus says YHWH. Since you freed the man of my חרם from (your) hand, let your life stand instead of his life, and your people instead of his people.

---

[38] H. Eising, "zākhar," *TDOT* IV, 76, cf. also 72-3.

[39] Normalization follows *CAD* E 96a.

[40] This section appears, in an earlier form in P.D. Stern,"The *ḥerem* in 1 Kgs 20,42 as a Hermeneutical Problem" *Bib* 71 (1990), 43-47.

The harsh judgement at the end of the verse condemns the whole people (or conceivably the army), because of Ahab's clemency towards Ben Hadad. Some commentator's have simply assumed that the חרם is mentioned as a normal part of Holy War.[41] There are excellent reasons to dispute that assumption. The concept of 'Holy War' is, in biblical studies, most closely associated with the name of Gerhard von Rad.[42] He believed that the חרם was an integral part of the Holy War.[43] This is, as I have argued before, a debatable claim. Holy War was not an Israelite invention, and its main practitioner and Israel's major model in the period of the monarchy was Assyria.[44] Yet C. H. W. Brekelmans' firm conclusion that Assyria never practiced an analogue to the חרם still holds true[45] As Assyria was the main actor on the stage, while Israel had a minor role, it is plain that the חרם was not normative Holy War practice

This was true too of Israel. Von Rad certainly regarded the wars of Deborah and Gideon as holy,[46] yet in these and other biblical holy war accounts the חרם is lacking. The account in 1 Kings 20 also lacks anything like 1 Sam 15:3 or Josh 6:17-19, where YHWH sent directions as to what the חרם was to entail. In the latter two instances, the חרם was of maximum severity, but Deut 2:1-5 illustrates a case where the Israelites were permitted to take liberal amounts of the spoils. There was thus no one recipe for the חרם that the prophet could have expected Ahab to follow in the absence of directions. Yet here the prophet does not even tell Ahab to initiate the חרם, as he should have after 1 Kgs 20:13 (the summons to war), according to the analogy of the three passages just cited. To sum up, the concept of 'Holy War' does not provide in itself an adequate explanation for the sudden appearance of the word חרם.

Others have assumed that the חרם was an expression of the working of the laws of war in Deuteronomy 20.[47] However, it is hard to see how these laws could have any application to 1 Kings 20. There are only three verses in the chapter that deal with the חרם, namely Deut 20:16-18:

16 רַק מֵעָרֵי הָעַמִּים הָאֵלֶּה אֲשֶׁר יְהוָה אֱלֹהֶיךָ נֹתֵן לְךָ נַחֲלָה לֹא תְחַיֶּה
כָּל־נְשָׁמָה׃ 17 כִּי־הַחֲרֵם תַּחֲרִימֵם הַחִתִּי וְהָאֱמֹרִי הַכְּנַעֲנִי וְהַפְּרִזִּי
הַחִוִּי וְהַיְבוּסִי כַּאֲשֶׁר צִוְּךָ יְהוָה אֱלֹהֶיךָ׃ 18 לְמַעַן אֲשֶׁר לֹא־

---

41 E,g, B. O, Long, *I Kings: With an Introduction to Historical Literature* (Grand Rapids, 1984), 207.

42 Due to his influential book, *Der Heilige Krieg im alten Israel*, (Zurich,1951).

43 G. von Rad, *Old Testament Theology I: The Theology of Israel's Historical Traditions* (New York, 1962), 17, *Der Heilige Krieg*, 25ff..

44 The two best treatments of Assyrian Holy War are those of R. Labat, *Le Caractère religieux de la royauté assyro-babylonienne*, ch. 3, "La guerre sainte," and M. Weippert, "'Heiliger Krieg' in Israel und Assyrien," *ZAW* 84 (1972), 460-493.

45 C. H. W. Brekelmans, *De ḥerem*, 134-139. Theoretically, the discovery of one document could overturn this conclusion.

46 G. von Rad, *Old Testament Theology* I, 328f..

47 R. D. Nelson, *First and Second Kings*,137. Also, *int. al*. J. Robinson. *The First Book of Kings* (Cambridge, 1972), 229,232, and passim.

יְלַמְּדוּ אֶתְכֶם֙ לַעֲשׂוֹת֙ כְּכֹל֙ תּוֹעֲבֹתָ֔ם אֲשֶׁ֥ר עָשׂ֖וּ לֵאלֹֽהֵיהֶ֑ם וַחֲטָאתֶ֖ם
לַיהוָ֥ה אֱלֹהֵיכֶֽם׃

16. Only from the cities of these peoples whose portion YHWH your God is giving you shall not allow a soul to live. 17. For you must devote them to destruction--the Hittites and the Amorites, the Canaanites and the Perizzites, the Hivites and the Jebusites--as YHWH your God has ordered you. 18. In order that they will not teach you to construct the like of their idols[48] which they make for their gods, thus sinning against YHWH.

These verses together with the first part of the chapter make it plain that the law of חרם is intended for offensive warfare under divine aegis against the earlier inhabitants of the land. The purpose is to prevent the spread of idolatry by imitation. In my view, none of this can apply to the situation of 1 Kings 20. Ahab is on the defensive, fighting a 'far away' people called the Arameans, who are not among the "primordial nations." Nor is he portrayed in the Bible or in 1 Kings 20 as a campaigner against idol-worship. Finally, in none of the other texts dealing with Aram or wars against Aram is there any intimation of the חרם. Consequently, Deuteronomy 20 is not the key to understanding 1 Kgs 20:42.

These considerations show that Ahab did not violate the חרם in the same sense that Saul did in 1 Samuel 15. If it were not for the last part of the verse, speaking of the wholesale destruction of the people, one would first think of חרם II, "net." The use of the net as a divine weapon goes back at least as far as the example of Eannatum of the First Dynasty of Lagash shows; his stele of the vultures depicts Ningirsu using a net against the enemies of the king (ANEP #298). YHWH, too, uses a net as his weapon (e.g. in Ezek 32:3). As it is, since the context deals with capturing the enemy king, we should view it as a double entendre. On one level, YHWH was angry because upon capturing Ben Hadad--acting as YHWH's net--Ahab let the fish swim free.[49] On another level, YHWH is condemning Ahab figuratively for, as it were, violating the חרם, even though there was none, technically speaking. This is, of course, a divine death sentence.

The appearance here of the חרם requires some fleshing out. In order to understand YHWH's anger in 1 Kgs 20:42, we must understand what YHWH told Ahab to see why the king's behavior so angered the deity. In 1 Kgs 20:13-15 we find a prophet approaching the king, saying, "All this great multitude I am giving into your hand today that you shall know that I am YHWH." Ahab asks, "Through whom?"

---

[48] Lit. "abominations." It is one of the usual Deuteronomic locutions for "idol," and is best so translated for clarity.

[49] The inscription accompanying the reliefs of the Stele of the Vultures refers to the king employing nets coming from various deities, like Utu and Enki. An English version is found in S.N. Kramer, *The Sumerians: Their History, Culture, and Character* (Chicago, 1963), 310-13. In 1 Kgs 20,42, a similar figure is implied, but here King Ahab has *failed* to use the 'net of YHWH.'

The prophet replies, "So says YHWH, 'through the soldiers of the provincial chiefs.'" Ahab asks one more question: מִי־יֶאְסֹר הַמִּלְחָמָה to which the reply is,"You!" Since Ahab proceeds to muster the soldiers, and since in the only appearance of the prophet before Ahab (1 Kgs 20:28) prior to the final scene of the condemnation (1 Kgs 20:35-43), nothing more is required of him, it is crucial to understand the question Ahab posed, מִי־יֶאְסֹר הַמִּלְחָמָה. It is translated as "who shall begin the battle?" by the lexica[50], and is derived from the need to hitch up the horses to the chariots before the battle can begin (אסר='bind')[51]. If that is all there is to it, then we may find nothing explicit in the chapter to account for the intensity of the divine wrath in 1 Kgs 20:42. After all, the sparing of defeated leaders was not unheard of in the ancient Near East (cf. Jehoiachin). J. Gray was dissatisfied with the translation of אסר as 'begin' and offered the following, "Who will clinch the fighting?"[52] He explains this diametrically opposed translation in these words:

> ʿāsar, usually taken as 'to begin' means literally 'to bind,' hence according to etymology and context, 'end' or 'close with,' hence our rendering 'clinch.'[53]

As YHWH was fighting with him, the king of Israel hardly needed to ask the trivial question put in his mouth, "who will begin the fighting," which advances the chapter's agenda not one whit.[54] However, Gray's translation helps to make sense of Ahab's offense. In letting Ben Hadad go free, Ahab was neglecting his God-given responsibility to clinch, put an end to the war by the logical means of killing the king. This is symbolized by the Aramean king coming to Ahab dressed in mourning and bringing with him cords to be bound in, making him an "אסיר מלחמה." By not taking the opportunity to bind the enemy king, who was מלחמה (war) personified, Ahab defied YHWH's will and received the condemnation of 1 Kgs 20:42.[55] Instead of knowing that "I am YHWH," as the prophet said, by spurning YHWH's gift, Ahab denied YHWH and became a man who was חרם in a way similar in principal to the offender of Exod 22:19, and disobedient like Saul who spared Agag.

The writer did his best to raise the ghost of Saul by using the word, חרם, even though the two situations were radically different. Without pretending to read the writer's mind, the reason he did this seems to have been out of a desire to emphasize the absolute quality of YHWH's rejection of Ahab, which extended also to his dynasty, as in the case of Saul (although in nei-

---

[50] *BDB* 63b-64a, *KBL* 73b.

[51] Ibid.

[52] J. Gray, *I and II Kings: A Commentary, OTL* (2nd ed., Philadelphia,1975), 419.

[53] Ibid. 425

[54] Nor is it what we would expect from elsewhere in the Bible. Cf. 2 Sam 19f. where David asks the Lord first if he should attack the enemy, then if he will win, to which the reply is 'yes.' Gray's rendering places this exchange in the same category, since the person who 'clinches' the victory is obviously the victor.

[55] 2 Chr 13:3a uses an almost identical expression, לאסור את המלחמה ב..., which evidently means the same thing as 2 Chr 13:3b's ערך מלחמה ב..., "to arrange (troops) in battle formation." Despite its verbal similarity, the idiom offers no help.

ther case did the dynasty expire immediately). However, unlike Ahab. Saul did violate the war-חרם in the full sense. Both kings spared an enemy monarch against YHWH's will; Ahab did not seek YHWH's forgiveness, unlike Saul. Probably the use of the expression 'man of my חרם' made Ahab understand that YHWH's anger was now intractable.

The logic of the prophetic parable in 1 Kgs 20:39f. extends as far as the exchange of Ahab's life for the fortunate Ben Hadad. Yet 1 Kgs 20:42 includes the people of Israel (who must die instead of the Arameans), making Israel in effect YHWH's עם חרמי (an expression found in Isa 34:5, also a call to judgement, as well as a cry for vengeance). It would seem to be a prediction (before or after the fact) of the doom of the Northern Kingdom, laying its demise at the feet of Ahab, a historically not untenable idea, since Ahab's leading role in the Battle of Qarqar was amply avenged by the Assyrians in the years to come.[56] The fact that the battle is not mentioned in the Bible does not mean that it was forgotten by Israel in biblical times. On the other hand, the Arameans continued to flourish despite Assyrian campaigns against them.

Some scholars believe that none of the wars between the Omrides and the Arameans took place at the time, but that they were actually retrojections of events that occurred later on, following the fall of the dynasty.[57] If this is true (and it is too large a matter to deal with in depth here) one can see why the hated Ahab was put into this position. He was seen by YHWHists as the *fons et origo* of all evil. At the same time, the argument originally raised by Jepsen that Israel and Aram could not have fought at this time because of the need to counter four Assyrian campaigns is not unassailable. Reluctant allies, they could have fought eagerly the moment the threat receded or was still over the horizon. The reason that Ahab released Ben Hadad, according to 1 Kings 20, was that they were 'brothers,' i.e. allies. This suggests that they were fighting for local dominance, knowing at the same time that they might need each other to fight a common foe. Damascus may well have supported Mesha's revolt by threat or deed, which is conceivably the reason why the king of Israel fled before Kemosh (MI 1.19); he had to guard the home front. One indication of the complexity of the problem is provided by H. Tadmor, who raises the possibility that one reason for the shift in the location of the capital of the Northern Kingdom was to move

---

[56] As Karl S. Erlich has pointed out to me, the Assyrians periodically wiped the slate clean, and the demise of Samaria is not due to Assyrian revenge over one hundred years later on Ahab. This does not mean that the ideological viewpoint of the Kings' writer paid attention to such facts. In this chapter, Ahab's evil takes on evil portent, and the writer puts all subsequent disaster on Ahab's head. Hence the use of the term, חרם. In this he takes on the character of a second Jereboam (cf. 2 Kings 17).

[57] E.g. K.-H. Bernhardt, "The Political Situation in the East of Jordan during the Time of King Mesha," in A. Hadidi, ed., *Studies in the History and Archeology of Jordan I* (Amman, 1982), 163-7, A. Jepsen, "Israel und Damaskus," *AfO* 13 (1941), 173-152, J. M. Miller,"The Elisha Cycle and the Accounts of the Omride Wars," *JBL* 85 (1966). 441-454. Miller agrees with Bernhardt that Jehosophat and Elisha do not belong in 2 Kings 3 (see ch. 2, appendix).

the capital westward to a location less exposed to Aramean attack.[58] This might be a rather concrete sign of the Omrides' relations with the Arameans. Further, B. Mazar has collected a number of circumstantial passages that together with archeological and epigraphic findings lend a plausibility to his more straightforward reconstruction of the relations between Israel and Aram as narrated in 1 Kings 20 and other chapters dealing with the Omrides and Aram.[59] Whatever the true historical background of the chapter, for the purpose of understanding the חרם in 1 Kgs 20:42 it is fortunately the hermeneutical approach which matters most, not the history, which must remain on any approach mired in obscurity and a subject of surmise.

I have tried to show that the use of the חרם in 1 Kgs 20:42 is far more difficult to explain than simple appeals to Holy War (or to Deut 20:16-18). In fact, Holy War in itself by no means implies the חרם, nor do the operation of Holy War motives in the chapter suffice to explain its presence in this verse. Even when not explicitly stated, as in Joshua 10-11, there is always a clear rationale for the execution of the חרם against a given enemy. In an instance like this, against a foe that is not normally the object of the war-חרם, Ahab could not be faulted for its violation unless the prophet had specifically prescribed it. I have further attempted to show that YHWH ordered the death of Ben Hadad, and that 1 Kings 20:42 gives a powerful but figurative condemnation of death upon his failing to do so. One may add that Ahab's making a covenant with Ben Hadad instead of adhering to the Covenant by obeying YHWH exacerbated the great wrath that the writer of 1 Kgs 20:42 felt brought suffering on all the people of Ephraim, which was precipitated at least in part by the incident related in 1 Kings 20. It is here that the real parallel with Saul lies. Like Saul, Ahab fecklessly failed to obey YHWH and execute the enemy king. Biblical writers understood that, just as children suffer for the sins of their parents, peoples suffer for the deficiencies of their rulers.

III: 1 KGS 9:20-22

This passage has several aspects of interest. It reads as follows:

> All the people who remain in the land from the Amorites, the Hittites, the Perizzites, the Hivites, and the Jebusites that are not Israelites. Their descendants who remained after them in the land, whom the Israelites were not able to devote to destruction (החרים), Solomon levied for forced labor, (מס עובד), but he did not place any Israelites in servitude, for they were his men of war....

[58] H. Tadmor, "On the History of Samaria in the Biblical Period," (Heb.), in *Eretz Shomron: The Thirtieth Archeological Conference, Septermber 1972* (Jerusalem, 1973), 68.

[59] B. Mazar, "The Aramean Empire and Its Relations with Israel," in Sh. Ahituv and B. A. Levine, eds., *The Early Biblical Period: Historical Studies* (Jerusalem, 1986), 157-160.

The passage is a little difficult towards the end. The expression מס עובד has been translated differently,[60] but for the purposes of this study, its precise meaning is unimportant. The general purport of the passage is simply that the members of the five peoples listed were required to shoulder burdens for Solomon that Israelites were not saddled with. This does not mean that Israelites were not subjected to the corvée, as 1 Kgs 5:26-32 describes in some detail. Yet the terminology is different in the latter passage, lacking the word עובד, with the low status attached to it, and it was not new in the ancient Near East for idle soldiers to be given assigned tasks.[61]

The list of nations is confined to five. One of the missing names is that of the Girgashites. As this is frequently lacking from the lists it is of no great consequence. More important is the absence of the Canaanites, which is deliberate. The LXX adds both, but it places the Canaanites in fourth position after the Perizzites, as happens in MT only in Exod 23:23.. Furthermore, the parallel verse, 2 Chr 8:7, contains the same five nations in slightly different order. However, the Canaanites are mentioned in connection with Pharaoh's expedition to Gezer, in what is commonly supposed to be an interpolation displaced from 1 Kgs 3:1.[62] However, this conclusion is scarcely irresistible. As it stands the Pharaoh and Solomon are shown acting on the same stage, enhancing Solomon's prestige. The writer is also careful to mention in this context Solomon's building of "store cities," a term found only here and in Exodus, when the Israelites were building the store cities of Egypt. Pharaoh's extirpation of the Canaanites of the Gezer area constituted for the writer (very probably of the Deuteronomic school), the elimination of the Canaanites as a significant group; hence the absence of the Canaanites from the list of those remaining. The writer, by omitting the Canaanites in this passage, perpetuated the tradition that the חרם did have an important role in the conquest and settlement of Canaan, and he integrated the Pharaoh's attack on Gezer into that tradition, making Pharaoh a tool of YHWH's will.

The passage is far more realistic than Joshua 10-11, where Joshua applied the חרם indiscriminately, wiping out vast numbers of autochthonous inhabitants of the land. The picture given is also in accordance with the MI. There, Mesha applied the חרם but he also used Israelite forced labor (ll.25-6); he employed his most closely-bound subjects (Dibonites) for one project (l.28), and expected Moabites to dig their own cisterns (l.24-5), not Israelites. Capital projects were enormously labor intensive in that era. Kings were glad to requisition as much of it as they could from the available sources, limited of course by the means which they had at their disposal to maintain control of the labor force, and to maintain it in general.

---

60 *KBL* 540b cites I. Mendelsohn's view "total slavery" although it does not adopt this translation. On this and other points see A. Biram, "מס עובד," *Tarbiz* 23 (1952/3) 137-42

61 Cf. A. L. Oppenheim, *Ancient Mesopotamia: Portrait of a Dead Civilization* (Rev. ed. E. Reiner, Chicago, 1977), 83. Here he speaks of "shiftless" workers pressed into hard labor and military service. Cf. also J. Gray, *The Legacy of Canaan SVT* 5 (2nd ed., 1965), 224.

62 J. Gray, *I and II Kings*, 241 note d.

The author of 1 Kings 9 clearly perceived the action of the divine will, so that even the king of Egypt served as God's tool to fulfill the promise to Israel to eliminate the peoples who barred the way to the Israelite settlement in Canaan. The use of the verb נותר indicates a left over portion that was not numerous. There was also a limit to how many laborers Solomon could employ in this way. Hence the need for the Israelite corvée as well.

The parallel in 2 Chr 8:9 uses the verb כלה in the piel instead of חרם. The writer does not follow exactly the Kings text of this section. It may not be coincidence that Chronicles omits to say that the Israelites were "not able" to ban all the peoples listed. 1 Kgs 9:21 לא יכלו and 2 Chr 8:9 כלום may be related. If a 'Kings' MS lacked a *yod* in the word יכלו, the Chronicler could have deleted להחרימם without changing the verse dramatically; or it may be a free variation. Whatever the case, the Chronicles use of כלה where the Kings text uses חרם, says nothing as to the meaning of the חרם in 1 Kings 9. There it plainly reflects the usage found in Deut 7,13, and 20, where as shown above, the verb means "to consecrate to destruction."

IV: 2 KGS 19:11=ISA 37:11

The principal question to be settled here is the meaning of the hiphil of חרם. Since the subject of the verb here is Assyria, and the object is the lands of Assyrian conquest (it is from the messengers of the Rabshekah, seeking the surrender of Jerusalem): "See, you have heard that which the kings of Assyria did to all the lands להחרימם; and you will be delivered?" In 2 Kgs 19:17 of the same chapter, in Hezekiah's prayer, we find the exact counterpart of this verse: "Truly, O YHWH, the kings of Assyria destroyed (החריב) the nations and their land." The two verses are virtually identical, but the first is addressed to Hezekiah from the Rabshekah, and the second from Hezekiah to YHWH (whether these statements were actually made as given is irrelevant to our concerns). Thus one approach would be that Hezekiah's statement to YHWH is a 'translation' of the Rabshekah's words, and that להחרימם is translated as החריבו because the two here are synonyms.

Another argument leading to this result is given by M. Cogan and H. Tadmor in their recent commentary on 2 Kings:

> Sanda's suggestion to emend the text...because of the improbability that the Assyrians practiced the Israelite form of *ḥerem*--ban--is unnecessary. In late BH, the verb *heḥerim* is used in the general sense of "to destroy"; cf. Jer 50:21, 26; 51:3; 2 Chr 20:23; Dan 11:44.[63]

This argument is somewhat oversimplified. The diachronic distinction is not based on sufficient evidence; as B. A. Levine pointed out to me, in actuality both meanings existed side by side, but we do not know from what pe-

---

[63] M. Cogan & H. Tadmor, *II Kings: A New Translation with Introduction and Commentary, AB* (Garden City, 1988), 234-5.

riod. The Jeremiah verses are uniformly exilic,[64] whereas late BH stems from the Persian period. There is a vast difference between the Hebrew of Jeremiah and that of Chronicles and Daniel, which come from the latest linguistic strata in the Hebrew Bible. Then there is Ezra 10:8, in which the verb החרים is still clearly differentiated from "destroy," and this is the case of a lexical subsystem of חרם in the scrolls of Qumran, according to the recent linguistic study of verbs of separation by A. Vivian.[65] 2 Kgs 19:11 is, at the latest, exilic by either Noth's original version of the deuteronomic hypothesis or by any variants of that hypothesis, but it could well be earlier. On the other hand, exilic prophecy's use of the חרם would be robbed of much of its effect if the root were lacking in its connotation of the sacred, as we shall see. J. Gray's explanation was that the verb here is used in a secondary sense, focusing on its destructive aspect.[66] However, the fact that in Arabic the eighth form of *ḫarama* (=חרם II) can mean, "kill, extirpate, destroy" inclines one to believe that the hiphil of חרם II is what is at stake here (see ch.1), especially as the occurrence of the word in 2 Kgs 19:11 does not fit in with a "late usage." As the hiphil of חרם I became less relevant, the use of the חרם II hiphil could be used more frequently in texts without causing unnecessary confusion, at least to the people of the biblical period. Distinguishing between the two roots could only be a problem in texts, not in popular speech..

C. H. W. Brekelmans pointed to the parallel between 2 Kgs 19:11 and the following verse, which repeats the basic contents of 2 Kgs 19:11 but substitutes the root שחת "destroy" for חרם, and I have already mentioned v.17 (prayer of Hezekiah) which uses another word for destroy, החריב. There is then every reason to see in the verb the simple meaning 'destroy.' After all, החרים seems to be used synonymously with 2 Kgs 19:12 שחתו and 2 Kgs 19:17 החריב.

The Book of Kings is the first biblical book since Genesis in which the war-חרם is not depicted as an extant practice in some shape or form. Of course, the actual chronology does not always follow the sequence of books, but it is nevertheless an important if superficial observation. It indicates that the laws of Deuteronomy 20, restricting the חרם to the aboriginal peoples of Canaan, reflect (as well as according to my hypothesis, helped shape) the behavior of Israel during the period of the monarchy. As an aside I shall try to respond to the position that the laws of חרם in Deuteronomy 20 are an expansion of the previous law of siege, and an unreal one at that.[67] They are an expansion, in the sense that the law relating to making peace with a ca-

---

[64] J. Bright, *Jeremiah: A New Translation with Introduction and Commentary, AB* (Garden City. 1965) 360.

[65] A. Vivian, *I campi lessicali della "separazione" nell'ebraico biblico, di Qumran e della Mishna: ovvere, applicabila della teoria dei campi lessicali all'ebraico* (Florence, 1978), 264. The dimension of 'sacrality' survives in Qumran to a limited degree; the same is true of the Mishna, 276.

[66] J. Gray, *I and II Kings*, 687.

[67] A. Biram, "מס עובד," 138.

pitulating city reflects the oldest practice of war; if one has to lay siege, the outcome is apt to be bitter (cf. Thucydides on the siege of Platea). Yet the Bible never portrays a successful Israelite siege, which makes Deut 20:10-14, too, look unreal.

The Book of Kings marks a watershed in the use of חרם in the Bible. It introduces the figurative, or not strictly literal use of the word, placed in the mouth of the biblical prophet (in 1 Kgs 20:42). In 1 Kgs 9:20, a writer makes novel use of the חרם tradition by combining it with the Egyptian assault on Gezer, leading (according to this writer) to the extirpation of the last of the Canaanites, and their consequent omission from the list of autochthonous peoples. Finally, 2 Kgs 19:11 gives us a clear cut example of the use of חרם, in my view חרם II with the meaning of "destroy." The Book of Kings employs the root חרם only two or three times, but no two uses are alike. The instances are therefore invaluable in disproportion to their number.

CHAPTER 9

THE LITERARY PROPHETS

I: ISAIAH 34

The dating of Isaiah 34 has been uncertain for a long time. G. A. Smith, writing in the early part of the century, was content to assign it a question mark,[1] and for my part, I am content with his verdict, restated more recently by Y. Hoffman with cogency.[2] The most common scholarly dating is exilic. Some place it in the post-exilic period, but the ferocious attitude towards Edom (which makes Isa 63:1-6 look quite anemic) argues that the prophet is reacting to the greatest misbehavior of Edom in Israel's history, its actions before and during the Babylonian conquest (the quarrel with Edom over its behavior towards Jerusalem is referred to explicitly in Isa 34:8).[3] As Smith noted (see n.1), other reactions are found in Obadiah, Ezek 35:10-15, and Ps 131:7. The archeological evidence proves that the Edomites had infiltrated into southern Judah even before Israel's fall.[4]

The attempt by Edom to dispossess Israel as it struggled against the nations who had made the attempt possible--the Edom oracle of Isaiah 34 illustrates just how high feelings ran--is what led the prophet to adopt the term חרם. The encroachment on the land of YHWH's promise represented, on top of all of Israel's other troubles, a threat that the forces of chaos would permanently replace the Israelite *Weltordnung*, making return impossible. As P. Bordreuil observed of the forces of chaos in another connection, "dans l'A.T., ces dernières figurent souvent les ennemis du peuple."[5] In this chapter, YHWH's actions, including above all the חרם, lead to the recoiling of chaos on its fomenters (Isa 34:11ff.) The prophet thus envisioned a total reversal of the sad situation that had arisen in Judah's history.

What means, then, the חרם in this chapter? As C. H. W. Brekelmans recognized, the חרם is used here metaphorically.[6] Here are the verses which employ חרם:

> Isa 34:2 For YHWH has rage against all the peoples, wrath at all their host; He has put them to the חרם, given them to the slaughter.
> Isa 34:5 My sword has drunk (blood) unto heaven. See, it will descend on Edom, on the people of my חרם, for judgement.

---

[1] G. A. Smith, *The Book of Isaiah,* vol. I *The Expositor's Bible* (London, 1908), 438ff., 454.

[2] Y. Hoffman, *The Prophecies against Foreign Nations in the Bible* (Tel Aviv, 1977), 103-5.

[3] W. Eichrodt, *Der Herr der Geschichte: Jesaja 13-23 und 28-39, Die Botschaft des alten Testaments* Bd. 17, II (Stuttgart,1965), 219.

[4] A recent article covering this ground is I. Beit-Arieh, "New Light on the Edomites," *BAR* XIV 2 (1988), 29-41.

[5] P. Bordreuil, "Michée 4:10-13 et ses parallèles ougaritiques," *Semitica* 21 (1971), 21-28.

[6] C. H. W. Brekelmans, *De ḥerem in het Oude Testament* (Nijmegen. 1959), 121.

We see in Isa 34:5 a usage similar to that of 1 Kgs 20:42, in which a prophet used the expression איש חרמי, "the man I set apart, i.e.consecrated for destruction." That was a figurative usage, and also in all probability a pun, since from חרם II comes a homonym, "net," an ancient Near Eastern divine weapon (e.g. of Marduk in *Enuma Elish)*. In this prophetic utterance, far removed from the realities of war, we have another figurative, or metaphorical usage.

According to Brekelmans we have here a witness to the "profanization" of החרים since one may understand החרים in v.2 by the continuation, נתנם לטבח, "given them to the slaughter."[7] However, not only is the sacral חרם used in parallel to words for slaughter in other biblical texts, but Ugaritic text KTU 1.13 has הרג/חרם, "slay" in parallel, and in this text the imperative of חרם is addressed to Anat.[8] So there is no need to speak of a secularized use here, particularly as YHWH is the subject in Isa 34:2 (as Anat was in KTU 1.13). As an army of Israel was lacking in the exilic period and thereafter, it was natural to use the imagery of YHWH as the agent of the חרם; something anticipated in KTU 1.13! In עם חרמי the sacral aspect is evident. In the figurative usage of Isa 34:2, since the Israelites were no longer able to execute YHWH's חרם, they were dispensed with and YHWH did it himself.

In support of this interpretation is the fact that this chapter, which was written after the fall of the kingdom of Judah, yet retains much of the flavor of the Mesha Inscription. In chapter two above, I pointed to Jer 46:10 and Isa 34:5 (the latter cited first by Brekelmans) as evidence of the meaning of the Moabite word רית, as cognate to Heb. רוה. In both scriptural passages, as well as in the Mesha Inscription, we are dealing with an incensed, insensate deity who is pictured as eager to glut himself with blood. This is especially true of Isaiah 34 and the MI, though Isaiah 34's portrayal of the deity's vengeful bloodlust is considerably more prolonged than the MI's. The basic issue at stake in both texts is occupation of the land, a fundamental issue which previous and subsequent history has proved to be fraught with the potential for bloodbaths. Isaiah 34's gory character thus flows from an urgent and agonizing historical situation to which the author reacted violently, and which he believed would cause YHWH to take the strongest possible action. There is therefore every reason to avoid the term 'apocalypse,' which is a transhistorical genre of text, in speaking of Isaiah 34.[9] In speaking of the חרם, however, it is hard to avoid the conclusion that Isaiah 34 is a testimony to the continuation of the basic ideas of חרם already embodied in the MI.

---

[7] Ibid.

[8] J. C. de Moor, "An Incantation against Infertility (KTU 1.13)," *UF* 12 (1980), 305.

[9] So, e.g. O. Kaiser, *Isaiah 13-39: A Commentary, OTL* (Phila., 1974), 353. G. A. Smith, *The Book of Isaiah* vol. I, 438ff. understood it also in purely historical terms. A more recent treatment, that of H. Wildberger, *Königsherrschaft Gottes: Jesaja 1-39. Teil 2: Die Nachfahren des Propheten und ihre Verkündigung, Kleine Biblische Bibliothek* (Neukirchen-Vluyn, 1984), 178-9, says that Isaiah 34 is not an apocalypse in the strict sense and is a distant parallel to chs.24-7.

There Israel had encroached upon Moab to a degree requiring similar radical measures. The usage in a prophetic address in a certain historical context where there was no question of actual military action is, naturally, both rhetorical and figurative. We shall see the like in Isa 43:28, which also places YHWH in the position of initiating the חרם, this time against Israel.

The use of the term זבח, "sacrifice," in Isa 34:6, may at first glance seem to give credence to the idea of חרם as sacrifice. However, the word is used in parallel with טבח, "slaughter," the slaughter YHWH is performing on Edom. The prophet employs the two in large part for their assonance, but in any case, YHWH does not sacrifice to YHWH! The use of the term "sacrifice" here is a literary device, an extremely strong and bitter literary device, but not evidence that the idea behind חרם is sacrifice, in which case YHWH would make the Carthaginian gods look tame.

Particularly portentous for the interpretation and my general theory of the חרם is the description of the fate of Edom in Isaiah 34 after application of the חרם. Like the Egyptian concept of returning the chaotic force of the enemy to chaos or the non-existent,[10] Isa 34:9-17 depicts the chaos that will befall the defeated Edom, which is a corollary of the establishment of world order for Israel. Chaos is pictured in the slaughter of domesticated animals, which are replaced by hovering night birds. Isa 34:11 speaks of the replacement of the measure and the weight--symbols of order--with chaos. Next, Isa 34:12 states that Edom will become an "unkingdom," (perhaps in this context to be understood as a biblical equivalent to the word, *Un-Welt*) where demons roam, including (Isa 34:14) a goat in demon form (a pun on Edom's name of Seir) and Lilith, another demon. All the assembled creatures of chaos will be given the parcelled-out Edom for a permanent dwelling-place, as the final verse, Isa 34:17, assures us.

Isa 34:5 ends with the word, למשפט, which I have translated, "for judgement." Given the provenance of the Isaiah 34, it is appropriate to cite the Second Isaiah, who in Isa 51:4b says:

כִּי תוֹרָה מֵאִתִּי תֵצֵא וּמִשְׁפָּטִי לְאוֹר עַמִּים

For my teaching from *Me* will go forth , and my judgement (will go out) as a light of peoples.

The above uses משפט in a far more peaceful context than does Isa 34:5, but both share the common denominator of YHWH's display of משפט in an international context, thus showing YHWH as the one who determines the order of the world.[11] This fits in well again with the MI, where Kemosh is

[10] E. Hornung, *Conceptions of God in Ancient Egypt: The One and the Many* (Ithaca, N.Y.: Cornell University Press, 1982), 172-84.

[11] The Hittites considered war to follow the model of a law suit. For a "juridical" model of biblical war, see R. Good, "The Just War in Ancient Israel," *JBL* 104 (1985) 385-400. Such a concept does not ordinarily come into expression in texts dealing with the חרם, and in any case in the context of the חרם, is subsumed under the broader idea of achieving *Weltordnung*.

plainly depicted in the same light.[12] It should be plain that there is no English equivalent to this term משפט which can convey its manifold connotations. In effect it is God's law which applies to not only Israel but other nations as well, according to these two passages. It is under YHWH's 'law' that Edom stands condemned, for the whole chapter expresses the feeling that Edom has followed such an unnatural path, one so opposed to YHWH's, that as in Deut 7:25-6, the abominable must be reincorporated into the sphere of God through the חרם. Like the use of חרם itself in Isaiah 34, the use of משפט in conjunction with it has a figurative, rhetorical side to it. This is the sole occasion in which they meet.

II: ISAIAH 11:15

I will not consider this verse, which has been roundly rejected as a witness to the חרם by the majority of scholars on text-critical and logical grounds. N. Lohfink's notable effort to defend MT (*TDOT* 5 141f.) does not quite work. The meaning "utterly destroy" does not fit the context; the Exodus (mentioned in v.16) did not involve destroying the sea; the "highway" of Isa 11:16 envisions a dry path through the sea, which points to החריב, "make dry." Most of the versions agree, as does even a midrash.[13] Furthermore, the argument in favor of retention of MT overlooks the evidence of a parallel passage, Isa 50:2, which like the pericope in which Isa 11:15 is found, pictures the redemption of the exiles as a new Exodus, complete with the image of the drying up of the sea (a couple of other verses could be adduced here as well).. The most important clause is this: הֵן בְּגַעֲרָתִי אַחֲרִיב יָם In my view, the use of the verb החריב. in Isa 50:2, is the single strongest argument against the correctness of החרים. in Isa 11:15. The support of the Qumran scroll merely shows the antiquity of the mistake which crept into the manuscript tradition. preserved in the MT.

---

[12] H. H. Schmid has stressed the concept of 'righteousness' as *Weltordnung* in his work, e.g. in his study, *Gerechtigkeit als Weltordnung, BHT* 40 (Tübingen, 1968), and in essays in his *Altorientalische Welt in der alttestamentlichen Theologie* (Zürich, 1974), but he does not deal with the חרם. צדק is never mentioned in connection with חרם, for what is at stake is not quite the same thing; any more than the fate of Uzza (2 Sam 6:6-7) involves צדק. The latter concept does not embrace all facets of the human relationship with God or of *Weltordnung*.

[13] For the same conclusion, see C. H. W. Brekelmans, *De ḥerem,* 119f.. N. Lohfink argues against it in "Ḥaram," *TDOT* 5, 181f.. But cf. already Midrash Tehillim §92.2 (401) cited by M. H. Goshen-Gottstein, *The Book of Isaiah: Sample Edition with Introduction* (Jerusalem, 1965), 53.

III: ISAIAH 43:28

The text of Isa 43:28 and the verses preceding it are troubled by some text-critical questions. Considering just three standard translations of the one verse, we may detect considerable disagreement:

> RSV: Therefore I profaned the princes of the sanctuary/I delivered Jacob to utter destruction, and Jacob to reviling.
> NEB (putting 28a with 27): Your first father transgressed,/your spokesmen rebelled against me/and your princes profaned my sanctuary; so I sent Jacob to his doom/and left Israel to execration.
> NJV: So I profaned the holy princes/I abandoned Israel to proscription/And Israel to mockery.

Of these three, it is the RSV which is most faithful to the MT; NEB follows LXX wherever possible, while NJV's attempt at fidelity to MT is compromised by an unfelicitous choice of words. It is possible, when dealing with such a construct phrase (here, שׂרי קדשׁ) to construe the second term as modifying the first as an alternative to using an adjectival form (the adjective may not be in actual use). But it is hard to understand the meaning of the phrase "holy princes." To whom does this refer? If the phrase applied to the kings of Judah, why was it not seized upon by subsequent pro-monarchical writers?

The more straightforward translation of RSV, "princes of the sanctuary" yields a better result, because this phrase, which is also found in 1 Chr 24:5, is far more intelligible (cp. also Ezra 10:5,8). It surely refers to the upper ranks of the priests: it runs parallel with "princes of God" in 1 Chr 24:5. However, the question of the MT translation should not be explored too far without reference to the NEB, which reflects the very different translation of the LXX. Isaiah 43:28, as translated by LXX and followed by NEB, differs from the MT greatly: "And the <u>rulers</u> defiled my holy places and I gave Jacob to be destroyed and Israel to reproach ."

In the past many scholars have preferred to follow the LXX translation: this includes B. Duhm, and in his wake have trailed O. C. Whitehouse, P. D. Volz &c., as well as more recently N. H. Snaith, BHS and, as noted, NEB.[14] C. Westermann follows his own school of thought. He deletes the phrase under discussion (Isa 43:28a) without any comment.[15] Less arbitrary is the clever reading of C. C. Torrey, who emended the text to read "my holy cities,"[16] though even this has won no support. C. F. Whitley preferred the reading, וחללו שׂריך שמי,[17] "your rulers profaned my name," which K. Elliger

---

[14] O. C. Whitehead, *Isaiah: XL-LXVI* v.2 *NCB* (New York, ND), 103 he cites as adherents to his position, Houbigant, Klosterman, and Cheyne. D. P. Volz *Jesaja II, KzAT* (Leipzig, 1932) 44, N. H. Snaith, "Isaiah 40-66: A Study of the Teaching of the Second Isaiah and its Consequences," in *Studies in the Second Part of the Book of Isaiah, SVT* 14 (1967), 183.

[15] C. Westermann, *Deutero-Isaiah: A Commentary, OTL* (London, 1969), 130.

[16] C. C. Torrey, *The Second Isaiah: A New Interpretation* (New York, 1928), 343.

[17] C. F. Whitley, "Textual Notes on Deutero-Isaiah," *VT* XI (1961), 457f..

rightly condemned as thoroughly unsound.[18] A third school accepts the MT, except that scholars agree that the pointing of Isa 43:28 must be adjusted to refer to the past rather than as a prediction of apocalypse.

The status of the LXX to Isaiah has been summarized by S. Jellicoe in his book, a basic book to Septuagint studies.[19] Aside from being imperfectly preserved, the conclusion Jellicoe reports is that the "text underlying the Greek version (was) virtually that of MT." Torrey went even further and said that the LXX was useless for textual criticism.[20] Even if he went too far, the scroll from Qumran, IQIsa[a] has affirmed the antiquity of the MT Isaiah textual tradition.

In the case of Isa 43:28, the Isaiah scroll agrees with the MT, except for some minor orthographic variations.[21] The reason for the difference in the LXX text could lie in a non-textual area. It seems probable that the text underlying the translations was also "virtually that of MT," but that a later editor (Jewish or Christian) had difficulty with the sentiment expressed for theological reasons. The role God assumes in that particular segment of Isa 43:28 may have repelled a later pietist, who preferred to put the onus on Israel, where it usually came to rest. Such prophetic statements were, after all, the norm, but Deutero-Isaiah delighted in turning conventions topsy-turvy. It therefore seems reasonable to conclude that the LXX is a poor guide to Isa 43:28.

The superiority of the MT to LXX is also clear from a literary analysis of the Hebrew text of 43:22-8, which is a passage typical of this prophet, full of ingenious exploitation of paradox, sarcasm, and his own unpredictable brand of parallelism. Part of the literary argument has already been made:

> (If the LXX reading were adapted) 28a should go with 27 to make up a tristich. It may be so; but 27 seems a comprehensive indictment enough as it stands, and if there must be a tristich, it is more likely to be in the final than in the penultimate verse. MT gives a perfectly good sense.[22]

Assuming that the passage does end in a tristich, then the verb חלל ("to profane") must be in the first person, so that Isa 43:28 gives the series of actions attributed to God in the MT. The sudden introduction of the past actions of Judah's ruler would be irrelevant. Another angle is that the pericope abounds in those elements of paradox and turning topsy-turvy to which I alluded above. Consider, for instance, Isa 43.23, which reads roughly: "You have not brought me your sacrificial sheep, nor have you honored me with your sacrifices / nor have I made you serve me with an offering, nor have I wearied you with frankincense." The verse offers more than one paradox.

---

[18] K. Elliger, *Deuterojesaja, BKAT* (Neukirchen-Vluyn, 1978), 386f..
[19] S. Jellicoe, *The Septuagint and Modern Study* (repr. Ann Arbor, 1978), 299-300.
[20] Ibid. 300.
[21] M. Burrows et al., *The Dead Sea Scrolls of St. Mark's Monastery,* Vol. 1: *The Isaiah Manuscript and the Habakuk Commentary, ASOR* (New Haven, 1950), Plate 37.
[22] C. R. North, *The Second Isaiah: Introduction, Translation, and Commentary to Chapters XL-LV* (Oxford, 1966), 127.

Taken at face value, it does not seem to square with the history of Israel's religion, which is one paradox. The second is in the relationship of the two parts of the verse, in which Isa 43:23b seems to offer superficial justification for the behavior complained of in Isa 43:23a. Yet one can be sure that the prophet's words were completely intelligible to his audience, and that they were calculated to have a powerful effect. Another example occurs in Isa 43:25-6. In Isa 43:25, carrying on from Isa 43:23, YHWH assures Israel that, if only for his own sake, He will dispose of the people's sins, rendering the object of much sacrifice rather academic. Then, using the root זכר in the qal and the hiphil as a hinge (אזכר followed by הזכרני),YHWH swings into a ringing challenge that Israel show itself innocent. This leads to the climactic paradox of the passage, wherein YHWH profanes what he has in the past deemed holy, and given his people to חרם:

וַאֲחַלֵּל שָׂרֵי קֹדֶשׁ וְאֶתְּנָה לַחֵרֶם יַעֲקֹב וְיִשְׂרָאֵל לְגִדּוּפִים׃

> I made profane the chiefs of the sanctuary, while I gave Jacob to the חרם, Israel to mockery.

One should note an ironic twist in the prophet's language. The notion of Israel as a holy people was of course this prophet's bread and butter. Given the sacral connotation of the word חרם, Deutero-Isaiah was also referring to God's having made Israel a people apart and holy even as he spoke of God's condemnation and the enemy's mockery.

Although C. North tried to make the case that שָׂרֵי קֹדֶשׁ referred to the kings of Judah, it does not make sense that the Chronicler, with his known partiality for the House of David, would have transferred such a glorious epithet to the priesthood, as North maintained.[23] Moreover, 1 Chr 24:5 is a verse that unmistakably speaks of priests,and uses שָׂרֵי קֹדֶשׁ in connection with priestly families. The importance of this for understanding both the verse and the pericope as well is immense; for Isa 43:28a is an allusion to what the prophet understood as YHWH's deliberate decision to put an end to his own temple in Jerusalem. The discussion of Isa 43:22-24/5 both provides context for and is put in context by Isa 43:28a.

Before finally arriving at the crucial phrase for a study of חרם, Isa 43:28b, let us dispose of Isa 43:28c: וְיִשְׂרָאֵל לְגִדּוּפִים. This is a reference to the derision of the enemies of the vanquished party, something alluded to through much of the Book of Lamentations but especially in Lam 4:21-5:2 (cf. 2 Sam 1:20--naturally the exultant enemy mocks the fallen foe). It also alludes to the terrible shame that accompanies defeat and the derision of the enemy. Of course, in this context the חרם is invoked as YHWH's judgement on Israel, and it sums up the catastrophe of the fall of Judah. The question is whether in this context the word employs the sense of consecration. In the first place, it is clearly a different usage from Josh 6:17. There, Israel was to devote the city (of Jericho) to YHWH. Here, YHWH is the subject and Is-

---

[23] Ibid 131.

rael (Jacob) is the object. Yet to translate חרם as some do, as simple "destruction" does not make sense because it does not describe the situation that the prophet faced. Israel had lost its national existence, but it had not lost its status as a people.

More important is the language of Isa 43:28, a verse that contains three semantically interrelated roots: הלל, קדש and חרם. The first two are simple opposites. The second and the third are related in a more complex way, but they are commensurable terms, as the levitical phrase equating חרם with קדש קדשים attests (Lev 27:28), as does Josh 7:1's use of מעל. The three words were selected from the same semantic field, that of holiness. Otherwise the verse would have no point. There is a definite progression going from Isa 43:28a-b: first YHWH has had to nullify the holiness of his priests and so deprived the whole people of its קדש. Secondly, God has had to punish the people for their religious lapses--by giving them to the חרם. Therefore the verse speaks both of the military defeat of Judah and the spiritual proscription of the people in the same breath. Those students of the text who appreciate that the use of חרם here cannot be simply to indicate destruction are therefore correct.[24]

Attention should be paid to the construction, וְאֶתְּנָה לַחֵרֶם, which is unique in its choice of verb and somewhat surprising in its pointing of ל with the definite article. Its closest analogue is Josh 6:18: וְשַׂמְתֶּם אֶת־מַחֲנֵה יִשְׂרָאֵל לְחֵרֶם, "you shall make the camp of Israel חרם." However, the definite article is always used for the objectified חרם, i.e. to denote a concrete object that has been devoted, as earlier in the same verse in Joshua, וּלְקַחְתֶּם מִן־הַחֵרֶם, "you take from the devoted spoil." Therefore in Isa 43:28 the prophet is depicting Israel as fallen to a divinely mandated חרם, to which Israel has been designated as part of the spoils consecrated to YHWH. The verse should thus read:

> I made profane the chiefs of the sanctuary, while I gave Jacob to the devoted spoil, Israel to mockery.[25]

The explosion of Israel's world order before the Babylonian host and its allies is thus portrayed in terms of חרם, just as a threat to it was described in repeated use of the root in Josh 6:18, and just as a prophet had used it in describing a hoped for destruction of the Edomite world order. To sum up Isa 43:38: those who had lost their moorings to the point that God felt compelled to place them in that unenviable, if figurative position of devoted spoils are then left to hear the revilings of the victorious and spiteful foes (see above) who may dispose of the land and the people as they wish. The Second Isaiah

---

[24] *Inter alia* J. L. Mackenzie, *Second Isaiah, AB* (Garden City, 1968), C. North, *The Second Isaiah,* R. D. Merendino, *Der Erste und der Letze: Eine Untersuchung von Jesaja 40-48, SVT* 31, RSV, NJV.

[25] NJV translates similarly, and suggests a possible emendation, to חרפה, "reproach." but it is unlikely that this prophet would have ended the verse, and the section, so lamely, with a tame synonomous parellelism that would not be typical for this prophet. The חרם has a stronger contextual claim.

has found a truly powerful way to utilize the חרם as an image in this deceptively diminuitive verse.

The passages of the exilic prophets whose writings found a place in the Book of Isaiah evince an acute awareness of the sacral connotations of the root חרם; and this is indicated by the context and/or subtext of their language and the figurative way they employed it. To read חרם as simple destruction would rob these passages of the rich religious resonances that these masterful exponents of Hebrew rhetoric drew on, intent on communicating in a poetic style that contrasts greatly with the rhetoric of the Greek orators. That they expected to be understood raises a whole set of questions about their intended audience. The nature of exilic prophetic discourse gave the idea of the חרם a new lease on life in Israel, possibly helping to bridge the gap between the war-חרם and the priestly חרם that came in its wake.

Indeed, the vitality of the concept of חרם is astonishing, and never more so than in the case of the prophets who used it for their own ends. It is curious that almost every single prophetic passage which mentions the חרם comes from the mouth of an anonymous prophet. The sole exception is a verse from the Book of Jeremiah, 25:9, where there is no reason to doubt that the prophet actually composed the passage. This curious fact mirrors the sometimes elusive character of the חרם in the popular mind of ancient Israel, compared to the easier to grasp concept of קדש. Despite the obstensible negativity of Isaiah 34, it contained latent within it a mirror image, the promise of a bright new world order for Israel. In Isa 43:28, the positive, sacral aspect still lingers, more than faintly discernable in the background.

IV: JEREMIAH 25:9

The attestations of חרם in the Book of Jeremiah fall naturally into two categories, that of Jer 25:9 and those of Jer 50-1 (Jer 50:21,26; 51:3). I will approach Jer 25:9 by comparing two translations, that of the NJV and that of J. Bright in his commentary:

> I am going to send for all the peoples of the north--declares the LORD--and for my servant, King Nebuchadnezzar of Babylon, and bring them against this land and its inhabitants, and against all those nations roundabout. I will exterminate them and make them a desolation, an object of hissing--ruins for all time (NJV). Believe me, I am going to send and get all the peoples of the north--Yahweh's word--that is, for Nebuchadnezzar, king of Babylon, my servant and I will bring them against this country and its citizens and against all the surrounding nations as well. I will devote them to wholesale destruction. I will make them a horrible and shocking spectacle, and an everlasting reproach (LXX vs. MT "ruins").[26]

The underlined portions of Bright's translation are text-critically questionable at best, considering the evidence of the LXX. This verse is part of a sweeping oracle against Judah for its idolatries, which are to bring on

[26] J. Bright, *Jeremiah: A New Translation with Introduction and Commentary, AB* (Garden City, 1965), 157.

YHWH's punishment in the form of an attack from the north. The reference to Nebuchadnezzar is, as Bright noted, syntactically awkward and most likely to be a later addition (note that the Book of Jeremiah speaks of a northern menace independent of Babylon from its first chapter);[26] but this matter is of limited significance for our subject.

The prophet who composed Jer 25:1-14 predicted YHWH's dooming of Judah through the instrumentality of foreign powers, in order to punish idolatry. The verb החרים was used of foreign enemies against Israelites in 2 Kgs 19:11. In that verse החרים meant simply "destroy" (see above), without any sacral connotation. Here YHWH himself is the subject of the verb החרים or its equivalent (as in two Isaianic verses). In one of the two verses in which YHWH is the subject, we have the unique phrase, וְאֶתְּנָה לַחֵרֶם יַעֲקֹב I have given Jacob to the חרם (Isa 43:28). As we have seen, this is a verse in which the sacral connotations of חרם are integral to the rhetorical effect. The other, Isa 34:2, occurs in a text that has some similarity to the MI.

Jer 25:1-14 is a speech from the period preceding the fall of Jerusalem, and hence Jer 25:9 is the earliest of the three verses in which YHWH is the executor of the חרם. Jeremiah was accustomed to radical rhetoric and gestures, and it is not surprising that he should have adopted החרים for such a purpose. Indeed, his use of the חרם is in a way extrapolated from that of the Book of Deuteronomy, which repeatedly links the חרם with idolatry, with death as the consequence (cf. Deut 7:25-6, 13:13-19. and so on). In Jer 25:5-6, the prophet lays out flatly the doctrine that the people had to act correctly to stay on the land, meaning that they could not serve other gods and expect YHWH to bless their presence on the land. This doctrine is much older than Deuteronomy, but it is certainly given enormous emphasis in that book, where its original function may have been to try to prevent the disaster of the fall of the Northern Kingdom, or at least learning from its example. In Deut 13:13ff., the community at large was expected to enforce the חרם against idolators; here, the community could not muster for the חרם. YHWH had to act using a foreign power as an instrument. Therefore I agree with Bright that החרים here should not be translated as "utterly destroy" as the NJV would have it, but as "consecrate to (wholesale) destruction."[26] Nowhere else in the book except for Jer 50-1 does the חרם appear, and most scholars have reached the conclusion that those chapters do not stem from Jeremiah. Yet even if they do stem, directly or indirectly, from Jeremiah, it is clear that the choice of words in this context is significant. There are many more mundane words for destruction that prophet could have used here. In any case, we see that the use of the sacral החרים is in Jer 25:9 purposeful and that this helps explicate the text, while the alternative does not. Nor is there anything incredible about YHWH using foreign armies to enforce the חרם, which the Judah had brought on itself with its idolatries. The refusal to repent of them constituted a trespass of YHWH's inviolability. The use of an enemy to punish the god's own people is illustrated by the MI, and

Near Eastern history furnishes other examples as well.[27] Retaliation of the gods was not limited to the ancient Near East, however, as the example of Helike and Bura shows. These two cities sank into the Corinthian Gulf after an earthquake in 373 B.C., whereupon "a story immediately sprung up that these two towns had been guilty of a sacrilege at the altar of Poseidon,"[28] who was, of course, the earth-shaker. Jeremiah was accusing Israel of rather more than a ritual offense. There is no good reason, then, to reduce החרים in the instance of Jer 25:9 merely to "utter destruction."

V: JEREMIAH 50-1

These two chapters which conclude the MT of the Book of Jeremiah contain three verses in which the root חרם appears: Jer 50:21,26 and 51:3. They appear in a context of prophetic virulence that was directed at Babylon, along with a projected return of Israel to its own soil. They read as follows:

> 50:21 Advance on the land of Marathaim,
> And on the inhabitants of Pekod,
> Attack and חרם after them--YHWH's word--and act just I have commanded you.
>
> 50:26 Come against her (Babylon) from all sides; open her granaries.
> Heap her up like piles (of sheaves) and החרימו her; don't leave a remnant of her!
>
> 51:3a (MT corrupt) 51:3b Have no mercy on her youths;
> החרימו all her army!

Again, previous translators have differed, rendering either "consecrate to destruction," or simply "destroy." The immediate contexts are not determinative, although they are not devoid altogether of indications. Jer 50:26, with its complementary "don't leave a remnant" is typical of the חרם-language in Deuteronomy (esp. chs.2-3), Joshua, and Samuel. Jer 51:3b pairs לא תחמלו and החרם, as only 1 Sam 15:3 does elsewhere (this would be still more meaningful if the prophet speaking here were Jeremiah, who we know was acquainted with the Samuel traditions). J. A. Thompson, a recent commentator who translates the verb consistently as "devote to destruction," has observed that:

> In the overthrow of Babylon there was a good reason to withhold from Israel the idolatrous city and its associated wealth which might taint Israel. In that case Babylon was to be "devoted to destruction."[29]

---

[27] B. Albrecht, *History and the Gods: An Essay on the Idea of Historical Events as Divine Manifestations in the Ancient Near East and in Israel, Coniectanea Biblica OT Series 1* (Lund, Sweden, 1967), 100-111.
[28] W. Burkert, *Greek Religion* (Cambridge, Mass., 1985), 137-8.
[29] J. A. Thompson, *The Book of Jeremiah, NICOT* (Grand Rapids, Mich., 1980), 741.

The principle he invokes in this argument is that of Deut 7:25-6, and hence the argument is strong. These texts deal with the violent overthrow of Babylon, an event which did not occur, so they must come from the exilic period, i.e. the middle of the 6th century, at the latest. At the earliest they come from the last period of Jeremiah's life, after the end of the kingdom of Judah. However, the dating of the text does not in itself fix the meaning of חרם The earlier חרם traditions were of course remembered. In addition, in biblical times and still later the sacral connotation of חרם still persisted alongside the secondary, secular meaning, which I have argued is from the other root. This is evident from the strong continuity between the war-חרם and priestly-חרם. Although the war-חרם had lapsed it was still alive in memory (cp. Josh 7 and 1 Chr 2:7).

Another approach is the theme of chaos vs. order. Babylon destroyed the world order of Judah. The prophet displays utter faith in YHWH's ability to restore the world order of his people Israel, and the חרם was a major divine instrument, earlier used in creating it. B. Childs has argued for a link between "The Enemy from the North and the Chaos Tradition."[30] He argues eloquently that רעש, "earthquake" is a term indicating chaos, particularly in Jeremiah in regard to the "enemy from the north." Both the enemy from the north and the root רעש appear in this unit (Jer. 50-1), so that if the prophet had chaos vs. order in mind it is probable from this angle alone that רעש is related to the anti-chaos vocabulary, "devote to destruction," and provides a meaningful context for it.

The motif of chaos may appear in yet another form. P. Bordreuil has pointed out that the depiction of the enemy (=chaos) as sheaves of grain to be trodden underfoot is common to Ugarit and other Near Eastern cultures.[31] In Ugaritic mythology Anat takes on bovine characteristics, and treads under chaos in the person of Môt.[32] These things are not conclusive in themselves; D. Hillers for one, dismissed Bordreuil's article out of hand[33]--in my opinion, incorrectly. The article focuses on Mic 4:13, however, and I shall return to it below. In any case, the cumulative effect of these indications of the order vs. chaos paradigm is to buttress the conclusion that Jer 50:26 does refer to the חרם proper. Jer 50:21 and 51:3 refer to mere destruction.

---

30 B. S. Childs, "The Enemy from the North and the Chaos Tradition" in ed. C. G. Perdue & B. W. Kovacs, *A Prophet to the Nations: Essays in Jeremiah Studies* (Winona Lake, Ind., 1984), 151-161.

31 P. Bordreuil, "Michée 14:11-13 et ses parallèles ougaritiques," *Semitica* 21 (1971), 25.

32 Ibid. 23f..

33 D. Hillers, *Micah: A Commentary on the Book of Micah* (Phila., 1984), 61.

VI: MICAH 4:13

Few indeed are the scholars who question that this verse is to be attributed to a much later prophet than Micah.[34] The majority place the verse and the chapter in the postexilic period.[35] That is interesting, if true, for in contrast to other of the late prophetic passages with which we have been dealing, the use here of the חרם here is straightforward and obviously used in the sense of consecration by destruction to the deity:

קוּמִי וָדוֹשִׁי בַת־צִיּוֹן כִּי־קַרְנֵךְ אָשִׂים בַּרְזֶל

Rise and thresh, O daughter of Zion,
For your horn I will make iron.

וּפַרְסֹתַיִךְ אָשִׂים נְחוּשָׁה וַהֲדִקּוֹת עַמִּים רַבִּים

And your hooves I will make bronze,
You shall pulverize many peoples.

וְהַחֲרַמְתִּי לַיהוָה בִּצְעָם וְחֵילָם לַאֲדוֹן כָּל־הָאָרֶץ׃

You(!) shall devote to YHWH their plunder,
And their wealth / army[36] to the Lord of the earth.

The figure of the daughter of Zion as a cow or bull has been illuminated by P. Bordreuil, in the article already cited.[37] His basic thesis is this:

> On a 'le l'existence d'un rapport entre nôtre texte (4:10-13) et le récit ougaritique bien connu du combat de la déesse Anat contre Mot: dans l'A.T., Anat est remplacée par le peuple, alors que dans le mythe ougaritique, c'est Anat qui, lorsque le blé est mûr, remporte la victoire sur Mot, personnification des forces du chaos; dans l'A.T. ces dernières figurent souvent les ennemis du peuple.[38]

This is not as far-fetched as idea as it may appear at first sight. Anat is portrayed as a heifer in several Ugaritic texts.[39] Bordreuil continues his exposition as follows:

> Le second élément du mythe ougaritique présent dans nôtre texte, est le grain que dépique la génisse. Ce grain représente les ennemis de la (*ᶜeglah) bat-ṣiyyon* et de

---

[34] S. R. Driver in *An Introduction to the Literature of the Old Testament* (repr. New York, 1956), 330, favors the possibility of Mic 4:13 stemming from Micah.
[35] Cf. among others, T. Lescow,"Redaktionsgeschichtliche Analyse von Micha," *ZAW* 84 (1972), 46-85, J. L. Mays, *Micah: A Commentary, OTL* (Phila., 1976), 108f.. They and others also detach 13 from 11f..
[36] So LXX. Perhaps the prophet wanted to suggest both.
[37] P. Bordreuil "Michée 14:11-13," 21-28.
[38] Ibid. 21.
[39] Ibid. 22.

YHWH, et le récit du massacre du Mot, l'ennemi de Anat et de Baal, rappelle la moisson et le dépiquage (C.T.A.. 6. II, 31-34).[40]

Bordreuil has illuminated the biblical imagery, showing that it is essentially the same as that of its precursor, the Ugaritic myth. He has drawn attention to the underlying problem of chaos as manifested in enemies threatening from the outside, in an idea of cosmos found in many cultures.. He even goes on to point to the occurrence of *bt ugrt* in a Ugaritic text with a similar context, and makes some observations which help solidify his parallel of the "daughter of Zion"and Anat.[37] Bordreuil has therefore shed light on what is otherwise a difficult verse. The חרם fits perfectly into the matrix of the fight against chaos = foreign foes sketched out by Bordreuil and basic to the Ugaritic myth. Other exegetes have failed to show what inspired the connection between the image of the threshing bovine and the חרם, which superficially seems a mere caprice of the poet.

Of course, Mic 4:13 is also a good example of extravagant (to us, not to the prophet) prophetic rhetoric. It justifies--a word that is slightly strong, as Micah was not trying to defend YHWH from criticism--the pulverizing of the "many peoples" (a phrase independent of history) by referring to YHWH as the "Lord of all the earth" (a title of Baal as well). In other words, the prophet wishes to portray Israel's victory over the "many peoples" as an exercise of YHWH's sovereignty over all the world. This reminds one (on a different level) of the Mesopotamian monarch styling himself *šar kiššati*, "king of the universe," and then feeling perfectly justified in subjugating all lesser powers within his reach. The Akk. term *kiššatu*, incidently, is worth remarking upon in the framework I have identified as appropriate for understanding the place of the חרם in ancient Israel's thought and practice. The *CAD* {K 457a) defines it as "entire inhabited world (as a politico-religious term)." The Akkadian word addresses the world, so to speak, not just in a territorial way, but with a mingling of the political and the religious that is characteristic, too, of the חרם. *kiššatu* is a word symptomatic of a broader way of thought that in Canaan led to one narrow application of it (which was by no means "inevitable"), namely the חרם.

The Hebrew phrase which the prophet uses, "I devoted their spoil to YHWH" (וְהַחֲרַמְתִּי לַיהוָה בִּצְעָם), is in itself interesting. Although it is written in the first person, the versions and modern commentators agree that it should be read in second feminine singular, in accordance with the previous verbs in the verse. One may speculate that the MT may be right, and that what was envisioned was this; in response to the prophet's forecast of victory, the people reply (in the first person) with a sort of bellicose doxology in which they devote the fruits of their forthcoming victory to YHWH.

However this may be (and I do not insist upon it), the use of the word בצע is unusual. According to the *BDB* (s.v.), it usually means ill-gotten gains. The prophet could easily have employed one of the many words for spoils in the Hebrew vocabulary. The "immorally won wealth" of the nations is best

[40] Ibid. 23.

submitted to the חרם, i.e. placed through destruction into a wholly other sphere, thus obviating any danger from foreign degeneracy (esp. "idols," cf. Deut 7:25-26), and falling into the proverbial "snare." This reference to the spoil of Babylon reminds us also of Joshua 7, and the devoted spoil which Achan took, which included a Babylonian cloak. Here the prophet conveys with a denigrating bravado that the enemy's wealth was not worth taking, when Israel had the "Lord of all the Earth" as its patron!

I therefore agree with P. Bordreuil in his locating the meaning of the imagery of this verse within the framework of 'Canaanite' myth involving the paradigm with which we have been working, namely chaos vs. order. The suggested idea of the חרם proposed in this work serves to strengthen his argument and it demonstrates the appropriateness of the bovine imagery appearing (otherwise bizarrely) in conjunction with the חרם. Of course, that imagery needed no explaining to the prophet's audience. If this verse is as late as the majority of scholars believe, it offers additional support to the above interpretation of other late prophetic passages preserved in Isaiah and Jeremiah. On the other hand, if this verse were by Micah, as S. R. Driver believed (see n.31), than it would offer unique testimony to the חרם from an eighth century prophet.

A verse not normally mentioned in connection with the חרם is Mic 7:2, which reads:

2 אָבַד חָסִיד מִן־הָאָרֶץ וְיָשָׁר בָּאָדָם אָיִן
כֻּלָּם לְדָמִים יֶאֱרֹבוּ אִישׁ אֶת־אָחִיהוּ יָצוּדוּ חֵרֶם׃

The faithful has vanished from the land, and the upright among humanity is nothingness; all of them lie in wait for blood, each man hunts his brother with a net.

This verse bears examination. In 1 Kgs 20:42 we had a pun where the two homonyms חרם I and II, were deliberately evoked in the prophet's words to Ahab. Here we are dealing primarily with חרם II, "net." The verse has some similarity to Mal 3:24, dealt with below. The pericope Mic 7:1-6 deals (especially in v.6) with the lack of harmony in Israel's family life. In Mal 3:24, this is cause for YHWH to threaten to "smite the land חרם." This is always seen as חרם I, "ban." It would seem that in Mic 7:2, the prophet probably wished to evoke the idea of the "ban" and its associated idea of slaughter in a secondary way. In Mal 3:24, where God smites the land חרם, a preposition is lacking, as in Mic 7:2, which adds to the two verses' general resemblance. The verse is Malachi may conceivably be the reverse of Mic 7:2, if it refers to חרם II, "net" a divine weapon of YHWH as of other gods (see 1 Kgs 20:42), in a secondary way, as a word play, as in 1 Kgs 20:42.. Mal 3:24 would thus contain a dual threat, that YHWH will employ the "ban" and the divine net against the people.

VII: MALACHI 3:24 AND ZECHARIAH 14:11

These two verses are the last and the latest attestations of the root חרם in the prophetical books, and both appear in the nominal form. Here they are:

Mal 3:24

וְהֵשִׁיב לֵב־אָבוֹת עַל־בָּנִים וְלֵב בָּנִים עַל־אֲבוֹתָם פֶּן־אָבוֹא וְהִכֵּיתִי אֶת־הָאָרֶץ חֵרֶם׃

He shall cause the heart of fathers to turn to (their) sons and the heart of sons to their fathers lest I come and smite the land (or people) חרם.

Zech 14:11

...וְחֵרֶם לֹא יִהְיֶה־עוֹד וְיָשְׁבָה יְרוּשָׁלִַם לָבֶטַח׃

And there will be no more חרם. and Jerusalem will dwell in security.

Scholars generally agree on a mid-fifth century date for the prophet Malachi.[41] Since the prophet of Zech 13-14 is clearly later than Zechariah, there can be no doubt that he or she comes well after Malachi, and despite the manifest difficulty of dating such material, some scholars are confident of dating Deutero-Zechariah (chs. 9-11) ca. 325.[42] Chapter 14 is even later. Now the verse from Malachi has traditionally been viewed as a postscript by a hand other than Malachi.[43] Whether this is true or not is beyond our purview, although a recent monograph by B. Glazier-McDonald attacks this notion vehemently.[44] However, even if the last verses of Malachi are an addendum, it is quite unlikely that this addendum postdates Zech 14:11 (Hellenistic period), since it is bears the authentic stamp of a Hebrew prophet. Moreover, while the Malachi verses are eschatological, they do not partake of the later genre of the apocalyptic as do Zech 13-14. Whether these particular considerations are sufficiently decisive or not, it seems probable that the Malachi verse is older. If so, it raises the interesting possibility that Zech 14:11 is, at least in part, a reaction to Mal 3:24. Scholars have long noted the inverse relation of the two verses.[45] It is time to focus, then, on the meaning and use of חרם in them.

The variety of possible translations is attested by AV "curse," modified in RSV with a footnote with the alternative "ban of utter destruction," NEB's "solemn ban" and NJV's "destruction" for Zech 14:11, "utter destruction" for

[41] B. Glazier-McDonald, *Malachi: The Divine Messenger, SBLDS* 98 (Atlanta, 1987), 16f..

[42] J. Kodell, *Lamentations, Haggai, Zechariah, Malachi, Obadiah, Joel, Second Zechariah, Baruch, Old Testament Message* (Wilmington, Delaware, 1982), 161.

[43] See commentaries.

[44] B. Glazier-McDonald, *Malachi,* 243ff..

[45] J. M. P. Smith, H. G. Mitchell, J. A. Bewer, *A Critical and Exegetical Commentary on Haggai, Zechariah, Malachi, and Jonah, ICC* (Edinburgh, 1912), 83.

Mal 3:24. The LXX, on the other hand uses "anathema" for the former verse (as does Vulgate), and "taken away utterly" for Malachi. Targum Onkelos, in another one of its interpretative translations, offers "killing" for Zech 14:11, but for MT "I will smite the land חרם," it substitutes "I will bring (lit. 'find') on all the earth destruction, and I shall smite it with total destruction."

Surprisingly, the translation "curse" has taken a new lease on life. J. Kodell uses it in the commentary just cited, the New Jerusalem Bible translates Zech 14:11 "the ban will be lifted." but reverts to "curse" for Mal 3:24, while B. Glazier-McDonald has recently embraced it in her monograph on Malachi. Such a translation has no etymological foundation, nor does it have any basis in usage. It is based in the first instance, not on the Hebrew word חרם but on the Greek. The Septuagint employs a sister word to "anathema"(differing only by one vowel) "anything dedicated," frequently, which can mean in addition to "dedicated thing," "accursed thing" or "curse."[46] Even in its primary meaning "anathema" like English equivalents such as "ban" or "proscribe," represented only a crude approximation of חרם, but its secondary and tertiary meanings have no bearing at all on the חרם.

In recent years, an attempt has been made to equate חרם with curse based on the supposed identity of Jud 5:23, which curses Meroz for not sending troops to the fight against the Canaanite kings, and Judges 21, which contains a story in which the חרם was applied against Jabesh Gilead for not joining in the war against Benjamin (see ch. 5).[47] The חרם cannot be identified with "curse," and any such equation is untenable because curse has its own disparate conceptual basis and functions. It is the curse, not חרם, which is invoked to enforce treaties in the ancient Near East, as well as the Covenant between God and Israel, e.g. Deut 28:16ff.. Note that Deut 29:20 uses the locution, והבדילו יהוה לרעה מכל שבטי ישראל,"YHWH will separate him for evil from the tribes of Israel." This comes after the strong language of Deut 29:19. Yet even after this and the prior reference to the gold and silver-plated idols of Deut 29:16 the חרם language of Deut 7:26 does not recur. והבדילו יהוה לרעה is neither a euphemism for חרם (this covenant curse, like most, eschews euphemism), nor a synonym; for as the element of consecration is lacking, this is a more negative expression which speaks of divine punishment.. H. C. Brichto was right to exclude the חרם from his monograph on the subject.[48]

Of the translations, ancient and modern, that were mentioned above, it seems to me that the Targum Onkelos's "killing" is closest to the meaning in Zech 14:11. The prophet is speaking figuratively, so that any literal rendering is bound to go astray, for the war-חרם had no application in the con-

---

46 H. G. Liddell, R. Scott, & H. S. Jones, *A Greek-English Lexicon* (Oxford, 1968), 104b.

47 R. de Vaux, *Ancient Israel: Its Life and Institutions*, v.1 (2nd ed., New York, 1965), 260.

48 H. C. Brichto, *The Problem of "Curse" in the Hebrew Bible, JBL Monograph Series* XIII (Phila., 1963), 203.

text of Zechariah 14. Nor do the renderings "destruction," or "utter destruction," fit as well as "killing," for it seems obvious that what the prophet is really projecting is an end to war, the war of the nations against Jerusalem, and the establishment of Jerusalem in security, as the verse concludes. חרם here is used metonymically for "war." It may also function as an antithesis to the grim scenario with which the chapter begins, in which the spoils of war were to be divided by Israel's enemies (Zech 14:1f.). Jerusalem is to be secure, but in future wars spoil need not be set apart for YHWH. Another possibility is that the prophet had in mind as well the kind of חרם mentioned in Isa 43:28, where YHWH wields the חרם against Israel. God's anger against Jerusalem shall cease.

The verse from Malachi (3:24) is more difficult. It should be understood in relation to Gen 32:12, which seems to have been the model on which this verse was built (even though the phrase אֵם עַל־בָּנִים recurs, only in this verse is such a relationship to Mal 3:24 discernible). Gen 32:12 comes from the story of Jacob's return to the land. Afraid that Esau would take revenge, Jacob prays to YHWH:

פֶּן־יָבוֹא וְהִכַּנִי אֵם עַל־בָּנִים

> Save me from the hand of my brother...for I fear him,
> lest he should come and kill me (and mine)--mother upon sons.

Mal 3:24:

וְהֵשִׁיב לֵב־אָבוֹת עַל־בָּנִים וְלֵב בָּנִים עַל־אֲבוֹתָם פֶּן־אָבוֹא וְהִכֵּיתִי אֶת־הָאָרֶץ חֵרֶם׃

> He shall cause the heart of fathers to turn to (their) sons and the heart of sons to their fathers lest I come and smite the land (or kill the people) חרם.

Not only is the language of Mal 3:24 extremely close to Gen 32:12, but the parallel extends to the situation. Jacob has been told by YHWH to return to the land, but he can only return safely if there is harmony between himself and his feared brother Esau. Malachi changes אֵם עַל־בָּנִים to אָבוֹת עַל־בָּנִים and makes dwelling in the land contingent on good relations between fathers and sons (presumably because of the way the land ordinarily passed from father to son).

In both situations access to the land, which belonged to YHWH, depended on family harmony.[49] According to Malachi, if the harmony was not achieved, YHWH would smite the land חרם, meaning that he would remove the land from the human sphere by force, for the world order could not be achieved by YHWH's word alone. It was necessary for the people to live harmoniously together (Ps 133). We have in this late text a recurrence of the land-god-people triangle to which I have referred to before in understanding the meaning of the חרם. The ultimate aim is for harmonious relationships among all three components of the triangle and within them; this is in fact

[49] B. Glazier-McDonald, *Malachi,* 256, suggested rendering 24a,b as "to turn the hearts of the fathers together with that of the children to Yahweh (implied)." This is forced.

another way of expressing the ideal *Weltordnung*. Therefore in this late and somewhat exceptional prophetic formulation, the essential idea of חרם is still present.

Zech 14:11 then comes to affirm that such a measure as the חרם will not be necessary, as well to speak of a time when Jerusalem will be safe from war. Whether this prophet was actually reacting to Malachi's words or to something else we cannot know.

The חרם in the prophetical books was used in a variety of powerful figurative or metaphorical connections, as with Malachi 3:24. It is interesting that the חרם took on rhetorical life only, as far as our evidence extends (which is admittedly not far), in the exilic and postexilic periods, with the possible exceptions of Jer 25:9 and Mic 4:13.. It would be futile to speculate as to why the earlier prophets, such as Amos, Hosea, and Isaiah, did not choose to employ the חרם as part of their formidable rhetorical arsenals. They may very well have done so; we have but a fragment of their life's work. The later prophets were, of course, farther removed from the actuality of the war-חרם, especially that of Moab in the ninth century, and this probably assisted in the making of the חרם imagery. Alongside the sacral חרם we see an increased incidence of the secular חרם with the meaning to destroy, which I attribute to חרם II. It crops up more in late texts (see next chapter) because the war-חרם is now a thing of the past, so there was less confusion in using the hiphil in written texts, or speeches that were written down. According to my calculations it is certain only in Jer 50:21, highly probable in the case of Jer 51:3. Since "net" (חרם II) is plainly excluded, Zech 14:11 uses חרם I figuratively, as a metonym for war and wrath. It is my contention that the prophets, who were nothing if not masters of rhetoric, seized on the word חרם with its sacral sense to express themselves with a word with no exact synonym in the language. Since Biblical Hebrew is rich in words for destruction, החרים, which carried with it additional associations and resonances, was used mainly in its religious sense (חרם I); for the prophetic enterprise was bound up in the creation of a great religious language to persuade audiences to follow and live by the word of YHWH.

CHAPTER 10

THE WRITINGS

I: EZRA 10:8

In the tripartite division of the Hebrew Bible, the Writings come last. In a discussion of the biblical חרם, they belong last. The material is scanty, consisting of a verse each in the Book of Ezra-Nehemiah and Daniel, and a total of four verses in Chronicles. The paucity of the material, as well as its mostly incidental nature, does not aid the exegete in controlling it, but fortunately the contexts are usually of help. Ezra 10:8, which is the most interesting attestation of the חרם in the Writings, is part of a narrative in which the word חרם is at the heart of the matter. The verse reads as follows:

וְכֹל אֲשֶׁר לֹא־יָבוֹא לִשְׁלֹשֶׁת הַיָּמִים כַּעֲצַת הַשָּׂרִים וְהַזְּקֵנִים
יָחֳרַם כָּל־רְכוּשׁוֹ וְהוּא יִבָּדֵל מִקְּהַל הַגּוֹלָה׃

> For all who fails to come in three days according to the counsel of the commanders and the elders. his property will be חרם, and he shall be barred from the congregation of the exiles.

The verse comes as a response to the sin of the exiles who had taken themselves foreign wives while in exile. Of course, traditionally in the pre-exilic period intermarriage was permitted. As we have seen, the legislation of Deut 21:10ff. sanctioned an Israelite's marriage to a woman captured in the course of war. However, the exiles were in a different situation, where group survival was not as assured. There were in any case two different varieties of intermarriage. An intermarriage which did not disrupt communal bonds or which strengthened them was fine (e.g. Ruth and Boaz). Similarly, the law of Deut 21:10-17 describes an induction process whereby the captive woman could shed her old identity and acquire certain rights. We are dealing in Ezra 10 with the opposite case. The model for this kind of intermarriage was that of Ahab and Jezebel, where the queen never relinquished her national identity and her cult, giving it preference over the cult of YHWH.

In Ezra 10:8 the objectionable intermarriages must have been those where the women had never entered into the "community of YHWH." Since there were apparently many such cases, the fragile community of returnees may not have been able to tolerate even the other kind of intermarriage, which under the circumstances was liable to arouse suspicion. In other words, the 'bad' type of intermarriage may have put all intermarriage in a bad light. Whether this was the case or not, Ezra apparently saw the issue as a kind of military threat. What occurred was virtually a muster (cf. the use of the word שרים vs. the שרי הכהנים והלוים of Ezra 10:5, although they clearly allude to the same thing. A penalty attached to failure to show up, as in Judges 21 where the men of Jabesh Gilead failed to report. The חרם of Judges 21 was in a modified (milder) form, as here (the Judges story may have acted as a partial precedent). After all, the Judges 21 story, too, involved a problem with women and marriage, although of a radically different kind.

Interesting though the congruences between this passage and Judges 21 may be, the failure to show up at this gathering was not deemed as radical a breach of the social order as the behavior of the tribe of Benjamin. The offender is to be barred, separated from the community (בדל), not actually deemed חרם and expunged (observe how Ezra 10:9 begins with וַיִּקָּבְצוּ, "gathered," a verb of inclusion, in order to oppose it to the verbs of exclusion (separation) in the previous verse--an intentional contrast).

In Ezra 10:8 the חרם applies to the property of the offender. As virtually all commentators note, this fits in with Lev 27:21 (שדה החרם), and Num 18:14 {Ezek 44:29).

In the priestly חרם, control of all property that has fallen under the חרם was placed in the hands of the priests. These texts are either late (as we saw, Leviticus 27 partakes of the two major divisions of the book and is the latest text in Leviticus) or found late application. It is more likely that these texts were designed for the conditions to which they were applied, whatever the degree of traditional residue they conserved (presumably considerable). In this respect, Ezra 10:8 indicates that a setting in the Persian period would be suitable. The authority of the priests and Levites as epitomized by the phrase of Ezra 10:5, שרי הכהנים והלוים, fits the pronouncements of Leviticus 27 precisely. In addition, J. Blenkinsopp points out that the confiscated goods of Ezra 10:8 were "destined to become property of the temple, as is explicitly noted in 1 Esd. 9:4, and Josephus (*Ant.* 11.148)."[1] This is what was to have been expected in a transaction involving the חרם. That the property should go to the temple links up with Num 18:14, giving what is חרם into the domain of the priests, and also it is what one could predict from the war-חרם. This passage shows that goods could be proscribed not only under the conditions mentioned or hinted at in the priestly writings, but also in these circumstances, in order to preserve the integrity of the community.

The person who failed to heed the call of the community of YHWH was to be severed from the community in precisely the way the community was to be severed from the "peoples of the lands and the foreign women" (Ezra 10:11). Note that the separation is indicated in both instances by בדל in the niphal. Note also that Ezra 9:1 gives a shopping list of those to be abhorred, including the long-gone Jebusites, Hittites, &c., but also adding the Ammonites, the Moabites, and the Egyptians. This gives us little idea as to the actual ethnic groups the exiles actually intermarried with in Babylonia or elsewhere. Ezra 10:11 connects this pericope with the list of peoples in Ezra 9:1, which also provides continuity between the use of חרם. here and the war-חרם. of Deuteronomy, in which the lists of nation play such a prominent part. In essence, the list expressed a principle, if not a reality (although intermarriage with the Transjordanians might have become a thing of the

[1] J. Blenkinsopp, *Ezra-Nehemiah: A Commentary, OTL* (Phila.,1988), 190. He sees no connection between the "leaders" of Ezra 10:8 and the priestly leaders mentioned in Ezra 10:5.

past following the Assyro-Babylonian occupations). The body of the list, however, represents the old enemy that always threatens to encroach, viz. the primordial nations which represented chaos.

According to the *KBL* (892a), רכוש means "property, goods" in Ezra 10:8. The malingerers, those who refuse to join in with the community, could not be allowed to retain their houses and lands in this situation. This would hardly effect the severing of ties called for in this verse, for they would still be living in the midst of YHWH's congregation. The verse may therefore elucidate the origin of at least one category of שדה החרם, or if not one category, illustrate one instance of how a landed property fell into that category. The verse (Ezra 10:8) lies in the domain of the hierocratic usage of חרם. Its significance for us lies in the fact that the חרם here still is being used to stave off a foreign threat (i.e. a form of chaos), which, left unchecked, would undermine the exiles attempt at *Weltordnung*.[2] The foreign wives threatened the character of the "community of YHWH," both by their inability to transmit YHWHistic tradition and by their ability to teach non-YHWHistic tradition. The exiles, or at least the writers who represent the community of exiles, were concerned with the restoration of Israel's *Weltordnung* on its ancestral soil. This is why the root חרם came into play. That the priests derived the priestly חרם from the war-חרם is self-evident (Exod 22:19 is an early example), but as has been seen, there are actual links between the two that the priests consciously created in order to preserve (albeit in a different setting) the aspect of חרם in the religion of Israel. For the priests, it was too fundamental an aspect to part with (revolving around holiness and the inviolability of God).

Returning to Ezra 10:8, the separation (בדל) spoken of, applied to those who disregarded the summons instead of that ultimate separation in degree and kind, the חרם, is at least partly attributable to circumstances. The Jewish authorities were not in a position to take lethal measures against a large group. This would have caused civil strife. The Persians wished to see nothing but peace and quiet in their Judean province. The laws of Lev 27:28ff. show that the lethal nature of the חרם had yet to fall into desuetude. That the authorities would have liked to invoke it in this instance, too, one can well imagine. It simply would have been impolitic to do so, and therefore impracticable.

The word מעל, "trespass against God,"[3] in Ezra 10:6, is significant in view of the occurrences of the term in the Book of Joshua (see discussion there). It indicates a certain conceptual continuity between two very different chapters, stemming from disparate eras. The remedy for מעל, is in both cases the חרם even if in the case of Ezra passage, the ultimate sanction is not at issue. Unfortunately, one cannot say on the basis of Ezra 10:8, or the chapter itself, what precise religious construction the returned exiles put on

---

[2] Questions of a historical nature, such as "did the returnees really have a monopoly on virtue (vs. the people who never left, for example)?" cannot be treated here.

[3] A sin against God, as we saw above in relation to Joshua 7 and Achan, may have the effect of endangering the world order and hence the community.

the חרם, but evidently they did construe it religiously. The חרם in this mild form still served to defend Israel against those who were carriers of the idolatry contagion, as prescribed in Deut 7:3. The emphasis on the collective in this chapter of Ezra is also found in Joshua 7, where Achan's sin caused such sinister complications for the community at large. Thus Ezra 10:8 reflects not only the priestly חרם, but it preserves many of the traditional implications of the much earlier (pre-exilic) חרם.

II: THE BOOK OF CHRONICLES AND THE BOOK OF DANIEL

The Book of Chronicles contains four verses which use the root חרם: 1 Chr 2:7, 4:41; 2 Chr 20:23, 32:14. The first, 1 Chr 2:7, reads as follows:

> The sons of Karmi; Achar the troubler of Israel who trespassed on (מעל) the חרם....

Obviously. this is a reminiscence of Joshua 7, and reflects the usage there, although it is subsumed under the gigantic genealogical framework with which the Chronicler launches the book. There is no need to enlarge on the passage, except to point out that the meaning of חרם as devoted (sacrosanct) spoil was retained here. The reference to the incident shows that even at the late date of this verse, the Achan incident created echoes and gave at least the writer of 1 Chr 2:7 food for thought. Also, the association with the term for trespass against God (מעל) is seized upon,as previously in Ezra 10:5-8 and Josh 7:1, 22:20. Here again, the mention of violating the Covenant in regard to Achan's taking from the proscribed booty is not seen as the most important aspect, since the Covenant is not mentioned in 1 Chr 2:7.

1 Chr 4:41 is a different story. Its text is flawed, although not badly. I quote from the middle:

> ...וַיַּכּוּ אֶת־אָהֳלֵיהֶם וְאֶת־הַמְּעִינִים [הַמְּעוּנִים] אֲשֶׁר נִמְצְאוּ־שָׁמָּה וַיַּחֲרִימֻם עַד־הַיּוֹם הַזֶּה וַיֵּשְׁבוּ תַּחְתֵּיהֶם כִּי־מִרְעֶה לְצֹאנָם שָׁם׃

> ...they struck the tents and the dwellings (or Meunites) that were found there and 'banned' them to this day and dwelt (there) in their stead, because there was pasture there for their flocks.

J. M. Myers has interpreted this passage as illustrating a non-religious nature of the proceedings, the object of the attack being to obtain good pasturage.[4] He has, however, gone so far as to translate וַיַּחֲרִימֻם as "banished them,"[5] which goes against the context, and would equate the root for the first time with גרש, a root previously kept distinct (see the end of ch. 2). At a minimum one must say that the tribe of Simeon undertook military action,

---

[4] J. M. Myers, *I Chronicles: A New Translation with Introduction and Commentary, AB* (Garden City, N.Y., 1965), 31.

[5] Ibid. 25.

and destroyed them. Perplexingly enough, in 1 Chr 4:43 there is no mention of the חרם, and this with regard to a people that already were subjected to it, the Amalekites (1 Samuel 15). It seems that the חרם was accompanied by such dubious behavior, that the Chronicler wanted to account for the disposal of Amalek without entering into the fall of Saul. It is remarkable that the Amalekites never again threatened Israel after Saul, although it would seem that David played a part in that (2 Sam 8:11-12). In Chronicles, it was understood without saying under what dispensation the Amalekites were being eliminated--a uniquely severe fate for a people who played a uniquely hideous role in the history of Israel, at least during the earlier periods. That is why 1 Chr 4:41 had to use the verb when one would have expected it with regard to Amalek instead.. The usage here follows at least the form (as Brekelmans noted)[6] of the traditional "consecration through destruction." A tribe of Israel is depicted as wiping out another entity on the land, and the achievement of the conditions necessary for *Weltordnung* is symbolized by the ability to pasture the sheep, as is found also near the very end of the Moabite Inscription (1.31).[7] Thus, the verse is not so straightforwardly non-religious as it seems, because the writer was conscious of the religious meaning of החרים employed in the older war narratives of Numbers-Samuel, and wished to evoke it, even if the writer did not necessarily wish to use it in a fully religious sense (which in the light of the above, may have indeed been the case). If my hypothesis regarding the origin of the secular החרים is correct (see end of ch.1), that it comes from חרם II, then this writer could conceivably be playing off one against the other as occasionally occurs with the nominal forms (see below).

It is fitting to treat of 2 Chr 20:23 in conjunction with Dan 11:44:

I. 2 Chr 20:23

עַל־יֹשְׁבֵי הַר־שֵׂעִיר לְמַשְׁחִית׃ לְהַחֲרִים וּלְהַשְׁמִיד וּכְכַלּוֹתָם בְּיוֹשְׁבֵי שֵׂעִיר עָזְרוּ אִישׁ־בְּרֵעֵהוּ
וַיַּעַמְדוּ בְּנֵי עַמּוֹן וּמוֹאָב

The Ammonites and Moab stood against the men of the hill country of Seir to הַחֲרִים and destroy them; and as soon as they annihilated the inhabitants of Seir as they fought each other to (their) destruction.

II. Dan 11:44

וּשְׁמֻעוֹת יְבַהֲלֻהוּ מִמִּזְרָח וּמִצָּפוֹן וְיָצָא בְּחֵמָא גְדֹלָה לְהַשְׁמִיד וּלְהַחֲרִים רַבִּים׃

---

[6] C. H. W. Brekelmans, *Die ḥerem in het Oude Testament* (Nijmegen, 1959), 91. He says that the religious form continues, but that the religious sense is lost.

[7] Consider the whole ancient Near Eastern and biblical use of the image of the pasturing sheep as the ideal condition for human beings, epitomized most famously by Ps 23. Note that in 2 Kgs 3:4, Israel boasted of the quantity of Moabite lambs and goats it took in tribute, while the MI nearly ends with an image of Moabite sheep under Moabite sovereignty.

Reports from the east and the north will alarm him and he will rise in a great wrath to destroy and to הַחֲרִים multitudes.

There is no difficulty in determining the meaning of הַחֲרִים in these two passages, where הַחֲרִים in each case is in hendiadys with לְהַשְׁמִיד, "to destroy." so that perhaps it would be better to translate the verbs together as "utterly extirpate." The Chronicles verse is part of a fantastical Holy War scenario painted by the Chronicler (it has no counterpart in Kings), woven around Jehosaphat, a king of Judah painted in Kings as a God-fearing man. In 2 Chr 20:33 the major enemies of Israel in Transjordan are pictured as destroying each other through the marvelous providence of YHWH. Similarly, in Dan 11:44, where the commentators agree that the king portrayed is none other than the notorious Antiochus Epiphanes,[8] there can be no question of the חרם proper. The hellenic culture effected a radical transformation in the ancient Near East, and the ancient practice was in any case irrelevant to the situation in Daniel. This is confirmed by the wording of the verse, which pertains only to destruction, and cannot possibly refer to consecrating anything to a deity through destruction (gross anachronisms are always possible, but not in this case).

Of course it is easy to toss out generalizations about Hellenism in Palestine, but for the less hellenizing Jews, a memory of חרם still could have relevance, if the situation demanded it. S. G. Dempster points to 1 Mac 5:5, where the LXX uses the verb, ajnaqema%otisen, a form of a verb used as an equivalent to החרים in the Greek translation of biblical Hebrew.[9] The verse includes the association of the חרם with fire, and the preceding verse speaks of an ambush on the road, evoking the shade of Amalek in listing the sins of the Bainites.

2 Chr 32:20 is a slight variation on 2 Kgs 19:11, which, as noted above, represented the earliest sure attestation of the root חרם (according to my theory חרם II} in the sense of non-sacral destruction. There can be no doubt, particularly in light of the other text just cited, that this is the sense here as well in this derivative verse.

We see that in the third traditional division of the Hebrew Scriptures, the Writings, the חרם is conspicuous by the meagerness of its appearances, if not by its absence altogether. Only two or three times does it display the sacral sense with which this study has been chiefly concerned.[10] If one considers the nature of the material in the Writings (and perhaps the relatively late process of writing and canonization through which it went--at a time when the practice was irrelevant at best), this meager attestation is not surprising. The Books of Job and Proverbs would scarcely employ such a term--the חרם is not the stuff of the more didactic kind of wisdom literature.

---

[8] So N. Porteous, *Daniel: A Commentary, OTL* (London, 1965), 157, and numerous others.

[9] S. G. Dempster, *The Prophetic Invocation of the Ban as a Covenant Curse: A Historical Analysis of a Prophetic Theme* (M.A. thesis, Westminster Theological Seminary, Chestnut Hill, Pa., 1978), 57.

[10] Ezra 10:8, 1 Chr 2:7, and at least partially in 1 Chr 4:41.

It is not a concept of much use in teaching the young student the wise way to act. In the Psalms there are many references to war, including episodes which involved the חרם, but the focus is on YHWH's saving acts on the battlefield, not on a practice which involved human participation. Chronicles glances over the periods and places Israelite historiographers recorded in connection with the practice of the חרם. For such reasons, and doubtless others as well, the חרם is eclipsed in the final division of the Hebrew Bible.

CHAPTER 11

CONCLUSION

This study represents an effort to understand the ancient Israelite practice of חרם in terms drawn from the ancient Near East (including the biblical texts). I have used the word "practice" to characterize the חרם instead of "institution" advisedly. If Joshua 10-11 were an historical account of the Israelite subjugation of Canaan, perhaps it would be justifiable to speak of the חרם as an institution (of war), in the sense of a normative, regular, and predictably repeated set of actions within set circumstances. Or it might seem on the face of it, that the laws of war in Deuteronomy provide grounds to consider the חרם an institution, in the sense of a legal institution. I have argued the opposite. The texts of Deuteronomy 20 and 7 were designed to help make the חרם a thing of the past, without application to the challenges faced by the law framers' contemporaries, although the laws themselves reflect many of the most important *realia* of the חרם--an indication that the memory of the living practice was still fresh. For one result of this investigation has been the conclusion that these laws date back to a time when the חרם was still something that loomed large in the memory, if not the praxis, of Northern Israel in the period following the Moabite חרם described in the MI. The aim of the laws was to prevent the inappropriate use of the חרם at a time when the "primordial" seven nations and Amalek, the barrier to Israel's world order in the Land, no longer constituted a threat. It was those nations who inhabited the Land (east of the Jordan) who were the proper object of the חרם, not Moab (Sihon and Og being the long past exception in Transjordan, due to historical circumstance as Israel sought to enter the land--according to the biblical view). Deuteronomy 20 I placed not in the time of Josiah, but rather in the time of Jereboam II, a king well placed to apply the חרם in revenge against Moab.

This account fits in with the fact that in the literature following Deuteronomy, the war-חרם as such fades away into figurative language and oblivion. The evidence of the biblical narratives decisively favors a view of the חרם as an ad hoc activity, brought about by the most elemental circumstances of a people's struggle for life and land. This ad hoc activity had its source in a broader ancient world view, which I have brought to bear on the problem, as well as in the particular circumstance that called it into expression. (see below) The war-חרם is occasioned only by direct divine order (Joshua 6, 1 Samuel 15), or, in one instance, by a vow striking a deal with the deity for his help (Num 21:1-3). That the חרם was a sharp deviation from the normal way of waging war is proved by the need to explain what its content was to be (e.g. Joshua 6),and the subsequent copy difficulty Israelites had in respecting it in its full rigor (Joshua 7, 1 Samuel 15).

A chief object of this inquiry was to try to reconstruct the mentality which produced the חרם and which enabled its execution to find a place in the warfare and the religious conceptions of Israel at the same time. Any such reconstruction had to be drawn from the ancient sources themselves. For this reason I made so little of the 'Holy War,' for as the author of *Der*

Heilige Krieg im alten Israel understood and acknowledged, the Holy War is a scholarly construct, a compendium. of diverse components which appeared in various war texts, with no one component or group of components necessarily appearing in a given situation meriting the label 'Holy War,' which is a modern rubric. Our attempt at reconstruction was inevitably also a construct, but not one built on top of a prior construction. If the Holy War was a defensive war, as G, von Rad first propounded in *Der Heilige Krieg*, the חרם would not in any case be subsumed under that rubric. However, if the Assyrian war of aggression was a Holy War, as it clearly was, then the war-חרם, which was in essence an attempt to wed warfare with consecration, is by definition a type of Holy War. But mere classification of this kind did not seem to lead to anything terribly illuminating, so that 'Holy War' has not been a major focus of this study.

The new (or refurbished) ancient Near Eastern parallels adduced, the philological evidence, as well as the better of the previously proposed parallels, and perhaps above all, the Mesha Inscription (the wording of which reveals that the חרם was part and parcel of Moabite religion, not just a recent borrowing from Israel), prove that the origins of the חרם lie in the broader world of pagan antiquity, and that its antecedents are exceedingly ancient. I have tried to show that Israel integrated the חרם into its religion because the חרם helped meet its need to bring order and security to a hostile and chaotic environment. Further, I have suggested that the sacral aspect of the חרם, which led Mesha to elevate Kemosh above any of the deities in his stele, was an integral part of the order vs. chaos aspect. The divine was, after all, responsible for creating the world, and for ordering it afterwards. Also, that quality of Israelite religion which H. W. F. Saggs labeled "exclusivistic" and "intolerant" vs. the "accretive" and "tolerant" required a term for holiness that would actively separate YHWH's holiness from that of foreign gods,"no-gods" whose worship was officially banned early on, in Exod 22:19. The חרם also served to enforce the early anti-iconic view of deity, which survived even though it was destined to be bitterly contested. In contrast, the early Romans had an aniconic religion but it succumbed to Etruscan influence. Although the exact timing and course of events that brought the term to Israel will never be known, short of a miracle, it shows that the Israelites were able to "accrete" a basic way of looking at holiness and adjust it to fit their own needs. It probably needed little adjusting (judging from the MI and some of the other parallels), which made it attractive to those first responsible for its use in Israel.

The war-חרם achieved its goal of turning the land of Canaan into a land of Israelite world order, according to Deuteronomy Joshua, (Judges), and Samuel. Perhaps it was a victim of its own success. Eventually, of course, the Israelite kingdoms were to lose their military option as great powers entered the arena. Such a practice could not survive forever; its turn came and it was naturally discontinued and even canonized--by elevating it to oblivion in the context of a day long gone by (Deuteronomy 7,20). Yet several prophets, including the prophet of 1 Kings 20, gave the חרם a new life as they took it and used it for purposes of their own, forging with it a radical rhetoric and finding in it a source of powerful imagery. Indeed, the prophet of Isaiah 34, whose חרם rhetoric is elaborate and late, had a firm grasp of the phenomenology of the חרם, as is illustrated by the chapter's affinities with the Mesha Inscription. The prophet explicitly described chaos descending upon Edom following the חרם. Nor could the priests dispense with its reinforcing of the inviolability and unique character of YHWH, and the special relationship between deity, people, and land which is the aim of the חרם. Indeed, Leviticus 27 places great emphasis on the sacral aspect of the חרם and the deity, people and land relationship.

The key text, without which our study would have been foredoomed, is the aforementioned Mesha Inscription, and it is from this text that I launched the investigation. It is mainly from this text that I first derived the hypothesis that the חרם represented the attempt to bring moral and physical order to the universe of the group that resorted to it. It appears that a mentality in which warfare in general was seen as a battle against the forces of chaos was widespread in the ancient Near East from long before the advent of Israel. This way of thinking was often expressed in myth. Finally, having tried to establish the ancient Near Eastern evidence, both large scale and in less encompassing points of contact, I applied the hypothesis to the varied biblical texts, to test its usefulness as a tool of interpreting the biblical חרם text. In my view, the results prove it a powerful tool for biblical exegesis, especially in such challenging but relatively full-bodied narratives as Joshua 6-7 and 1 Samuel 15.

The חרם has been a problem for biblical theologians. The view of the חרם as a way of achieving moral and physical order in the world helps explain why neither Mesha nor the biblical writers hesitated to record the practice and assign a deity a leading role with regard to it. For to the Moabites and Israelites, the חרם was a reenactment of creation, a way of achieving a world order (literally creating sacred space) in which they could live and thrive. The laws of Deuteronomy as I have interpreted them may seem to contradict this. But if Jeroboam II had gone to Moab and retaliated for the still unavenged deaths of his compatriots at Mesha's hands (blood-feuds have frequently lasted for generations, as the language of the Bible with regard to Edom and Moab attests), applying the חרם himself, it would not have contributed to the establishment of the Israelite world order as such. Retaliation could easily assume another form. (2 Kings 3 is a work of apologetic theology; the success of the revolt against Ahab's heir was due to the wrath of YHWH Jehoram inherited from the Naboth episode (1 Kgs 21:29) and to Jehoram's own wickedness. The peculiar ending of 2 Kings 3 reflects the actuality of Moabite independence without giving a historical account.)

In the eyes of Mesha, Israel represented the forces of chaos that were preventing Moab from living in its own proper world order. The Omride suzerainty was understood as a divine punishment (of Moab's god Kemosh), an old theme in the Near East. Mesha took a series of religiously dictated steps. He took blood-vengeance to satiate his god and nation, and then he sanctified Nebo--the Moabite seat of YHWH--by destroying it and devoting it to Kemosh. The positive connotation of the root חרם, "sacred" (cf. the personal names scattered across the Semitic languages, including Hebrew) was operational in the religious use of the verb in war, as C. H. W. Brekelmans recognized. One has to be aware of the tremendous emphasis the peoples of the ancient Near East placed on the destructive power of their deities. This was manifest in storms and natural disasters, and particularly manifest in war, when the god's or goddess's fury was, one hoped and prayed, turned on the enemy, not on oneself. Israel shared in this common view. With the חרם, the means might be destructive, but the object was to create a holier world, which required the divine general to lead the people in war (so one might interpret YHWH's war leader, who appears before the battle of Jericho in this light, since even if the pericope comes originally from a different source than Joshua 6, someone put the sources together to depict him, Joshua and Jericho, in one context).

Mesha went on from Nebo to renew and rededicate Moabite cult centers, and he rebuilt the land of Moab from the ground up. In brief, Kemosh and Mesha re-sanctified Moab, and vanquished the forces opposed to Moabite world order, the forces of chaos. These were personified by Gad, Israel, and YHWH, whose name had its first known written appearance as a result of the Nebo temple of YHWH being an object of the חרם. The world order sought by those who practiced the חרם may be schematized as the harmonious working together of the elements of what I have characterized as the people-god-land triangle. This meant that the people lived freely and prosperously on its land, under the guidance and good will of its god.

The חרם mentality which I have detected in ancient sources typically found expression in myth or mythic thought. This is one of the strengths of my hypothesis, for as we have seen, the חרם itself is deeply rooted in mythic conceptions. So the mythic elements present in Joshua 6 attest, or Deut 3:11, where it is associated with the idea of primordial giants, like Og himself. The whole battle against the Amorites seems, as J. van Seters has argued, to be mythic (cf. Am 2:9-10, and the place of the Amorites in the list of primordial peoples). The cosmogonic character of the perpetual struggle for order against chaos not only lent itself to mythic expression but in the ancient world, demanded it. As a result.this discussion has utilized cosmogonic myths of Babylon, Egypt, Ugarit, and Israel, and doubtless other ancient myths could have been employed.

It might be objected that the proposed chaos/order paradigm for the חרם is both too abstract and too general. Actually, nothing could be more palpable than the human longing to dwell in a livable environment. In the real life of ancient Israel, this 'abstraction' to which the חרם was a specific response, was conditioned by the belief of a group of people that it had to assure its survival through its exclusivistic relationship with YHWH. For this reason biblical religion built on the etymological association of the root with the sacred to link the חרם with the most stringent anti-idolatry laws (e.g. Exod 22:19, Deut 7:24-5). For this reason (among others) it is wrong to see this linkage as secondary. In fact, it flows directly from the חרם's role as a unique expression of the ancient perception of the holy, and it afforded a unique opportunity for Israel to participate with YHWH in fighting the forces of chaos.

This alliance had its price. The spoils which in the normal course of events would accrue to the victors became inviolably attached to the deity. I have indicated, however, that the 'economics' of the חרם were not simply those of sacrifice to no purpose. As I. J. Gelb has noted, a social group had to be at a sufficiently high level of economic organization to absorb the vanquished soldiers *en masse* as slaves, and one should add that they had to have the will to do so. Solomon and Mesha did not hesitate, although a later editor censured Solomon for so doing. In Israel the demands of religion and economics did not conflict as one might have predicted. Consider, after all, the enormous social benefits to be gained from eliminating a predatory people like the Amalekites (as a factor--the חרם was not modern genocide, and Amalekites remained--cf. 2 Samuel 1; 1 Chr 4:43, the final elimination of Amalek, is more likely to be ideology at work than history). Hence the historical plausibility of an Amalekite war even in the beleaguered reign of Saul.

The aspect of renunciation was necessary for the Israelites to find favor and secure the cooperation of YHWH. In the case of mass idolatry in Deut 13:13-19, the חרם served to assuage the wrath of God and this was operative also in the victory Num 21:1-3, where the vow of חרם was the extreme means of placating YHWH's anger and displeasure. The חרם of the Mesha Inscription undoubtedly played a role in placating the wrath of Kemosh so glancingly and tantalizingly mentioned early in the inscription.

The Bible provides us with a good analogy to those who made such a vow of renunciation. The Nazirite, too, had to renounce certain things in order to reach the requisite level of holiness. Samson died because he breached such a requirement, just as Saul lost the Battle of Gilboa for failing to observe the rigor of the חרם. The economic side of the חרם, with the partial exception of the levitical חרם, in which the priests controlled property which fell חרם, interested the biblical writers very little. But from the religious point of view such renunciations were highly practical when adhered to, and this is one reason why the sanction for breaking them was severe. The חרם was not just a figment of the religious imagination, however. With the text of Osorkon in mind, with its mythological references which are contemporary to the action, it should not amaze the student of religion that the חרם, the stuff of a mythic world view, was actualized in history.

Returning to the question of the חרם and idolatry, touched on above, it must be reemphasized that the connection between these two is not secondary or fortuitous. Given the nature of the root as dealing with the sacred, the way it is used is definitely a statement about God. In biblical religion, this is expressed in a view of the nature of God as being of an aniconic character. Albrecht Alt emended Exod 22:19 and cut out the word חרם. However, as I showed above, he did this without support from the versions. The verse stands as a proof that the connection between the two is not secondary, but is as at least as early as the Covenant Code. YHWH would allow no sacrifices to other gods. Together with Deut 7:24-5, 13:13-19, the חרם in Exod 22:19 appears in intimate relation to that most distinctive and most celebrated aspect of ancient Israel's religion, the acknowledgement of YHWH alone. This aspect of the חרם is of itself sufficient to demonstrate that the חרם is an important concept for the understanding of monotheism or its historical development. Deut 7:24-5, the prohibition against stripping idols, is a refinement of Exod 22:19. As a method for dealing with the abominable, it partakes of an ancient form; its origins should not lightly be consigned to a late period. It shows how the abominable and the sacred sphere of YHWH somehow meet in full circle; they are not polar opposites or most distant points in a linear continuum. The abominable must be destroyed or swallowed up in the sacred sphere of God's holiness so that things in the world of human beings may take their proper place as well..

Further, the Mesha Inscription is centered wholly on Kemosh as the god who speaks, feels and acts, and authorizes the חרם. YHWH's cult was not allowed to continue at Nebo. The inscription of ^{d}Idi-Sin (Early Old Babylonian), which despite its fairly compact account provides us with an interesting parallel to the חרם, also shows a tendency to concentrate on one deity, albeit by dedicating its cultic observance to one god in each of three versions. We may see a certain exclusivistic tendency in the ^{d}Idi-Sin text but the Mesha Inscription provides firm support for the contention that the חרם proper was based on an exclusivistic kind of relationship with the deity, something found in its most extreme form in biblical religion. I cannot enter much more deeply into the question of monotheism here, but in antiquity, religion was not merely a passive question as to what one believed, but much more how one practised, and the prohibition of Exod 22:19 reflected the norm embraced by biblical religion. ^{d}Idi-Sin's text is a remarkable early example of the idea of "consecration through destruction."

In the same vein, the association of the חרם with the anti-iconic tendencies that manifested themselves early on in the history of the religion of Israel (e.g. the ark had images of the cherubim but none of YHWH) was an important development in the religion of ancient Israel.. Its importance was recognized by the priests, who held on to the חרם as living practice. Num 18:14, assigning devoted property and objects to the priests, may have been a cherished principle to the priests (it is hard to imagine otherwise). The complex history of the חרם, known only in bits and pieces, shows that in the matter of God's image, the subject leaves little room for a simple evolutionism that the religion of Israel must have evolved from "lower" to "higher" forms.

There are interesting counterexamples which have cropped up in the course of our research: 1) as already mentioned, ancient Roman religion was apparently aniconic and the gods were non-anthropomorphic, but this early phase gave way to Etruscan influence and a full-blooded image-using polytheism and 2) according to the account given in an Egyptian document of the Second Intermediary Period (Hyksos), "The Quarrel of Seqenenre and Apophis," Apophis is denigrated for his exclusive worship of a god named Sutekh (who was associated with Syro-Palestine and identified with Seth), which offended the sensibilities of the Egyptians. The idea of exclusive worship of one deity had long preceded Akhenaton, and did not need a long evolution over time in Israel.[1] There need be no doubt that the connection between the חרם and monolatry and iconoclasm was early and intrinsic to the Israelite conception of חרם.

The חרם was an important component of Israelite theology at a second level. It is an extremely pragmatic level, wherein abstention from some or all of the spoils of war leads to the manifestation of the warrior god, YHWH, and the triumph of the divine order over chaos. Here Israel shows how much it owed to its ancient Near Eastern background. In Egypt, the god Re was viewed as the deity ultimately responsible for maintaining the order of the world; in Babylon, Marduk. Yet in Egypt other gods such as Sekhmet played important roles in the fight against chaos, as we have seen. The Mesha Inscription restricts that role to Kemosh, the Bible to YHWH.

It is not desirable to leave the term "chaos" an unreal abstraction. In the context of חרם we are dealing with a concrete idea of chaos. It is, very simply, the enemies who threaten the world order of a group from within or without. Indeed, this is how ancient Egypt and Mesopotamia viewed the matter (with individual refinements), among others. This concept was then "reified" into the mythology, a major way a people has at its disposal of expressing its collective view of reality. The tendency to mythicize one's enemies transcends specific times and cultures. One has only to consider the role the Communists played in the minds (and under the beds) of many Americans in recent decades. The myth sets the stage for the extreme measures the group will feel compelled to take (or justifies them after the fact). The form in which the tendency to mythicize crystallizes is the result of a complex web of historical and cultural factors, but the guiding impulse is to further the group's ability to survive in a world aswarm with hostile forces. Nature's own prickliness in an era of primitive agricultural practices meant that the sanctification of the land of which I have spoken was no joke to the ancients. who survived if the god rained on them. Due to this perception of the world (found also in the MI), early Israel had plenty of incentive to adopt the cosmogonic, sacral term חרם, which was pregnant with myth-making potential. It could thus provide the adherents of YHWH with a down to earth and practical avenue for urgent, myth-based action to help insure the survival of a fairly small group surrounded by potential enemies.

The mythicizing of the enemy--evident in the חרם narratives of Deuteronomy 2-3, Joshua 6, and elsewhere--enabled the mass destruction of the enemy to take place, as J. Yoyotte pointed out in relation to the much more richly documented domain of ancient Egypt. Nevertheless, the mythic had its limits when competing with basic human acquisitiveness. There were always those who were tempted to defy the rigor of the חרם. One can only imagine how this process would have intensified in the case of the idolatrous

---

[1] For the closest approach in Babylonian religion to monotheism, see W. G. Lambert, "The Historical Development of the Mesopotamian Pantheon: A Study in Sophisticated Polytheism," in H. Goedicke & J.J. Roberts, eds., *Unity and Diversity: Essays in the History, Literature, and Religion of the Ancient Near East*, (Baltimore, 1975), 191-200.

city of Deut 13:13-19. The fury a society may vent on its external foes is likely to be a pale thing compared to the rage it hurls at its own members who have become the enemy. Deuteronomy 20 and 7 focused first and foremost on the six or seven nations defunct by the time of the composition of the chapters. In contrast, the חרם of Deuteronomy 13, which dealt with the Israelites themselves was a possibility throughout the period of the monarchy. It would be foolish to assume that such a thing never occurred or never was contemplated. A story in which the חרם was levied against Israelites is found in Judges 21. The fact that the Bible has no record of an application of the legislation of Deuteronomy 13 tells us very little. The pericope bears witness to the fact that the legislator and those who preserved his legislation felt that the conception should continue to play a part in the society in which they lived. The linking of the חרם to the exclusive worship of YHWH is therefore one of the keys to its understanding. It should be clear that in a society in which YHWH alone was the source of order (Exod 22:19, Deut 6:4), a practice like the חרם could function only through loyalty to the God of Israel. Few things could be more fearful to those who accepted this role of YHWH than an internal plague of worship of other gods, that might spread from place to place, bringing disorder and disaster in its wake, as in Sodom and Gomorrah. One might conclude, then, that Deut 13:13-19 was written with serious intent, even though we cannot know whether it reflected an actual Israelite practice.

A practice like the חרם reflects a certain mythicization of the enemy as the monster of chaos, which helped justify the massacre of large populations. Yet with it one enters the realm of the sacred. This is what is most difficult for us as products of modern secular culture to grasp, although a crusading knight might well have grasped it more easily. The חרם was a sort of philosopher's stone, with the ability to transmute disorder and chaos into the consecrated order of God. As the sacred was involved, there could be no room for error. In dealing with the deity, all ancient Near Eastern religions had set ways of bridging the gap between mortal and divine in order to avert the divine wrath insofar as it was possible. The most widespread means of accomplishing this in the ancient world was through sacrifice. However, the חרם comes to realization in more extreme circumstances. The cases of Achan (Joshua 7) and Saul (1 Samuel 15) illustrate this point vividly. Achan was executed on the spot with his family (Israelites had already died in the first, vain, foray against Ai). Doom was not only Saul's fate, but as a result of his sin he led Israel to another military defeat, and his line was supplanted by that of David. Subjective considerations of justice have no place here. When one tampered with the deity's projection of the sacral sphere on this earth--for YHWH was not omnipresent, rather manifestations of YHWH (e.g. כבוד) radiated in every direction--one is subject to the penalty imposed by the elemental nature of God. Experience demonstrated that such tampering was risky.

The חרם has been labelled a taboo partly because of the association with danger. But I have noted that the taboo was not isolated in its original setting, but part of a complex of ideas expressed by terms, two of which at least (*noa, mana*) are integral to taboo but lacking any counterpart in biblical language and thought. Another factor, the supposed contagious nature of the חרם, is not all that similar to the contagion of taboo. For instance, no one had any fear of touching the banned objects which Achan stole. The real 'contagion' is that the intrusion on what deity has set up as an inviolable object or border invariably is fatal. The phenomenon of the war-חרם has many parallels from antiquity (of greater or lesser value), but it is not something paralleled in the annals of modern cultural anthropology. It was primarily an urban phenomenon, the product of high civilization and long-literate cultures. The urban nature of the phenomenon is certain. Practically every instance of the חרם is directed at a city with the exception of the Amalekites, who were a menace to Israelite cities, such as Ziklag (1 Samuel 30). Even the deuteronomic law of חרם aimed at the 6 (or 7) autocthonous peoples speaks in terms of their cities. Therefore the חרם reflected the urbanized condition of ancient Palestine, and was not a 'primitive' rite.

Since the חרם cannot be satisfactorily understood from Polynesian taboo and the terms associated with it, I examined the terms made available by the sources. The war-חרם does appear as part of a complex of terms that define the semantic domain of the חרם, and thus help clarify the context and the quality of the חרם as it was perceived in ancient times. Some of the most important of these were גרש,"expel," הרג, "slay," ירש, "take possession," and אחז,"capture." The verbs, common to both the MI and the Exodus-Conquest narratives of the Bible, form part of the authentic verbal "matrix" within which the war-חרם took its place, a matrix very different from that of the Polynesian "tapoo."

A basic feature of the חרם emerges from looking at these four roots. Together they form a small glossary which could be used to describe the struggle for control of land. Such a struggle was inevitable given the number of peoples on it, its small size, and its strategic location. The four terms divide nicely. Two describe ways of dealing with the enemy ("killing, expelling"). The other two deal with occupying and possessing the land (although the Bible has only remnants of MI's usage of אחז). גרש in both Moabite and Hebrew usage.takes the deity as subject.

The חרם represents the most intensely religious form of action, taking the land and dealing with the enemy, thus uniting both poles. Paradoxically, the war-חרם unites the pragmatic with an idealistic yearning for the sanctification of life (of one's own folk). This duality gave the חרם a special place in the religious conceptualizing of war in Moab and Israel.

Another, rather different point arises out of the matrix of terms in which the חרם was embedded in the MI and the Bible. I drew the Hebrew roots from Exodus-and-conquest narratives of the Pentateuch. YHWH speaks prospectively to the Israelites about how they will come to possess the land sworn to the forefathers (and incidentally already made sacred by God's promise to them and their presence there in 'primordial' times). However, we find the same terms used, significantly, in a context of a rooted people's attempt to assert mastery over its land. A partial biblical example is Judges

11 (Jephthah and the Ammonites) where ירשׁ plays a major role. In Jud 11:24 both Kemosh and YHWH are the subject of the verb. The chapter also calls attention to two other roots found in the MI, לחם "to wage war," and ישׁב, "to settle, colonize." This yields the following matrix, which is in itself incomplete.

	חרם	
ירשׁ		הרג
ישׁב		גרשׁ
אחז		לחם

We could add, on the basis of our reading of KTU 1.13, כלה, "annihilate," and still others (the left column relates mostly to treatment of land, the right to treatment of the enemy people, the חרם of both). From this matrix I concluded that the biblical use of these verbs in the context of Exodus and conquest had its source in this complex of verbs for interstate warfare, via retrojection them into the idealized, Mosaic past. The complex actually arose from the post-settlement situation, in Israel as in Moab. The content of Judges 11, Jephthah's long speech to the Ammonites embraces both periods, and helps confirm this deduction. The struggle for land and the willingness to fight for it, (and one's freedom) were taken up into the emotional and intellectual life of the people and transformed by myth into a chaos vs. order paradigm or set of paradigms. A great biblical result of such a myth-forming process is Joshua 6, a cosmogonic myth in which order wins over chaos (the enemy forces). YHWH intervenes directly, but the Israelites participated through the obedient execution of the חרם. A gateway to the land had opened. The struggle for land was equally an effort to create "sacred space," a space consecrated by the presence of God in which the people could serve deity and in turn be blessed with the dignity and deserts of a "people of YHWH." The חרם was linked (philologically) to concepts of sacred space in the first chapter, with Arabic *ḥaram,* and if I am correct, with the irregular and in many ways mysterious sacred space of Akkadian *bīt ḫamri*. The חרם was a projection of and reaction to basic realities and human needs. It was an expression of the search for life for the individual and the community (under the aegis of the national god), as well as for fruitfulness and holiness. It was an expression fully integrated into biblical religion from paganism, playing a role not only in war but even in times of peace. It helped a people suffering from an inchoate or fractured world order to find the way to walk. The faithful saw it as ultimately one of the דרכי יהוה, the "paths of YHWH," of which prophets, sages, and psalmists spoke and sang, in a world where paths were often crooked. It was a world where disorder and death, epitomized for the YHWHist by the gold and silver plated idols that people worshipped, were never far away.

SELECT BIBLIOGRAPHY

Abel, F. M. "L'anathème de Jericho et la maison de Rahab," *RB* 57 (1950), 321-330.

Aharoni, Y. The Land of the Bible: A Historical Geography, (Rev. ed., Philadelphia, 1979).

Albright, W. F. Archeology and the Religion of Israel, (Baltimore, 1968).
---, From the Stone Age to Christianity: Monotheism and the Historical Process, (2nd ed., Garden City, N.Y., 1957).
---, "Two Little Understood Amarna Letters from the Middle Jordan Valley," *BASOR* 89 (1943), 7-21.

Albrecht, B. History and the Gods: An Essay on the Idea of Historical Events as Divine Manifestations in the Ancient Near East and in Israel, *Coniectanea Biblica OT Series 1* (Lund, Sweden, 1967).

Alt, A. Essays on Old Testament History and Religion (Garden City, 1968).

Anbar (Bernstein), M. "Le châtiment du crime de sacrilège d'après la Bible et un texte hépatascopique paléo-babylonien," *RA* 68 (1974), 172-3.

Bartlett, J. R. "The 'United' Campaign against Moab in 2 Kings 3:4-27," in J. F. A. Sawyer & D. J. A. Clines Midian, Edom and Moab, *JSOT* Sup 24 (1983), 135-146.
---, "Sihon and Og, Kings of the Amorites," *VT* 20 (1970), 257-77.
---, "The Conquest of Sihon's Kingdom; A Literary Examination," *JBL* 97 (1978), 347-51.

Beeston, A. F. L. "Mesha and Ataroth," *JRAS* 1985, 143-9.
---, "Warfare in Ancient South Arabia (2nd-3rd centuries A.D.)," *QAHTAN: Studies in old South Arabian Epigraphy* Fasc. 3 (1976).

Beit-Arieh, I. "New Light on the Edomites," *BAR* XIV 2 (1988), 29-41.

Blau, J. "Short Philological Notes on the Inscription of Mesha," *Maarav* 2/2 (1979-80), 146-48.

Bordreuil, P. "Michée 4:10-13 et ses parallèles ougaritiques," *Semitica* 21 (1971), 21-28.

Brekelmans, C. H. W. De herem in het Oude Testament, (Nijmegen, 1959).
---, "Le ḥerem chez les prophètes du royaume du Nord et dans le Deutéronome," *Sacra Pagina I. BETL* 12/13 (1959), 77-83.

---, "*ḥerem*, Bann," 635-39 in E. Jenni and C. Westerman, eds. *Theologische Handwörterbuch zum Alten Testament* I (Munich, 1971).

Brueggeman, W. "The Kerygma of the Priestly Writers," *ZAW* 84 (1972), 397-413..

Burkert, W. Greek Religion, (Cambridge, Mass., 1985).

Callaway, J. A. "New Evidence in the Conquest of Ai," *JBL* 87 (1968), 312-320.

Caloz, M. "Exode XIII 3-16 et le Deutéronome," *RB* 75 (1968), 5-62.

Caquot, A. & Sznycer, M. Ugaritic Religion, *Iconogragraphy of Religions* XV, 8 (Leiden, 1980).

Childs, B. S. "The Enemy from the North and the Chaos Tradition," in C. G. Perdue & B. W. Kovacs, eds. A Prophet to the Nations: Essays in Jeremiah Studies (Winona Lake, Ind., 1984), 151-161.

Cross, F. M. Canaanite Myth and Hebrew Epic: Essays in the History of the Religion of Israel, (Cambridge, Mass., 1973)
---, and Freedman, D. N. Early Hebrew Orthography; a Study of the Epigraphic Evidence, *AOS Series* 36 (New Haven, 1952).

Dearman, A. Studies in the Mesha Inscription and Moab, *ASOR/SBL Archeology and Biblical Studies* 2 (Atlanta, 1989).

Deller, K. Rev. of R. de Vaux Les sacrifices de l'Ancien Testament, *Or* N.S. 34 (1965), 382-6.

Delporte, J. "L'anathème de Jahveh," *Recherches de Science Religieuses,* 297-338.

Dempster, S. G. The Prophetic Invocation of the Ban as Covenant Curse: A Historical Analysis of a Prophetic Theme (M.A. thesis, Westminster Theological Seminary, Chestnut Hill, Pa., 1978)

Driver, S. R. An Introduction to the Literature of the Old Testament, (repr. N.Y., 1956).

Edelstein, D. "Saul's Battle Against Amaleq (I Sam 15)," *JSOT* 35 (1986), 71-84.

Ehrlich, A. B. Mikra ki-Pheshuto: Scholien und kritische Bemerkungen zu den heiligen Schriften der Hebräer: III Die prosaischen Schriften. (repr. New York, 1969).

Eliade, M. The Sacred and the Profane: The Nature of Religion. (San Diego, 1959).
---, Cosmos and History: The Myth of the Eternal Return. (New York, 1959)

Elitsur, Y. "The Plan of Conquest in the Book of Joshua," (Heb.) in Lurya, B., ed., Studies in the Book of Joshua (Jerusalem, 1960/61), 1-7.

Fernandez. A. "El ḥerem biblico," *Bib* 5 (1924), 1-25.

al-Fouadi, A. "Inscriptions and Reliefs from Bitwata," *Sumer* 34 (1978), 122-129.

Gelb, I. J. "The Arua Institution," *RA* 66 (1972), 1-21.
---, "Prisoners of War in Early Mesopotamia," *JNES* 32 (1973), 70-98.

Gevirtz, S. "Jericho and Shechem: A Religio-Literary Aspect of City Destruction," *VT* 13 (1963), 52-62.

Gibson, J. C. L. Textbook of Syrian Semitic Inscriptions I: Hebrew and Moabite Inscriptions. (Oxford, 1971).

Ginsberg, H. L. The Israelian Heritage of Judaism. (New York, 1982).

Glassner, J. J. "Sargon, 'roi de combat'" *RA* 79 (1985), 115-26.

Glazier-McDonald, B. Malachi: The Divine Messenger. *SBLDS* 98 (Atlanta, 1987).

Gosse, B. "Le recueil d'oracles contre les nations du livre d'Amos et l''histoire deutéronomique,'" *VT* 38 (1988), 22-40.

Gottwald, N. K. The Tribes of Yahweh: A Sociology of the Religion of Liberated Israel. (Maryknoll, N.Y., 1980).
---, "'Holy War' in Deuteronomy: Analysis and Critique," *Review and Expositor* 61 (1964), 296-310.

Greenberg, M. "Ḥerem," *EJ* H, 344-51.

Grintz, J. M. "The Treaty of Joshua with the Gibeonites," *JAOS* 86 (1966), 113-26.

Hallo, W. W. "Biblical Abominations and Sumerian Taboos," *JQR* 76 (1985), 21-40.
---, "New Moons and Sabbaths: A Case-study in the Contrastive Approach," *HUCA* 48 (1977), 1-18.
---, "Simurrum and the Hurrian Frontier," *RHA* 36 (1978), 71-81.
---,. & Dijk, J. J. A. van. The Exaltation of Inanna, (New Haven, 1968).

Hirsch, H. Untersuchungen zur altassyrischen Religion, *AfO* Bhft. 13/14 (1961).
---, "Die Inschiften der Könige von Agade," *AfO* 20 (1961), 1-84.
Hoffman, K. "Anathema," *RAC* I, 427-30.

Hoffner, H. A. jr. "Histories and Historians of the Ancient Near East: The Hittites," *Or* 49 (1980) 283-332.

Hornung, E. Conceptions of God in Ancient Egypt:The One and the Many, (Ithaca, 1982).

Huehnergard, J. Ugaritic Vocabulary in Syllabic Transcription, *HSS* 32, (1987).

Ishida, T. "The Structure and Historical Implications of the Lists of the Pre-Israelite Nations," *Bib* 60 (1979), 461-90.

Jacobsen, T. The Treasures of Darkness: A History of Mesopotamian Religion, (New Haven, 1976).

Kaiser, W. The Ugaritic Pantheon, diss. (Ann Arbor, Mich., 1973).

Kang, S.-M. Divine War in the Old Testament and in the Ancient Near East, *BZAW* 177 (Berlin, 1989)

Klein, R. Textual Criticism of the Old Testament, (Philadelphia, 1974).

Koppel, U. Das deuteronomische Geschichtswerk und seine Quellen: Die Absicht der deuteronomischen Geschichtsdarstellung aufgrund des Vergleichs zwischen Num. 21, 21-35 und Dtn 2, 26-3,3., *Europäische Hochschulschriften*, Reihe XXIII, Bd. 122 (Bern, 1979).

Krebernick, M. Zu Syllabar und Orthographer der lexicalischen Texte aus Ebla, *ZA* 73 (1983), 1-47.

Labat, R. Le caractère religieux de la royauté assyro-babylonienne, (Paris, 1939).

Lete, G. del Olmo. "La conquista de Jerico y la leyenda ugaritica de KRT," *Sefarad* 25 (1965), 3-15.

Levine, B. A. In the Presence of the Lord: A Study of Cult and Some Cultic Terms in Ancient Israel, (Leiden, 1974).
---, "The Deir 'Allah Plaster Inscriptions," *JAOS* 101 (1981), 195-205.
---, "Late Language in the Priestly Source: Some Literary and Historical Observations," *WJCS* 8 (1983), 69-82.
---, & Tarragon, J.-M. de. "Dead Kings and Rephaim: The Patrons of the Ugaritic Dynasty," *JAOS* 104 (1984), 149-59.
---, Leviticus: The Traditional Hebrew Text with the New JPS Translation *The JPS Torah Commentary* (Phila., 1989).

Lind, M. C. Yahweh is a Warrior: The Theology of Warfare in Ancient Israel, (Scottdale, Pa., 1980).

Lipinski, E. "Notes on the Meša' Inscription," *Or* N.S. 40 (1971), 325-40.

Liver, J. "The Wars of Mesha, King of Moab," *PEQ* 99 (1967), 14-31.
---, "The War of Mesha, King of Moab," (Heb.) in Lurya, B. Z. ed., Studies in the Book of Kings: II (Jerusalem, 1985) 193-210.

Lohfink, N., "Ḥaram," *TDOT*, vol 5, (Grand Rapids, 1986), 180-191.

Lowenstaum, Sh. "*ḥerem*," *EM* 3;290-2.

Lurya, B. Z., "The Incident of the Concubine at Gibea" (Heb.) in idem ed., Studies in the Book of Judges (Jerusalem, 1966), 394-463.

Maag, V. Kultur, Kulturkontakt und Religion: Gesammelte Studien zur allgemeinen und alttestamentlichen Religiongeschichte, (Göttingen, 1980).

Malamat, A. "The Ban in Mari and the Bible," Biblical Essays: 1966, *OuTWP* (Stellenbosch, 1967) 40-9.

Milgrom, J. Cult and Conscience: the ASHAM and the Priestly Doctrine of Repentance, *Studies in Judaism in Late Antiquity* 18 (Leiden, 1976).
---, Numbers: The Traditional Hebrew Text with the New JPS Translation, *The JPS Torah Commentary* (Phila., 1990}.

Miller, M. "The Mesha Stone as a Memorial Stela," *PEQ* 106 (1974), 9-18.

Miller, P. D. The Divine Warrior in Early Israel, (Cambridge, Mass., 1973).
---, "A Note on the Mesha Inscription," *Or* N.S. 38 (1969), 461-64.

Moor. J. C. de. "An Incantation against Infertility," (KTU 1.13) *UF* 12 (1980), 305-10.
---, "*Rāpi'ūma*- Rephaim," *ZAW* 88 (1976), 323-345.
---, & Spronk, K. A Cuneiform Anthology of Religious Texts from Ugarit, *Semitic Study Series* 6 (1987).

Moran, W. L. "New Evidence from Mari on the History of Prophecy," *Bib* 50 (1969), 15-56.

Oglivie, R. M. Early Rome and the Etruscans, *Fontana History of the Ancient World* (Glasgow, 1976).

Oppenheim, A. L. Ancient Mesopotamia: Portrait of a Dead Civilization, (Rev. ed. E. Reiner, Chicago, 1977).

Paul, S. "Amos 1:3-2:3: A Concatenous Literary Pattern," *JBL* 90 (1971), 397-403.

Pettinato, G. "Il Calendrio di Ebla al Tempo del Re Ibbi-Sipis sulla base di TM 75.G. 427.," *AfO* 25 (1978), 1-36.
---, "Il Calendario semitico del 3. millennio ricostruito sulla base dei testi di Ebla," *OA* 16 (1977), 257-285.
---, Ebla: An Empire Inscribed in Clay, (Garden City, N.Y., 1981).

Pickett, W. The Meaning and Function of T'B/TO'EVAH in the Hebrew Bible, diss. HUC-JIR (Cincinatti, 1985).

Rad, G. von. Old Testament Theology, *OTL* (N.Y., 1962-5) 2 vols..
---, Studies in Deuteronomy, (London, 1953).
---, Der Heilige Krieg im alten Israel, (Zurich, 1951).

Rendsberg, G. "A Reconstruction of Moabite-Israelite History," *JANES* 13 (1981), 67-73.

Saggs, H. W. F. The Encounter with the Divine in Mesopotamia and Israel, (London, 1978).

Schäfer-Lichtenberger, C. "Das gibeonitische Bündnis im Lichte deuteronomischer Kriegsgebote. Zum Verhältnis von Tradition und Interpretation in Jos 9." *BN* 34 (1986), 58-81.

Schmitt, G. Du sollst keinen Frieden schliessen mit dem Bewohnern des Landes, *BWANT* V 11 (1970).

Schwally, F. Semitische Kriegsaltertümer I Der heilige Krieg im alten Israel. (Leipzig, 1901).

Segert, S. "Die Sprache der moabitischen Königsinschrift," *ArOr* 29 (1961), 197-267.

Seters, J. van "The Terms 'Amorite' and 'Hittite in the Old Testament," *VT* 22 (1972), 64-81.
---, "The Conquest of Sihon's Kingdom: A Literary Examination," *JBL* 91 (1972), 182-97.
---, "Once Again--The Conquest of Sihon's Kingdom," *JBL* 99 (1980), 117-19.

Sherlock, C. "The Meaning of ḤRM in the Old Testament," *Colloquium* 14 (1982), 13-26.

Smith, M. "A Note on Burning Babies," *JAOS* 95 (1975), 477-79.

Spalinger, A. "A Canaanite Ritual Found in Egyptian Reliefs," *Journal of the Society for the Study of Egyptian Antiquities* 8 (1978), 47-58.

Sperling, S. D. "Joshua 24 Re-examined," *HUCA* LVIII (1987), 119-136.

Sternberg, M. "The Bible's Art of Persuasion: Ideology, Rhetoric, and Poetics in Saul's Fall," *HUCA* LIV (1983) 45-82.

Tadmor, H. "Assyria and the West: The Ninth Century and Its Aftermath," in H. Goedicke and J. J .M. Roberts, eds., Unity and Diversity: Essays in the History, Literature, and Religion of the Ancient Near East. (Baltimore, 1975), 36-48..
---, "Autobiographical Apology in Royal Assyrian Inscriptions," in H. Tadmor & M. Weinfeld eds. History, Historiography and Interpretation: Studies in Biblical and Cuneiform literatures. (Jerusalem, 1983), 36-67.
---, "History and Ideology in the Assyrian Royal Inscriptions" in F. M. Fales, ed. Assyrian Royal Inscriptions: New Horizons in Literary, Ideological, and Historical Analysis. (Rome, 1981), 13-33.
---, & Cogan M.. II Kings: A New Translation with Introduction and Commentary. *AB* (Garden City, 1988).
---, "On the History of Samaria in the Biblical Period," in Eretz Shomron: The Thirttieth Archeological Convention, September 1972 (Jerusalem, 1973), 67-74.

Timm, S. Die Dynastie Omri: Quellen und Untersuchung zum Geschichte Israels. (Göttingen, 1982).

Toorn, K. van der "Ḥerem-Bethel and Elephantine Oath Procedure," *ZAW* 98 (1986), 282-285.

---, Sin and Sanction in Israel and Mesopotamia. *Studia Semitica Neerlandica* 22 (Assen/Maastrict, Netherlands, 1985).

Vivian, A. I campi lessicali della separazione nell'ebraico biblico, di Qumran e della Mishna: ovvero, applicabilita della teoria dei campi lessicali all'ebraico. (Florence, 1978).

Weinfeld, M. Deuteronomy and the Deuteronomic School. (Oxford, 1972).
---, "The Extent of the Promised Land--the Status of Transjordan" in G. Strecher, ed. Das Land Israel in biblischer Zeit: Jerusalem-Symposium 1981. *GThA* 25 (1983) 59-75.
---, "The Worship of Molech and of the Queen of Heaven and its Background," *UF* 4 (1972), 133-54.
---, "The Deuteronomic Movement" in N. Lohfink Das Deuteronomium: Enstehung, Gestalt, und Botschaft. *BETL* 68 76-96.

Weippert, M. "'Heiliger Krieg' in Israel und Assyrien," *ZAW* LXXXIV (1972), 460-493.

Weiss, R. Studies in the Language and Text of the Bible. (Jerusalem, 1981).

Wijngaards, J. "*hwṣi'* and *hᶜlh*: A Twofold Approach to the Exodus," *VT* 15 (1965), 91-102.

Wyatt, N. "Who Killed the Dragon?" *Aula Orientalis* V (1987), 185-198.

Zevit, Z. "Archeological and Literary Stratigraphy in Joshua 7-8," *BASOR* 254 (1983), 23-36.

Zyl, A. H. van. The Moabites. *POS* III (1960).

INDEX

Achan (violator of *ḥerem*), 1, 57, 58, 64, 109, 114 n. 58, 131, 139, 140, 145, 147, 149-56, 163, 173, 175, 203, 211 n.3, 212, 224, 225. Other violators, see Ahab and Saul.
Agag, 173, 175-6, 181.
Ahab, 20, 24-6, 28, 53, 179-183, 203, 209.
Amalek, 70, 71, 72, 92-3, 95, 142, 213, 214, 217, 221, 225; *ḥerem* of, 165-178.
Ammonite, Citadel Inscription, 47; suggested influence of language on Moabite, 44, n.73.
Ammonite(s), 19, 28, 29, 30, 48-9, 210, 213.
Amon-Re, nature of combination, 37.
Amorites, 27, 89, 90, 91, 117, 119, 137, 144, 158, 180, 183, 220; In Amos; 94-6, 101-102, 119, 220.
Anat, 33, 85; 201-02; "Incantation of Fertility" to, 5-6, 79-80; Anat-Yahu, 14, 37.
Arabic, 11, 13-14, 15, 16; *ḥaram*, 9,11, 17, 226; Muharram, 12, 17; Old South Arabic, 7, 13, 17; *hrg*, 60.
Aramaic, PN's of Elephantine, 14-15, 17, 37; Hazael booty inscription, 100; Syriac (use of root *ḥrm*), 15, 17.
Aramean(s), 23, 28, 99-100; against Ahab, 178-83.
Archeology and *ḥerem*, 65-6, 139, 154; archeological-medical interpretation of *ḥerem*, 143
asakku. See Mari.
Ashtar, *Ashtar-Kemosh, 34-8, 40
Assyria(n), 8, 9, 10, 11, 21-24, 26, 28, 31, 42, 53, 61, 73, 76, 86, 98, 100-1, 103, 105, 108-09, 114, 143, 145, 149, 157, 171, 175, 177, 178, 179, 182, 185, 218.
Ataroth, 23, 29, 31, 32, 33, 38, 42, 44, 55.

Baal, 5, 6, 21 (n.7), 35, 38, 40, 79- 80, 141, 171-2, 202; in PNs, 21, 55-6
Babylon, -ians, 1, 23, 26, 34, 41, 53, 57, 78, 86, 115, 148, 151, 152, 171, 177, 189, 196-200, 211, 220, 223.
Bathsheba, 27.
Ben Hadad, 92, 179-183.
bīt ḫamri, 8, 10, 11, 15, 226.
Booty. See Spoils of War.

Canaanite(s), 19, 35, 49, 66, 89-90, 95, 99, 136-7, 144, 161, 180, 187, 202, 204.
Chaos, in relation to *ḥerem*, 2-3, 41-43, 50, 110, 117, 119, 121, 141, 142, 153, 171, 172, 174, 175, 177, 189, 191, 200, 211, 218-220, 223, 224, 226; in Egyptian parallel, 83-85, 86, 110, 172 in Babylonian & Hebrew myth, 171-72; in Ugaritic myth, 171; Ug. parallel, 80; in Utuḫegal Inscription, 71. See also Disorder, "non-existence," and *Weltordnung*.
Chronology, of Mesha stone, 20-25; of 2 Kgs 3, 50-2, 54; relative chronology, of Amos 1-2:8, 91-93; of Deuteronomy 7, 101-103, 113-115; of Deuteronomy 20, 89, 96-103, of 1 Samuel 15, 165-169, 178.

Consecration (devotion), 1, 7, 19, 40, 59, 72, 78, 118, 119, 129, 141, 142, 144, 218, 224, 226; to/through destruction (*ḥerem*), 1, 7, 16, 19, 33, 36, 37- 39, 46, 55, 74, 78, 92, 104,106, 107, 109, 125, 128, 130, 132-4, 137, 142, 144, 147, 148-49, 152, 161, 175, 180, 183,184, 185, 190, 195, 196, 198-202, 203, 212, 213, 214, 222; at Mari, 69; in Egypt, 81-2; in Hittite ritual, 75-7; in Latin sources, 61-3.; in Ugaritic ritual, 6-7,79.
Cosmogony, as aspect of *ḥerem*, 2, 41-2, 118, 141, 171-3, 220, 223, 226. See also Creation.
Covenant, 183, 205, 212; in relation to *ḥerem*, 109, 155-6.
Covenant Code, 123, 125, 221.
Creation (see also Cosmogony), 40-41, 77, 80, 83, 84, 85, 86, 104-106, 110, 118, 141-2, 144, 152-53, 163, 171, 172, 178, 200, 211, 218, 219, 226.

David, 20, 23, 30, 30 n. 27, 44, 45, 52, 71, 77, 95, 127, 149, 170, 195, 224.
Deity, land, people triangle, 50, 130, 206-07, 218-19. See *Weltordnung*, World order.
Deuteronomic school, deuteronomists, &c., 47, 53, 89, 90, 91, 95-105, 107, 108, 110-121, 124, 144, 145, 156-60, 184, 186, 225; and 1 Samuel 15, 165-9, 173, 176, 177.
Dibon, -ite, 22, 30, 42, 55-56 (MI), 184.
Disorder, "non-existence," 41, 80, 83, 85, 110, 153, 172-73, 178,191, 224, 226. See akso Chaos, *Weltordnung*.

Ebla, Eblaite, 12-13, 17, 21 n.7, 37, 48.
Edom, ite(s), 6, 19, 22, 32, 51-52, 54, 91-3, 94, 95, 115, 137, 161, 180, 184, 187; 196; Amos's prophecy against; 101-03; YHWH's *ḥerem* against, 91-95.
Egypt, ian(s), 15, 17, 27, 31, 41, 45, 71, 78, 80, 90, 94, 95, 97, 102, 103, 105, 110, 157, 166, 168, 170-3, 184, 185, 187, 191, 210, 220, 222; parallel to *ḥerem*; 81-85, 221.
Etruscans, 105, 122,

Hammurapi, 78, 129, 151.
Hittite(s), 10, 57, 59, 89, 90, 94, 95, 99, 108-09, 129, 157, 180, 183, 210; Hittite parallel to *ḥerem*; 72-77, 79, 87.
Holy, holiness, etc., 9, 10, 14-16, 21,25,27, 36, 58-60, 62, 74, 76, 77, 80, 102, 104, 106, 107, 111, 115, 118, 121, 125-8, 130, 132-35, 147-48, 154, 161, 169, 175, 186, 190, 193, 195-8, 200, 207, 211, 212, 214, 220-22, 224-26.
Holy War, 42, 49, 61, 63, 67-68, 69, 86, 92, 101, 120, 133, 143-43, 165, 179, 183, 215, 218.
Hurrian, -s, 10, 35, 79.

Idols, idolatry, 1, 40, 47, 96, 104, 105, 107, 109-15, 126, 135, 152, 180, 197-98, 199, 203, 205 212, 220, 221-3, 226.
Inscriptions, texts, exerpted from, Akkadian: ARM X 8, 67, ARM V 72, 149-50, *Enuma Elish* 1, I:1, 178, ^{d}Idi Sin, 38, hepatoscopic sacrilege text, 151, Inscription of Rimush, 67-8, middle Babylonian *kudurru*, 177, TCL 9 57:18; 10, Aramaic: Elephantine courtroom text, 14, Hazael booty inscription, 100, Greek: LXX to 2 Sam 23:20,

Aeschines, *Against Ctesiphon* 107-113; Latin, Livy VIII IX, 61, Tacitus xiii. 57; OSA; A. Jamme, *Sabaean Inscriptions*, #575, 60; Ugaritic: KTU l.13, "An Incantation for Fertility," 5-6, 79, Krt [100-03], 98, omen text, 157, *UT* 129, 34-5.
Ishtar, 27, 35, 38, 68.
Israel, Israelite(s), 2, 3, 8, 16 ,58, 59, 62, 64, 65, 69, 74, 75, 76, 77, 78, 79, 81, 83, 84, 85, 86, 87, 90-99, 101-110, 111, 114, 115, 116, 117, 118, 119, 120,121, 122, 126, 127, 131, 132, 134, 149, 151, 153, 155, 157, 160, 179, 181-7, 202, 203, 205, 206,209, 211, 212, 213, 214, 215, 217-226 against Amalek, 165-178.; against Jericho, 139-45; and Moab, 19-56; 63, 64, 67, 72,, 92, 93, 101-03, 115-17, 191, 219-20; in Isaiah, 189-97; in Jeremiah, 198-200; in most intensive use of *ḥerem*,158-161, united action in Judges, 161-163, vows *ḥerem*, 136-8.

Jephthah, 11, 28, 48-9, 51, 120, 131-32, 162, 226.
Jereboam, 24, 124, 181 n.56.
Jereboam II, 19, 121, 168, 217.
Jericho, 1, 13, 70, 74, 76, 139-145, 150, 154, 157, 195, 220.
Joshua, 31, 45, 46, 63, 74-75, 94-95, 103, 129, 144, 148, 148, 153-54, 158-59, 162, 184, 220.

Kemosh, 20-22, 25-28, 31-38, 40-45, 47-50, 53, 55-56, 61-62, 73, 104, 109, 140, 169, 174, 182, 191, 218, 219.

Laws, of war and *ḥerem*, 3, 89-121, 156-57, 159-60, 179-80, 212.

Mari, 15, 23, 29, 38, 63, 65; *asakku* at, 57-58, 145, 148-152, 156, *ḥerem* parallel, 67-70.
Mars, 61-3, 105.
Mesha, 19-29, 31, 33-36, 38, 40-43, 45, 47, 49, 50-55, 62, 73,81, 82, 86, 92, 93, 101, 108, 121, 162, 218-221.
Mesha Inscription, 2, 3, 57,60-63, 66, 69, 70, 71, 72, 78, 80, 87, 89, 104, 108, 118, 140, 142, 143, 144,155, 156, 162, 163, 169, 182, 184, 190, 191, 198, 217-219, 221-23, 225-26; implications of, 19-56, 213 n.7; in translation, 55-56.
Moab, Moabite(s}, 2, 3, 16, 19, 20-36, 21 n.7, 40-51, 53-55, 60, 62, 64, 65, 67, 72, 81, 86, 87, 89, 91-94, 95, 101-02, 102, 116, 118, 121, 143, 184, 190, 191, 207, 210, 213, 217, 123-6.
Moses, 19, 44, 47, 93, 97, 101, 102, 105, 116, 127, 137, 158, 160, 167, 169, 172.
Myth, -ic, 2, 22, 35, 36, 41, 50, 52, 76, 80, 83-85, 86, 103, 116-18, 119, 121, 139, 141-2, 152, 154, 163, 170-73, 176, 200, 219-20.

Nations, Seven primordial, listed, 89; non-stereotyped use, table, 95.
Nabatean, -s, 14, 17, 146.
New Year, Egyptian, 82, 84.
"Non-existence," Egyptian concept, of, 85, 41. See Disorder, "non-existence."

Omnasticon, names using *ḥerem*, chart of, 17.
Omri, 23-6, 28, 48-9, 52, 54-55.
Oracle, 20, 33, 58-9, 63, 67-8, 181 n.54; Prophetic, 93, 96, 101, 119, 121, 162, 176, 181. 189, 197, and see ch. 9.

Origins, of *ḥerem*, 7-8, 12, 15, 39-40, 42, 48, 50, 62-65, 72, 77-80, 85-86, 104-5, 109, 110, 130, 141-2, 153, 172, 201, 202, 217-226.

Palmyran, 14.
Phalanx, 166.
Phoenician -s, 15, 17, 31, 85, 85, 99.
Plunder. See Spoils of war.
Priest, (ess), priesthood, etc., 2, 14, 45, 62, 64, 140, 144, 145, 151, 154-55, 158, 193, 195-96, 200, 211, 219, 222. Priestly *ḥerem*, 2, 125-135, 147, 156, 197, 200, 210, 211, 212, 221-22.
Promised Land, 19, 139, 155.

Rephaim, 96, 116-18.
Rome, an, 59, 61-3, 65, 73, 105, 106, 125, 138, 166, 218, 22.

Sacrifice, 1, 13, 40, 43, 53, 59, 61, 104, 109, 126, 131, 133-5, 191, 194-95, 224; Deuteronomic metaphor, 106-07; in Egypt; 81-83; to other gods, 107, 123-5; 221; of spoils of *ḥerem*, 169, 173, 175-76.
Sacrilege, 50-60, 62, 147, 150, 151, 175, 199.
Samuel, 63, 93, 101, 103, 108, 165, 169-70, 173, 175-76, 199.
Saul, 45, 64, 92, 159, 162, 165-66, 170, 173-76, 180-83, 221, 224.
Septuagint (LXX), 29-30, 58, 91, 97, 123-5, 144, 148, 180, 184, 193-94, 197, 205, 214.
Siege, 3, 29, 52-54, 92, 111-12, 120, 186-87.
Solomon, 20, 22, 27, 37, 183, 184, 185, 221.
Spoils of war, 1, 32, 33-4, 36, 38, 39, 57, 58, 60, 62, 63, 64, 73, 75, 96, 99-100, 106, 108, 121, 126, 133, 137, 138, 143, 145, 148-152, 154, 160, 165, 169, 173, 175, 178, 196, 201, 202, 203, 206, 212, 221, 223.

Taboo, 14, 57, 77, 115, 146-8, 151, 156, 224-25.
Texts used, see Inscriptions.
Transjordan (ian), 29, 30, 31, 43, 44, 49, 52, 54, 91-3, 102-03, 116-17, 121, 132-38, 154-55, 210, 214, 217.

Ugarit, -ic, 5-8, 15, 17, 26, 31, 33, 79-80, 98-99, 117, 141, 149, 157, 171-72, 190, 200-02, 220.

Vengeance, 32, 48, 102, 166, 174, 182, 190, 206, 217, 219.

War(fare), war-*ḥerem*, 1-3, 7, 13,19, 23, 28-30, 35-39, 41, 43, 45, 49, 54-55, 58, 60, 64, 67-72, 79, 125, 131, 132, 134, 135, 137, 138, 141-44, 146-48, 150-54, 156, 166, 167, 170, 172, 175-76, 178-79, 181-83, 186-87, 190, 197, 200, 205-06, 207, 209-11, 213-14, 217-21, 223, 225-26; in Egypt, 80-82; in Hittite culture, 73-77, 99, 108, 157; in Roman writers, 61-63; war legislation, 3, 89-121, 156-57, 159-60, 179-80, 212.
Weltordnung, 2, 41, 50, 102, 106, 116, 116, 118, 138, 138, 152, 153, 156, 178. See next entry and Deity, land, people triangle.
World order, 2, 36, 41, 50, 70, 71, 83, 95, 106, 109, 110, 118-19, 125, 131-32, 141, 156, 160, 163, 171, 173, 191, 196, 197, 200, 206, 217-20, 223. See previous entry, and Chaos.

Brown Judaic Studies

140001	*Approaches to Ancient Judaism I*	William S. Green
140002	*The Traditions of Eleazar Ben Azariah*	Tzvee Zahavy
140003	*Persons and Institutions in Early Rabbinic Judaism*	William S. Green
140004	*Claude Goldsmid Montefiore on the Ancient Rabbis*	Joshua B. Stein
140005	*The Ecumenical Perspective and the Modernization of Jewish Religion*	S. Daniel Breslauer
140006	*The Sabbath-Law of Rabbi Meir*	Robert Goldenberg
140007	*Rabbi Tarfon*	Joel Gereboff
140008	*Rabban Gamaliel II*	Shamai Kanter
140009	*Approaches to Ancient Judaism II*	William S. Green
140010	*Method and Meaning in Ancient Judaism*	Jacob Neusner
140011	*Approaches to Ancient Judaism III*	William S. Green
140012	*Turning Point: Zionism and Reform Judaism*	Howard R. Greenstein
140013	*Buber on God and the Perfect Man*	Pamela Vermes
140014	*Scholastic Rabbinism*	Anthony J. Saldarini
140015	*Method and Meaning in Ancient Judaism II*	Jacob Neusner
140016	*Method and Meaning in Ancient Judaism III*	Jacob Neusner
140017	*Post Mishnaic Judaism in Transition*	Baruch M. Bokser
140018	*A History of the Mishnaic Law of Agriculture: Tractate Maaser Sheni*	Peter J. Haas
140019	*Mishnah's Theology of Tithing*	Martin S. Jaffee
140020	*The Priestly Gift in Mishnah: A Study of Tractate Terumot*	Alan. J. Peck
140021	*History of Judaism: The Next Ten Years*	Baruch M. Bokser
140022	*Ancient Synagogues*	Joseph Gutmann
140023	*Warrant for Genocide*	Norman Cohn
140024	*The Creation of the World According to Gersonides*	Jacob J. Staub
140025	*Two Treatises of Philo of Alexandria: A Commentary on De Gigantibus and Quod Deus Sit Immutabilis*	David Winston/John Dillon
140026	*A History of the Mishnaic Law of Agriculture: Kilayim*	Irving Mandelbaum
140027	*Approaches to Ancient Judaism IV*	William S. Green
140028	*Judaism in the American Humanities*	Jacob Neusner
140029	*Handbook of Synagogue Architecture*	Marilyn Chiat
140030	*The Book of Mirrors*	Daniel C. Matt
140031	*Ideas in Fiction: The Works of Hayim Hazaz*	Warren Bargad
140032	*Approaches to Ancient Judaism V*	William S. Green
140033	*Sectarian Law in the Dead Sea Scrolls: Courts, Testimony and the Penal Code*	Lawrence H. Schiffman
140034	*A History of the United Jewish Appeal: 1939-1982*	Marc L. Raphael
140035	*The Academic Study of Judaism*	Jacob Neusner
140036	*Woman Leaders in the Ancient Synagogue*	Bernadette Brooten
140037	*Formative Judaism: Religious, Historical, and Literary Studies*	Jacob Neusner
140038	*Ben Sira's View of Women: A Literary Analysis*	Warren C. Trenchard
140039	*Barukh Kurzweil and Modern Hebrew Literature*	James S. Diamond

140040 *Israeli Childhood Stories of the Sixties: Yizhar, Aloni,Shahar, Kahana-Carmon* Gideon Telpaz
140041 *Formative Judaism II: Religious, Historical, and Literary Studies* Jacob Neusner
140042 *Judaism in the American Humanities II: Jewish Learning and the New Humanities* Jacob Neusner
140043 *Support for the Poor in the Mishnaic Law of Agriculture: Tractate Peah* Roger Brooks
140044 *The Sanctity of the Seventh Year: A Study of Mishnah Tractate Shebiit* Louis E. Newman
140045 *Character and Context: Studies in the Fiction of Abramovitsh, Brenner, and Agnon* Jeffrey Fleck
140046 *Formative Judaism III: Religious, Historical, and Literary Studies* Jacob Neusner
140047 *Pharaoh's Counsellors: Job, Jethro, and Balaam in Rabbinic and Patristic Tradition* Judith Baskin
140048 *The Scrolls and Christian Origins: Studies in the Jewish Background of the New Testament* Matthew Black
140049 *Approaches to Modern Judaism I* Marc Lee Raphael
140050 *Mysterious Encounters at Mamre and Jabbok* William T. Miller
140051 *The Mishnah Before 70* Jacob Neusner
140052 *Sparda by the Bitter Sea: Imperial Interaction in Western Anatolia* Jack Martin Balcer
140053 *Hermann Cohen: The Challenge of a Religion of Reason* William Kluback
140054 *Approaches to Judaism in Medieval Times I* David R. Blumenthal
140055 *In the Margins of the Yerushalmi: Glosses on the English Translation* Jacob Neusner
140056 *Approaches to Modern Judaism II* Marc Lee Raphael
140057 *Approaches to Judaism in Medieval Times II* David R. Blumenthal
140058 *Midrash as Literature: The Primacy of Documentary Discourse* JacobNeusner
140059 *The Commerce of the Sacred: Mediation of the Divine Among Jews in the Graeco-Roman Diaspora* Jack N. Lightstone
140060 *Major Trends in Formative Judaism I: Society and Symbol in Political Crisis* Jacob Neusner
140061 *Major Trends in Formative Judaism II: Texts, Contents, and Contexts* Jacob Neusner
140062 *A History of the Jews in Babylonia I: The Parthian Period* Jacob Neusner
140063 *The Talmud of Babylonia: An American Translation. XXXII: Tractate Arakhin* Jacob Neusner
140064 *Ancient Judaism: Debates and Disputes* Jacob Neusner
140065 *Prayers Alleged to Be Jewish: An Examination of the Constitutiones Apostolorum* David Fiensy
140066 *The Legal Methodology of Hai Gaon* Tsvi Groner
140067 *From Mishnah to Scripture: The Problem of the Unattributed Saying* Jacob Neusner
140068 *Halakhah in a Theological Dimension* David Novak

140069	*From Philo to Origen: Middle Platonism in Transition*	Robert M. Berchman
140070	*In Search of Talmudic Biography: The Problem of the Attributed Saying*	Jacob Neusner
140071	*The Death of the Old and the Birth of the New: The Framework of the Book of Numbers and the Pentateuch*	Dennis T. Olson
140072	*The Talmud of Babylonia: An American Translation. XVII: Tractate Sotah*	Jacob Neusner
140073	*Understanding Seeking Faith: Essays on the Case of Judaism. Volume Two: Literature, Religion and the Social Study of Judiasm*	JacobNeusner
140074	*The Talmud of Babylonia: An American Translation. VI: Tractate Sukkah*	Jacob Neusner
140075	*Fear Not Warrior: A Study of 'al tira' Pericopes in the Hebrew Scriptures*	Edgar W. Conrad
140076	*Formative Judaism IV: Religious, Historical, and Literary Studies*	Jacob Neusner
140077	*Biblical Patterns in Modern Literature*	David H. Hirsch/ Nehama Aschkenasy
140078	*The Talmud of Babylonia: An American Translation I: Tractate Berakhot*	Jacob Neusner
140079	*Mishnah's Division of Agriculture: A History and Theology of Seder Zeraim*	Alan J. Avery-Peck
140080	*From Tradition to Imitation: The Plan and Program of Pesiqta Rabbati and Pesiqta deRab Kahana*	Jacob Neusner
140081	*The Talmud of Babylonia: An American Translation. XXIIIA: Tractate Sanhedrin, Chapters 1-3*	Jacob Neusner
140082	*Jewish Presence in T. S. Eliot and Franz Kafka*	Melvin Wilk
140083	*School, Court, Public Administration: Judaism and its Institutions in Talmudic Babylonia*	Jacob Neusner
140084	*The Talmud of Babylonia: An American Translation. XXIIIB: Tractate Sanhedrin, Chapters 4-8*	Jacob Neusner
140085	*The Bavli and Its Sources: The Question of Tradition in the Case of Tractate Sukkah*	Jacob Neusner
140086	*From Description to Conviction: Essays on the History and Theology of Judaism*	Jacob Neusner
140087	*The Talmud of Babylonia: An American Translation. XXIIIC: Tractate Sanhedrin, Chapters 9-11*	Jacob Neusner
140088	*Mishnaic Law of Blessings and Prayers: Tractate Berakhot*	Tzvee Zahavy
140089	*The Peripatetic Saying: The Problem of the Thrice-Told Tale in Talmudic Literature*	Jacob Neusner
140090	*The Talmud of Babylonia: An American Translation. XXVI: Tractate Horayot*	Martin S. Jaffee
140091	*Formative Judaism V: Religious, Historical, and Literary Studies*	Jacob Neusner
140092	*Essays on Biblical Method and Translation*	Edward Greenstein
140093	*The Integrity of Leviticus Rabbah*	Jacob Neusner
140094	*Behind the Essenes: History and Ideology of the Dead Sea Scrolls*	Philip R. Davies

140095	*Approaches to Judaism in Medieval Times, Volume III*	David R. Blumenthal
140096	*The Memorized Torah: The Mnemonic System of the Mishnah*	Jacob Neusner
140097	*Knowledge and Illumination*	Hossein Ziai
140098	*Sifre to Deuteronomy: An Analytical Translation. Volume One: Pisqaot One through One Hundred Forty-Three. Debarim, Waethanan, Eqeb*	Jacob Neusner
140099	*Major Trends in Formative Judaism III: The Three Stages in the Formation of Judaism*	Jacob Neusner
140101	*Sifre to Deuteronomy: An Analytical Translation. Volume Two: Pisqaot One Hundred Forty-Four through Three Hundred Fifty-Seven. Shofetim, Ki Tese, Ki Tabo, Nesabim, Ha'azinu, Zot Habberakhah*	Jacob Neusner
140102	*Sifra: The Rabbinic Commentary on Leviticus*	Jacob Neusner/ Roger Brooks
140103	*The Human Will in Judaism*	Howard Eilberg-Schwartz
140104	*Genesis Rabbah: Volume 1. Genesis 1:1 to 8:14*	Jacob Neusner
140105	*Genesis Rabbah: Volume 2. Genesis 8:15 to 28:9*	Jacob Neusner
140106	*Genesis Rabbah: Volume 3. Genesis 28:10 to 50:26*	Jacob Neusner
140107	*First Principles of Systemic Analysis*	Jacob Neusner
140108	*Genesis and Judaism*	Jacob Neusner
140109	*The Talmud of Babylonia: An American Translation. XXXV: Tractates Meilah and Tamid*	Peter J. Haas
140110	*Studies in Islamic and Judaic Traditions*	William Brinner/Stephen Ricks
140111	*Comparative Midrash: The Plan and Program of Genesis Rabbah and Leviticus Rabbah*	Jacob Neusner
140112	*The Tosefta: Its Structure and its Sources*	Jacob Neusner
140113	*Reading and Believing*	Jacob Neusner
140114	*The Fathers According to Rabbi Nathan*	Jacob Neusner
140115	*Etymology in Early Jewish Interpretation: The Hebrew Names in Philo*	Lester L. Grabbe
140116	*Understanding Seeking Faith: Essays on the Case of Judaism. Volume One: Debates on Method, Reports of Results*	Jacob Neusner
140117	*The Talmud of Babylonia. An American Translation. VII: Tractate Besah*	Alan J. Avery-Peck
140118	*Sifre to Numbers: An American Translation and Explanation, Volume One: Sifre to Numbers 1-58*	Jacob Neusner
140119	*Sifre to Numbers: An American Translation and Explanation, Volume Two: Sifre to Numbers 59-115*	Jacob Neusner
140120	*Cohen and Troeltsch: Ethical Monotheistic Religion and Theory of Culture*	Wendell S. Dietrich
140121	*Goodenough on the History of Religion and on Judaism*	Jacob Neusner/ Ernest Frerichs
140122	*Pesiqta deRab Kahana I: Pisqaot One through Fourteen*	Jacob Neusner
140123	*Pesiqta deRab Kahana II: Pisqaot Fifteen through Twenty-Eight and Introduction to Pesiqta deRab Kahana*	Jacob Neusner
140124	*Sifre to Deuteronomy: Introduction*	Jacob Neusner

140126	*A Conceptual Commentary on Midrash Leviticus Rabbah: Value Concepts in Jewish Thought*	Max Kadushin
140127	*The Other Judaisms of Late Antiquity*	Alan F. Segal
140128	*Josephus as a Historical Source in Patristic Literature through Eusebius*	Michael Hardwick
140129	*Judaism: The Evidence of the Mishnah*	Jacob Neusner
140131	*Philo, John and Paul: New Perspectives on Judaism and Early Christianity*	Peder Borgen
140132	*Babylonian Witchcraft Literature*	Tzvi Abusch
140133	*The Making of the Mind of Judaism: The Formative Age*	Jacob Neusner
140135	*Why No Gospels in Talmudic Judaism?*	Jacob Neusner
140136	*Torah: From Scroll to Symbol Part III: Doctrine*	Jacob Neusner
140137	*The Systemic Analysis of Judaism*	Jacob Neusner
140138	*Sifra: An Analytical Translation Vol. 1*	Jacob Neusner
140139	*Sifra: An Analytical Translation Vol. 2*	Jacob Neusner
140140	*Sifra: An Analytical Translation Vol. 3*	Jacob Neusner
140141	*Midrash in Context: Exegesis in Formative Judaism*	Jacob Neusner
140143	*Oxen, Women or Citizens? Slaves in the System of Mishnah*	Paul V. Flesher
140144	*The Book of the Pomegranate*	Elliot R. Wolfson
140145	*Wrong Ways and Right Ways in the Study of Formative Judaism*	Jacob Neusner
140146	*Sifra in Perspective: The Documentary Comparison of the Midrashim of Ancient Judaism*	Jacob Neusner
140148	*Mekhilta According to Rabbi Ishmael: An Analytical Translation Volume I*	Jacob Neusner
140149	*The Doctrine of the Divine Name: An Introduction to Classical Kabbalistic Theology*	Stephen G. Wald
140150	*Water into Wine and the Beheading of John the Baptist*	Roger Aus
140151	*The Formation of the Jewish Intellect*	Jacob Neusner
140152	*Mekhilta According to Rabbi Ishmael: An Introduction to Judaism's First Scriptural Encyclopaedia*	Jacob Neusner
140153	*Understanding Seeking Faith. Volume Three*	Jacob Neusner
140154	*Mekhilta According to Rabbi Ishmael: An Analytical Translation Volume Two*	Jacob Neusner
140155	*Goyim: Gentiles and Israelites in Mishnah-Tosefta*	Gary P. Porton
140156	*A Religion of Pots and Pans?*	Jacob Neusner
140157	*Claude Montefiore and Christianity*	Maurice Gerald Bowler
140158	*The Philosopical Mishnah Volume III*	Jacob Neusner
140159	*From Ancient Israel to Modern Judaism Volume 1: Intellect in Quest of Understanding*	Neusner/Frerichs/Sarna
140160	*The Social Study of Judaism Volume I*	Jacob Neusner
140161	*Philo's Jewish Identity*	Alan Mendelson
140162	*The Social Study of Judaism Volume II*	Jacob Neusner
140163	*The Philosophical Mishnah Volume I : The Initial Probe*	Jacob Neusner
140164	*The Philosophical Mishnah Volume II : The Tractates Agenda: From Abodah Zarah Through Moed Qatan*	Jacob Neusner

140166	*Women's Earliest Records*	Barbara S. Lesko
140167	*The Legacy of Hermann Cohen*	William Kluback
140168	*Method and Meaning in Ancient Judaism*	Jacob Neusner
140169	*The Role of the Messenger and Message in the Ancient Near East*	John T. Greene
140171	*Abraham Heschel's Idea of Revelation*	Lawerence Perlman
140172	*The Philosophical Mishnah Volume IV: The Repertoire*	Jacob Neusner
140173	*From Ancient Israel to Modern Judaism Volume 2: Intellect in Quest of Understanding*	Neusner/Frerichs/Sarna
140174	*From Ancient Israel to Modern Judaism Volume 3: Intellect in Quest of Understanding*	Neusner/Frerichs/Sarna
140175	*From Ancient Israel to Modern Judaism Volume 4: Intellect in Quest of Understanding*	Neusner/Frerichs/Sarna
140176	*Translating the Classics of Judaism: In Theory and In Practice*	Jacob Neusner
140177	*Profiles of a Rabbi: Synoptic Opportunities in Reading About Jesus*	Bruce Chilton
140178	*Studies in Islamic and Judaic Traditions II*	William Brinner/Stephen Ricks
140179	*Medium and Message in Judaism: First Series*	Jacob Neusner
140180	*Making the Classics of Judaism: The Three Stages of Literary Formation*	Jacob Neusner
140181	*The Law of Jealousy: Anthropology of Sotah*	Adriana Destro
140182	*Esther Rabbah I: An Analytical Translation*	Jacob Neusner
140183	*Ruth Rabbah: An Analytical Translation*	Jacob Neusner
140184	*Formative Judaism: Religious, Historical and Literary Studies*	Jacob Neusner
140185	*The Studia Philonica Annual*	David T. Runia
140186	*The Setting of the Sermon on the Mount*	W.D. Davies
140187	*The Midrash Compilations of the Sixth and Seventh Centuries Volume One*	Jacob Neusner
140188	*The Midrash Compilations of the Sixth and Seventh Centuries Volume Two*	Jacob Neusner
140189	*The Midrash Compilations of the Sixth and Seventh Centuries Volume Three*	Jacob Neusner
140190	*The Midrash Compilations of the Sixth and Seventh Centuries Volume Four*	Jacob Neusner
140191	*The Religious World of Contemporary Judaism: Observations and Convictions*	Jacob Neusner
140192	*Approaches to Ancient Judaism: Volume VI*	Jacob Neusner/ Ernest S. Frerichs
140193	*Lamentations Rabbah: An Analytical Translation*	Jacob Neusner
140194	*Early Christian Texts on Jews and Judaism*	Robert S. MacLennan
140196	*Torah and the Chronicler's History Work*	Judson R. Shaver
140197	*Song of Songs Rabbah: An Analytical Translation Volume One*	Jacob Neusner
140198	*Song of Songs Rabbah: An Analytical Translation Volume Two*	Jacob Neusner
140199	*From Literature to Theology in Formative Judaism*	Jacob Neusner
140202	*Maimonides on Perfection*	Menachem Kellner

140203	*The Martyr's Conviction*	Eugene Weiner/Anita Weiner
140204	*Judaism, Christianity, and Zoroastrianism in Talmudic Babylonia*	Jacob Neusner
140205	*Tzedakah: Can Jewish Philanthropy Buy Jewish Survival?*	Jacob Neusner
140206	*New Perspectives on Ancient Judaism: Volume 1*	Neusner/Borgen Frerichs/Horsley
140207	*Scriptures of the Oral Torah*	Jacob Neusner
140208	*Christian Faith and the Bible of Judaism*	Jacob Neusner
140209	*Philo's Perception of Women*	Dorothy Sly
140210	*Case Citation in the Babylonian Talmud: The Evidence Tractate* Neziqin	Eliezer Segal
140211	*The Biblical Ḥerem: A Window on Israel's Religious Experience*	Philip D. Stern
140212	*Goodenough on the Beginnings of Christianity*	A.T. Kraabel
140213	*The Talmud of Babylonia: An American Translation XXIA: Tractate Bava Mesia Chapters 1-2*	Jacob Neusner
140214	*The Talmud of Babylonia: An American Translation XXIB: Tractate Bava Mesia Chapters 3-4*	Jacob Neusner
140215	*The Talmud of Babylonia: An American Translation XXIC: Tractate Bava Mesia Chapters 5-6*	Jacob Neusner
140216	*The Talmud of Babylonia: An American Translation XXID: Tractate Bava Mesia Chapters 7-10*	Jacob Neusner
140217	*Semites, Iranians, Greeks and Romans: Studies in their Interactions*	Jonathan A. Goldstein
140218	*The Talmud of Babylonia: An American Translation XXXIII: Temurah*	Jacob Neusner
140219	*The Talmud of Babylonia: An American Translation XXXIA: Tractate Bekhorot Chapters 1-4*	Jacob Neusner
140220	*The Talmud of Babylonia: An American Translation XXXIB: Tractate Bekhorot Chapters 5-9*	Jacob Neusner
140221	*The Talmud of Babylonia: An American Translation XXXVIA: Tractate Niddah Chapters 1-3*	Jacob Neusner
140222	*The Talmud of Babylonia: An American Translation XXXVIB: Tractate Niddah Chapters 4-10*	Jacob Neusner

Brown Studies on Jews and Their Societies

145001	*American Jewish Fertility*	Calvin Goldscheider
145003	*The American Jewish Community*	Calvin Goldscheider
145004	*The Naturalized Jews of the Grand Duchy of Posen in 1834 and 1835*	Edward David Luft
145005	*Suburban Communities: The Jewishness of American Reform Jews*	Gerald L. Showstack
145007	*Ethnic Survival in America*	David Schoem

Brown Studies in Religion

147001	*Religious Writings and Religious Systems Volume 1*	Jacob Neusner, et al
147002	*Religious Writings and Religious Systems Volume 2*	Jacob Neusner, et al
147003	*Religion and the Social Sciences*	Robert Segal